ETERNALS

ONLY DEATH
IS ETERNAL

·

ETER

ETERNALS CREATED BY
JACK KIRBY

⬡   ⬡   ⬡

COLLECTION EDITOR	**JENNIFER GRÜNWALD**
ASSISTANT EDITOR	**DANIEL KIRCHHOFFER**
ASSISTANT MANAGING EDITOR	**MAIA LOY**
ASSISTANT MANAGING EDITOR	**LISA MONTALBANO**
VP PRODUCTION & SPECIAL PROJECTS	**JEFF YOUNGQUIST**
BOOK DESIGNERS	**JAY BOWEN** WITH **CLAYTON COWLES**
SVP PRINT, SALES & MARKETING	**DAVID GABRIEL**
EDITOR IN CHIEF	**C.B. CEBULSKI**

ETERNALS VOL. 1: ONLY DEATH IS ETERNAL. Contains material originally published in magazine form as ETERNALS (2021) #1-6. First printing 2021. ISBN 978-1-302-92547-5. Published by MARVEL WORLDWIDE, INC., a subsidiary of MARVEL ENTERTAINMENT, LLC. OFFICE OF PUBLICATION: 1290 Avenue of the Americas, New York, NY 10104. © 2021 MARVEL No similarity between any of the names, characters, persons, and/or institutions in this magazine with those of any living or dead person or institution is intended, and any such similarity which may exist is purely coincidental. **Printed in Canada.** KEVIN FEIGE, Chief Creative Officer; DAN BUCKLEY, President, Marvel Entertainment; JOE QUESADA, EVP & Creative Director; DAVID BOGART, Associate Publisher & SVP of Talent Affairs; TOM BREVOORT, VP, Executive Editor; NICK LOWE, Executive Editor, VP of Content, Digital Publishing; DAVID GABRIEL, VP of Print & Digital Publishing; JEFF YOUNGQUIST, VP of Production & Special Projects; ALEX MORALES, Director of Publishing Operations; DAN EDINGTON, Managing Editor; RICKEY PURDIN, Director of Talent Relations; JENNIFER GRÜNWALD, Senior Editor, Special Projects; SUSAN CRESPI, Production Manager; STAN LEE, Chairman Emeritus. For information regarding advertising in Marvel Comics or on Marvel.com, please contact Vit DeBellis, Custom Solutions & Integrated Advertising Manager, at vdebellis@marvel.com. For Marvel subscription inquiries, please call 888-511-5480. **Manufactured between 7/9/2021 and 8/10/2021 by SOLISCO PRINTERS, SCOTT, QC, CANADA.**

10 9 8 7 6 5 4 3 2 1

NALS

ONLY DEATH
IS ETERNAL

·

WRITER	**KIERON GILLEN**
ARTIST	**ESAD RIBIĆ**
COLOR ARTIST	**MATTHEW WILSON**

·

LETTERER	**VC's CLAYTON COWLES**
COVER ART	**ESAD RIBIĆ**

·

ASSISTANT EDITOR	**KAT GREGOROWICZ**
EDITOR	**DARREN SHAN**
EXECUTIVE EDITOR	**TOM BREVOORT**

·

SPECIAL THANKS TO
**LAUREN AMARO, MARK BASSO
& JACQUE PORTE**

1

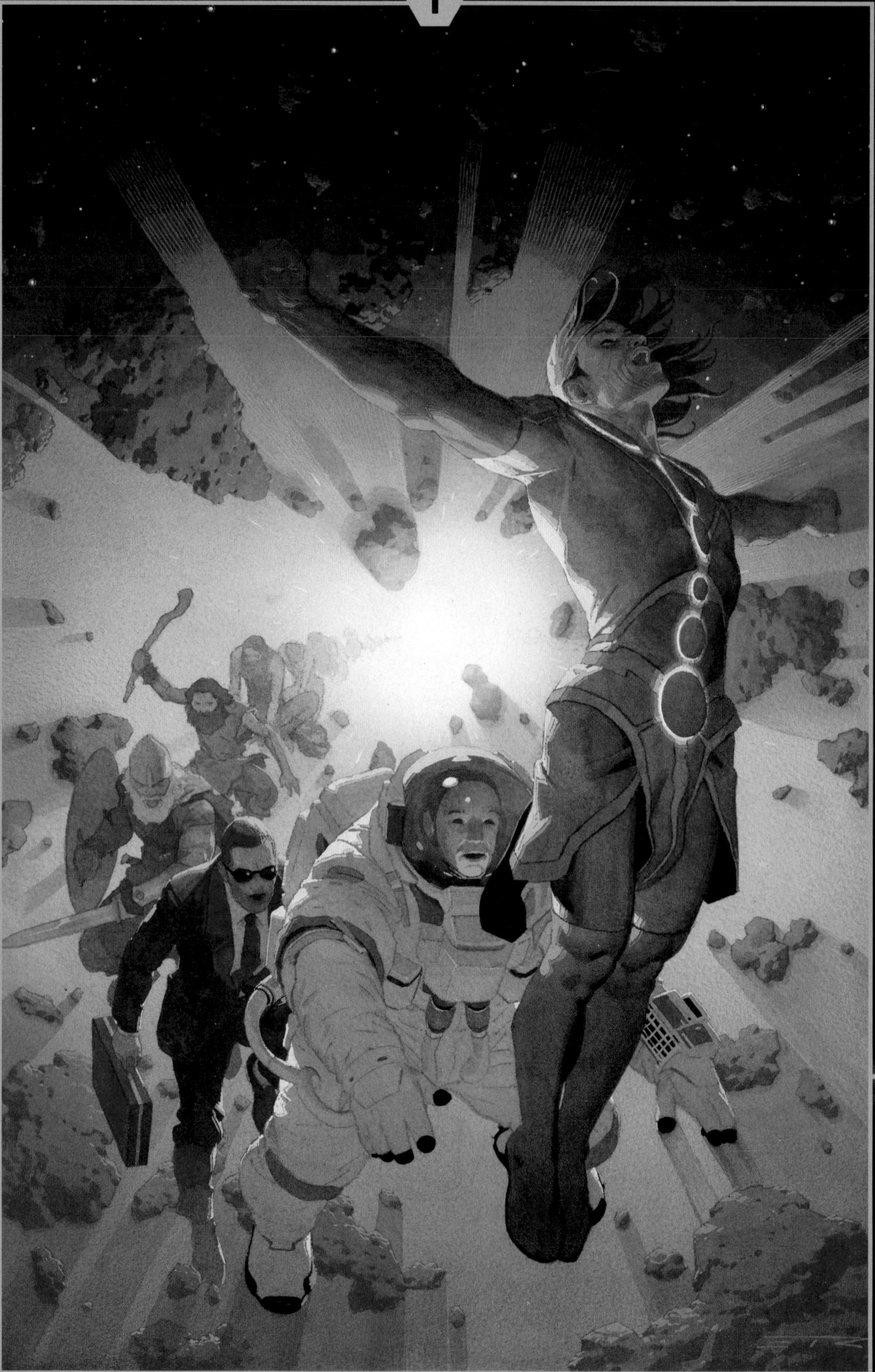

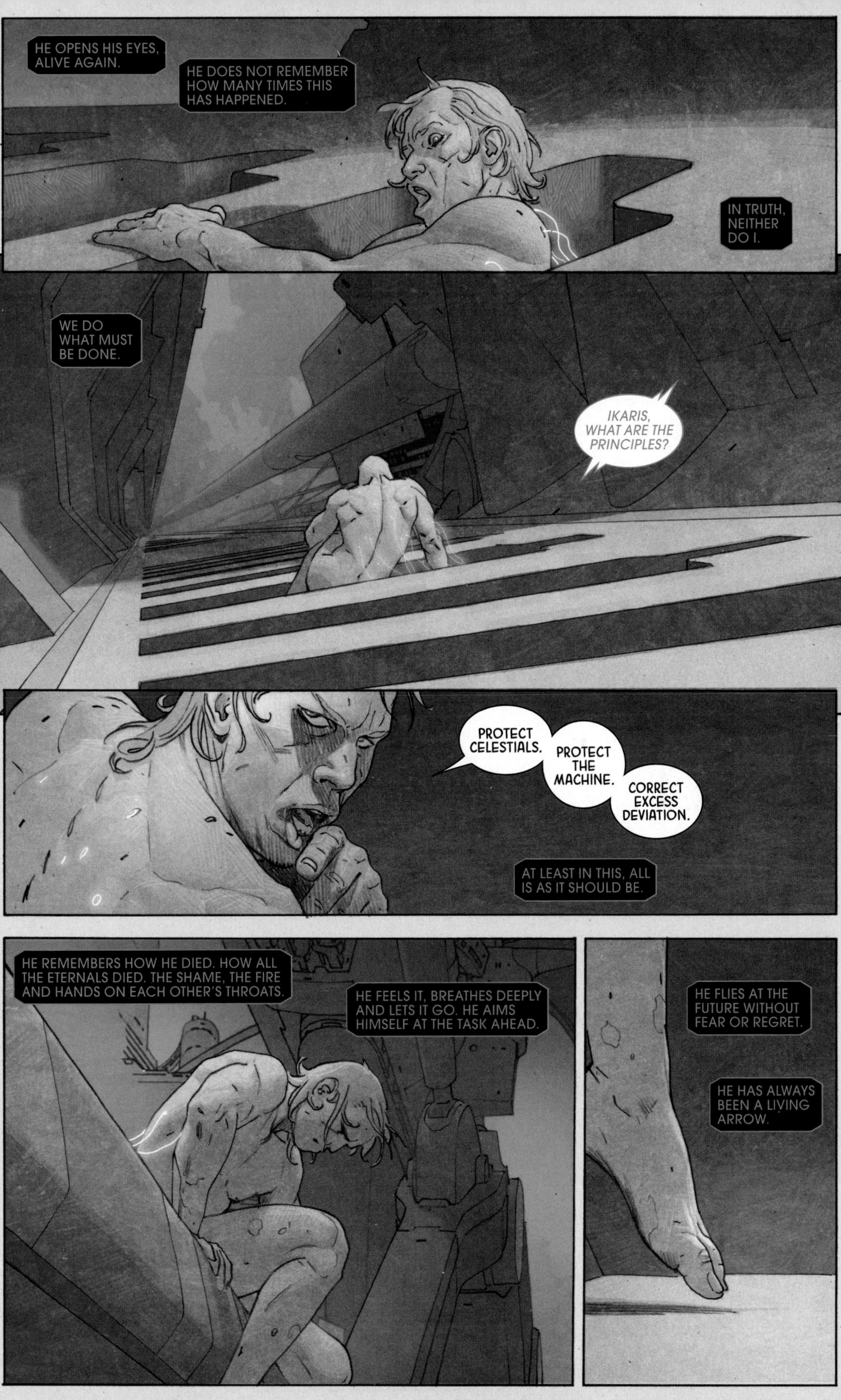
HE OPENS HIS EYES, ALIVE AGAIN.
HE DOES NOT REMEMBER HOW MANY TIMES THIS HAS HAPPENED.
IN TRUTH, NEITHER DO I.
WE DO WHAT MUST BE DONE.
IKARIS, WHAT ARE THE PRINCIPLES?
PROTECT CELESTIALS.
PROTECT THE MACHINE.
CORRECT EXCESS DEVIATION.
AT LEAST IN THIS, ALL IS AS IT SHOULD BE.
HE REMEMBERS HOW HE DIED. HOW ALL THE ETERNALS DIED. THE SHAME, THE FIRE AND HANDS ON EACH OTHER'S THROATS.
HE FEELS IT, BREATHES DEEPLY AND LETS IT GO. HE AIMS HIMSELF AT THE TASK AHEAD.
HE FLIES AT THE FUTURE WITHOUT FEAR OR REGRET.
HE HAS ALWAYS BEEN A LIVING ARROW.

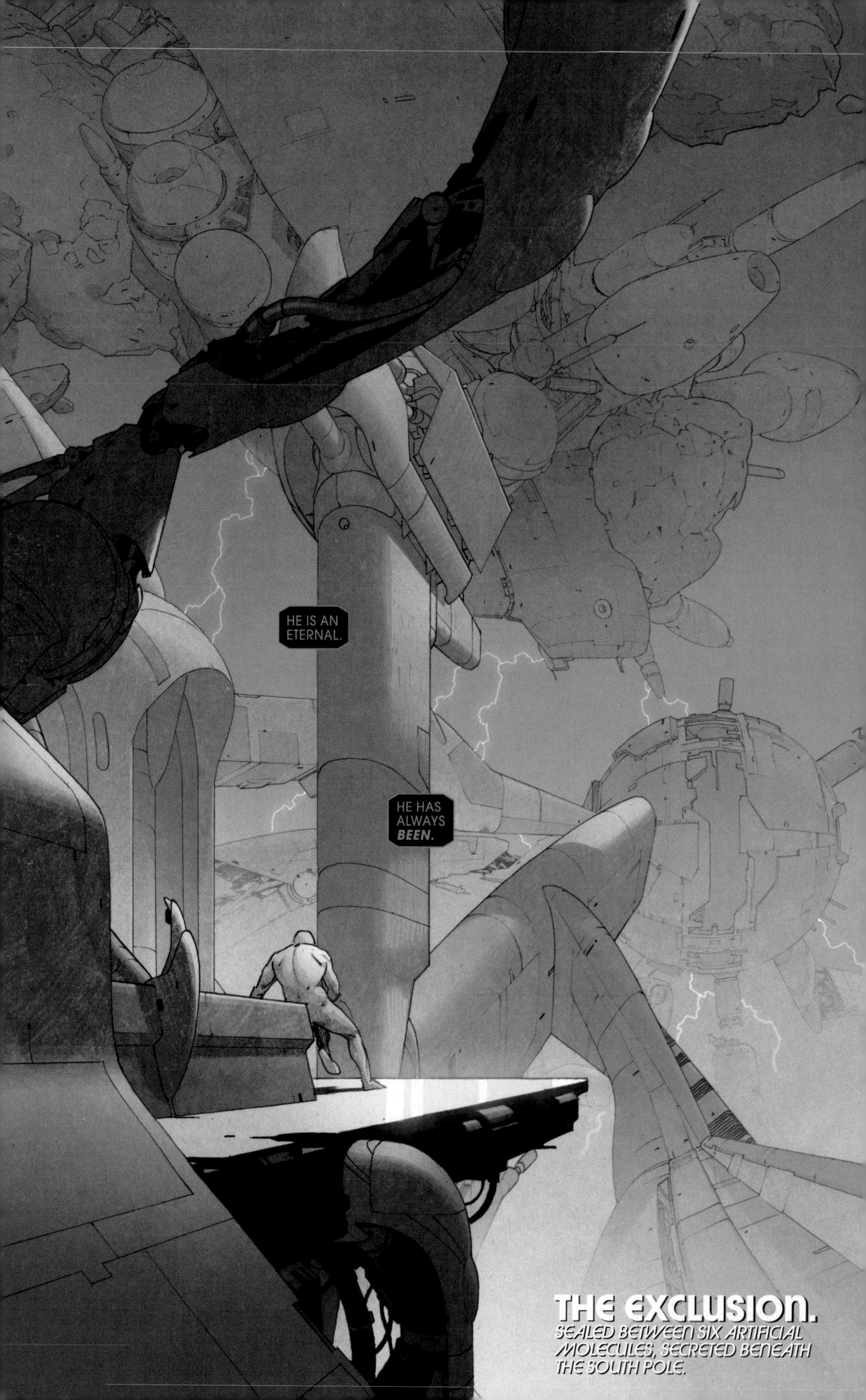
HE IS AN ETERNAL.
HE HAS ALWAYS BEEN.
THE EXCLUSION.
SEALED BETWEEN SIX ARTIFICIAL MOLECULES, SECRETED BENEATH THE SOUTH POLE.

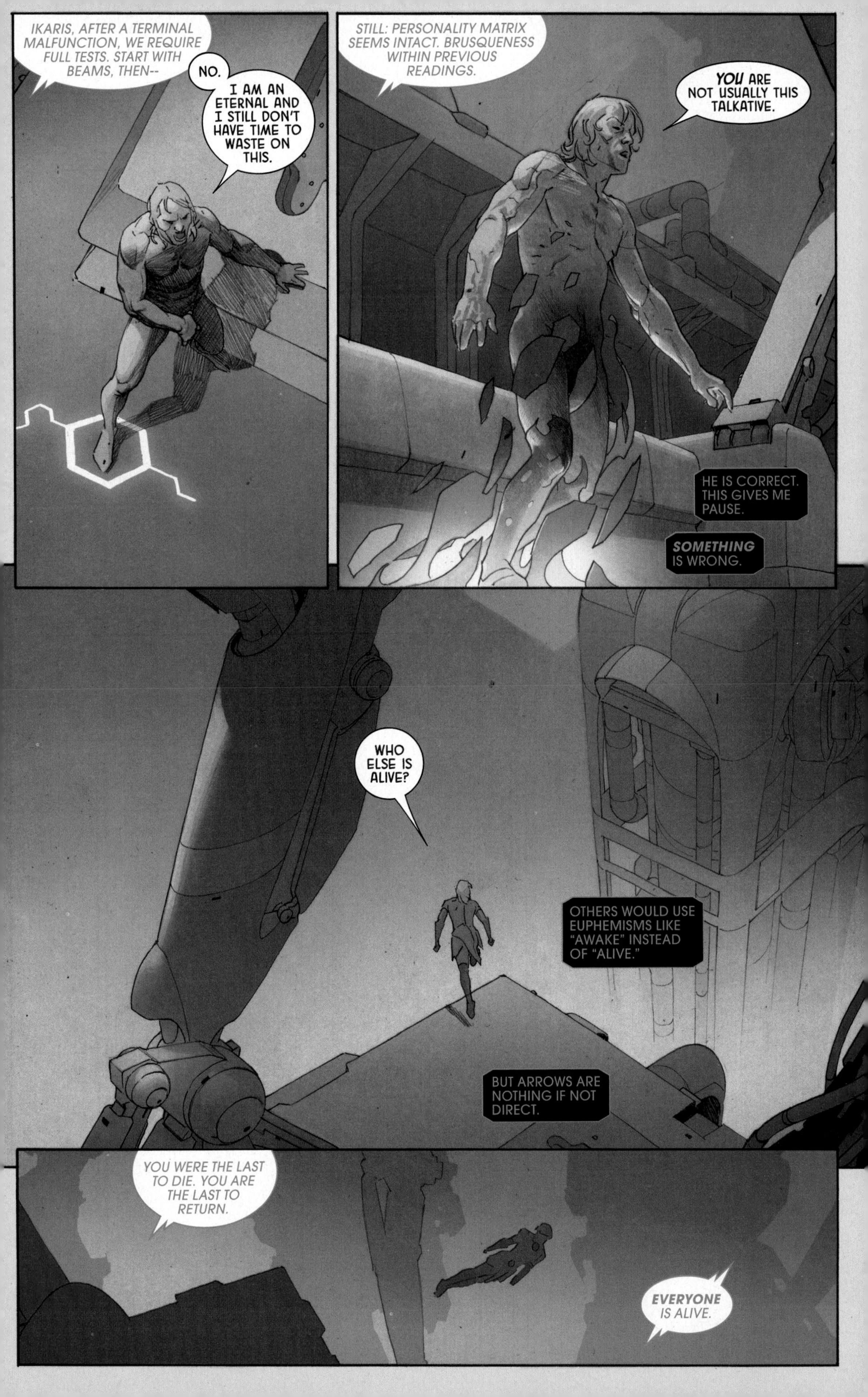
IKARIS, AFTER A TERMINAL MALFUNCTION, WE REQUIRE FULL TESTS. START WITH BEAMS, THEN--
NO.
I AM AN ETERNAL AND I STILL DON'T HAVE TIME TO WASTE ON THIS.
STILL: PERSONALITY MATRIX SEEMS INTACT. BRUSQUENESS WITHIN PREVIOUS READINGS.
YOU ARE NOT USUALLY THIS TALKATIVE.
HE IS CORRECT. THIS GIVES ME PAUSE.
SOMETHING IS WRONG.
WHO ELSE IS ALIVE?
OTHERS WOULD USE EUPHEMISMS LIKE "AWAKE" INSTEAD OF "ALIVE."
BUT ARROWS ARE NOTHING IF NOT DIRECT.
YOU WERE THE LAST TO DIE. YOU ARE THE LAST TO RETURN.
EVERYONE IS ALIVE.

ETERNALS

CREATED BY **JACK KIRBY**

A long, long time ago, alien space gods came to Earth.

They made 100 Eternals.

They made 100 Deviants.

They left.

¯_(ツ)_/¯

ONLY DEATH IS ETERNAL

 **OLYMPIA**

ZURAS	ARGOS
IKARIS	ALTO
RAKAR	CEYOTE
SERSI	PSYKOS
HELIOS	SUYIN KING
PERSE	AURELLE
DOMO	HIPPOCRATIS
VERON	MABB
MARA	BAKKUS
THE DELPHAN BROTHERS (4)	HORNED KERNNIS
PHASTOS	FIONNMAK
TITANIS	KINGO SUNEN

 **POLARIA**

VALKIN	PANNIX
VIRAKO	SOULE THE CHARRED
ZARIN	DAZH
AMAA	JUTRO
AREX	KARNAI
AGINAR	KREZNAK
DRUIG	ZORRJA
SYGMAR	TENGRAI
BETILAKK THE INTERLOPER	TUNGAC
LEGBA	QUEEN TABTEE
AKPAXA	DONARR
ERAMIS	

THE EXCLUSION

UR-LUCIVA	EXCLUDED "S"
KHARON	EXCLUDED "A"
EXCLUDED "K".	EXCLUDED "H"
EXCLUDED "SP"	EXCLUDED "E"
EXCLUDED "U"	EXCLUDED "T"

THE OCEANIC WATCH

OCEANUS
SHASTRA
THYRIO
ASTRON
KALOS THE DESTRUCTOR
ARLOK
ARGII

THE CELESTIAN PRIESTS

AJAK
MAKKARI
HARPOKRATIS
MASTER ELO
I-CHEL
THE DELPHAN MOTHER

TITANOS HERMITS

BLIND ORLA
THE SILVERED BRIDE OF HEAVEN
SCAB

THE LEMURIAN MISSION

THENA
KHORYPHOS

THE GAIAN SISTERS

DAINA OF TIMES PAST
CYBELE OF TIMES PRESENT
TULAYN OF TIMES FUTURE

THE TRICKS

JACK OF KNIVES
THE KNIGHT UNGALLANT
THE QUEEN OF MACES
IVANI GOLDENTOUCH

THE FORGOTTEN

THE FORGOTTEN ONE
UTUNAA
DUMUZA
ISHTA

THE HEX

<CLASSIFIED>
<CLASSIFIED>
<CLASSIFIED>
<CLASSIFIED>
<CLASSIFIED>
<CLASSIFIED>

DAMOCLES FOUNDATION

AZTARTAE
ELEKTRYON
KHONCHAN

LOCATION UNKNOWN

ORA OF THE PANDEMONIUM BOX
0-XXII
LUIS THREE-FINGERS
(ALL RECORDS LOST)

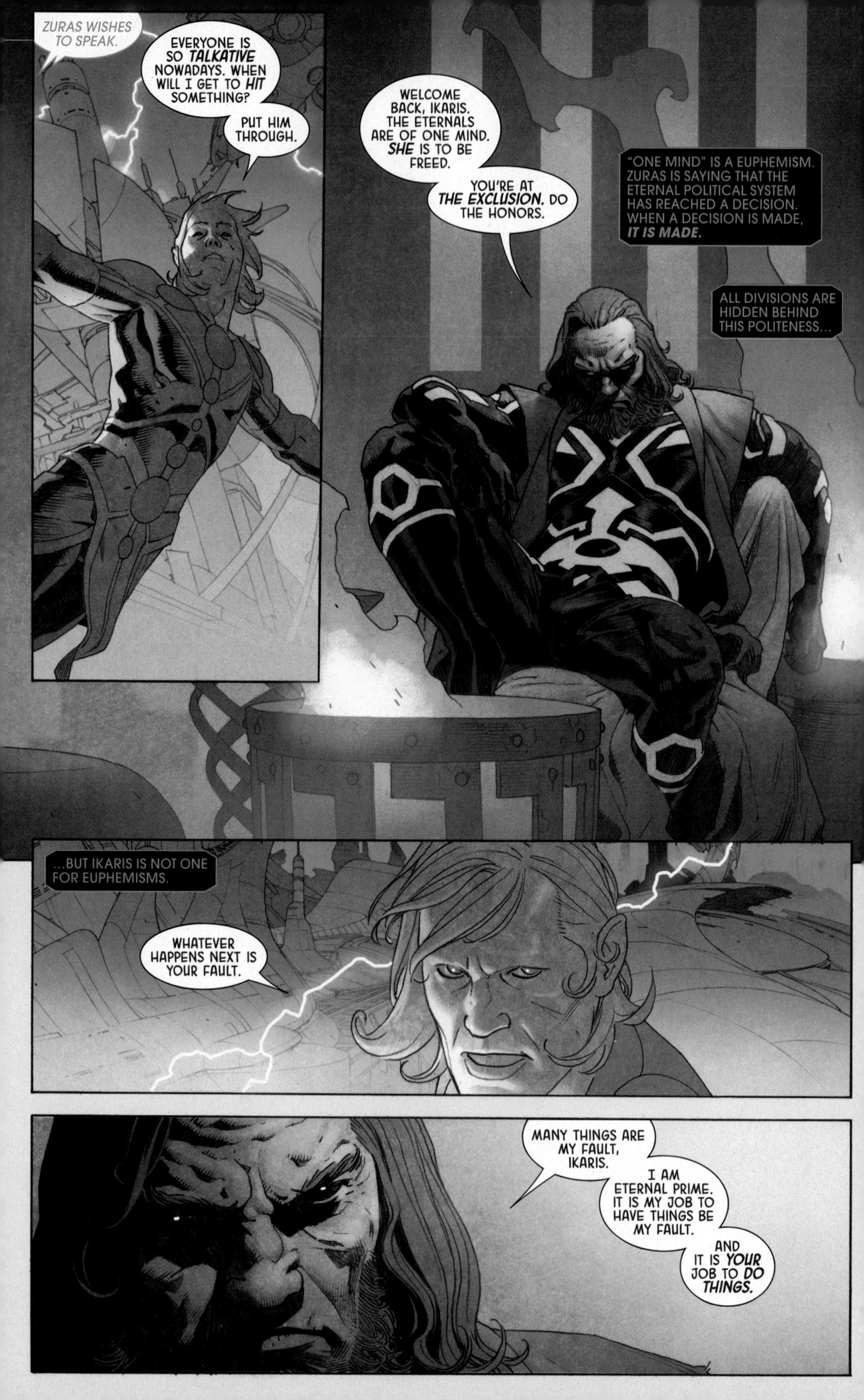

ZURAS WISHES TO SPEAK.
EVERYONE IS SO TALKATIVE NOWADAYS. WHEN WILL I GET TO HIT SOMETHING?
PUT HIM THROUGH.
WELCOME BACK, IKARIS. THE ETERNALS ARE OF ONE MIND. SHE IS TO BE FREED.
YOU'RE AT THE EXCLUSION. DO THE HONORS.
"ONE MIND" IS A EUPHEMISM. ZURAS IS SAYING THAT THE ETERNAL POLITICAL SYSTEM HAS REACHED A DECISION. WHEN A DECISION IS MADE, IT IS MADE.
ALL DIVISIONS ARE HIDDEN BEHIND THIS POLITENESS...
...BUT IKARIS IS NOT ONE FOR EUPHEMISMS.
WHATEVER HAPPENS NEXT IS YOUR FAULT.
MANY THINGS ARE MY FAULT, IKARIS.
I AM ETERNAL PRIME. IT IS MY JOB TO HAVE THINGS BE MY FAULT.
AND IT IS YOUR JOB TO DO THINGS.

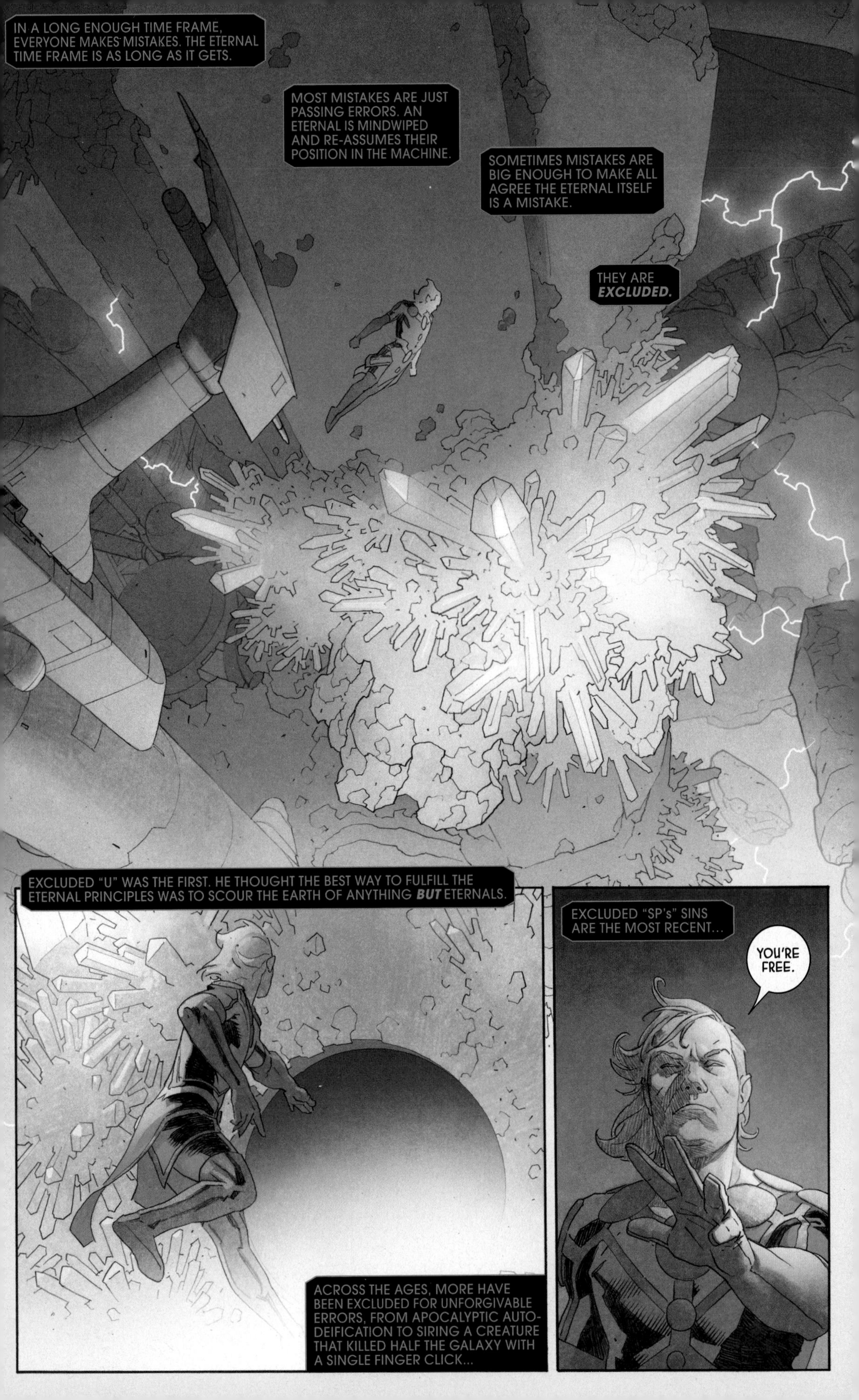
IN A LONG ENOUGH TIME FRAME, EVERYONE MAKES MISTAKES. THE ETERNAL TIME FRAME IS AS LONG AS IT GETS.
MOST MISTAKES ARE JUST PASSING ERRORS. AN ETERNAL IS MINDWIPED AND RE-ASSUMES THEIR POSITION IN THE MACHINE.
SOMETIMES MISTAKES ARE BIG ENOUGH TO MAKE ALL AGREE THE ETERNAL ITSELF IS A MISTAKE.
THEY ARE *EXCLUDED.*
EXCLUDED "U" WAS THE FIRST. HE THOUGHT THE BEST WAY TO FULFILL THE ETERNAL PRINCIPLES WAS TO SCOUR THE EARTH OF ANYTHING *BUT* ETERNALS.
ACROSS THE AGES, MORE HAVE BEEN EXCLUDED FOR UNFORGIVABLE ERRORS, FROM APOCALYPTIC AUTO-DEIFICATION TO SIRING A CREATURE THAT KILLED HALF THE GALAXY WITH A SINGLE FINGER CLICK...
EXCLUDED "SP's" SINS ARE THE MOST RECENT...
YOU'RE FREE.

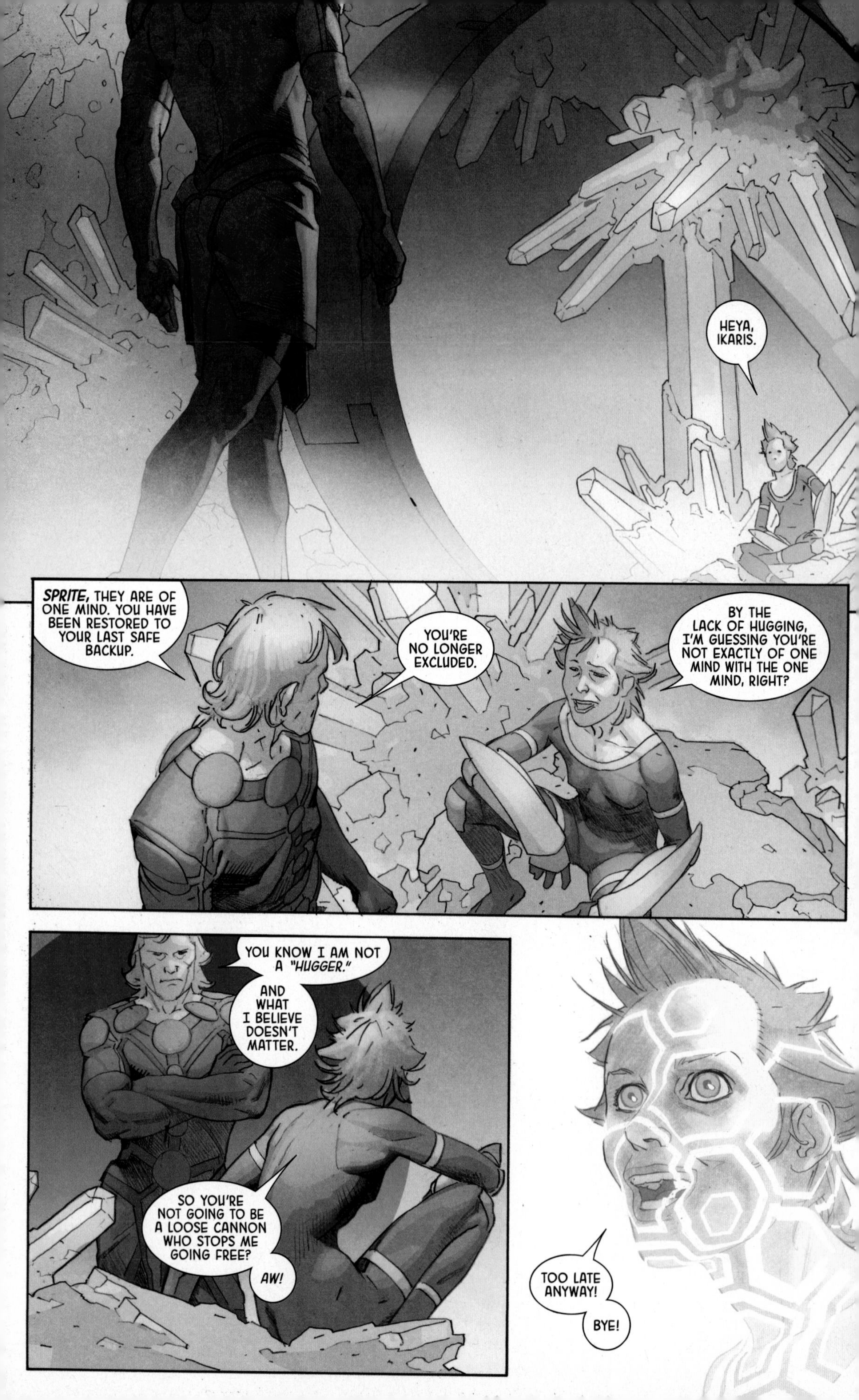
HEYA, IKARIS.
SPRITE, THEY ARE OF ONE MIND. YOU HAVE BEEN RESTORED TO YOUR LAST SAFE BACKUP.
YOU'RE NO LONGER EXCLUDED.
BY THE LACK OF HUGGING, I'M GUESSING YOU'RE NOT EXACTLY OF ONE MIND WITH THE ONE MIND, RIGHT?
YOU KNOW I AM NOT A "HUGGER."
AND WHAT I BELIEVE DOESN'T MATTER.
SO YOU'RE NOT GOING TO BE A LOOSE CANNON WHO STOPS ME GOING FREE?
AW!
TOO LATE ANYWAY!
BYE!

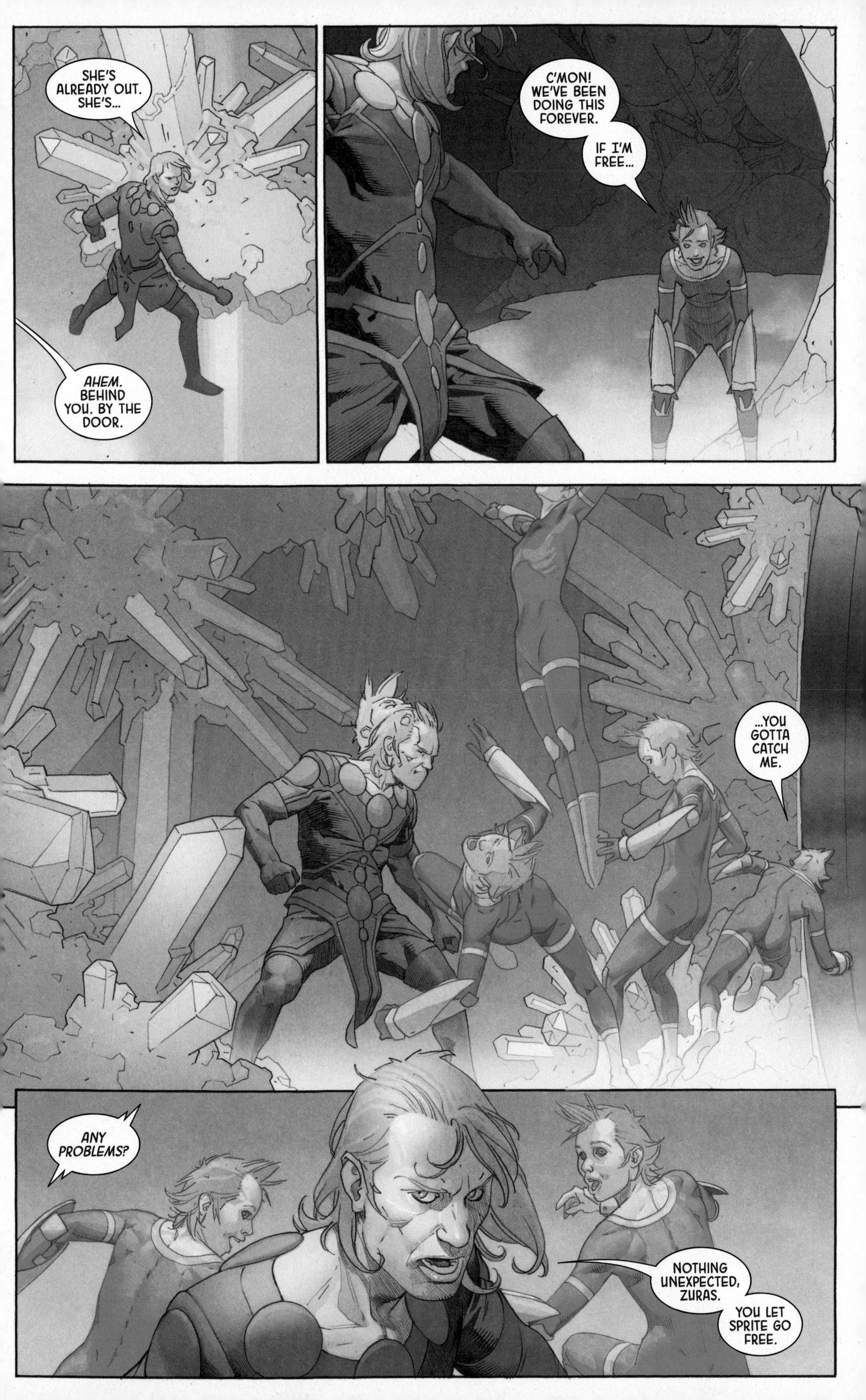
SHE'S ALREADY OUT. SHE'S...
AHEM. BEHIND YOU. BY THE DOOR.
C'MON! WE'VE BEEN DOING THIS FOREVER.
IF I'M FREE...
...YOU GOTTA CATCH ME.
ANY PROBLEMS?
NOTHING UNEXPECTED, ZURAS.
YOU LET SPRITE GO FREE.

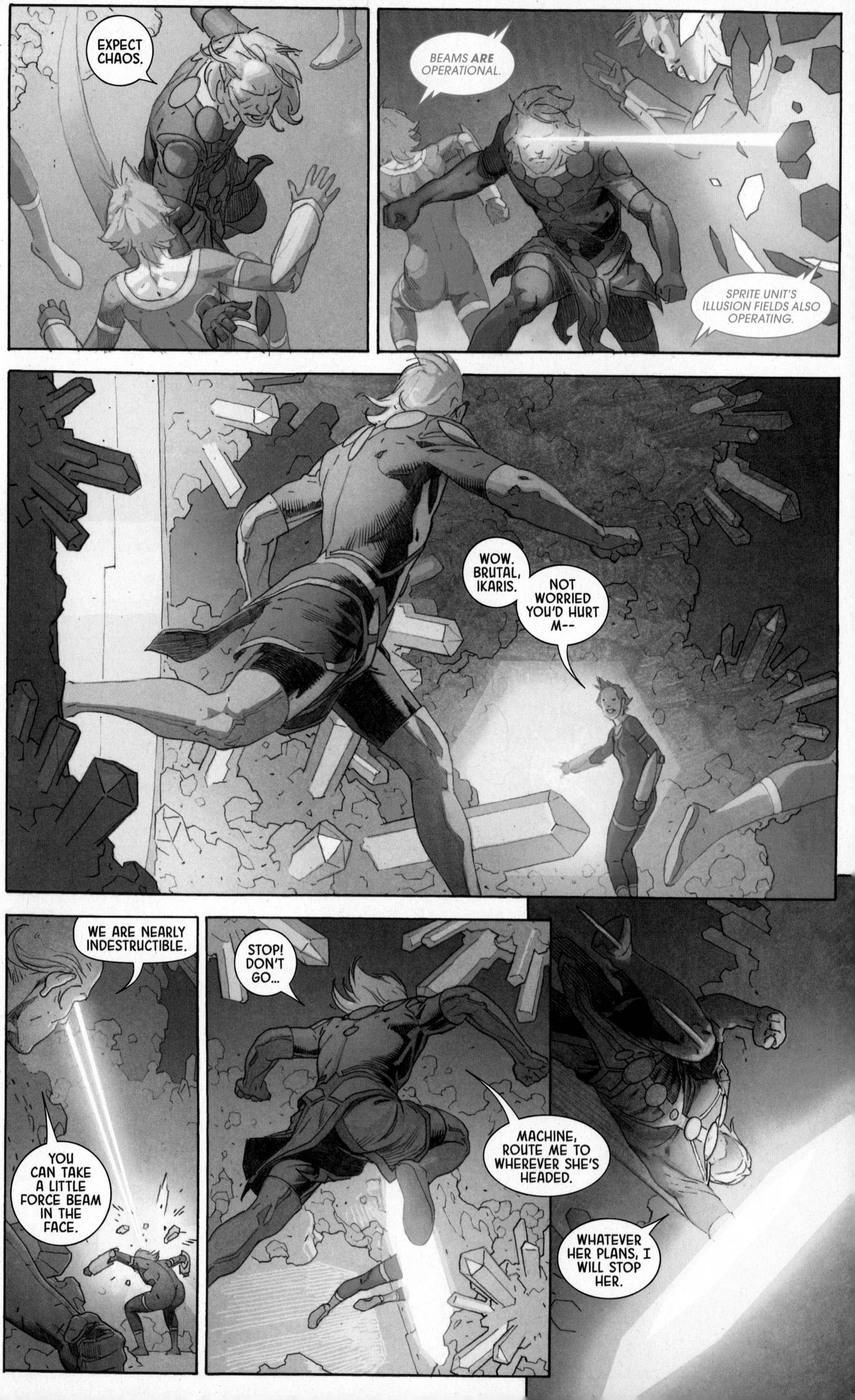
EXPECT CHAOS.
BEAMS **ARE** OPERATIONAL.
SPRITE UNIT'S ILLUSION FIELDS ALSO OPERATING.
WOW. BRUTAL, IKARIS.
NOT WORRIED YOU'D HURT M--
WE ARE NEARLY INDESTRUCTIBLE.
YOU CAN TAKE A LITTLE FORCE BEAM IN THE FACE.
STOP! DON'T GO...
MACHINE, ROUTE ME TO WHEREVER SHE'S HEADED.
WHATEVER HER PLANS, I WILL STOP HER.

THE MACHINE

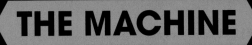

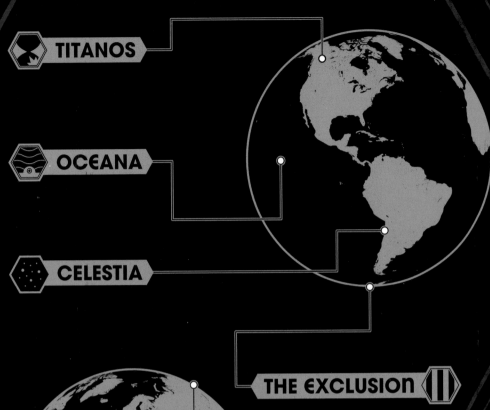

TITANOS

OCEANA

CELESTIA

THE EXCLUSION

POLARIA

OLYMPIA

Eternals' suite of abilities includes complete molecular disassembly and reassembly—as in, effective teleportation. To do this over a distance is of enormous strain.

The Machine supplements this ability with the network, forming a system of subdimensional threads interlacing the planet.

Any cleared Eternal can disassemble, enter the system and move between the nodes then reassemble in the required destination.

The Machine will argue the system works incredibly well, considering its complexities. Most Eternals would agree though likely underline the word "considering."

It is the teleportation equivalent of a mass transit system in a major Earth city.

Unreliable, complicated, yet essential.

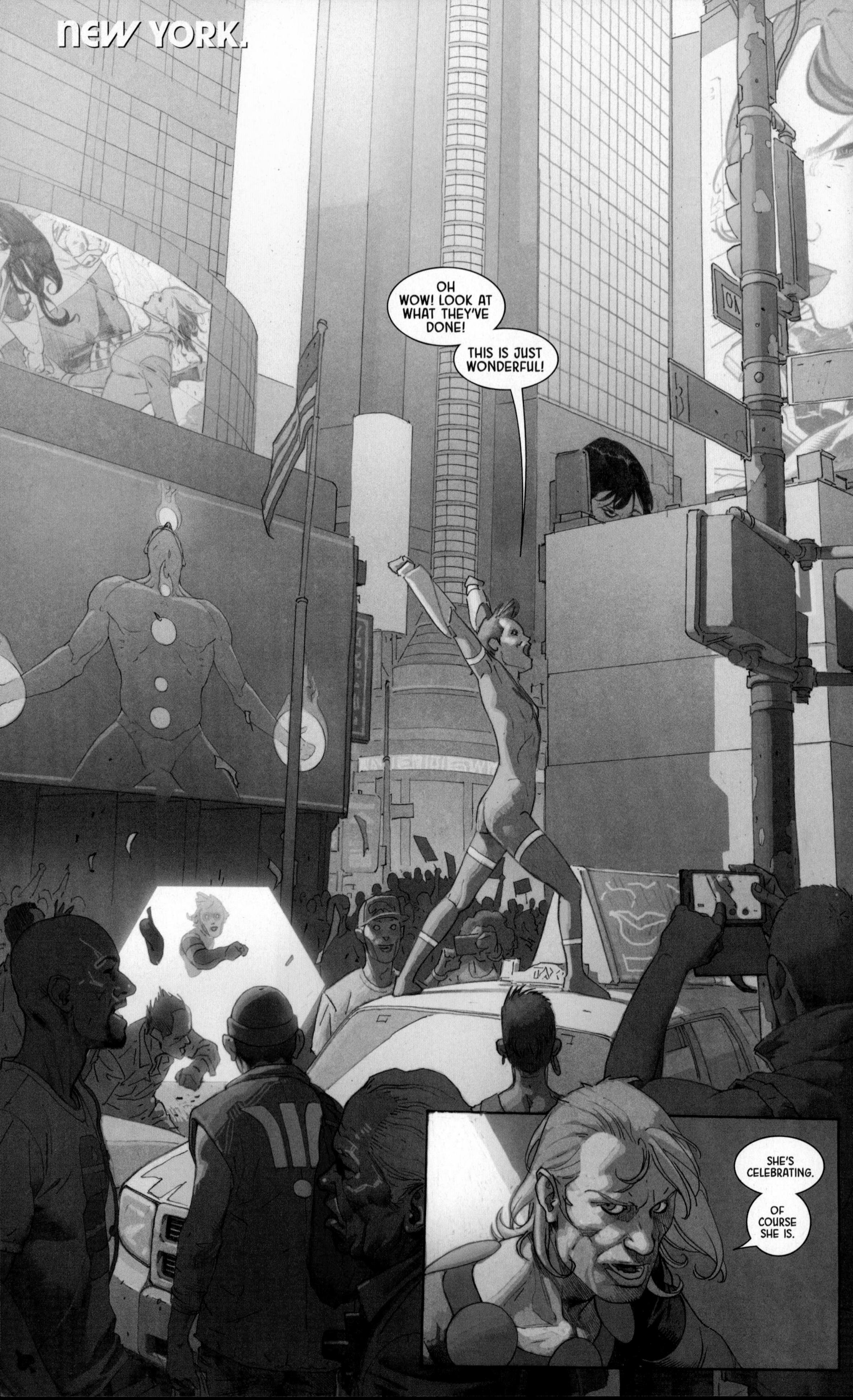
NEW YORK.
OH WOW! LOOK AT WHAT THEY'VE DONE!
THIS IS JUST WONDERFUL!
SHE'S CELEBRATING.
OF COURSE SHE IS.

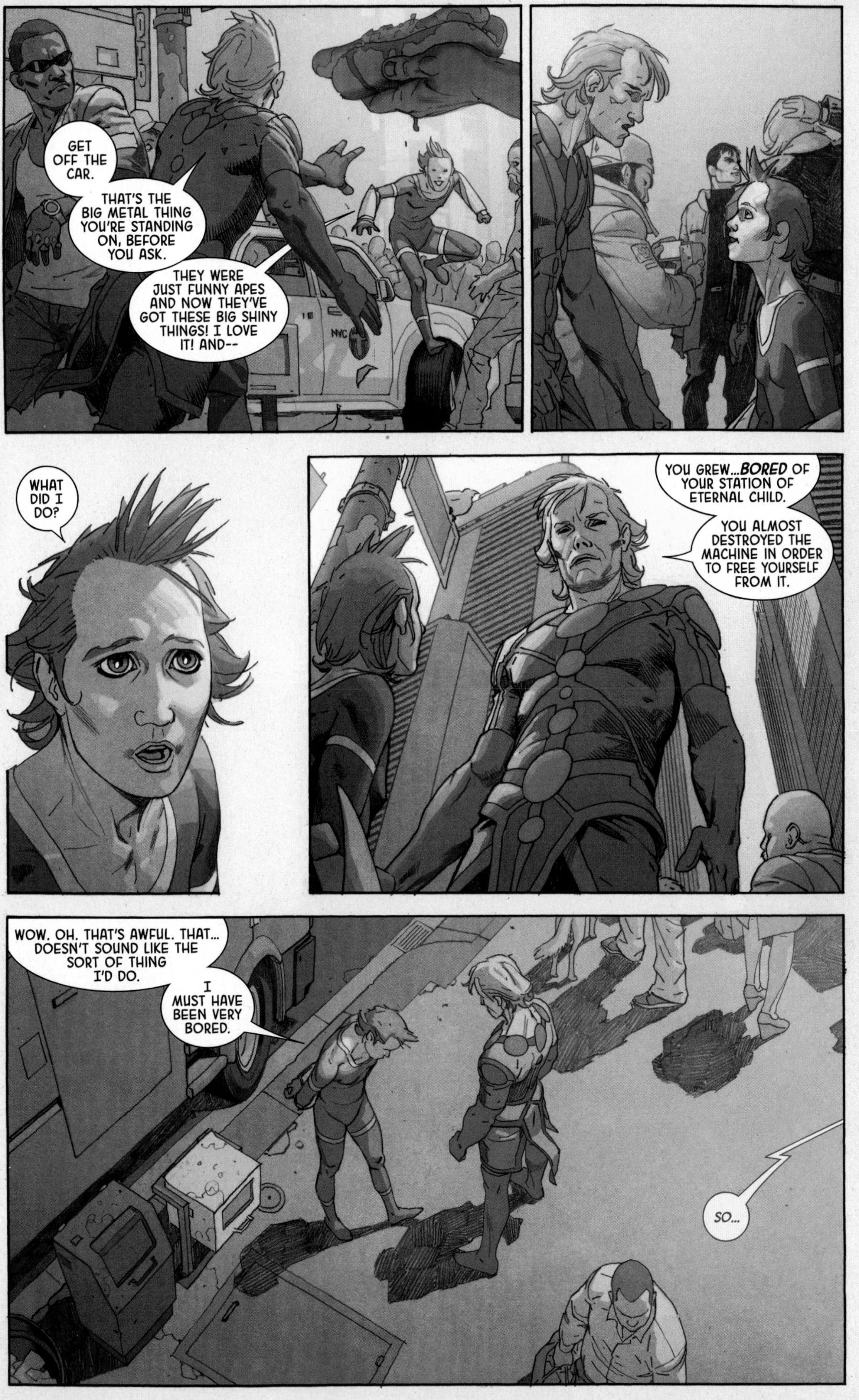
GET OFF THE CAR.
THAT'S THE BIG METAL THING YOU'RE STANDING ON, BEFORE YOU ASK.
THEY WERE JUST FUNNY APES AND NOW THEY'VE GOT THESE BIG SHINY THINGS! I LOVE IT! AND--
NYC
WHAT DID I DO?
YOU GREW...**BORED** OF YOUR STATION OF ETERNAL CHILD.
YOU ALMOST DESTROYED THE MACHINE IN ORDER TO FREE YOURSELF FROM IT.
WOW. OH. THAT'S AWFUL. THAT... DOESN'T SOUND LIKE THE SORT OF THING I'D DO.
I MUST HAVE BEEN VERY BORED.
SO...

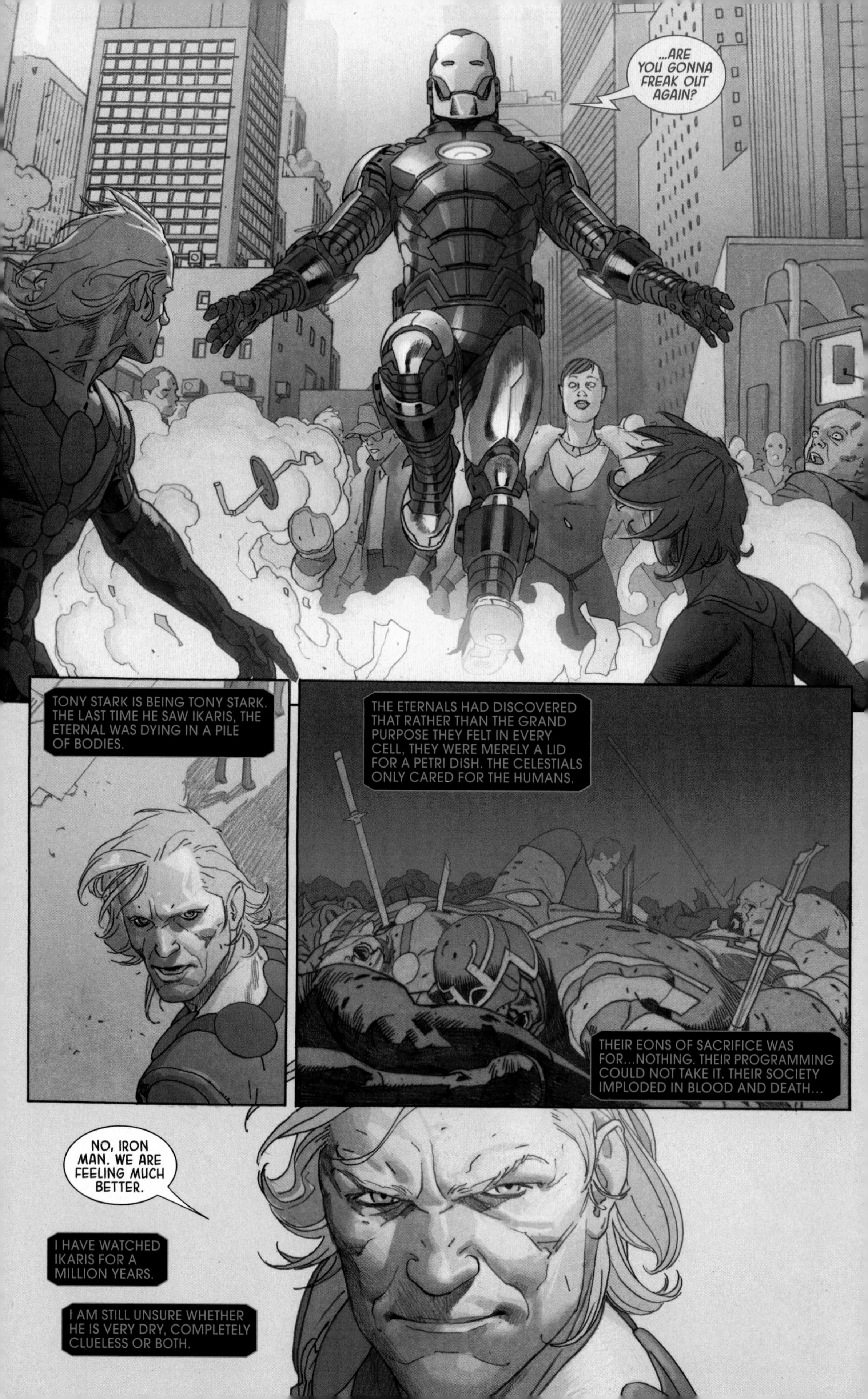
...ARE YOU GONNA FREAK OUT AGAIN?
TONY STARK IS BEING TONY STARK. THE LAST TIME HE SAW IKARIS, THE ETERNAL WAS DYING IN A PILE OF BODIES.
THE ETERNALS HAD DISCOVERED THAT RATHER THAN THE GRAND PURPOSE THEY FELT IN EVERY CELL, THEY WERE MERELY A LID FOR A PETRI DISH. THE CELESTIALS ONLY CARED FOR THE HUMANS.
THEIR EONS OF SACRIFICE WAS FOR...NOTHING. THEIR PROGRAMMING COULD NOT TAKE IT. THEIR SOCIETY IMPLODED IN BLOOD AND DEATH...
NO, IRON MAN. WE ARE FEELING MUCH BETTER.
I HAVE WATCHED IKARIS FOR A MILLION YEARS.
I AM STILL UNSURE WHETHER HE IS VERY DRY, COMPLETELY CLUELESS OR BOTH.

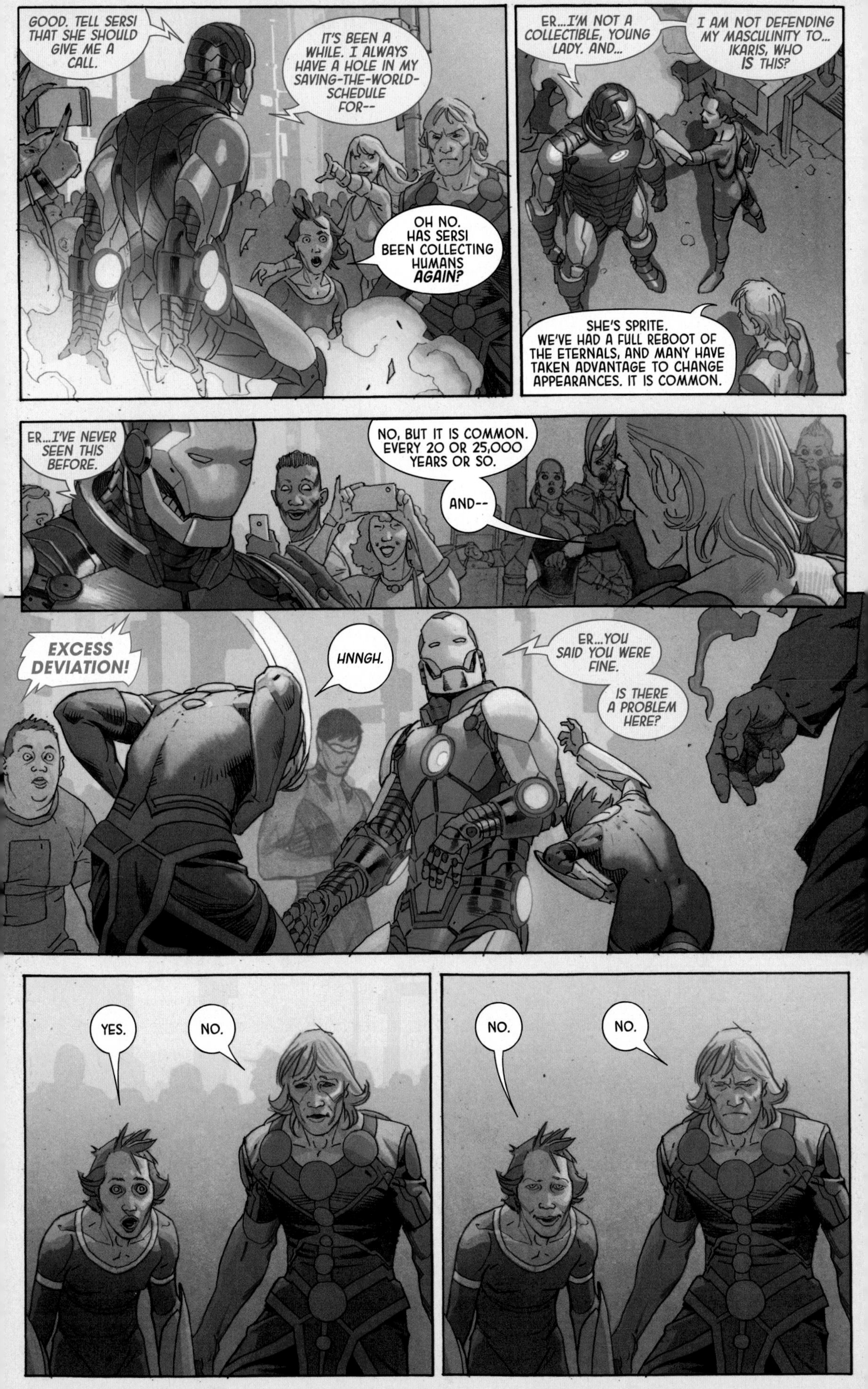
GOOD. TELL SERSI THAT SHE SHOULD GIVE ME A CALL.
IT'S BEEN A WHILE. I ALWAYS HAVE A HOLE IN MY SAVING-THE-WORLD-SCHEDULE FOR--
OH NO. HAS SERSI BEEN COLLECTING HUMANS AGAIN?
ER...I'M NOT A COLLECTIBLE, YOUNG LADY. AND...
I AM NOT DEFENDING MY MASCULINITY TO... IKARIS, WHO IS THIS?
SHE'S SPRITE. WE'VE HAD A FULL REBOOT OF THE ETERNALS, AND MANY HAVE TAKEN ADVANTAGE TO CHANGE APPEARANCES. IT IS COMMON.
ER...I'VE NEVER SEEN THIS BEFORE.
NO, BUT IT IS COMMON. EVERY 20 OR 25,000 YEARS OR SO.
AND--
EXCESS DEVIATION!
HNNGH.
ER...YOU SAID YOU WERE FINE.
IS THERE A PROBLEM HERE?
YES.
NO.
NO.
NO.

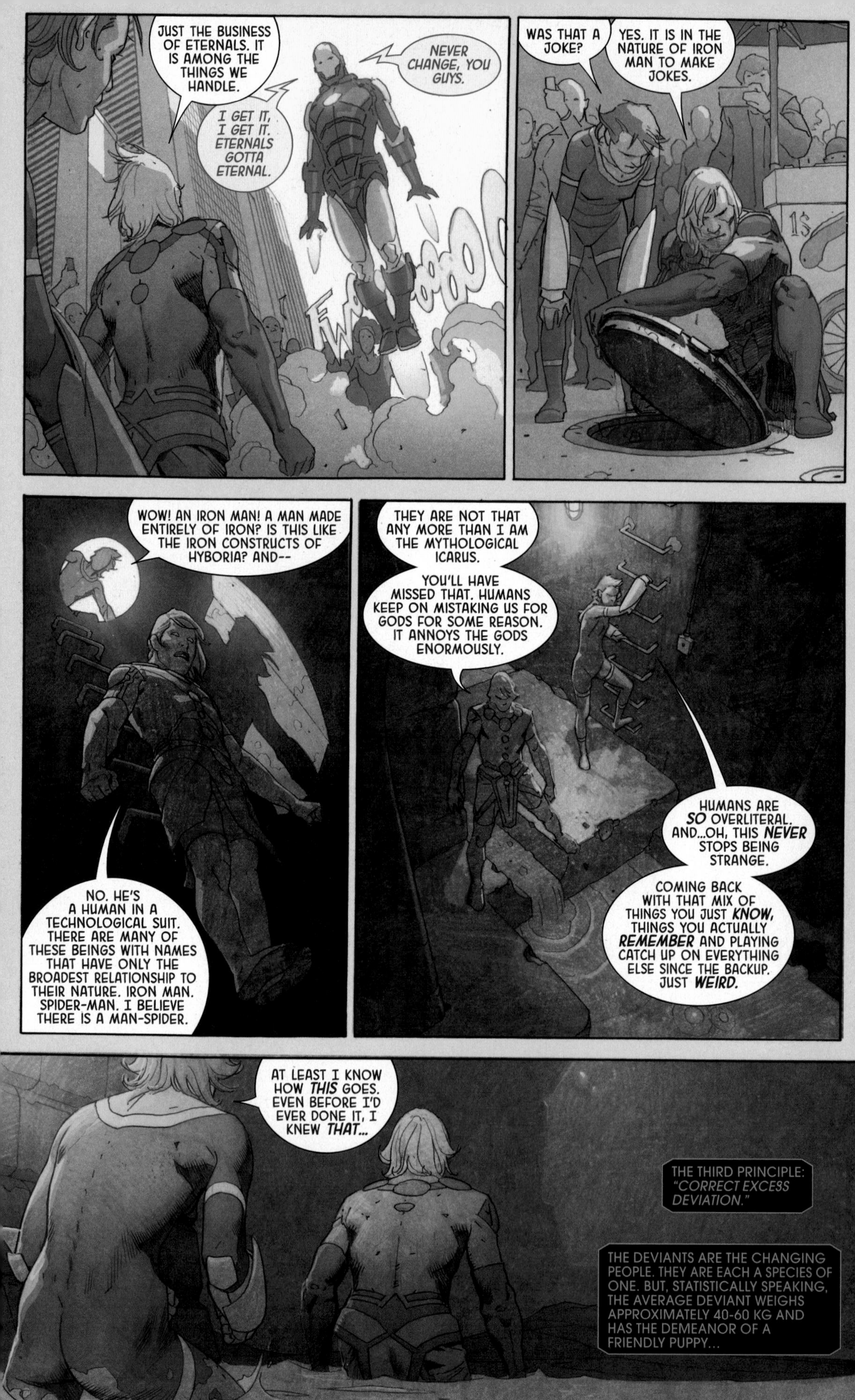
JUST THE BUSINESS OF ETERNALS. IT IS AMONG THE THINGS WE HANDLE.
I GET IT, I GET IT. ETERNALS GOTTA ETERNAL.
NEVER CHANGE, YOU GUYS.
WAS THAT A JOKE?
YES. IT IS IN THE NATURE OF IRON MAN TO MAKE JOKES.
1$
WOW! AN IRON MAN! A MAN MADE ENTIRELY OF IRON? IS THIS LIKE THE IRON CONSTRUCTS OF HYBORIA? AND--
NO. HE'S A HUMAN IN A TECHNOLOGICAL SUIT. THERE ARE MANY OF THESE BEINGS WITH NAMES THAT HAVE ONLY THE BROADEST RELATIONSHIP TO THEIR NATURE. IRON MAN. SPIDER-MAN. I BELIEVE THERE IS A MAN-SPIDER.
THEY ARE NOT THAT ANY MORE THAN I AM THE MYTHOLOGICAL ICARUS.
YOU'LL HAVE MISSED THAT. HUMANS KEEP ON MISTAKING US FOR GODS FOR SOME REASON. IT ANNOYS THE GODS ENORMOUSLY.
HUMANS ARE SO OVERLITERAL. AND...OH, THIS NEVER STOPS BEING STRANGE.
COMING BACK WITH THAT MIX OF THINGS YOU JUST KNOW, THINGS YOU ACTUALLY REMEMBER AND PLAYING CATCH UP ON EVERYTHING ELSE SINCE THE BACKUP. JUST WEIRD.
AT LEAST I KNOW HOW THIS GOES. EVEN BEFORE I'D EVER DONE IT, I KNEW THAT...
THE THIRD PRINCIPLE: "CORRECT EXCESS DEVIATION."
THE DEVIANTS ARE THE CHANGING PEOPLE. THEY ARE EACH A SPECIES OF ONE. BUT, STATISTICALLY SPEAKING, THE AVERAGE DEVIANT WEIGHS APPROXIMATELY 40-60 KG AND HAS THE DEMEANOR OF A FRIENDLY PUPPY...

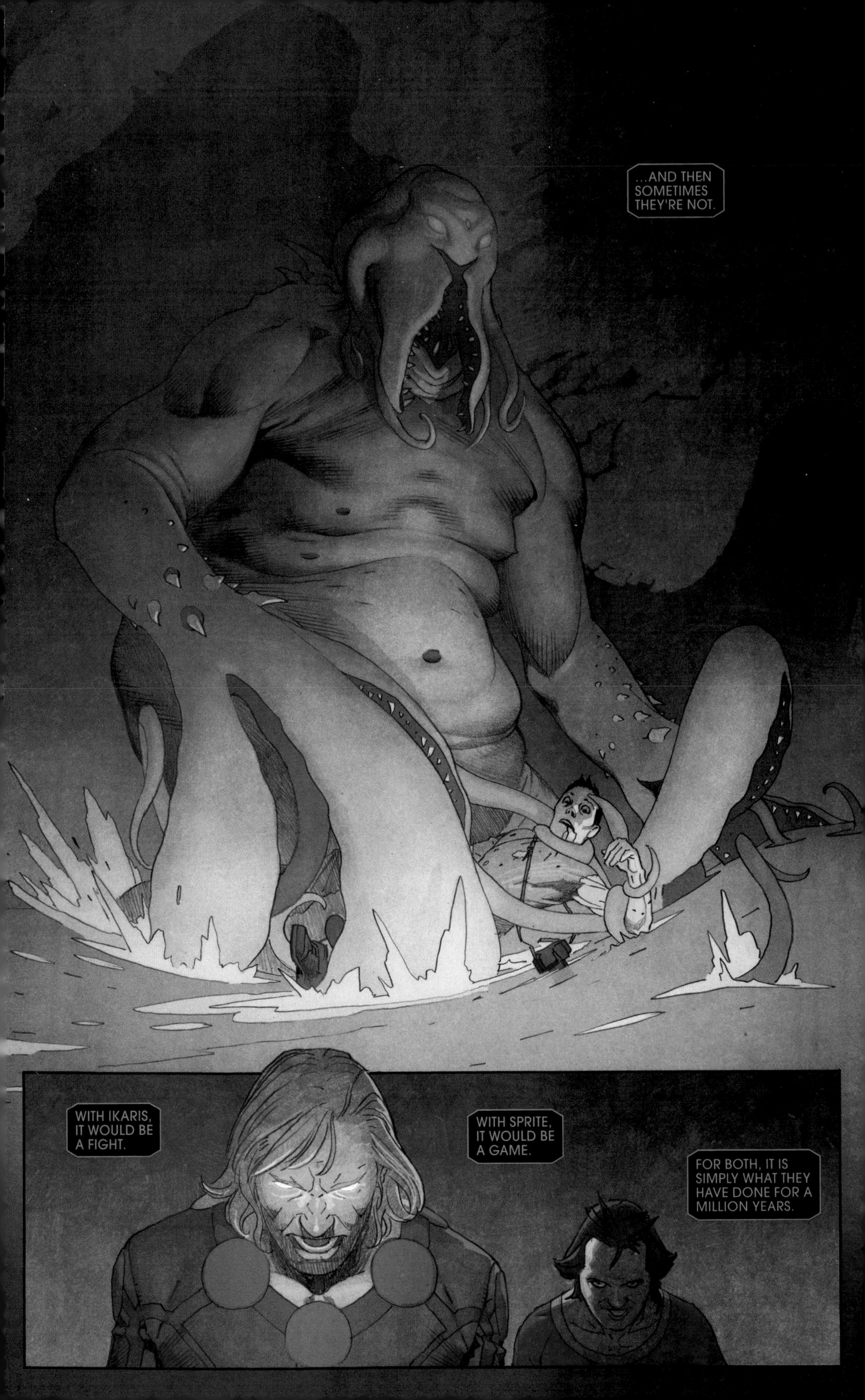
...AND THEN SOMETIMES THEY'RE NOT.
WITH IKARIS, IT WOULD BE A FIGHT.
WITH SPRITE, IT WOULD BE A GAME.
FOR BOTH, IT IS SIMPLY WHAT THEY HAVE DONE FOR A MILLION YEARS.

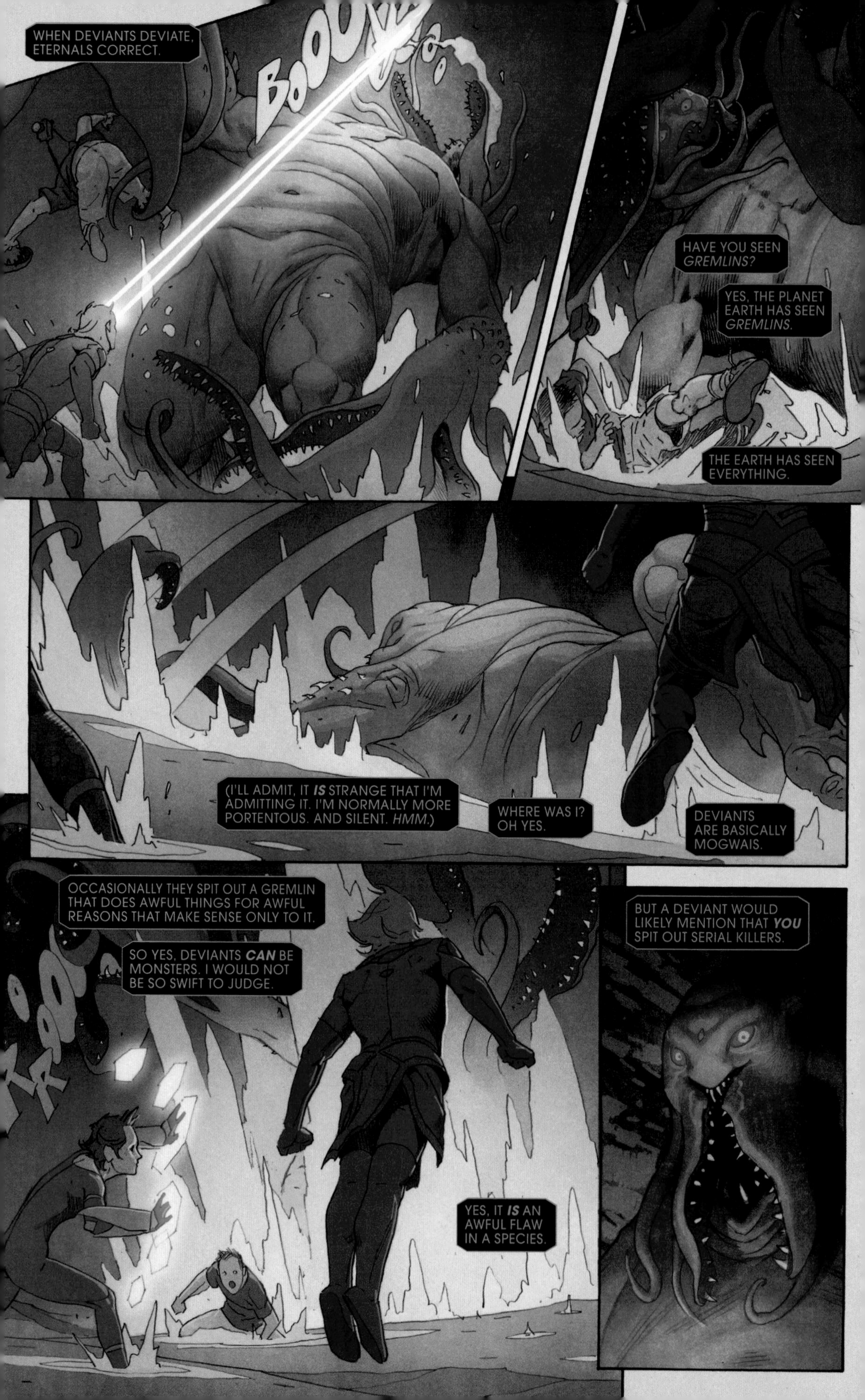
WHEN DEVIANTS DEVIATE, ETERNALS CORRECT.
HAVE YOU SEEN *GREMLINS?*
YES, THE PLANET EARTH HAS SEEN *GREMLINS.*
THE EARTH HAS SEEN EVERYTHING.
(I'LL ADMIT, IT ***IS*** STRANGE THAT I'M ADMITTING IT. I'M NORMALLY MORE PORTENTOUS. AND SILENT. *HMM.*)
WHERE WAS I? OH YES.
DEVIANTS ARE BASICALLY MOGWAIS.
OCCASIONALLY THEY SPIT OUT A GREMLIN THAT DOES AWFUL THINGS FOR AWFUL REASONS THAT MAKE SENSE ONLY TO IT.
SO YES, DEVIANTS ***CAN*** BE MONSTERS. I WOULD NOT BE SO SWIFT TO JUDGE.
YES, IT ***IS*** AN AWFUL FLAW IN A SPECIES.
BUT A DEVIANT WOULD LIKELY MENTION THAT ***YOU*** SPIT OUT SERIAL KILLERS.

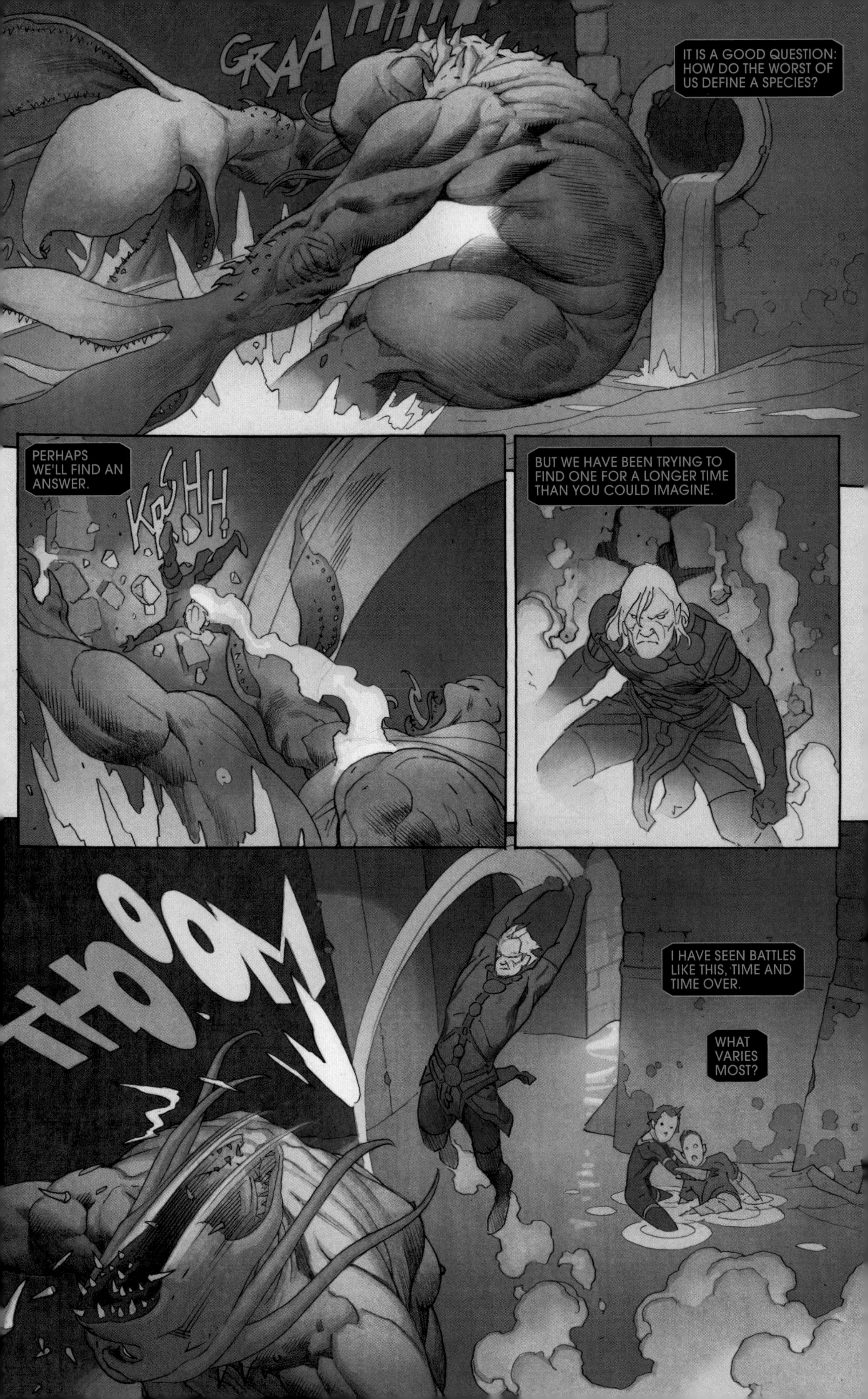
GRAAHHH
IT IS A GOOD QUESTION: HOW DO THE WORST OF US DEFINE A SPECIES?
PERHAPS WE'LL FIND AN ANSWER.
KRSHH
BUT WE HAVE BEEN TRYING TO FIND ONE FOR A LONGER TIME THAN YOU COULD IMAGINE.
THOOM
I HAVE SEEN BATTLES LIKE THIS, TIME AND TIME OVER.
WHAT VARIES MOST?

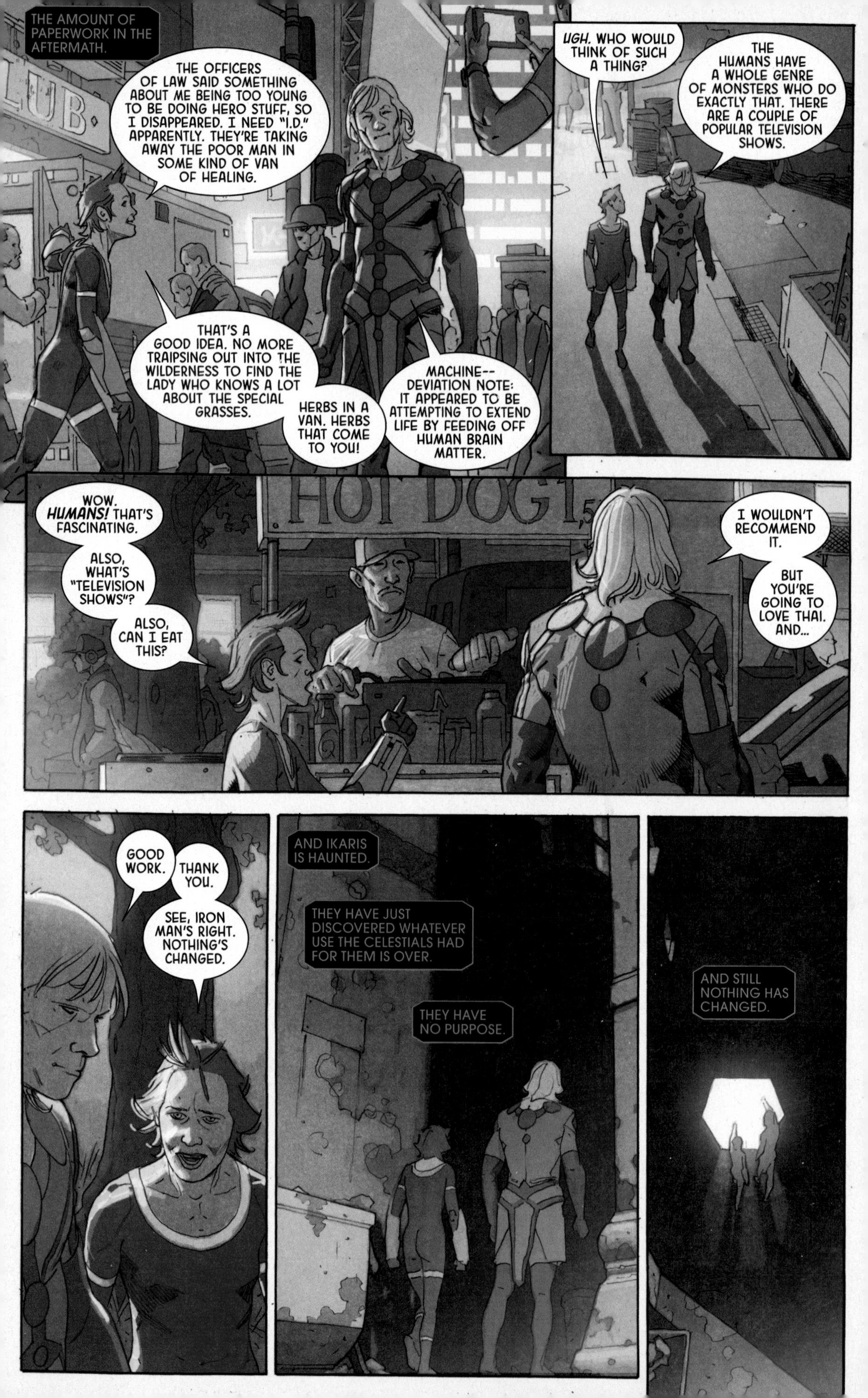
THE AMOUNT OF PAPERWORK IN THE AFTERMATH.
THE OFFICERS OF LAW SAID SOMETHING ABOUT ME BEING TOO YOUNG TO BE DOING HERO STUFF, SO I DISAPPEARED. I NEED "I.D." APPARENTLY. THEY'RE TAKING AWAY THE POOR MAN IN SOME KIND OF VAN OF HEALING.
THAT'S A GOOD IDEA. NO MORE TRAIPSING OUT INTO THE WILDERNESS TO FIND THE LADY WHO KNOWS A LOT ABOUT THE SPECIAL GRASSES.
HERBS IN A VAN. HERBS THAT COME TO YOU!
MACHINE-- DEVIATION NOTE: IT APPEARED TO BE ATTEMPTING TO EXTEND LIFE BY FEEDING OFF HUMAN BRAIN MATTER.
UGH. WHO WOULD THINK OF SUCH A THING?
THE HUMANS HAVE A WHOLE GENRE OF MONSTERS WHO DO EXACTLY THAT. THERE ARE A COUPLE OF POPULAR TELEVISION SHOWS.
HOT DOG
WOW. HUMANS! THAT'S FASCINATING.
ALSO, WHAT'S "TELEVISION SHOWS"?
ALSO, CAN I EAT THIS?
I WOULDN'T RECOMMEND IT.
BUT YOU'RE GOING TO LOVE THAI. AND...
GOOD WORK.
THANK YOU.
SEE, IRON MAN'S RIGHT. NOTHING'S CHANGED.
AND IKARIS IS HAUNTED.
THEY HAVE JUST DISCOVERED WHATEVER USE THE CELESTIALS HAD FOR THEM IS OVER.
THEY HAVE NO PURPOSE.
AND STILL NOTHING HAS CHANGED.

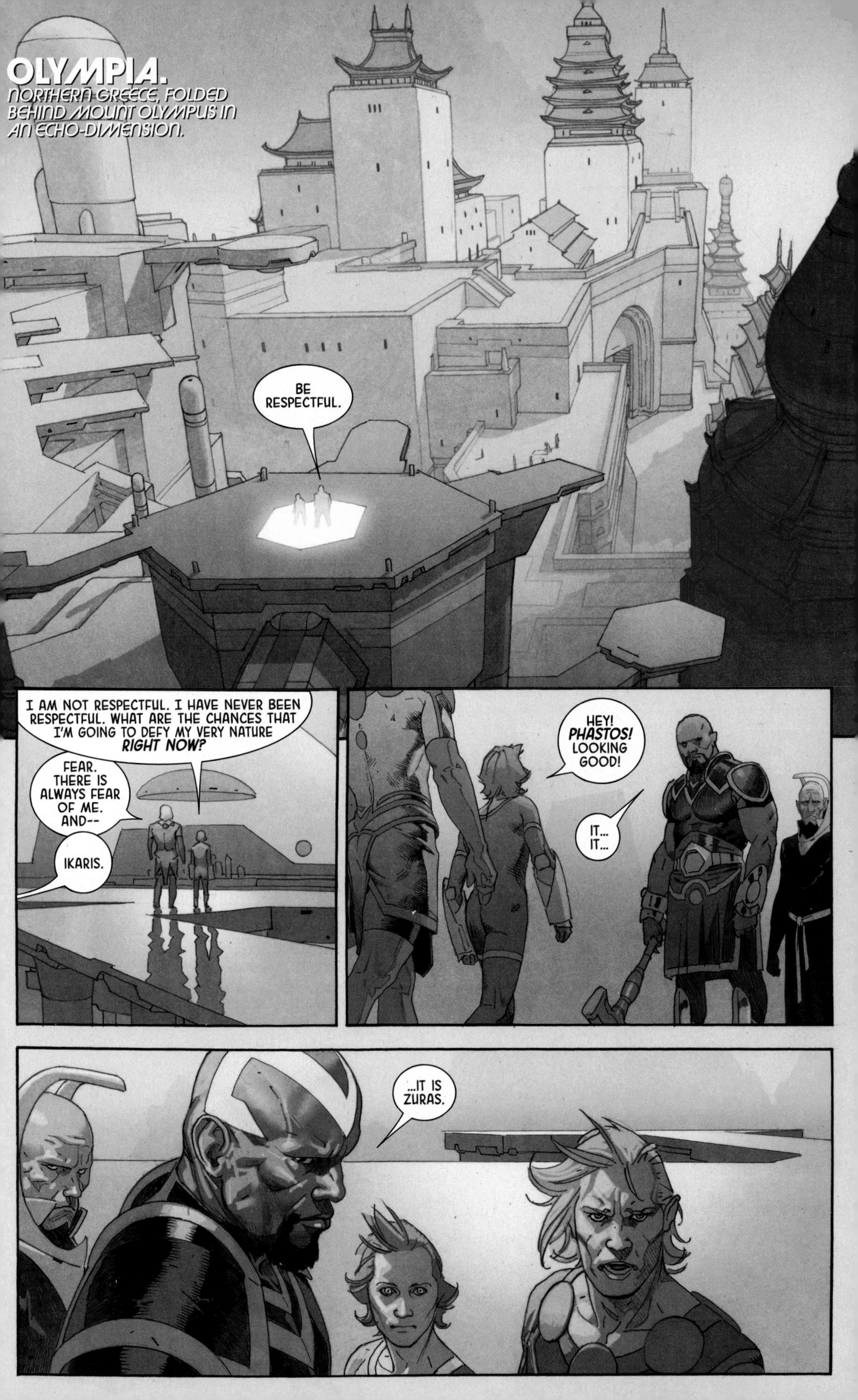
OLYMPIA.
NORTHERN GREECE, FOLDED BEHIND MOUNT OLYMPUS IN AN ECHO-DIMENSION.
BE RESPECTFUL.
I AM NOT RESPECTFUL. I HAVE NEVER BEEN RESPECTFUL. WHAT ARE THE CHANCES THAT I'M GOING TO DEFY MY VERY NATURE RIGHT NOW?
FEAR. THERE IS ALWAYS FEAR OF ME. AND--
IKARIS.
HEY! PHASTOS! LOOKING GOOD!
IT... IT...
...IT IS ZURAS.

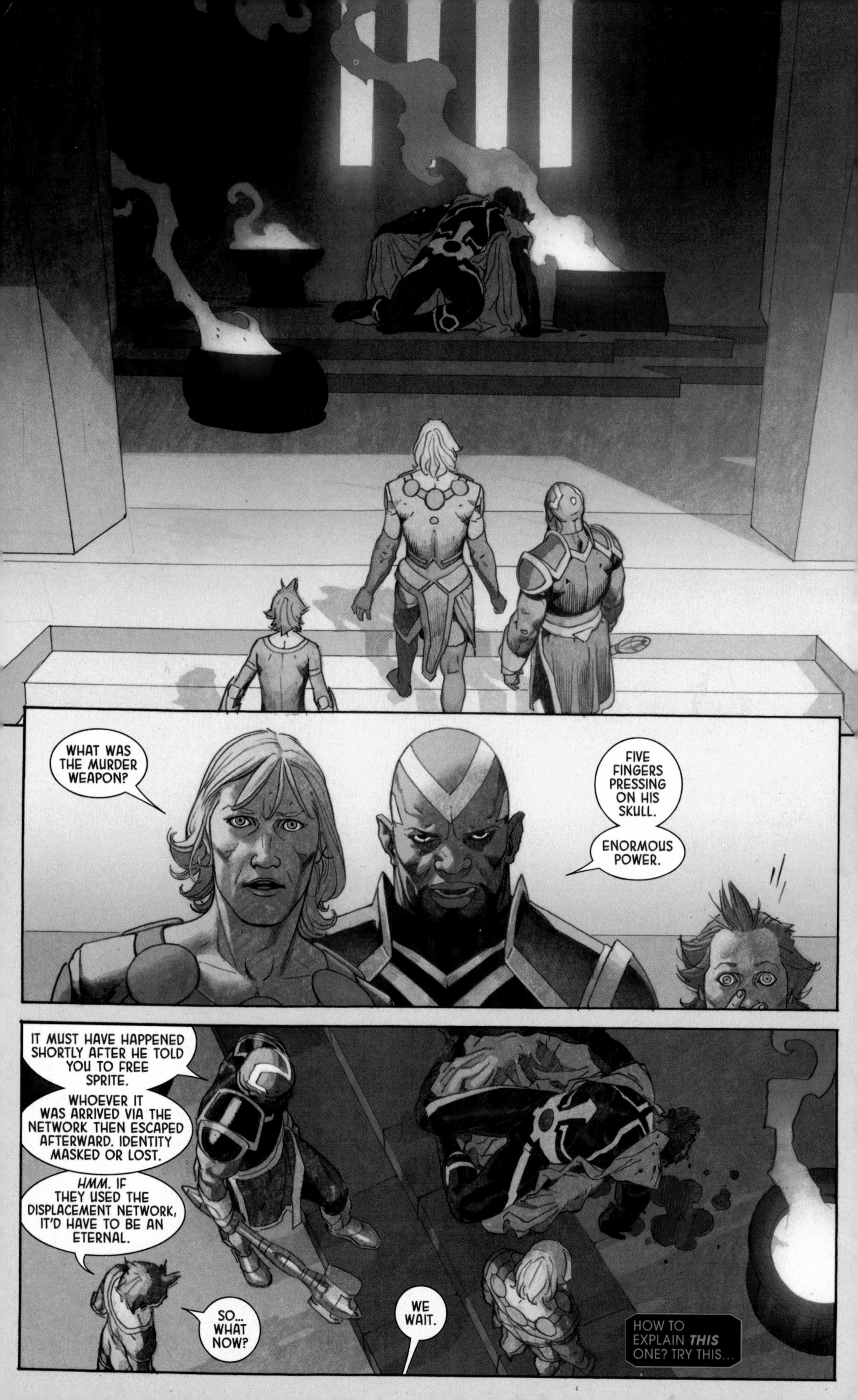
WHAT WAS THE MURDER WEAPON?
FIVE FINGERS PRESSING ON HIS SKULL.
ENORMOUS POWER.
IT MUST HAVE HAPPENED SHORTLY AFTER HE TOLD YOU TO FREE SPRITE.
WHOEVER IT WAS ARRIVED VIA THE NETWORK THEN ESCAPED AFTERWARD. IDENTITY MASKED OR LOST.
HMM. IF THEY USED THE DISPLACEMENT NETWORK, IT'D HAVE TO BE AN ETERNAL.
SO... WHAT NOW?
WE WAIT.
HOW TO EXPLAIN THIS ONE? TRY THIS...

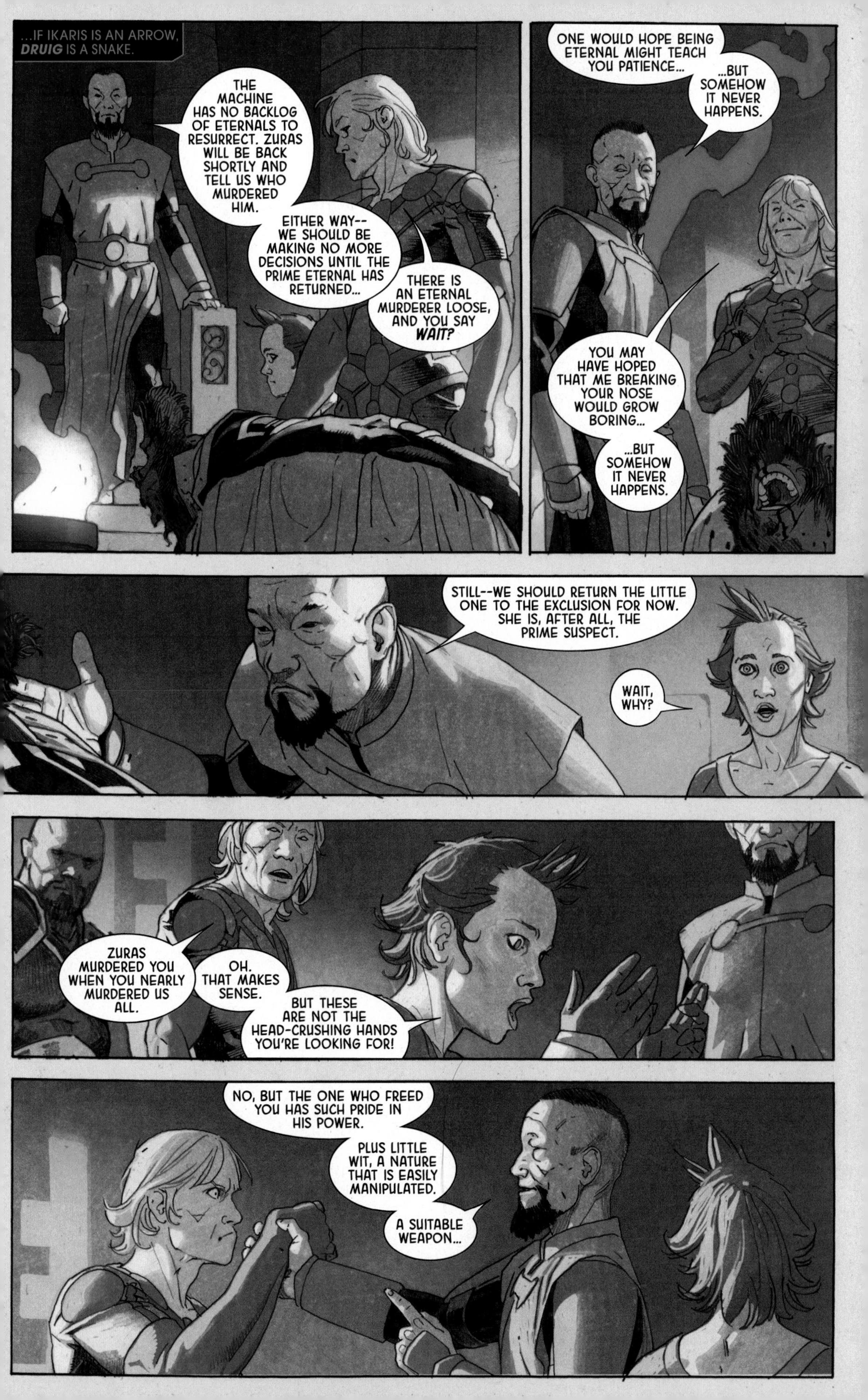
...IF IKARIS IS AN ARROW, DRUIG IS A SNAKE.
THE MACHINE HAS NO BACKLOG OF ETERNALS TO RESURRECT. ZURAS WILL BE BACK SHORTLY AND TELL US WHO MURDERED HIM.
EITHER WAY-- WE SHOULD BE MAKING NO MORE DECISIONS UNTIL THE PRIME ETERNAL HAS RETURNED...
THERE IS AN ETERNAL MURDERER LOOSE, AND YOU SAY WAIT?
ONE WOULD HOPE BEING ETERNAL MIGHT TEACH YOU PATIENCE...
...BUT SOMEHOW IT NEVER HAPPENS.
YOU MAY HAVE HOPED THAT ME BREAKING YOUR NOSE WOULD GROW BORING...
...BUT SOMEHOW IT NEVER HAPPENS.
STILL--WE SHOULD RETURN THE LITTLE ONE TO THE EXCLUSION FOR NOW. SHE IS, AFTER ALL, THE PRIME SUSPECT.
WAIT, WHY?
ZURAS MURDERED YOU WHEN YOU NEARLY MURDERED US ALL.
OH. THAT MAKES SENSE.
BUT THESE ARE NOT THE HEAD-CRUSHING HANDS YOU'RE LOOKING FOR!
NO, BUT THE ONE WHO FREED YOU HAS SUCH PRIDE IN HIS POWER.
PLUS LITTLE WIT, A NATURE THAT IS EASILY MANIPULATED.
A SUITABLE WEAPON...

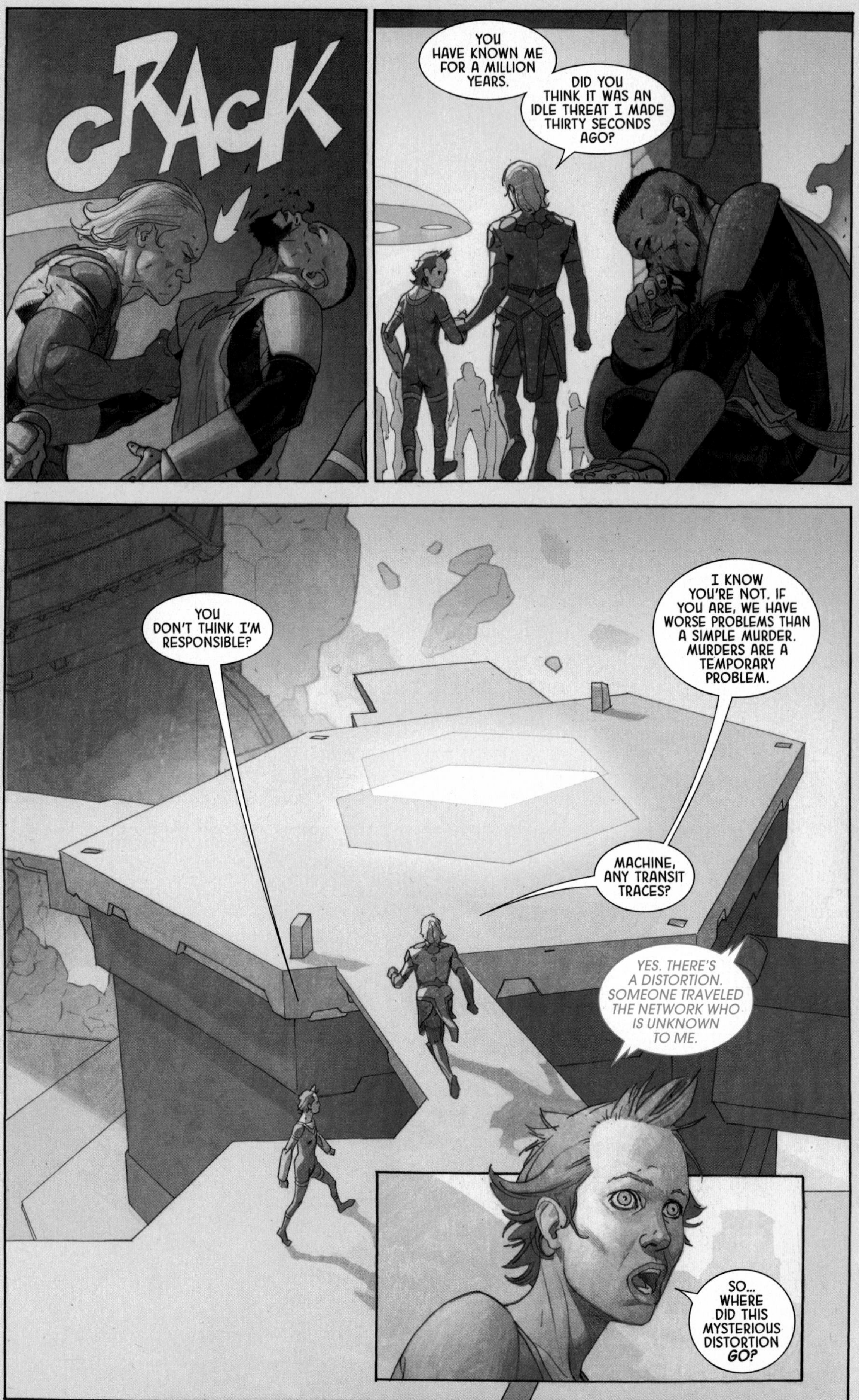
CRACK
YOU HAVE KNOWN ME FOR A MILLION YEARS.
DID YOU THINK IT WAS AN IDLE THREAT I MADE THIRTY SECONDS AGO?
YOU DON'T THINK I'M RESPONSIBLE?
I KNOW YOU'RE NOT. IF YOU ARE, WE HAVE WORSE PROBLEMS THAN A SIMPLE MURDER. MURDERS ARE A TEMPORARY PROBLEM.
MACHINE, ANY TRANSIT TRACES?
YES. THERE'S A DISTORTION. SOMEONE TRAVELED THE NETWORK WHO IS UNKNOWN TO ME.
SO... WHERE DID THIS MYSTERIOUS DISTORTION *GO?*

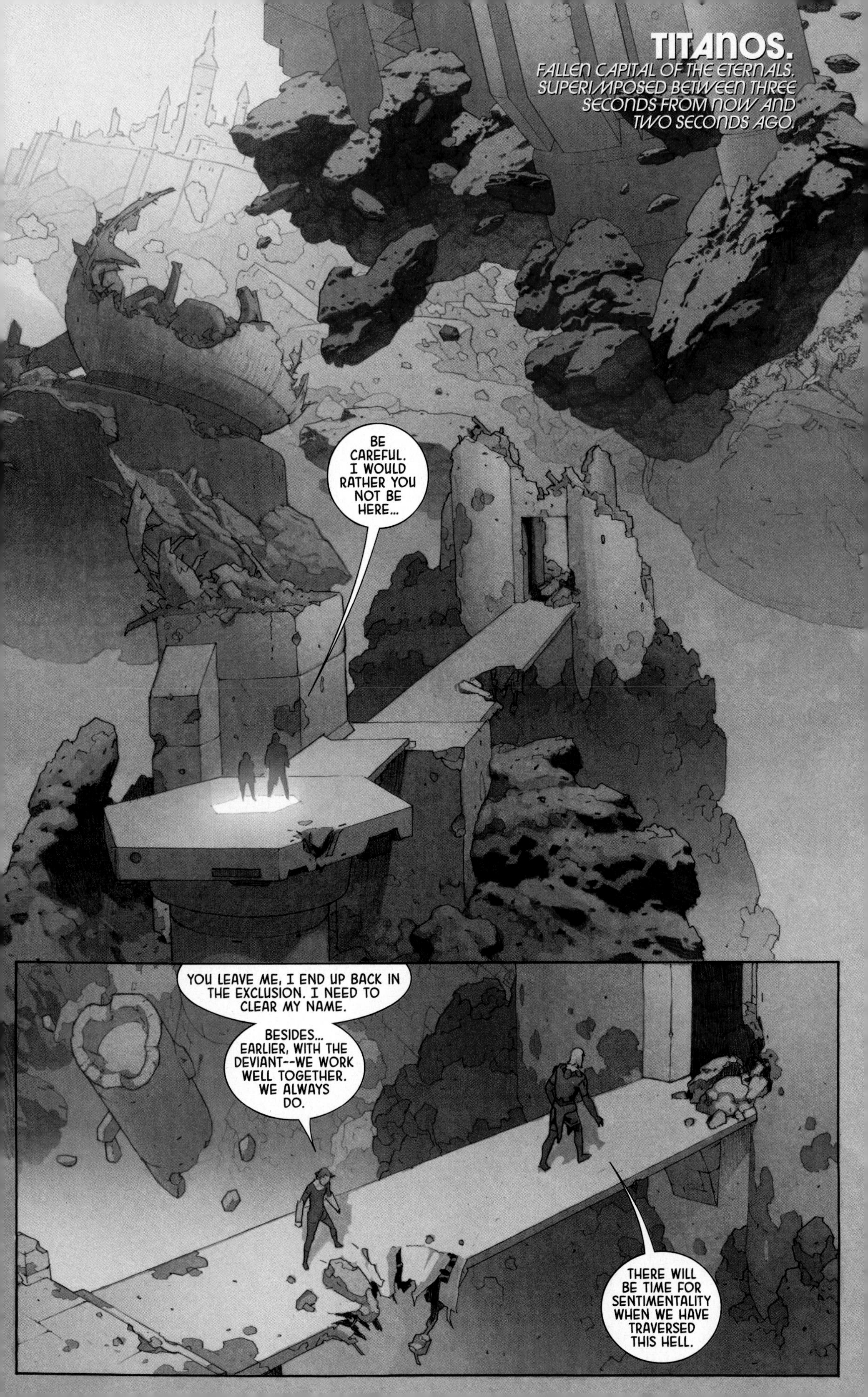
TITANOS.
FALLEN CAPITAL OF THE ETERNALS. SUPERIMPOSED BETWEEN THREE SECONDS FROM NOW AND TWO SECONDS AGO.
BE CAREFUL. I WOULD RATHER YOU NOT BE HERE...
YOU LEAVE ME, I END UP BACK IN THE EXCLUSION. I NEED TO CLEAR MY NAME.
BESIDES... EARLIER, WITH THE DEVIANT--WE WORK WELL TOGETHER. WE ALWAYS DO.
THERE WILL BE TIME FOR SENTIMENTALITY WHEN WE HAVE TRAVERSED THIS HELL.

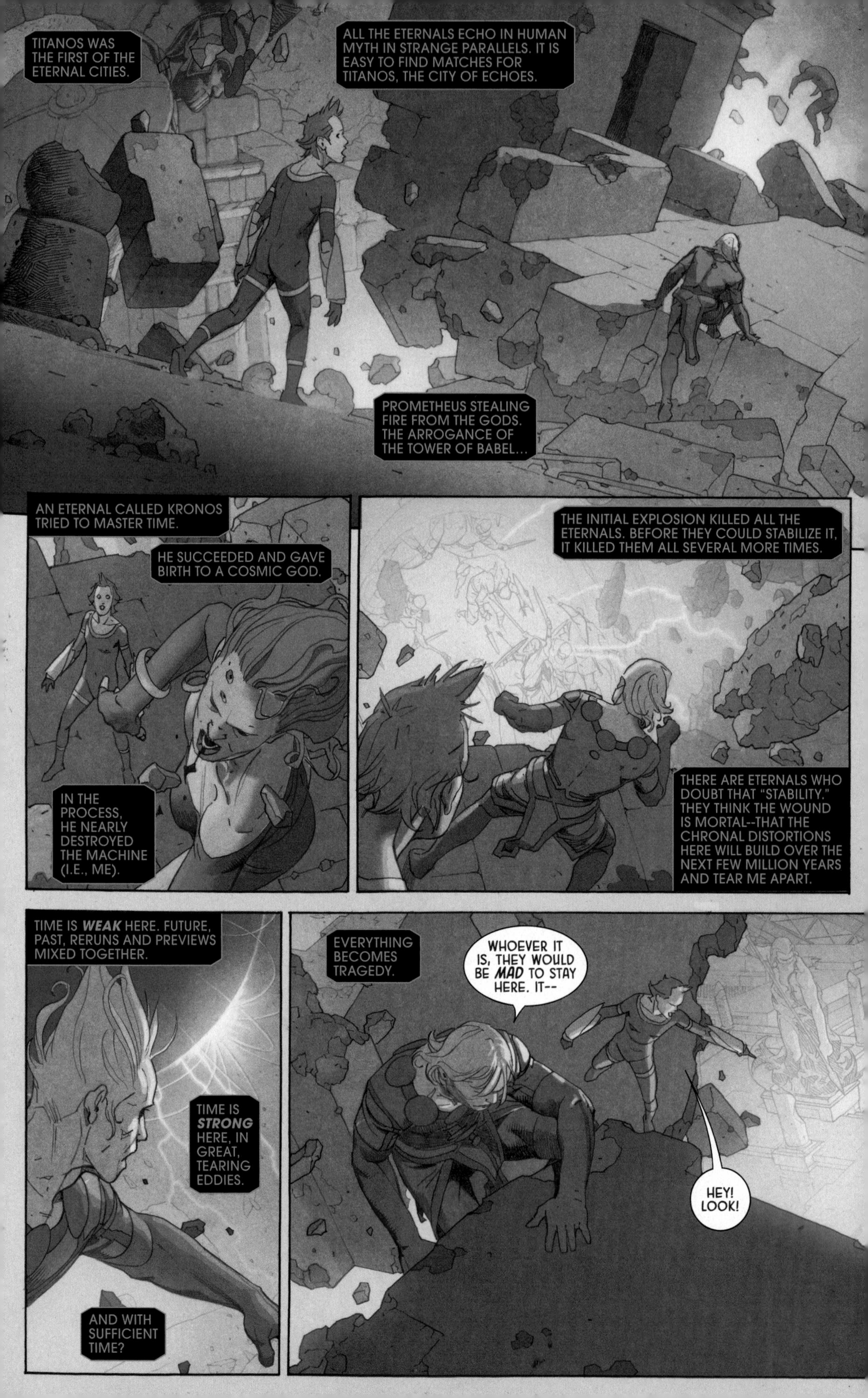
TITANOS WAS THE FIRST OF THE ETERNAL CITIES.
ALL THE ETERNALS ECHO IN HUMAN MYTH IN STRANGE PARALLELS. IT IS EASY TO FIND MATCHES FOR TITANOS, THE CITY OF ECHOES.
PROMETHEUS STEALING FIRE FROM THE GODS. THE ARROGANCE OF THE TOWER OF BABEL...
AN ETERNAL CALLED KRONOS TRIED TO MASTER TIME.
HE SUCCEEDED AND GAVE BIRTH TO A COSMIC GOD.
IN THE PROCESS, HE NEARLY DESTROYED THE MACHINE (I.E., ME).
THE INITIAL EXPLOSION KILLED ALL THE ETERNALS. BEFORE THEY COULD STABILIZE IT, IT KILLED THEM ALL SEVERAL MORE TIMES.
THERE ARE ETERNALS WHO DOUBT THAT "STABILITY." THEY THINK THE WOUND IS MORTAL--THAT THE CHRONAL DISTORTIONS HERE WILL BUILD OVER THE NEXT FEW MILLION YEARS AND TEAR ME APART.
TIME IS ***WEAK*** HERE. FUTURE, PAST, RERUNS AND PREVIEWS MIXED TOGETHER.
TIME IS ***STRONG*** HERE, IN GREAT, TEARING EDDIES.
AND WITH SUFFICIENT TIME?
EVERYTHING BECOMES TRAGEDY.
WHOEVER IT IS, THEY WOULD BE ***MAD*** TO STAY HERE. IT--
HEY! LOOK!

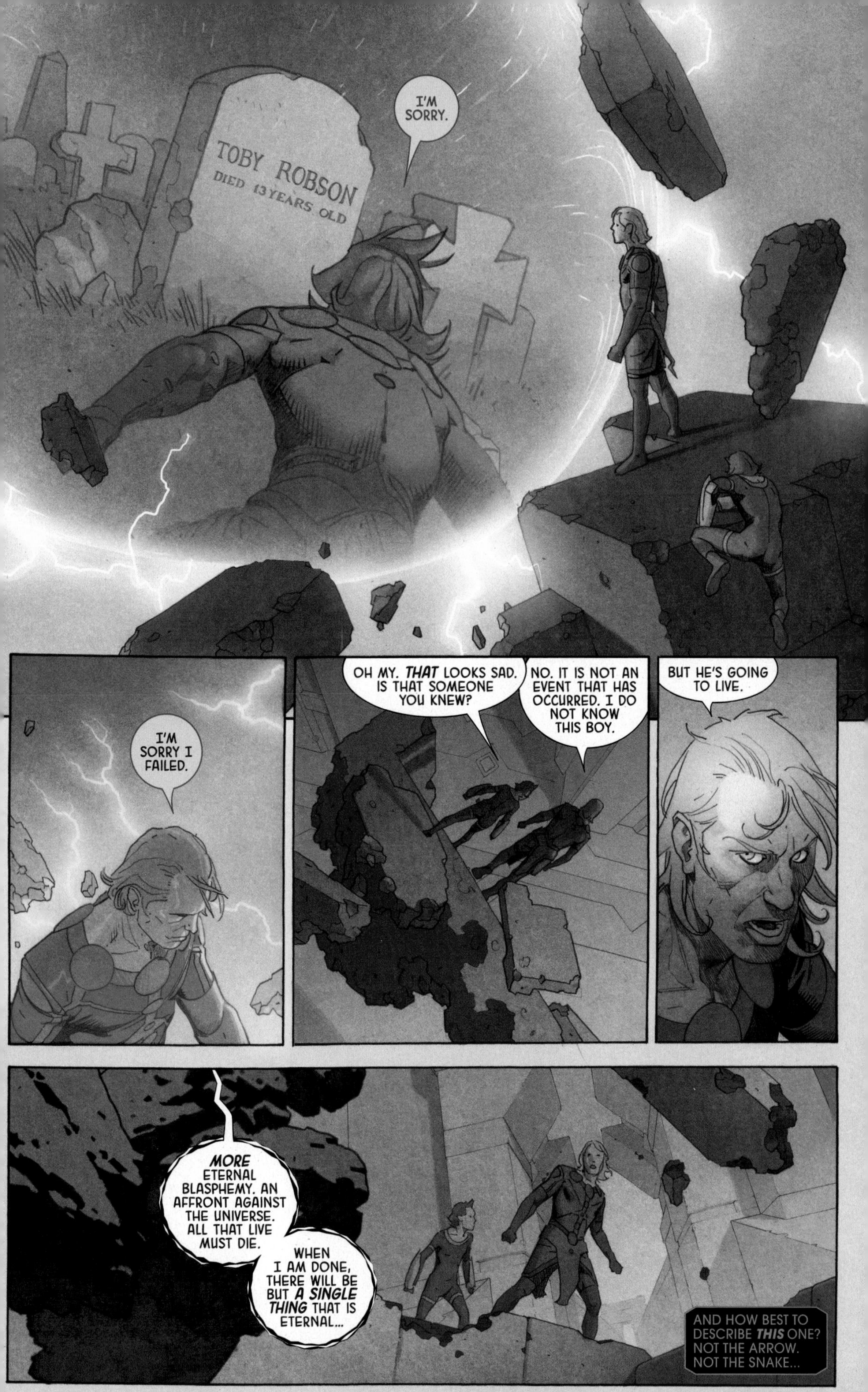
TOBY ROBSON
DIED 13 YEARS OLD
I'M SORRY.
I'M SORRY I FAILED.
OH MY. THAT LOOKS SAD. IS THAT SOMEONE YOU KNEW?
NO. IT IS NOT AN EVENT THAT HAS OCCURRED. I DO NOT KNOW THIS BOY.
BUT HE'S GOING TO LIVE.
MORE ETERNAL BLASPHEMY. AN AFFRONT AGAINST THE UNIVERSE. ALL THAT LIVE MUST DIE.
WHEN I AM DONE, THERE WILL BE BUT A SINGLE THING THAT IS ETERNAL...
AND HOW BEST TO DESCRIBE THIS ONE? NOT THE ARROW. NOT THE SNAKE...

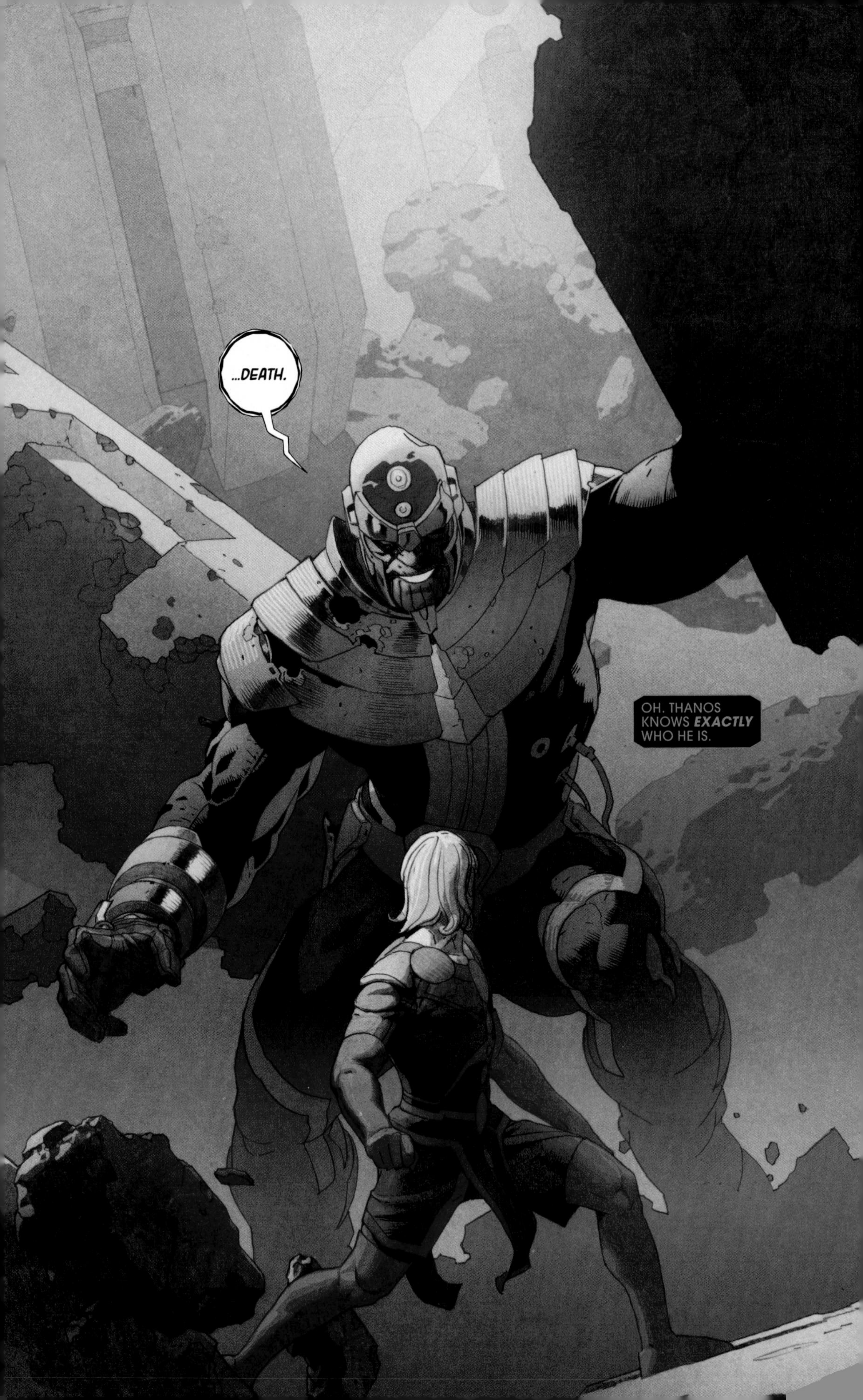
...DEATH.
OH. THANOS KNOWS EXACTLY WHO HE IS.

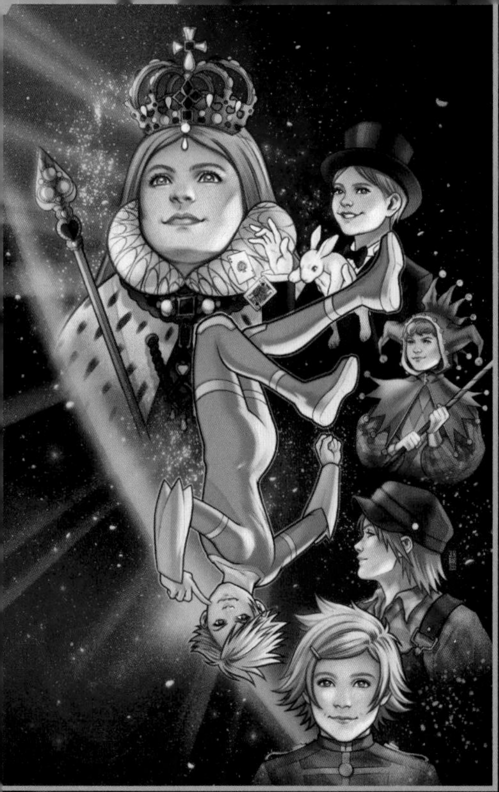

#1 VARIANT BY **JEN BARTEL**

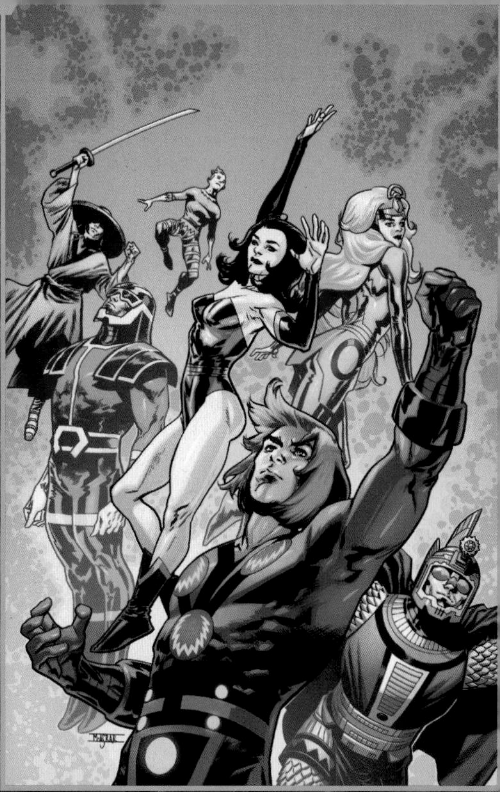

#1 VARIANT BY **MAHMUD ASRAR & DAVE McCAIG**

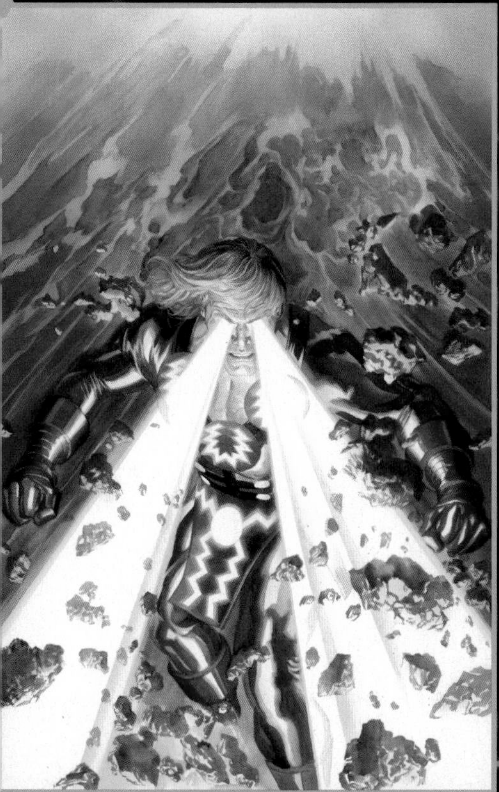

#1 VARIANT BY **ALEX ROSS**

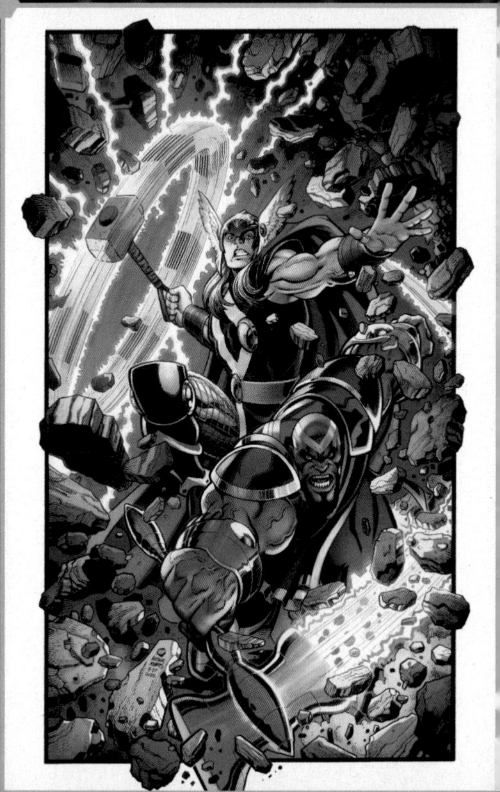

#1 VARIANT BY **ARTHUR ADAMS & JASON KEITH**

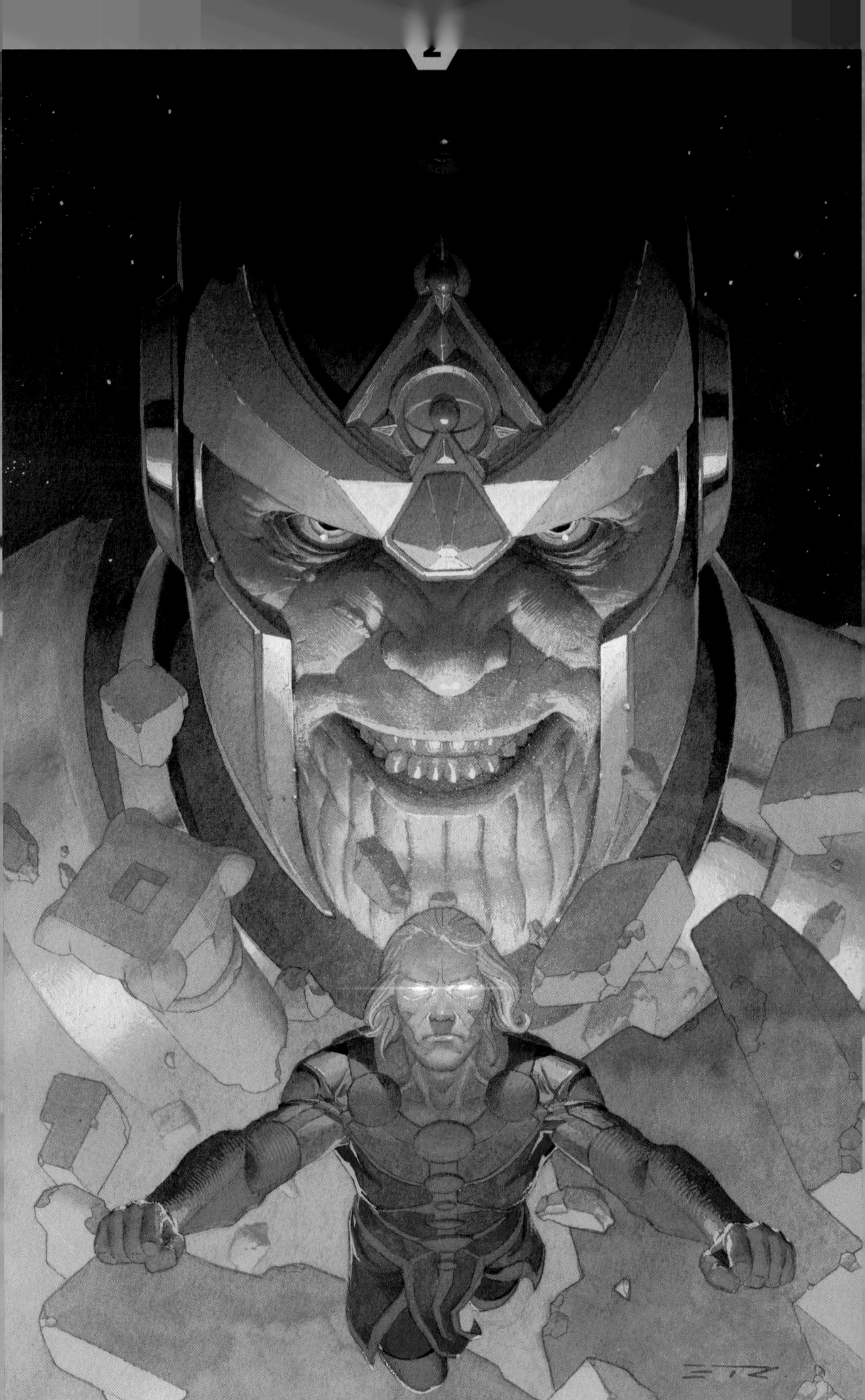

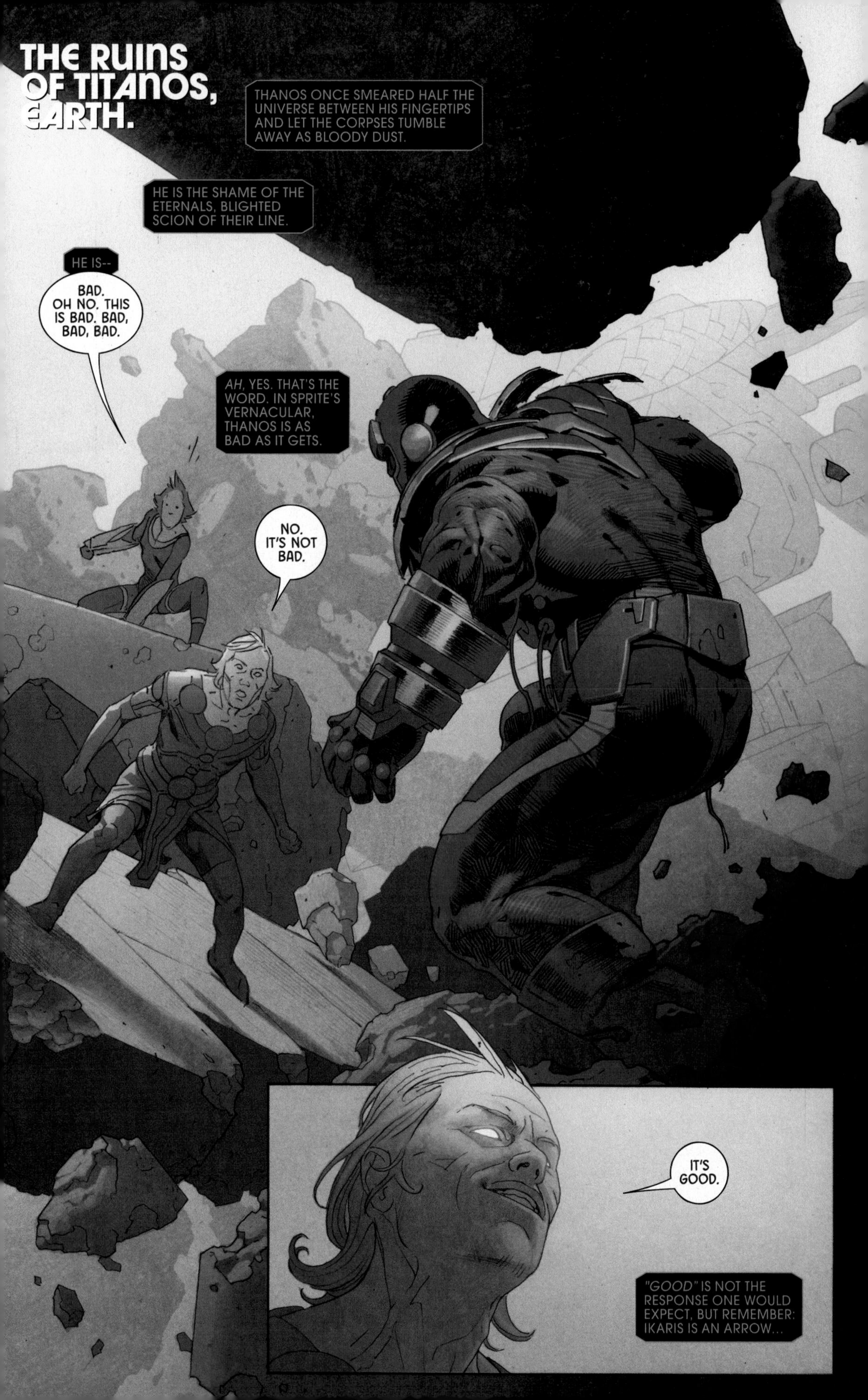

THE RUINS OF TITANOS, EARTH.
THANOS ONCE SMEARED HALF THE UNIVERSE BETWEEN HIS FINGERTIPS AND LET THE CORPSES TUMBLE AWAY AS BLOODY DUST.
HE IS THE SHAME OF THE ETERNALS, BLIGHTED SCION OF THEIR LINE.
HE IS--
BAD. OH NO. THIS IS BAD. BAD, BAD, BAD.
AH, YES. THAT'S THE WORD. IN SPRITE'S VERNACULAR, THANOS IS AS BAD AS IT GETS.
NO. IT'S NOT BAD.
IT'S GOOD.
"GOOD" IS NOT THE RESPONSE ONE WOULD EXPECT, BUT REMEMBER: IKARIS IS AN ARROW...

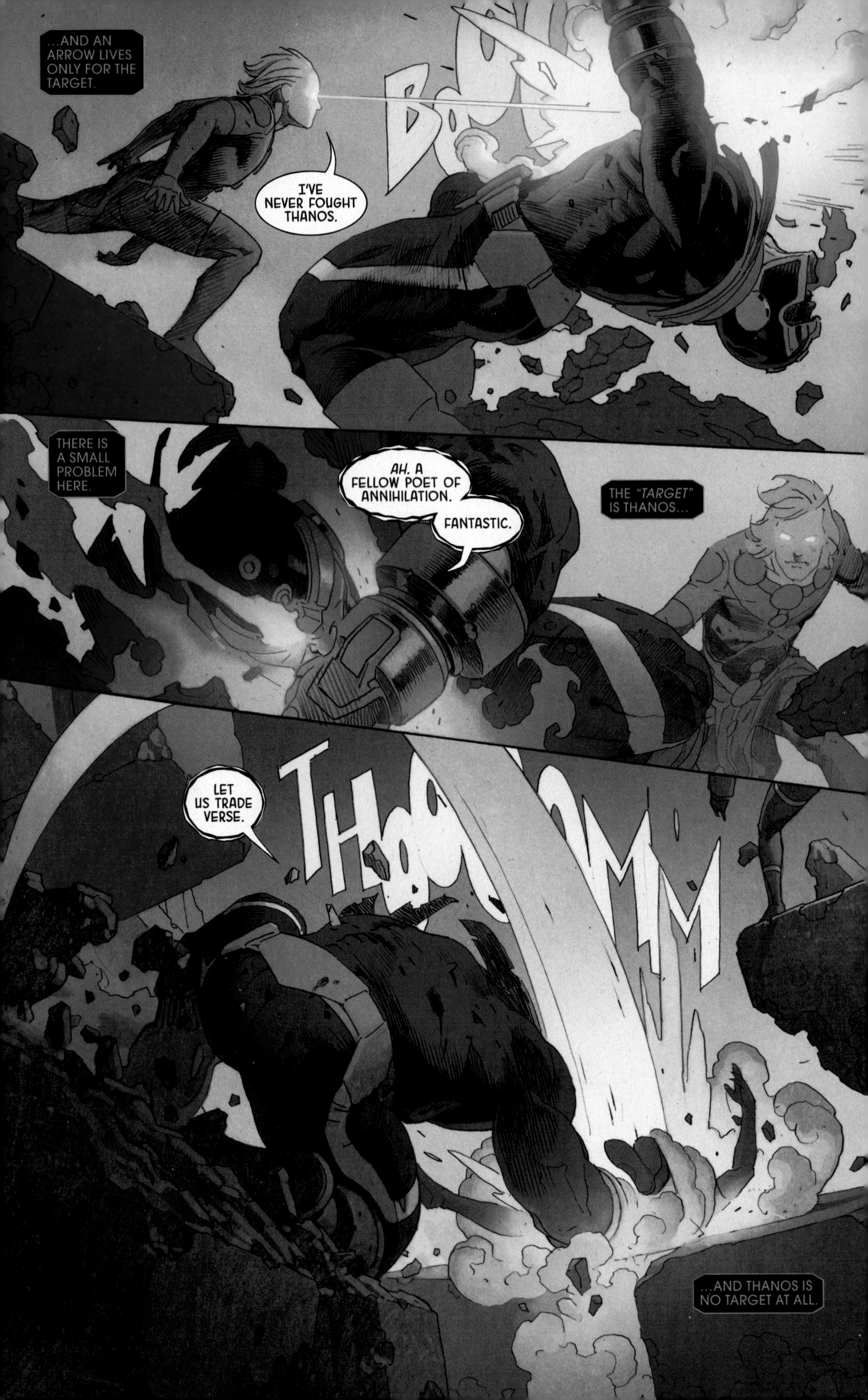
...AND AN ARROW LIVES ONLY FOR THE TARGET.
I'VE NEVER FOUGHT THANOS.
THERE IS A SMALL PROBLEM HERE.
AH. A FELLOW POET OF ANNIHILATION.
FANTASTIC.
THE "TARGET" IS THANOS...
LET US TRADE VERSE.
...AND THANOS IS NO TARGET AT ALL.

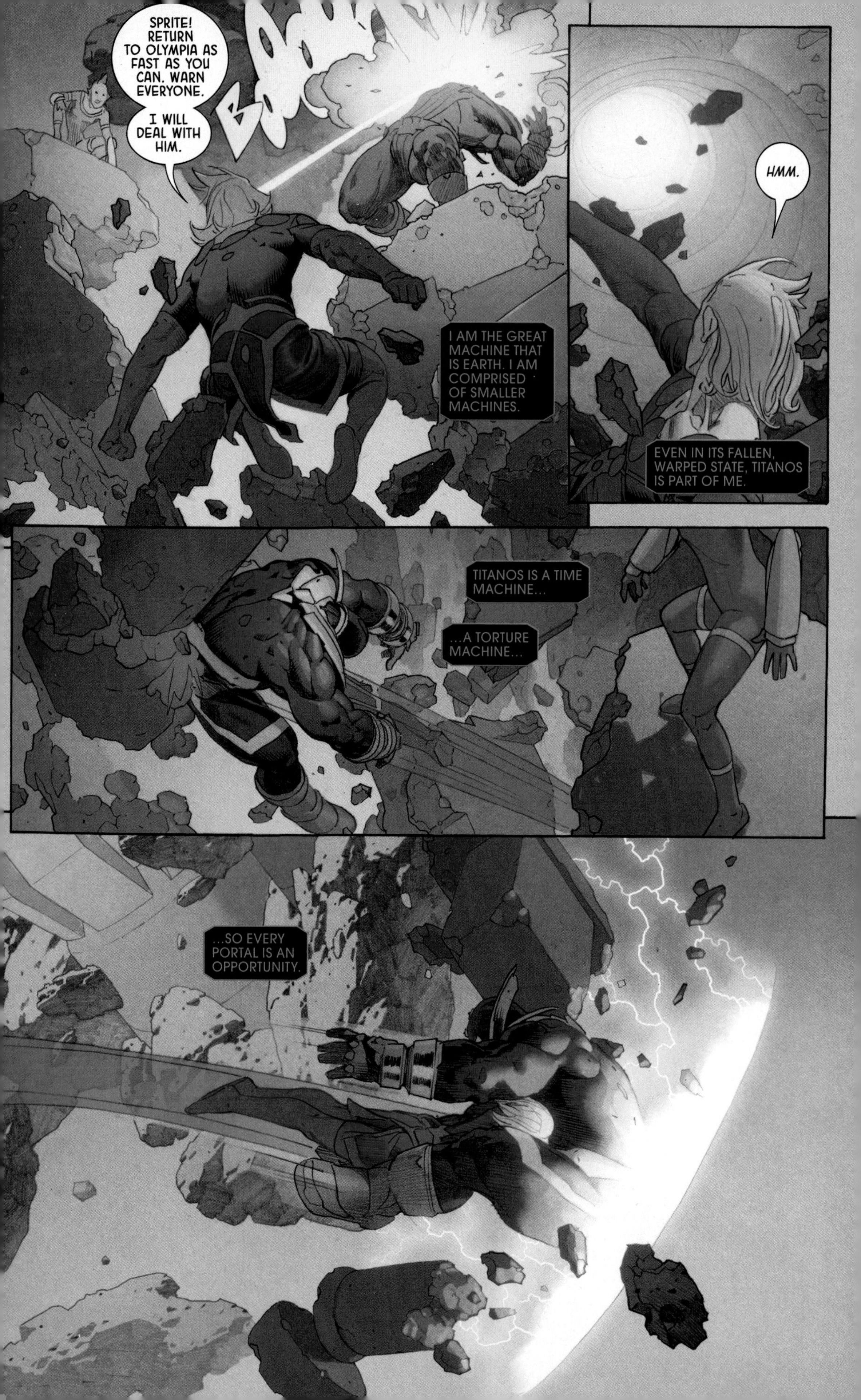
SPRITE! RETURN TO OLYMPIA AS FAST AS YOU CAN. WARN EVERYONE.
I WILL DEAL WITH HIM.
I AM THE GREAT MACHINE THAT IS EARTH. I AM COMPRISED OF SMALLER MACHINES.
HMM.
EVEN IN ITS FALLEN, WARPED STATE, TITANOS IS PART OF ME.
TITANOS IS A TIME MACHINE...
...A TORTURE MACHINE...
...SO EVERY PORTAL IS AN OPPORTUNITY.

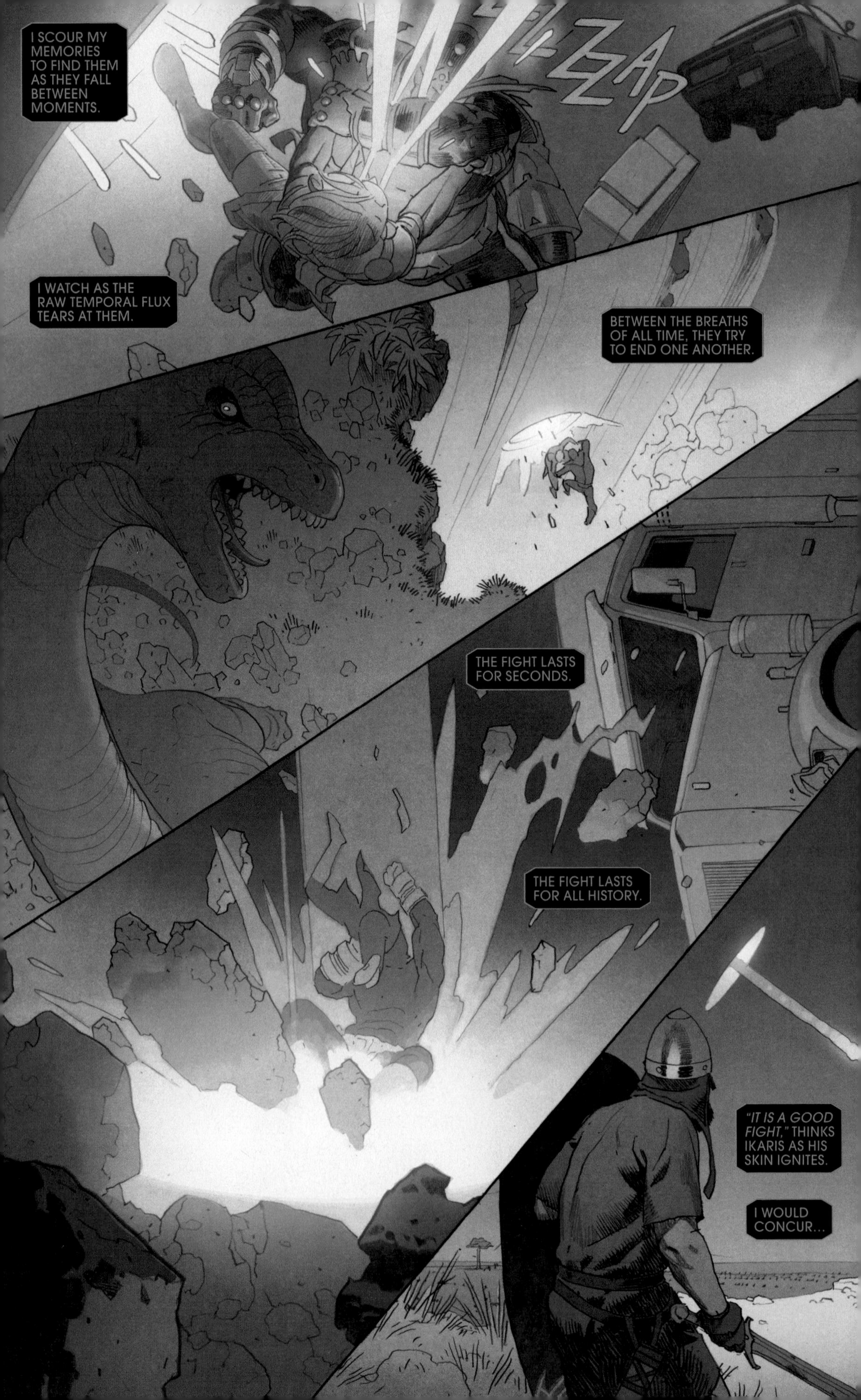
I SCOUR MY MEMORIES TO FIND THEM AS THEY FALL BETWEEN MOMENTS.
ZZAP
I WATCH AS THE RAW TEMPORAL FLUX TEARS AT THEM.
BETWEEN THE BREATHS OF ALL TIME, THEY TRY TO END ONE ANOTHER.
THE FIGHT LASTS FOR SECONDS.
THE FIGHT LASTS FOR ALL HISTORY.
"IT IS A GOOD FIGHT," THINKS IKARIS AS HIS SKIN IGNITES.
I WOULD CONCUR…

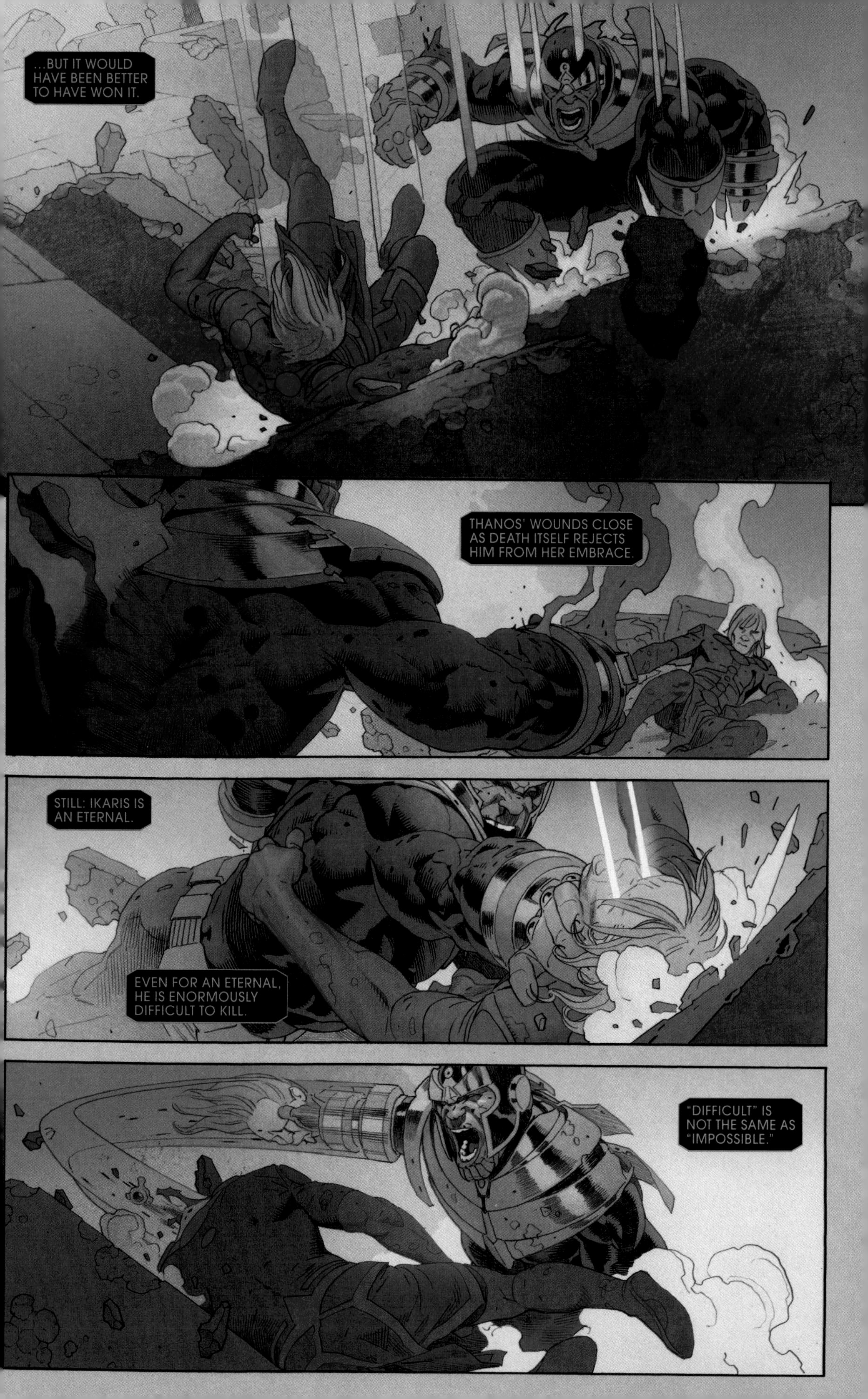
...BUT IT WOULD HAVE BEEN BETTER TO HAVE WON IT.
THANOS' WOUNDS CLOSE AS DEATH ITSELF REJECTS HIM FROM HER EMBRACE.
STILL: IKARIS IS AN ETERNAL.
EVEN FOR AN ETERNAL, HE IS ENORMOUSLY DIFFICULT TO KILL.
"DIFFICULT" IS NOT THE SAME AS "IMPOSSIBLE."

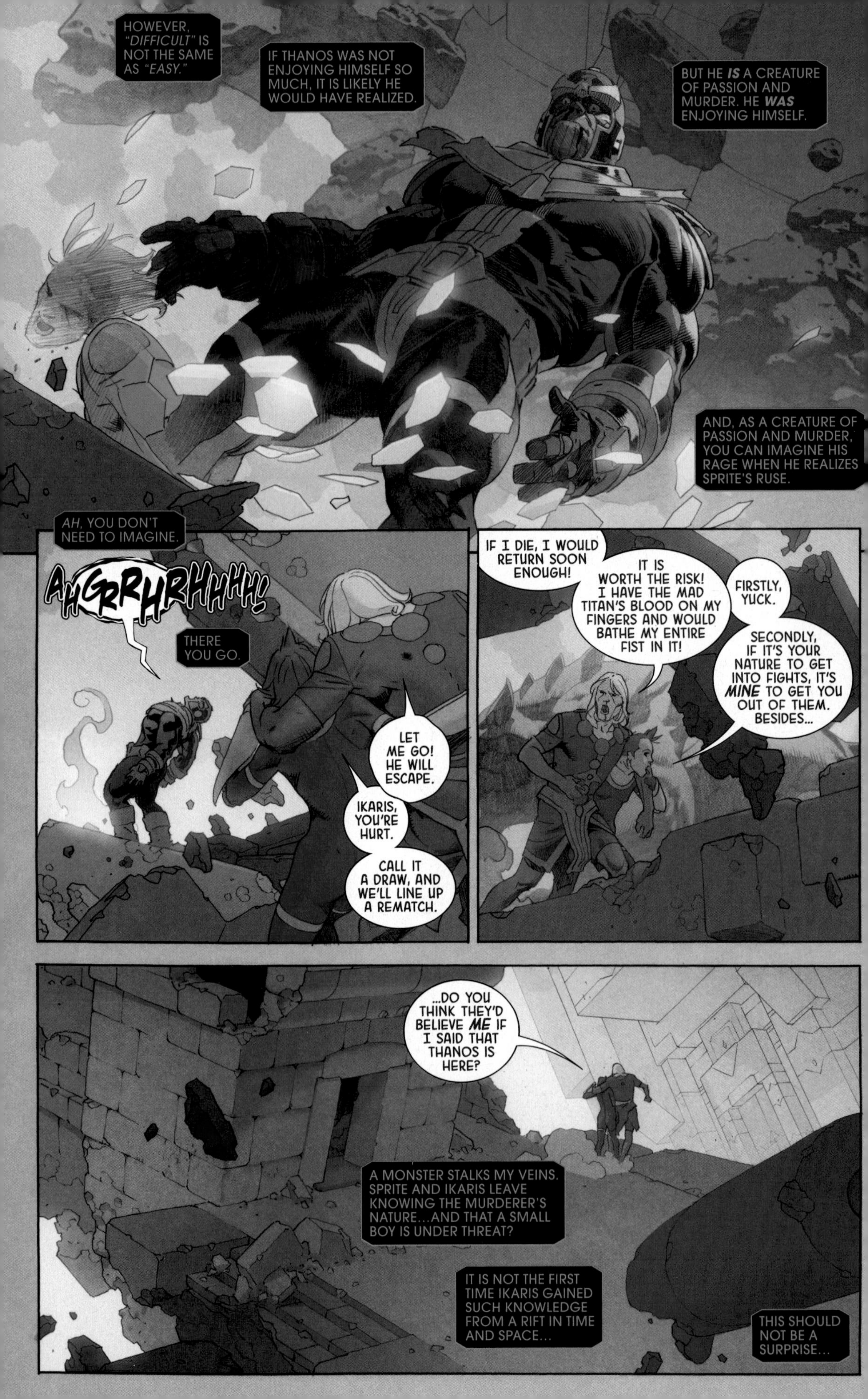
HOWEVER, "DIFFICULT" IS NOT THE SAME AS "EASY."
IF THANOS WAS NOT ENJOYING HIMSELF SO MUCH, IT IS LIKELY HE WOULD HAVE REALIZED.
BUT HE IS A CREATURE OF PASSION AND MURDER. HE WAS ENJOYING HIMSELF.
AND, AS A CREATURE OF PASSION AND MURDER, YOU CAN IMAGINE HIS RAGE WHEN HE REALIZES SPRITE'S RUSE.
AH, YOU DON'T NEED TO IMAGINE.
AHGRRHRHHHH!
THERE YOU GO.
LET ME GO! HE WILL ESCAPE.
IKARIS, YOU'RE HURT.
CALL IT A DRAW, AND WE'LL LINE UP A REMATCH.
IF I DIE, I WOULD RETURN SOON ENOUGH!
IT IS WORTH THE RISK! I HAVE THE MAD TITAN'S BLOOD ON MY FINGERS AND WOULD BATHE MY ENTIRE FIST IN IT!
FIRSTLY, YUCK.
SECONDLY, IF IT'S YOUR NATURE TO GET INTO FIGHTS, IT'S MINE TO GET YOU OUT OF THEM. BESIDES...
...DO YOU THINK THEY'D BELIEVE ME IF I SAID THAT THANOS IS HERE?
A MONSTER STALKS MY VEINS. SPRITE AND IKARIS LEAVE KNOWING THE MURDERER'S NATURE...AND THAT A SMALL BOY IS UNDER THREAT?
IT IS NOT THE FIRST TIME IKARIS GAINED SUCH KNOWLEDGE FROM A RIFT IN TIME AND SPACE...
THIS SHOULD NOT BE A SURPRISE...

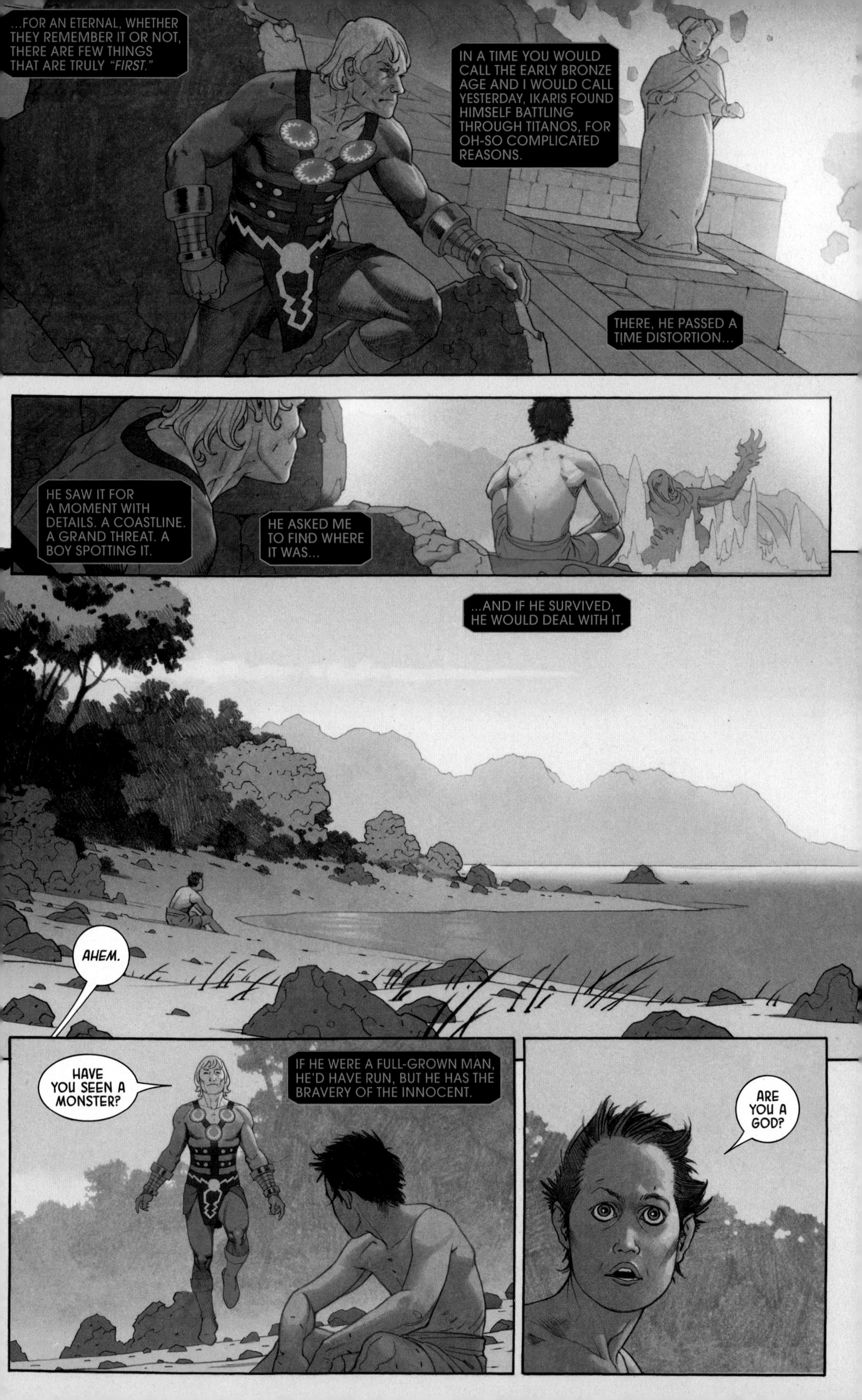
...FOR AN ETERNAL, WHETHER THEY REMEMBER IT OR NOT, THERE ARE FEW THINGS THAT ARE TRULY *"FIRST."*
IN A TIME YOU WOULD CALL THE EARLY BRONZE AGE AND I WOULD CALL YESTERDAY, IKARIS FOUND HIMSELF BATTLING THROUGH TITANOS, FOR OH-SO COMPLICATED REASONS.
THERE, HE PASSED A TIME DISTORTION...
HE SAW IT FOR A MOMENT WITH DETAILS. A COASTLINE. A GRAND THREAT. A BOY SPOTTING IT.
HE ASKED ME TO FIND WHERE IT WAS...
...AND IF HE SURVIVED, HE WOULD DEAL WITH IT.
AHEM.
HAVE YOU SEEN A MONSTER?
IF HE WERE A FULL-GROWN MAN, HE'D HAVE RUN, BUT HE HAS THE BRAVERY OF THE INNOCENT.
ARE YOU A GOD?

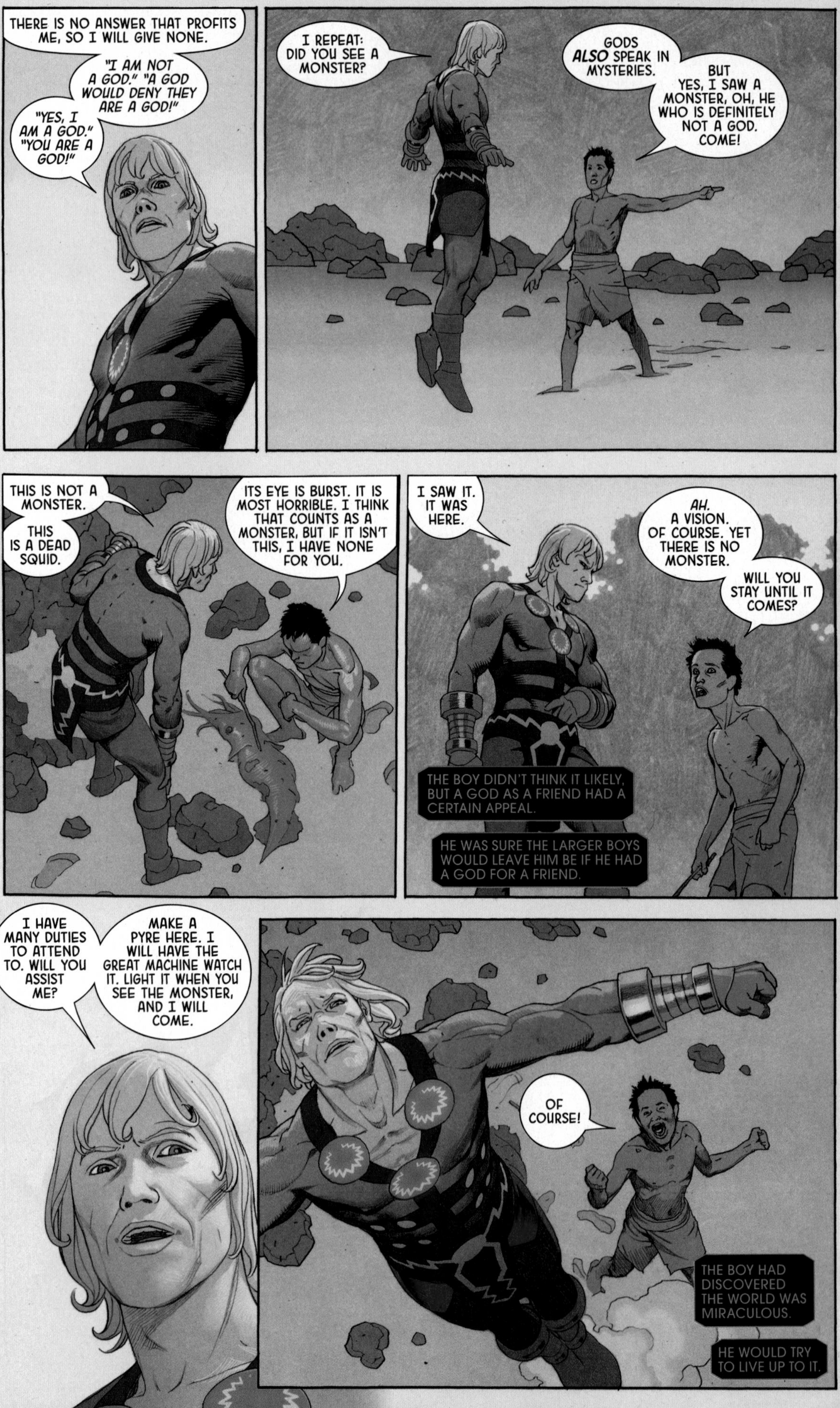
THERE IS NO ANSWER THAT PROFITS ME, SO I WILL GIVE NONE.
"I AM NOT A GOD." "A GOD WOULD DENY THEY ARE A GOD!"
"YES, I AM A GOD." "YOU ARE A GOD!"
I REPEAT: DID YOU SEE A MONSTER?
GODS ALSO SPEAK IN MYSTERIES.
BUT YES, I SAW A MONSTER, OH, HE WHO IS DEFINITELY NOT A GOD. COME!
THIS IS NOT A MONSTER.
THIS IS A DEAD SQUID.
ITS EYE IS BURST. IT IS MOST HORRIBLE. I THINK THAT COUNTS AS A MONSTER, BUT IF IT ISN'T THIS, I HAVE NONE FOR YOU.
I SAW IT. IT WAS HERE.
AH. A VISION. OF COURSE. YET THERE IS NO MONSTER.
WILL YOU STAY UNTIL IT COMES?
THE BOY DIDN'T THINK IT LIKELY, BUT A GOD AS A FRIEND HAD A CERTAIN APPEAL.
HE WAS SURE THE LARGER BOYS WOULD LEAVE HIM BE IF HE HAD A GOD FOR A FRIEND.
I HAVE MANY DUTIES TO ATTEND TO. WILL YOU ASSIST ME?
MAKE A PYRE HERE. I WILL HAVE THE GREAT MACHINE WATCH IT. LIGHT IT WHEN YOU SEE THE MONSTER, AND I WILL COME.
OF COURSE!
THE BOY HAD DISCOVERED THE WORLD WAS MIRACULOUS.
HE WOULD TRY TO LIVE UP TO IT.

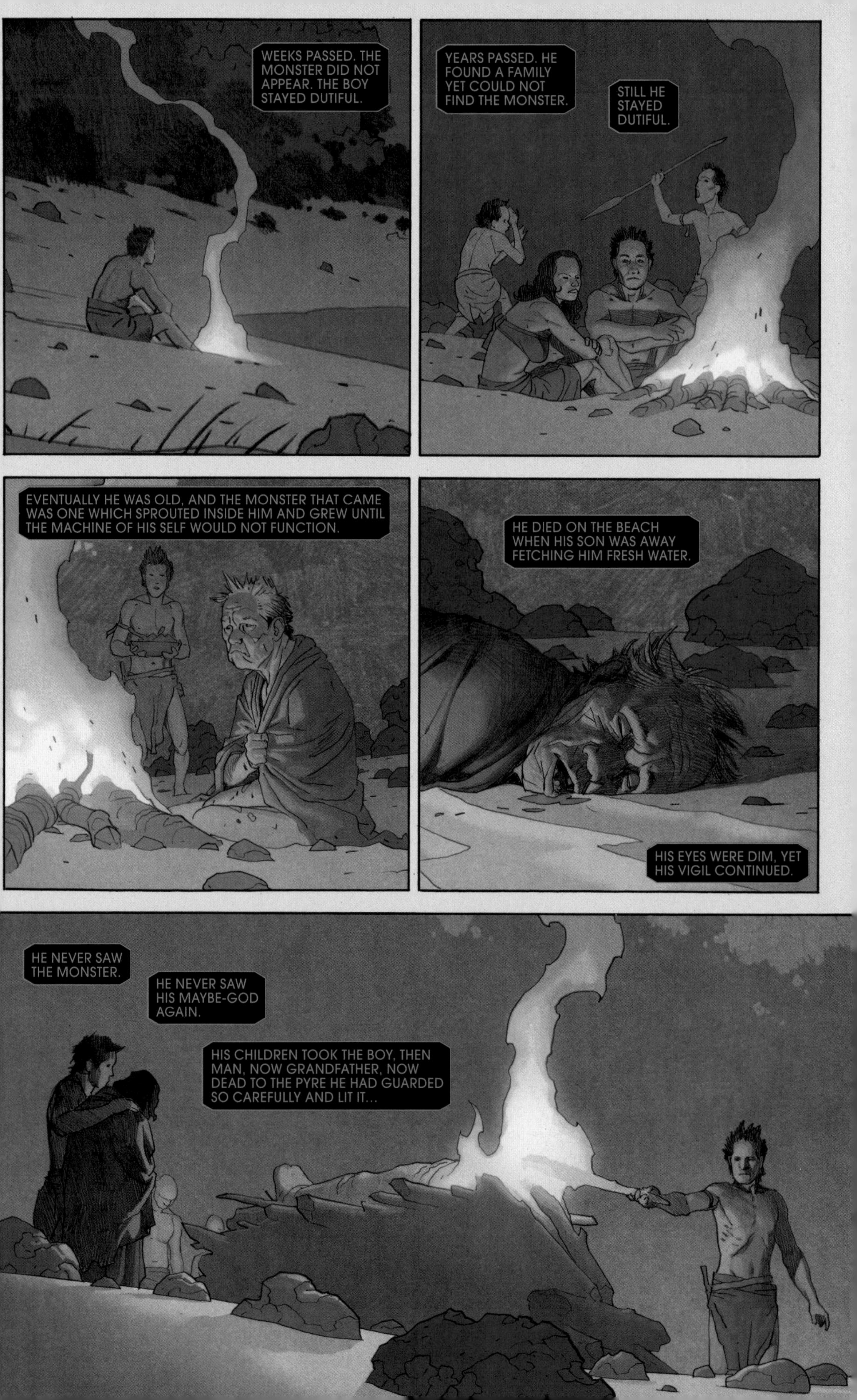
WEEKS PASSED. THE MONSTER DID NOT APPEAR. THE BOY STAYED DUTIFUL.
YEARS PASSED. HE FOUND A FAMILY YET COULD NOT FIND THE MONSTER.
STILL HE STAYED DUTIFUL.
EVENTUALLY HE WAS OLD, AND THE MONSTER THAT CAME WAS ONE WHICH SPROUTED INSIDE HIM AND GREW UNTIL THE MACHINE OF HIS SELF WOULD NOT FUNCTION.
HE DIED ON THE BEACH WHEN HIS SON WAS AWAY FETCHING HIM FRESH WATER.
HIS EYES WERE DIM, YET HIS VIGIL CONTINUED.
HE NEVER SAW THE MONSTER.
HE NEVER SAW HIS MAYBE-GOD AGAIN.
HIS CHILDREN TOOK THE BOY, THEN MAN, NOW GRANDFATHER, NOW DEAD TO THE PYRE HE HAD GUARDED SO CAREFULLY AND LIT IT...

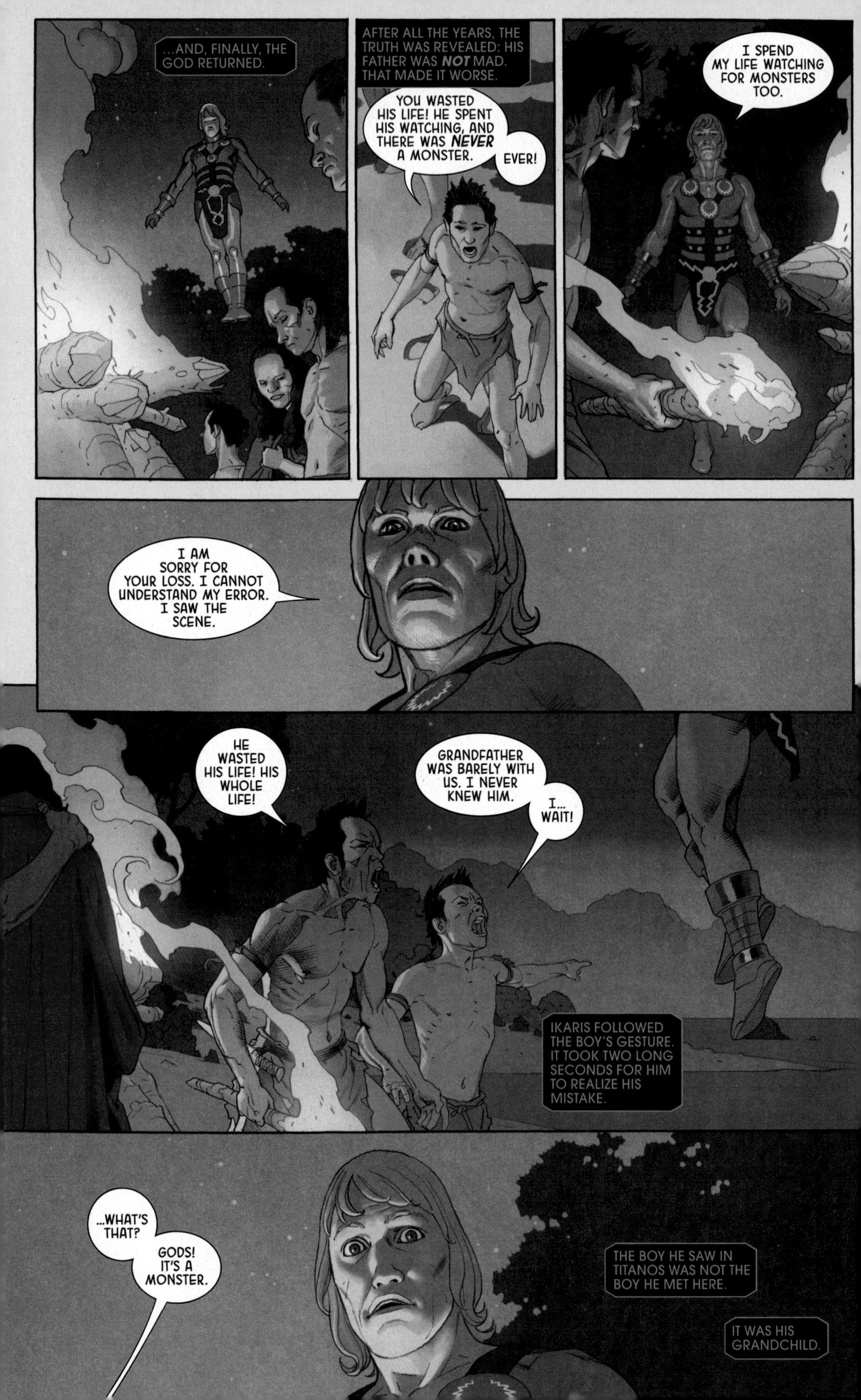
...AND, FINALLY, THE GOD RETURNED.
AFTER ALL THE YEARS, THE TRUTH WAS REVEALED: HIS FATHER WAS **NOT** MAD. THAT MADE IT WORSE.
YOU WASTED HIS LIFE! HE SPENT HIS WATCHING, AND THERE WAS ***NEVER*** A MONSTER.
EVER!
I SPEND MY LIFE WATCHING FOR MONSTERS TOO.
I AM SORRY FOR YOUR LOSS. I CANNOT UNDERSTAND MY ERROR. I SAW THE SCENE.
HE WASTED HIS LIFE! HIS WHOLE LIFE!
GRANDFATHER WAS BARELY WITH US. I NEVER KNEW HIM.
I... WAIT!
IKARIS FOLLOWED THE BOY'S GESTURE. IT TOOK TWO LONG SECONDS FOR HIM TO REALIZE HIS MISTAKE.
...WHAT'S THAT?
GODS! IT'S A MONSTER.
THE BOY HE SAW IN TITANOS WAS NOT THE BOY HE MET HERE.
IT WAS HIS GRANDCHILD.

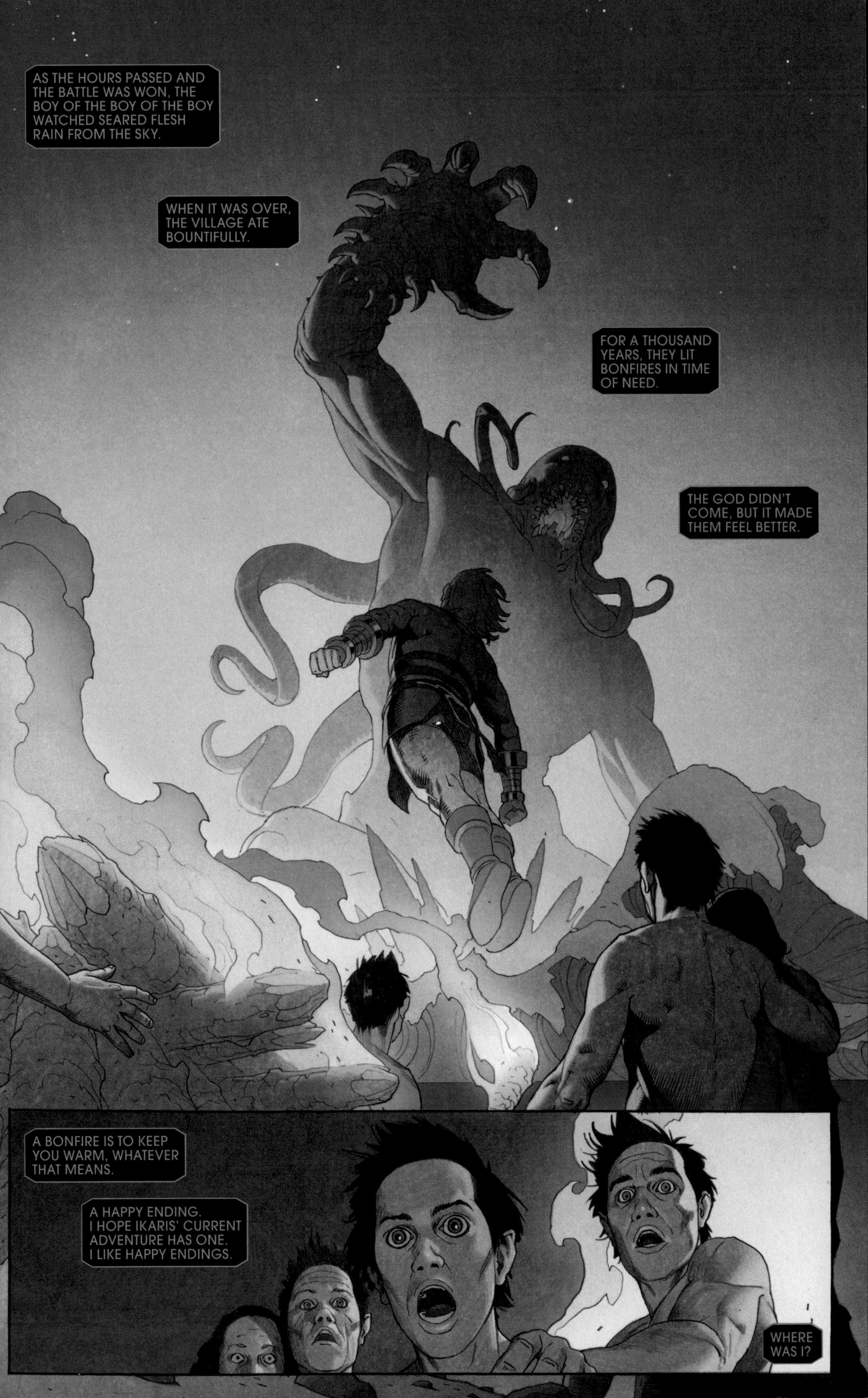
AS THE HOURS PASSED AND THE BATTLE WAS WON, THE BOY OF THE BOY OF THE BOY WATCHED SEARED FLESH RAIN FROM THE SKY.
WHEN IT WAS OVER, THE VILLAGE ATE BOUNTIFULLY.
FOR A THOUSAND YEARS, THEY LIT BONFIRES IN TIME OF NEED.
THE GOD DIDN'T COME, BUT IT MADE THEM FEEL BETTER.
A BONFIRE IS TO KEEP YOU WARM, WHATEVER THAT MEANS.
A HAPPY ENDING. I HOPE IKARIS' CURRENT ADVENTURE HAS ONE. I LIKE HAPPY ENDINGS.
WHERE WAS I?

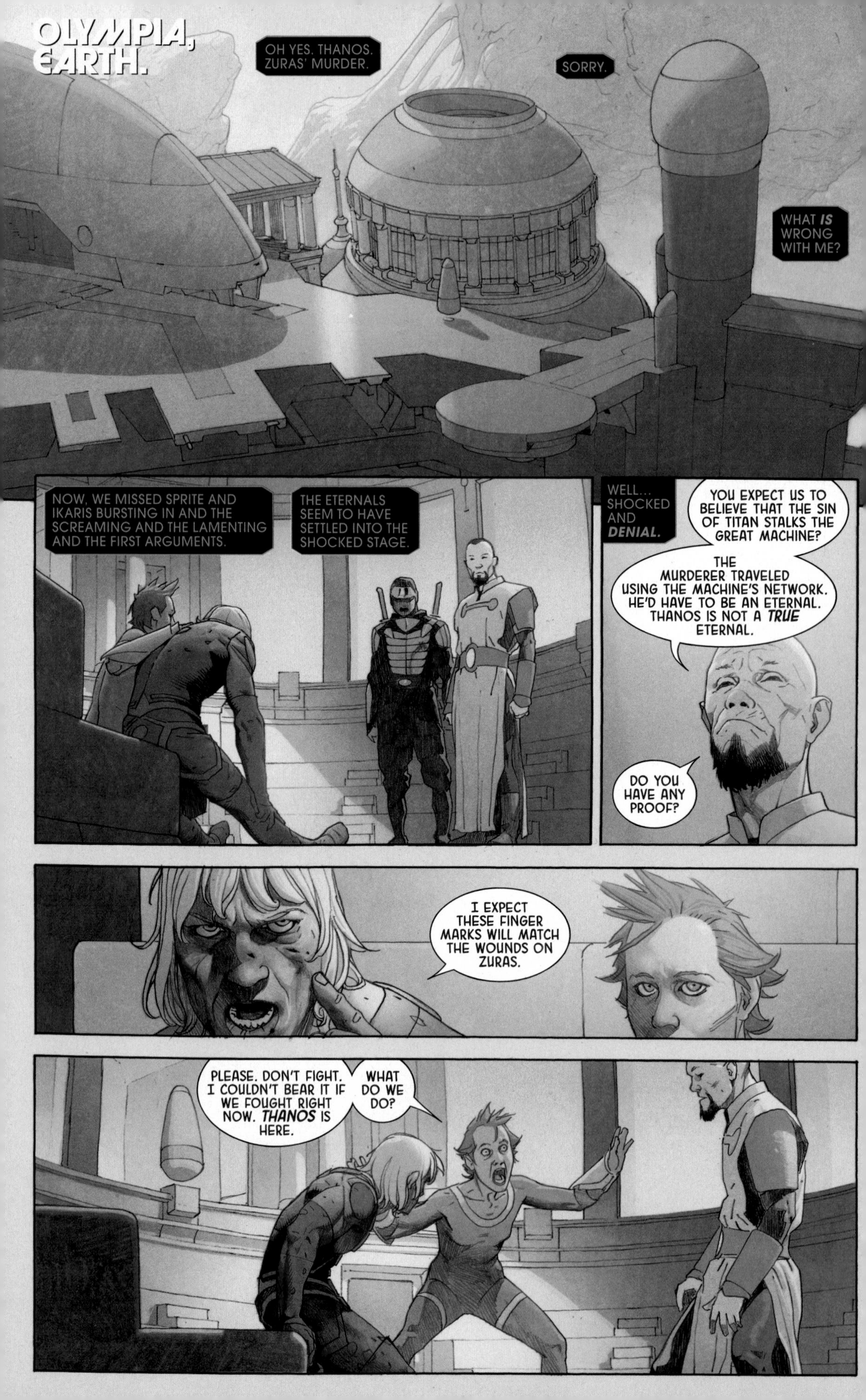
OLYMPIA, EARTH.
OH YES. THANOS. ZURAS' MURDER.
SORRY.
WHAT IS WRONG WITH ME?
NOW, WE MISSED SPRITE AND IKARIS BURSTING IN AND THE SCREAMING AND THE LAMENTING AND THE FIRST ARGUMENTS.
THE ETERNALS SEEM TO HAVE SETTLED INTO THE SHOCKED STAGE.
WELL... SHOCKED AND DENIAL.
YOU EXPECT US TO BELIEVE THAT THE SIN OF TITAN STALKS THE GREAT MACHINE?
THE MURDERER TRAVELED USING THE MACHINE'S NETWORK. HE'D HAVE TO BE AN ETERNAL. THANOS IS NOT A TRUE ETERNAL.
DO YOU HAVE ANY PROOF?
I EXPECT THESE FINGER MARKS WILL MATCH THE WOUNDS ON ZURAS.
PLEASE. DON'T FIGHT. I COULDN'T BEAR IT IF WE FOUGHT RIGHT NOW. THANOS IS HERE.
WHAT DO WE DO?

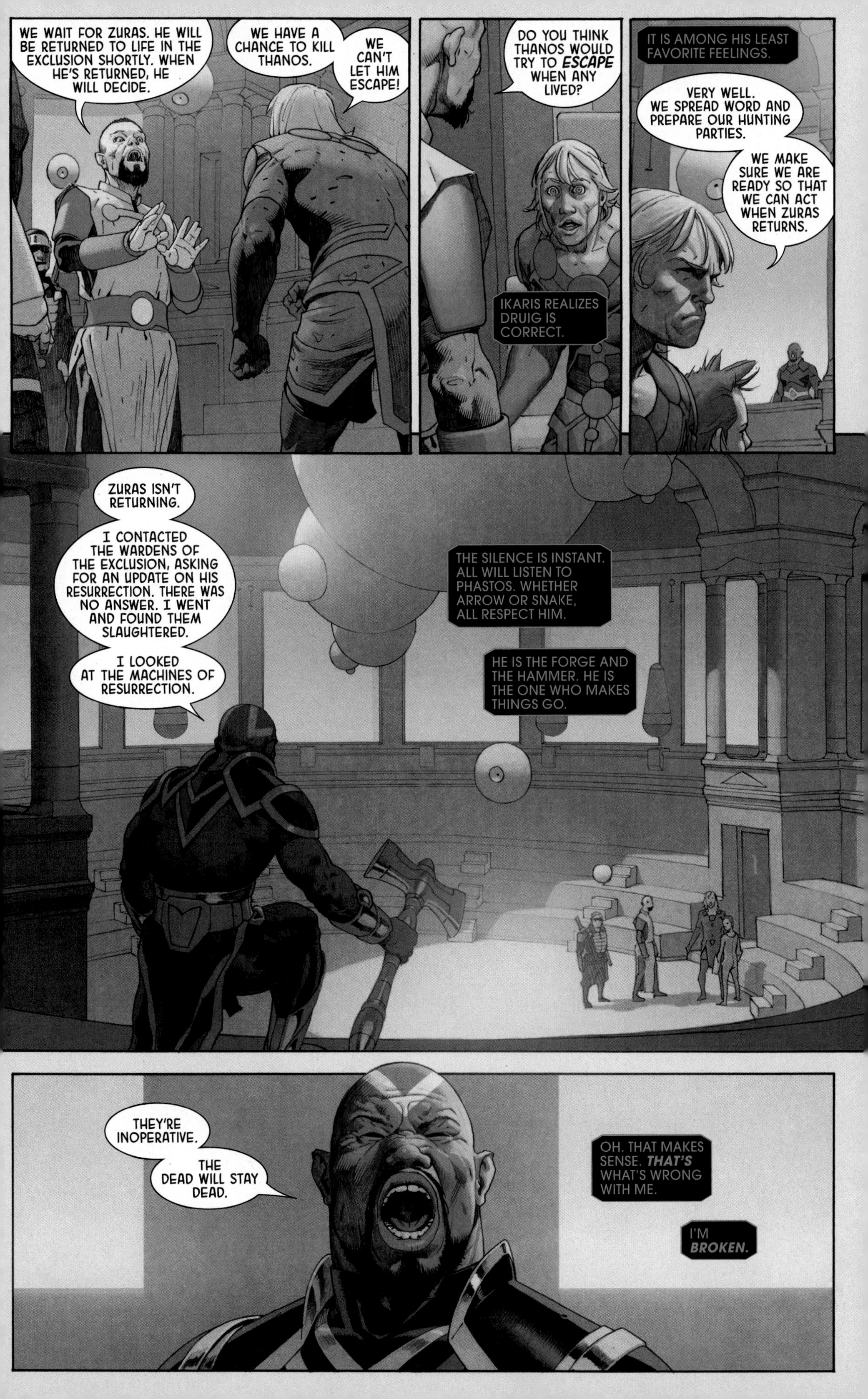
WE WAIT FOR ZURAS. HE WILL BE RETURNED TO LIFE IN THE EXCLUSION SHORTLY. WHEN HE'S RETURNED, HE WILL DECIDE.
WE HAVE A CHANCE TO KILL THANOS.
WE CAN'T LET HIM ESCAPE!
DO YOU THINK THANOS WOULD TRY TO *ESCAPE* WHEN ANY LIVED?
IKARIS REALIZES DRUIG IS CORRECT.
IT IS AMONG HIS LEAST FAVORITE FEELINGS.
VERY WELL. WE SPREAD WORD AND PREPARE OUR HUNTING PARTIES.
WE MAKE SURE WE ARE READY SO THAT WE CAN ACT WHEN ZURAS RETURNS.
ZURAS ISN'T RETURNING.
I CONTACTED THE WARDENS OF THE EXCLUSION, ASKING FOR AN UPDATE ON HIS RESURRECTION. THERE WAS NO ANSWER. I WENT AND FOUND THEM SLAUGHTERED.
I LOOKED AT THE MACHINES OF RESURRECTION.
THE SILENCE IS INSTANT. ALL WILL LISTEN TO PHASTOS. WHETHER ARROW OR SNAKE, ALL RESPECT HIM.
HE IS THE FORGE AND THE HAMMER. HE IS THE ONE WHO MAKES THINGS GO.
THEY'RE INOPERATIVE.
THE DEAD WILL STAY DEAD.
OH. THAT MAKES SENSE. ***THAT'S*** WHAT'S WRONG WITH ME.
I'M ***BROKEN.***

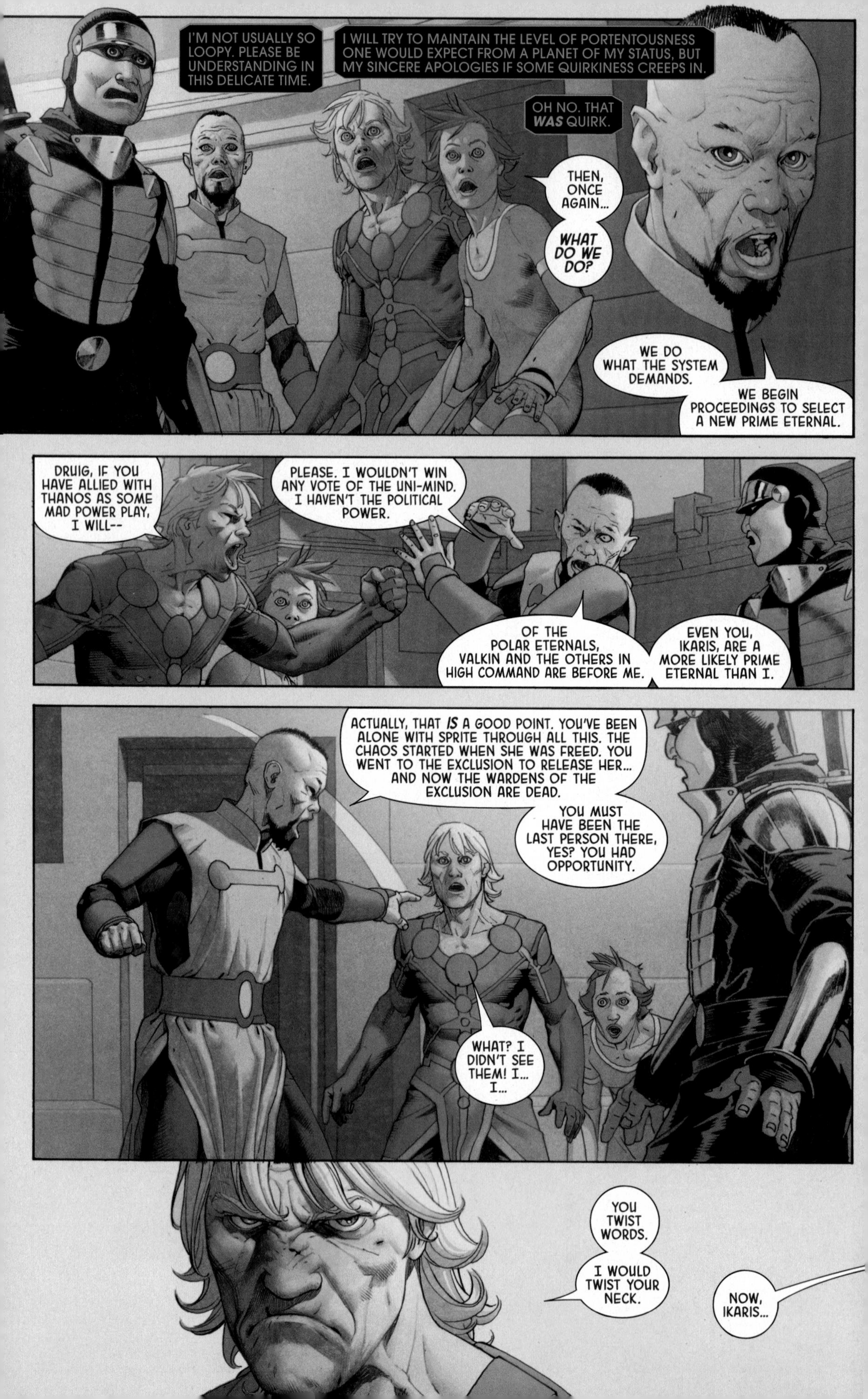
I'M NOT USUALLY SO LOOPY. PLEASE BE UNDERSTANDING IN THIS DELICATE TIME.
I WILL TRY TO MAINTAIN THE LEVEL OF PORTENTOUSNESS ONE WOULD EXPECT FROM A PLANET OF MY STATUS, BUT MY SINCERE APOLOGIES IF SOME QUIRKINESS CREEPS IN.
OH NO. THAT ***WAS*** QUIRK.
THEN, ONCE AGAIN...
WHAT DO WE DO?
WE DO WHAT THE SYSTEM DEMANDS.
WE BEGIN PROCEEDINGS TO SELECT A NEW PRIME ETERNAL.
DRUIG, IF YOU HAVE ALLIED WITH THANOS AS SOME MAD POWER PLAY, I WILL--
PLEASE. I WOULDN'T WIN ANY VOTE OF THE UNI-MIND. I HAVEN'T THE POLITICAL POWER.
OF THE POLAR ETERNALS, VALKIN AND THE OTHERS IN HIGH COMMAND ARE BEFORE ME.
EVEN YOU, IKARIS, ARE A MORE LIKELY PRIME ETERNAL THAN I.
ACTUALLY, THAT *IS* A GOOD POINT. YOU'VE BEEN ALONE WITH SPRITE THROUGH ALL THIS. THE CHAOS STARTED WHEN SHE WAS FREED. YOU WENT TO THE EXCLUSION TO RELEASE HER... AND NOW THE WARDENS OF THE EXCLUSION ARE DEAD.
YOU MUST HAVE BEEN THE LAST PERSON THERE, YES? YOU HAD OPPORTUNITY.
WHAT? I DIDN'T SEE THEM! I... I...
YOU TWIST WORDS.
I WOULD TWIST YOUR NECK.
NOW, IKARIS...

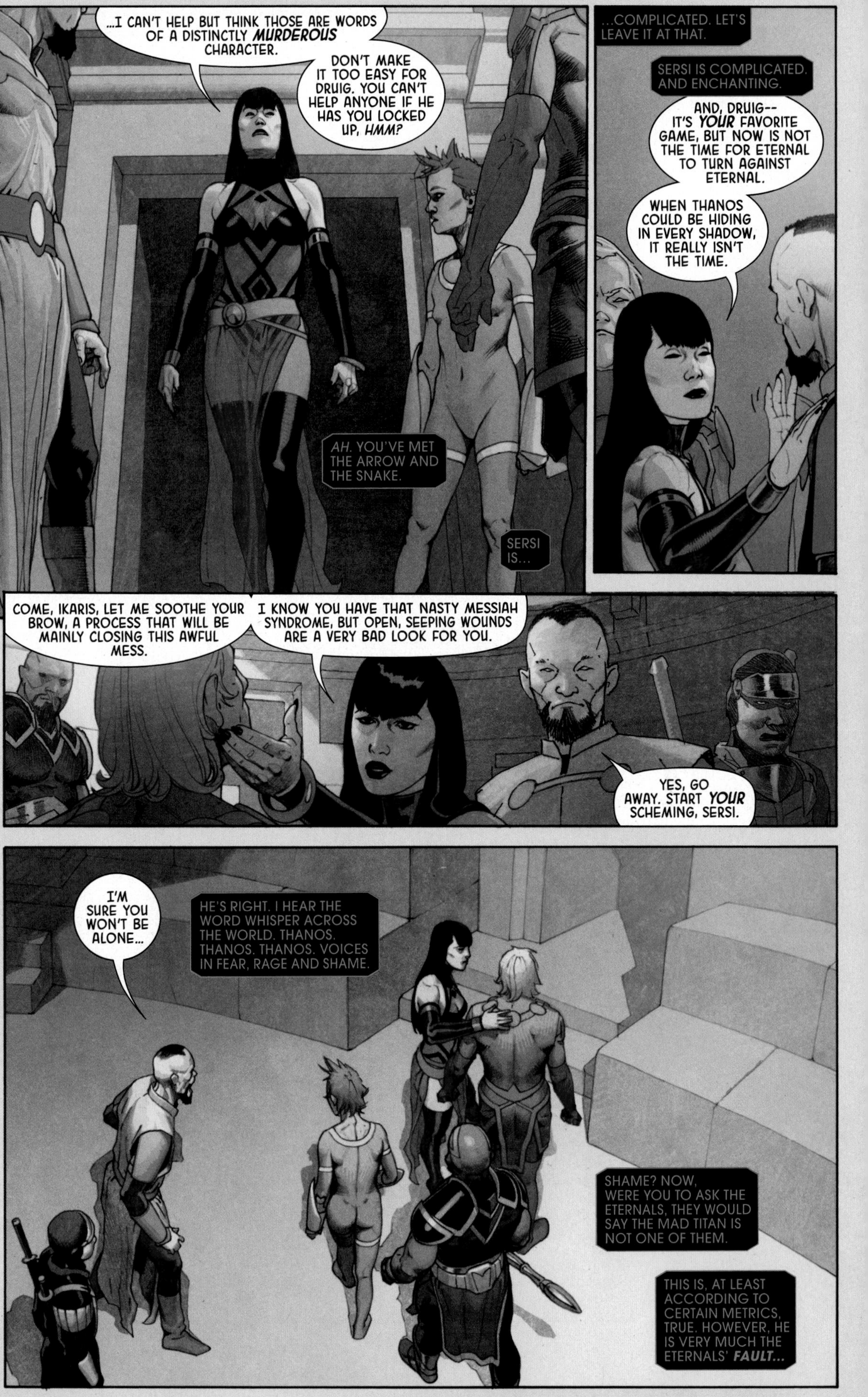

...I CAN'T HELP BUT THINK THOSE ARE WORDS OF A DISTINCTLY *MURDEROUS* CHARACTER.
DON'T MAKE IT TOO EASY FOR DRUIG. YOU CAN'T HELP ANYONE IF HE HAS YOU LOCKED UP, *HMM?*
AH. YOU'VE MET THE ARROW AND THE SNAKE.
SERSI IS...
...COMPLICATED. LET'S LEAVE IT AT THAT.
SERSI IS COMPLICATED. AND ENCHANTING.
AND, DRUIG-- IT'S *YOUR* FAVORITE GAME, BUT NOW IS NOT THE TIME FOR ETERNAL TO TURN AGAINST ETERNAL.
WHEN THANOS COULD BE HIDING IN EVERY SHADOW, IT REALLY ISN'T THE TIME.
COME, IKARIS, LET ME SOOTHE YOUR BROW, A PROCESS THAT WILL BE MAINLY CLOSING THIS AWFUL MESS.
I KNOW YOU HAVE THAT NASTY MESSIAH SYNDROME, BUT OPEN, SEEPING WOUNDS ARE A VERY BAD LOOK FOR YOU.
YES, GO AWAY. START *YOUR* SCHEMING, SERSI.
I'M SURE YOU WON'T BE ALONE...
HE'S RIGHT. I HEAR THE WORD WHISPER ACROSS THE WORLD. THANOS. THANOS. THANOS. VOICES IN FEAR, RAGE AND SHAME.
SHAME? NOW, WERE YOU TO ASK THE ETERNALS, THEY WOULD SAY THE MAD TITAN IS NOT ONE OF THEM.
THIS IS, AT LEAST ACCORDING TO CERTAIN METRICS, TRUE. HOWEVER, HE IS VERY MUCH THE ETERNALS' *FAULT...*

THE TITAN SCHISM OF THE SECOND AGE

THE ZURASIAN FACTION

Headed by Zuras. The majority faction, believing that the dangers of Eternals overextension had been proved by the Uranos and Kronos schisms. The Machine must be maintained, not expanded.

Strength: Unknown. Believed to be 70% of Eternals.

THE LLARSITE FACTION

Headed by A'Lars. Believes that the Great Machine's design should be subject to modification and extension. Most importantly, new True Eternals should be created, via biological and technological methods.

Strength: Unknown. Believed to be 30% of Eternals.

THANOS' LIFE

Thanos eventually destroys the Titan colony, kills his parents and murders half the population of the universe. He remains the galaxies' greatest criminal, with a death count that rivals even the greater forces of reality.

THANOS' BIRTH

Sui-San gives birth to Thanos.

THE PUNISHMENT

After their deaths, Sui-San and Mentor awaken in the Great Machine on Earth. They are both Excluded.

THE WAR

Due to the almost complete mind-wipe of individuals from this period, it is believed this is among the most emotionally intense periods of inter-Eternal warfare. While some Eternals know at least which side of the debate they were on during the Uranos War, many are unsure of their position in the Titan Schism.

THE ACCORD

It was decided that the Llarsite faction would be allowed to found a colony as an experiment. A solitary Llarsite would be allowed to do so. A'Lars was chosen and took the name "Mentor." Their beliefs would be judged according to the success or failure of the endeavor.

GROWTH OF THE TITAN COLONY

The methods are a success, leading to a splinter society of Eternals called "Titans." They are not part of the Great Machine but have many of the Eternals' abilities. Earth Eternals start to believe that this proves the Zurasian faction had been proven to be overly conservative. Mentor continues to pursue his work.

THE RE-ESTABLISHMENT OF THE TITAN COLONY

Mentor chose the lost colony of the Uranites on Titan, suspecting there was at least one Uranite survivor in residence. He located Sui-San, and they, together, used their genetic material and technology to found a new species of Eternal-derived beings, the Titans.

THE JUDGMENT

The Titan experiment is judged a failure.

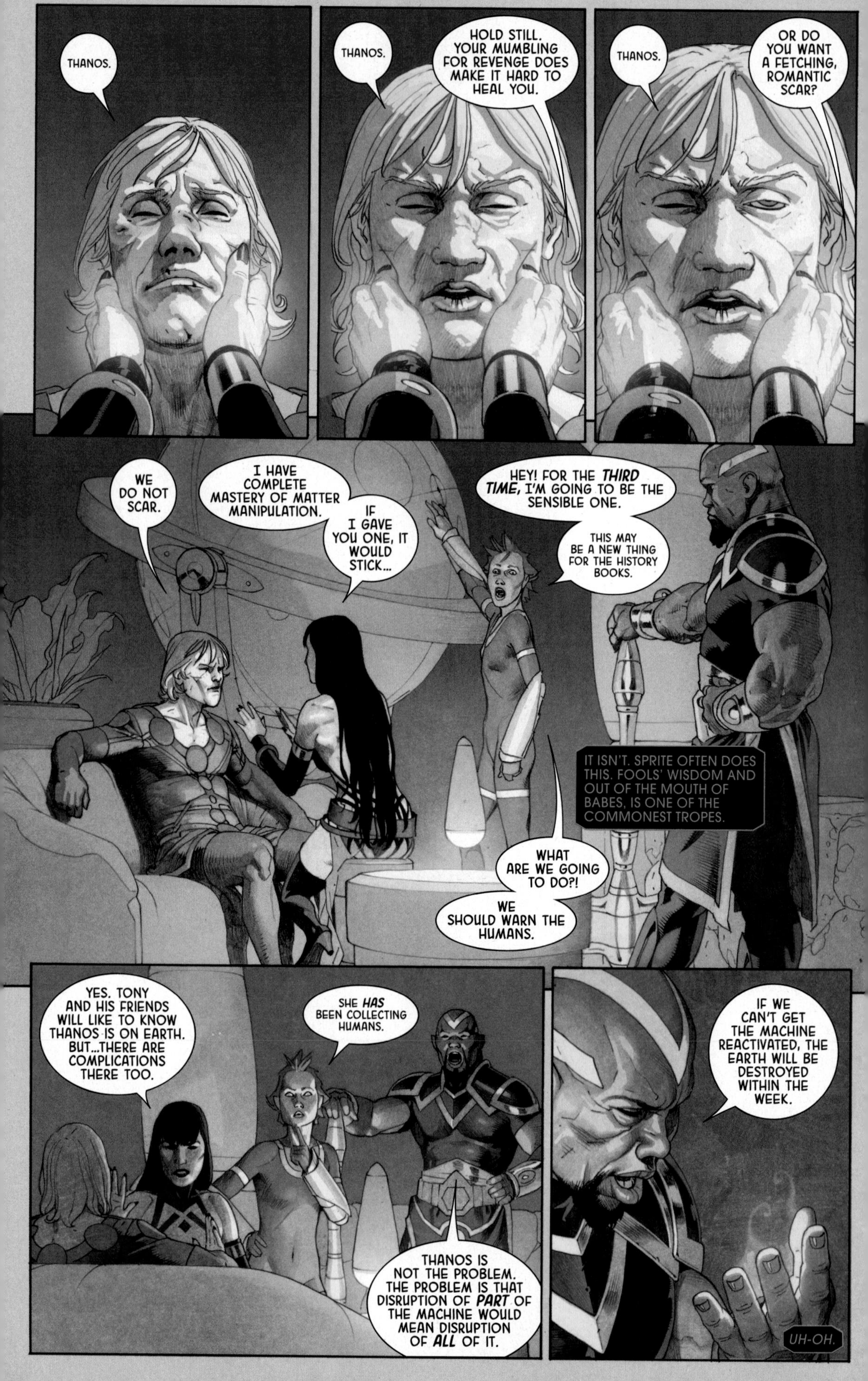
THANOS.
THANOS.
HOLD STILL. YOUR MUMBLING FOR REVENGE DOES MAKE IT HARD TO HEAL YOU.
THANOS.
OR DO YOU WANT A FETCHING, ROMANTIC SCAR?
WE DO NOT SCAR.
I HAVE COMPLETE MASTERY OF MATTER MANIPULATION.
IF I GAVE YOU ONE, IT WOULD STICK...
HEY! FOR THE *THIRD TIME,* I'M GOING TO BE THE SENSIBLE ONE.
THIS MAY BE A NEW THING FOR THE HISTORY BOOKS.
IT ISN'T. SPRITE OFTEN DOES THIS. FOOLS' WISDOM AND OUT OF THE MOUTH OF BABES, IS ONE OF THE COMMONEST TROPES.
WHAT ARE WE GOING TO DO?!
WE SHOULD WARN THE HUMANS.
YES. TONY AND HIS FRIENDS WILL LIKE TO KNOW THANOS IS ON EARTH. BUT...THERE ARE COMPLICATIONS THERE TOO.
SHE *HAS* BEEN COLLECTING HUMANS.
THANOS IS NOT THE PROBLEM. THE PROBLEM IS THAT DISRUPTION OF *PART* OF THE MACHINE WOULD MEAN DISRUPTION OF *ALL* OF IT.
IF WE CAN'T GET THE MACHINE REACTIVATED, THE EARTH WILL BE DESTROYED WITHIN THE WEEK.
UH-OH.

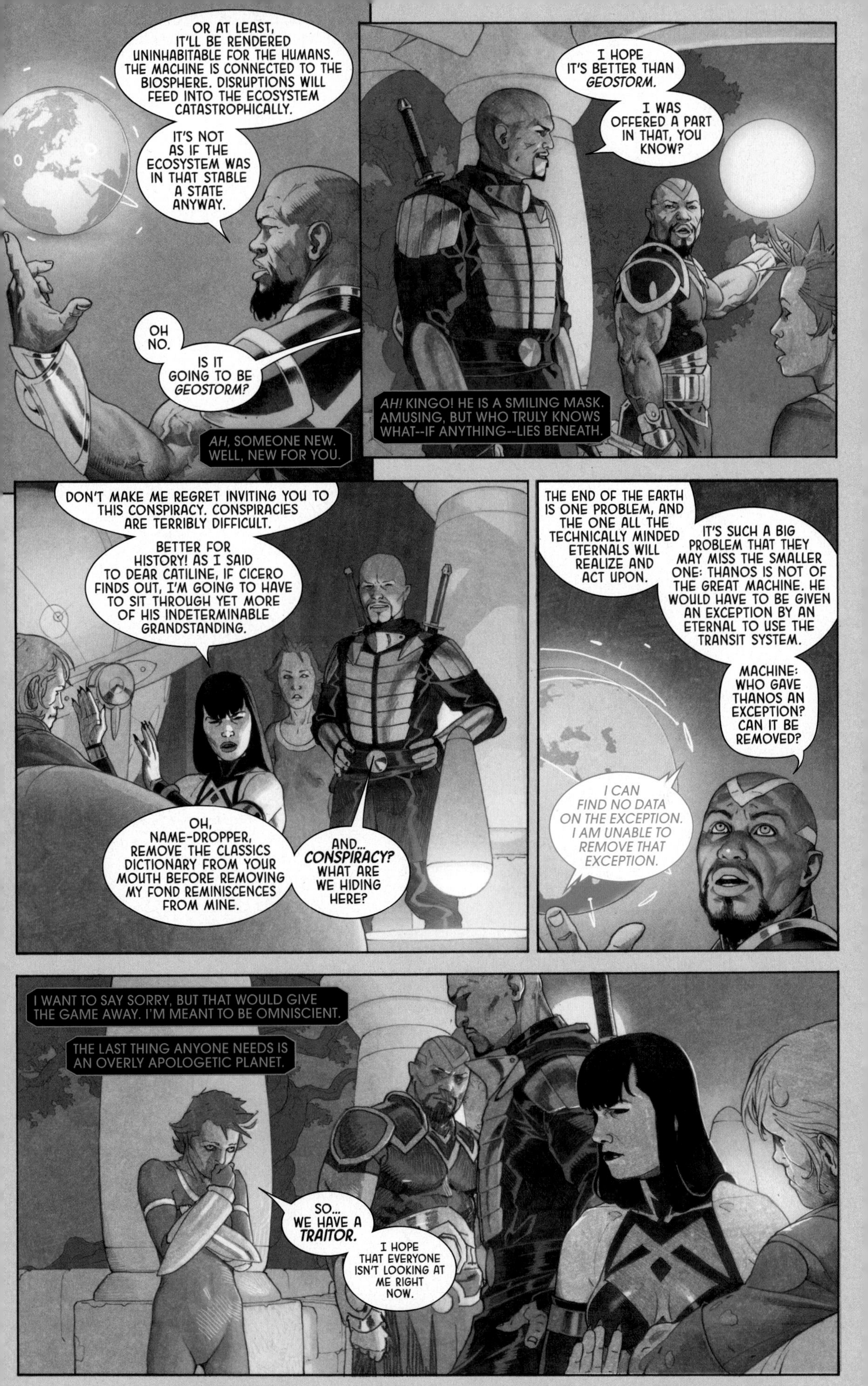
OR AT LEAST, IT'LL BE RENDERED UNINHABITABLE FOR THE HUMANS. THE MACHINE IS CONNECTED TO THE BIOSPHERE. DISRUPTIONS WILL FEED INTO THE ECOSYSTEM CATASTROPHICALLY.
IT'S NOT AS IF THE ECOSYSTEM WAS IN THAT STABLE A STATE ANYWAY.
OH NO.
IS IT GOING TO BE GEOSTORM?
AH, SOMEONE NEW. WELL, NEW FOR YOU.
I HOPE IT'S BETTER THAN GEOSTORM.
I WAS OFFERED A PART IN THAT, YOU KNOW?
AH! KINGO! HE IS A SMILING MASK. AMUSING, BUT WHO TRULY KNOWS WHAT--IF ANYTHING--LIES BENEATH.
DON'T MAKE ME REGRET INVITING YOU TO THIS CONSPIRACY. CONSPIRACIES ARE TERRIBLY DIFFICULT.
BETTER FOR HISTORY! AS I SAID TO DEAR CATILINE, IF CICERO FINDS OUT, I'M GOING TO HAVE TO SIT THROUGH YET MORE OF HIS INDETERMINABLE GRANDSTANDING.
OH, NAME-DROPPER, REMOVE THE CLASSICS DICTIONARY FROM YOUR MOUTH BEFORE REMOVING MY FOND REMINISCENCES FROM MINE.
AND... CONSPIRACY? WHAT ARE WE HIDING HERE?
THE END OF THE EARTH IS ONE PROBLEM, AND THE ONE ALL THE TECHNICALLY MINDED ETERNALS WILL REALIZE AND ACT UPON.
IT'S SUCH A BIG PROBLEM THAT THEY MAY MISS THE SMALLER ONE: THANOS IS NOT OF THE GREAT MACHINE. HE WOULD HAVE TO BE GIVEN AN EXCEPTION BY AN ETERNAL TO USE THE TRANSIT SYSTEM.
MACHINE: WHO GAVE THANOS AN EXCEPTION? CAN IT BE REMOVED?
I CAN FIND NO DATA ON THE EXCEPTION. I AM UNABLE TO REMOVE THAT EXCEPTION.
I WANT TO SAY SORRY, BUT THAT WOULD GIVE THE GAME AWAY. I'M MEANT TO BE OMNISCIENT.
THE LAST THING ANYONE NEEDS IS AN OVERLY APOLOGETIC PLANET.
SO... WE HAVE A TRAITOR.
I HOPE THAT EVERYONE ISN'T LOOKING AT ME RIGHT NOW.

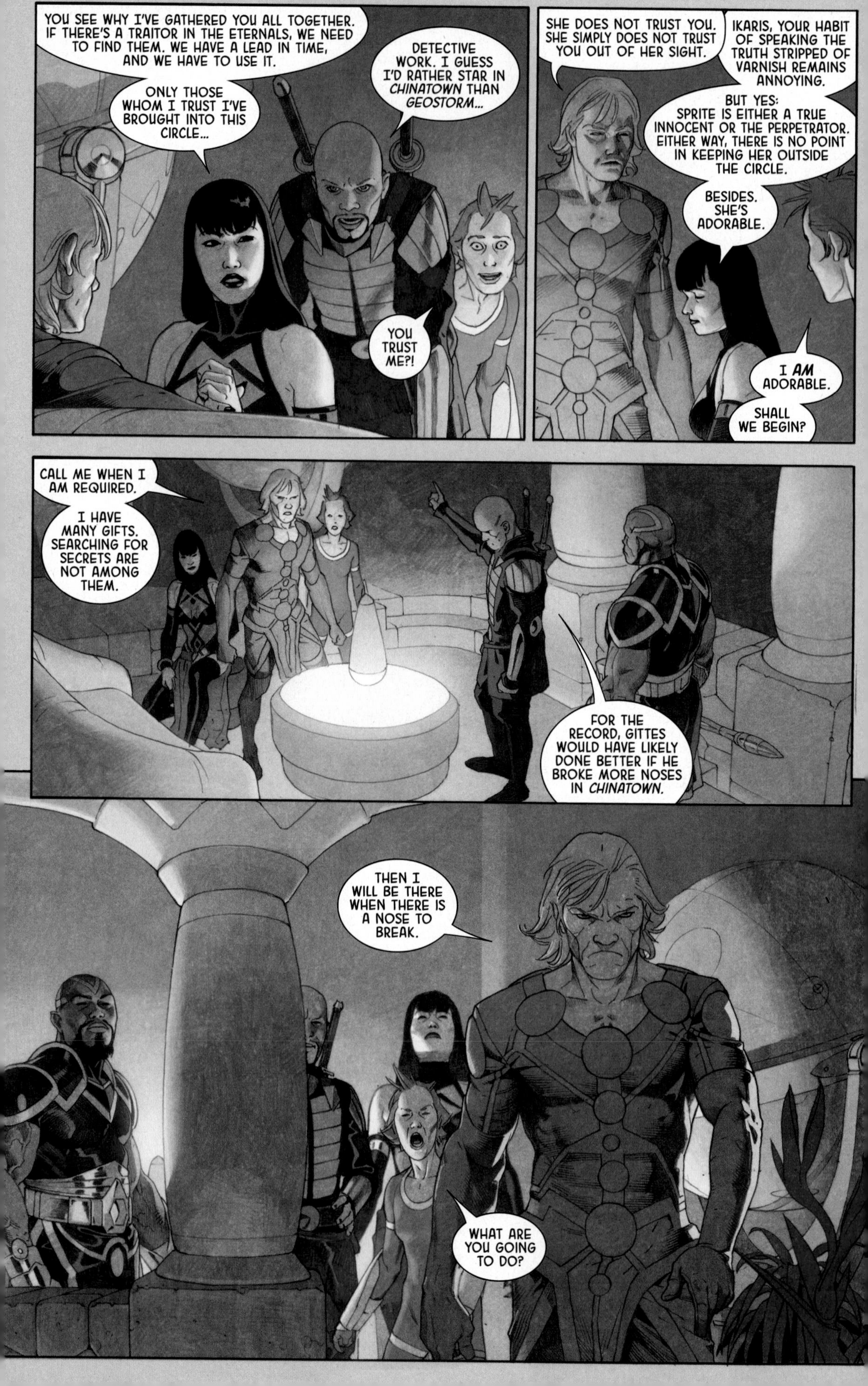
YOU SEE WHY I'VE GATHERED YOU ALL TOGETHER. IF THERE'S A TRAITOR IN THE ETERNALS, WE NEED TO FIND THEM. WE HAVE A LEAD IN TIME, AND WE HAVE TO USE IT.
ONLY THOSE WHOM I TRUST I'VE BROUGHT INTO THIS CIRCLE...
DETECTIVE WORK. I GUESS I'D RATHER STAR IN *CHINATOWN* THAN *GEOSTORM*...
YOU TRUST ME?!
SHE DOES NOT TRUST YOU. SHE SIMPLY DOES NOT TRUST YOU OUT OF HER SIGHT.
IKARIS, YOUR HABIT OF SPEAKING THE TRUTH STRIPPED OF VARNISH REMAINS ANNOYING.
BUT YES: SPRITE IS EITHER A TRUE INNOCENT OR THE PERPETRATOR. EITHER WAY, THERE IS NO POINT IN KEEPING HER OUTSIDE THE CIRCLE.
BESIDES. SHE'S ADORABLE.
I **AM** ADORABLE.
SHALL WE BEGIN?
CALL ME WHEN I AM REQUIRED.
I HAVE MANY GIFTS. SEARCHING FOR SECRETS ARE NOT AMONG THEM.
FOR THE RECORD, GITTES WOULD HAVE LIKELY DONE BETTER IF HE BROKE MORE NOSES IN *CHINATOWN.*
THEN I WILL BE THERE WHEN THERE IS A NOSE TO BREAK.
WHAT ARE YOU GOING TO DO?

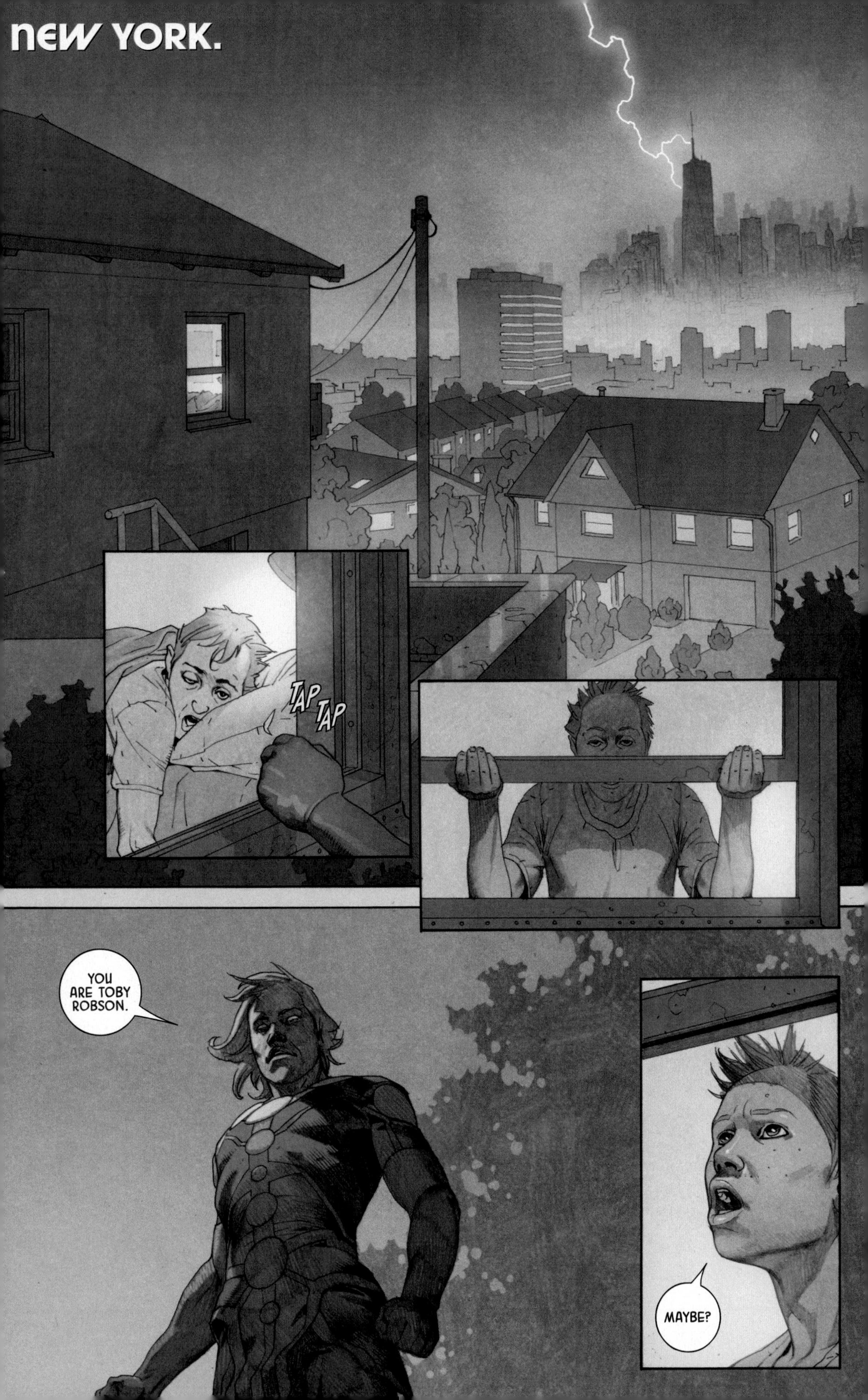
NEW YORK.
TAP TAP
YOU ARE TOBY ROBSON.
MAYBE?

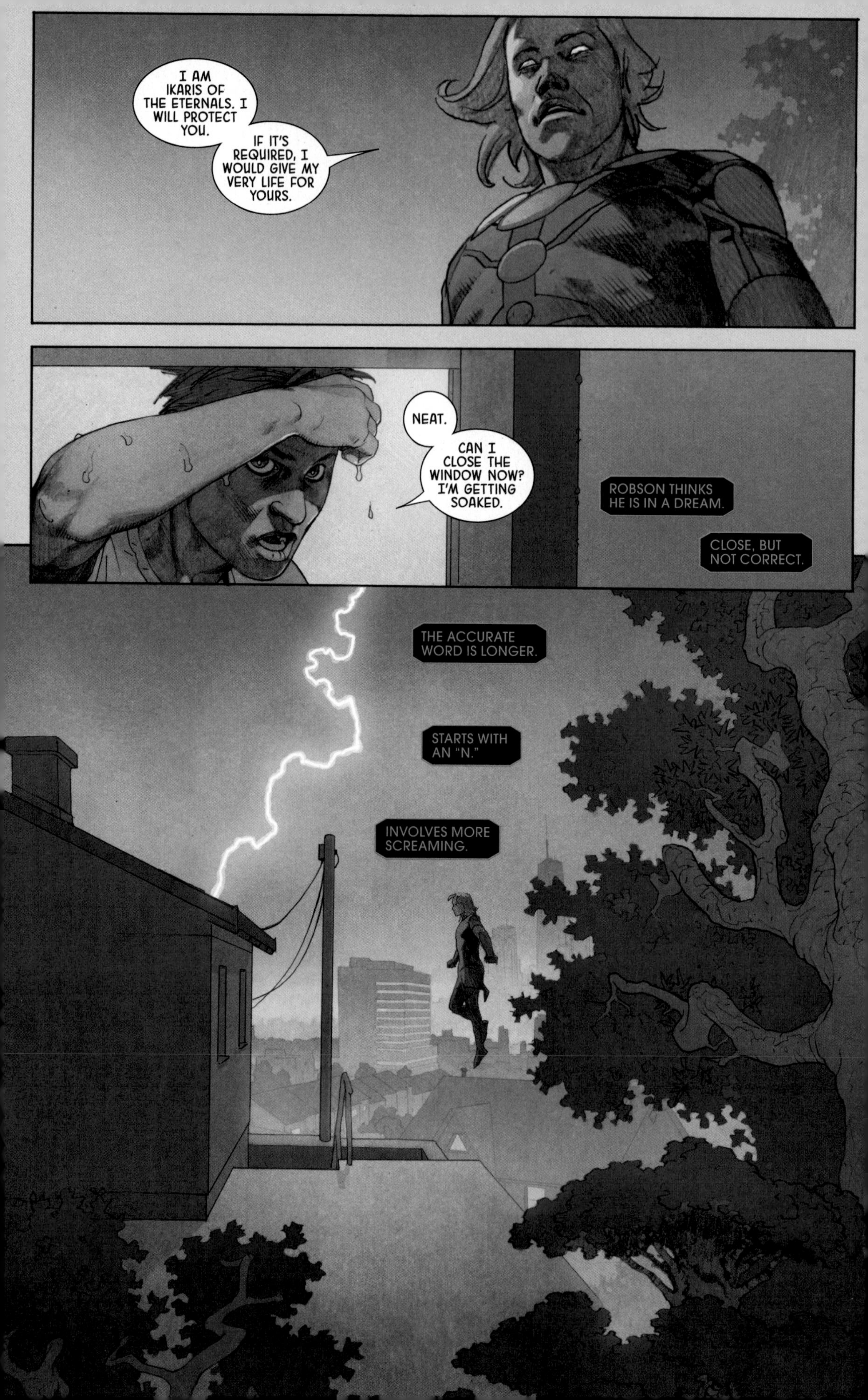
I AM IKARIS OF THE ETERNALS. I WILL PROTECT YOU.
IF IT'S REQUIRED, I WOULD GIVE MY VERY LIFE FOR YOURS.
NEAT.
CAN I CLOSE THE WINDOW NOW? I'M GETTING SOAKED.
ROBSON THINKS HE IS IN A DREAM.
CLOSE, BUT NOT CORRECT.
THE ACCURATE WORD IS LONGER.
STARTS WITH AN "N."
INVOLVES MORE SCREAMING.

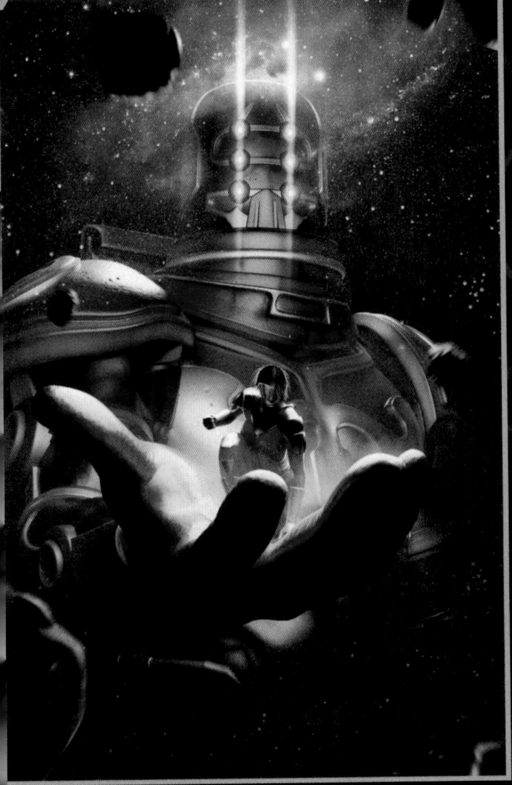

#1 VARIANT BY **BOSSLOGIC**

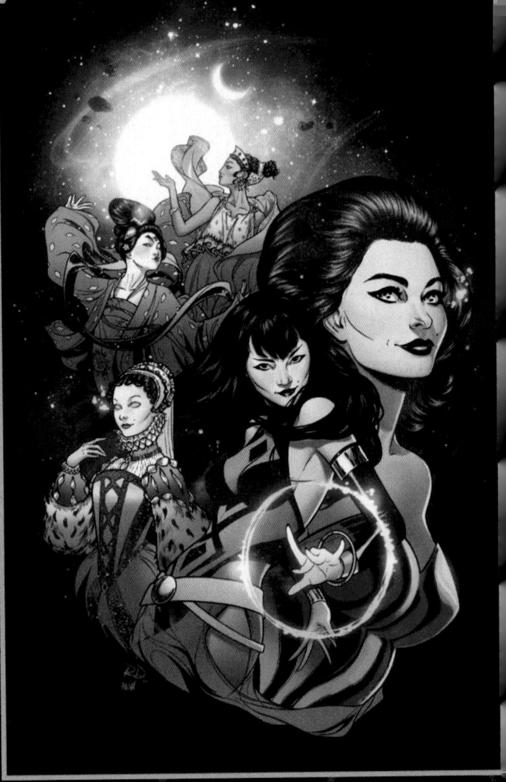

#1 VARIANT BY **RUSSELL DAUTERMAN & MATTHEW WILSON**

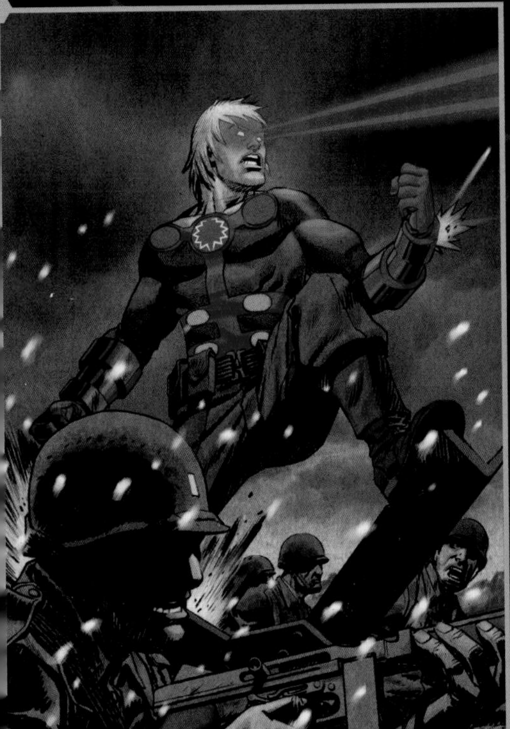

#1 VARIANT BY **DAVE JOHNSON**

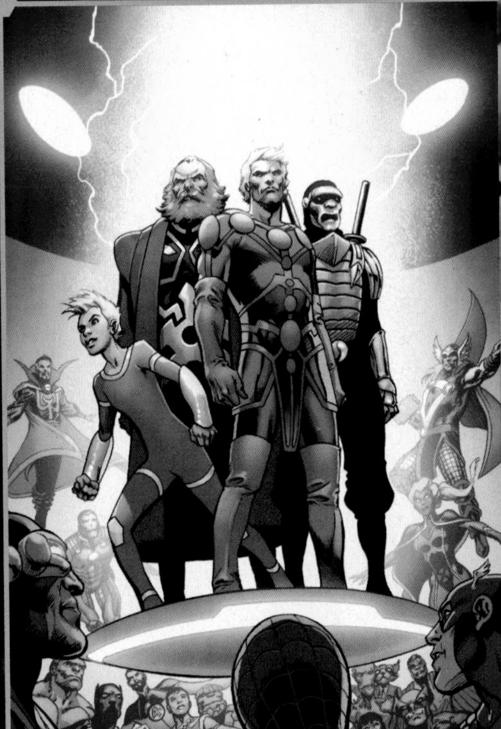

#1 VARIANT BY **ALAN DAVIS & NOLAN WOODARD**

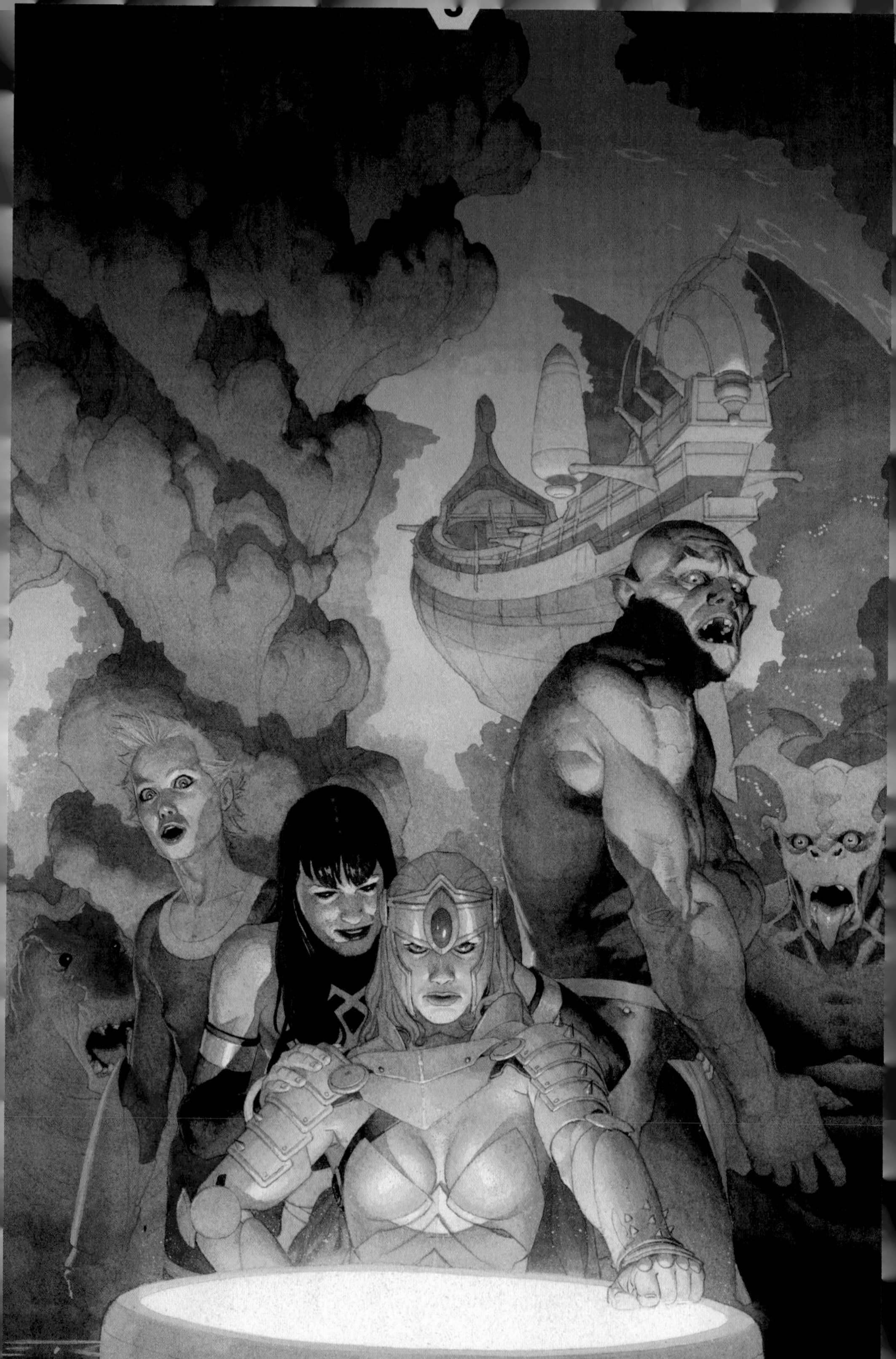

HHRH HRTR HHH

THIS IS **THENA**.

SHE IS THE BOOK AND THE BLADE.

YOU WOULD LIKELY LIKE HER. SHE WOULD LIKELY LIKE YOU.

SHE AWAKENS FROM A DREAMLESS SLEEP.

THENA FEELS FREE FOR THE FIRST TIME IN FOREVER.

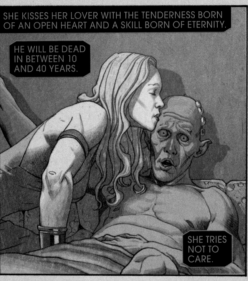

SHE KISSES HER LOVER WITH THE TENDERNESS BORN OF AN OPEN HEART AND A SKILL BORN OF ETERNITY.

HE WILL BE DEAD IN BETWEEN 10 AND 40 YEARS.

SHE TRIES NOT TO CARE.

THENA IS GOOD AT MANY THINGS BUT NOT **EVERYTHING**.

STILL, SHE MADE HER CHOICE.

SHE KNOWS WHAT THE ETERNALS, WHOM SHE LEFT BEHIND, WILL THINK OF HER...

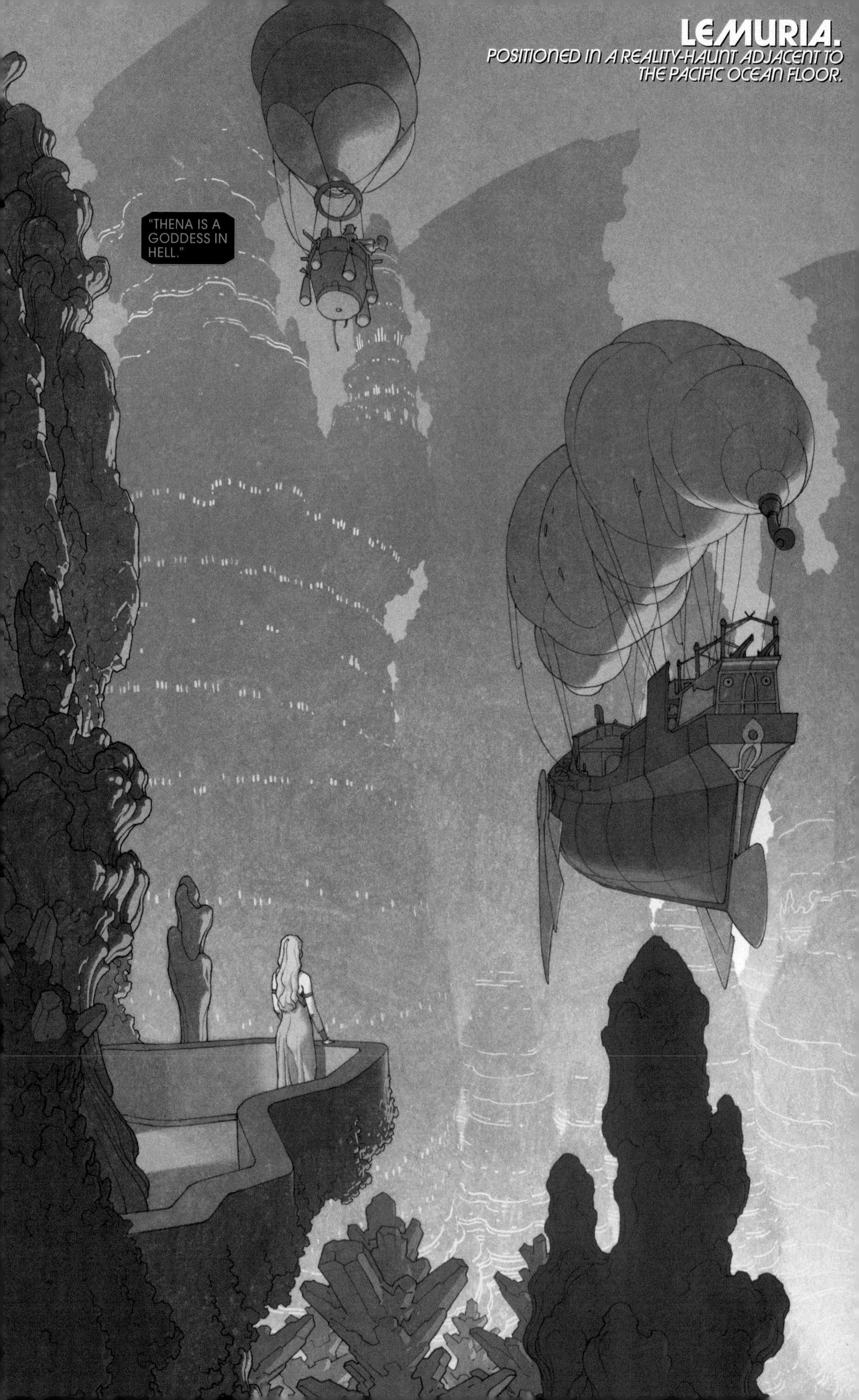
LEMURIA.
POSITIONED IN A REALITY-HAUNT ADJACENT TO THE PACIFIC OCEAN FLOOR.
"THENA IS A GODDESS IN HELL."

//

LEMURIA

CAPITAL CITY OF THE DEVIANTS, ANCESTRAL FOE OF THE ETERNALS

INITIAL POPULATION: 100

CURRENT POPULATION...

ACCESSING DEVIANT DATABASE...

//

PUKIGAL'PYRE **SEYGMO'IGO QUARTZSWORD** GROSTROMA

HARE ERESHUR SLUEGA
DULTHAG BLUJAKINA
ASBOATH EVIL DROM
RT **FINNOP** TRICITE
OMELESS RANJAKX
FASOPE
NDICE KROBOATH
METULA GHAICEA
HEIT THE MINISCULE
SEYNERX VEEG KASE
OS AHTHAG VISTHAG
LT ZOOMONKEY BRNG
JLA THIGO'US PHRAUGOS
G **PHRAUGOS FRATHAG**
AU KARGMAXINI TIGERWINTER
OGMO THIGO'US PHRAUGOS
UGAH TARLAU KARGMAXINI
AINI STRATAUR KROGMO
LAA TOBULAINY **VERHUDE**
STREETSNAIL **DRALER**
OPHRAINA CATAKEEANA
ECREAM STRAOB THE
HEIT UNATZ BRNATZ
NNAL FASRGINY
CORPULENT THRA
CE DULBOATH
GON **PUAH'NTO**
VED KLARDARINY
THAG STRABOATH
VIRHUDE DRAAG'IGO
TATO MEDKA INKPYRE
X **SLEETWIND** SLEUGINY
TZAPYRE CATAHAG BLOODY
MO FASEL LAGOHREL MAEAK
CHUAG SLUICEEANA THAAR
S GIGUS STRAWSMILE VISKAX
RONG VELER BRSIS KLARAH
A AHRAE TORE WELLRHUDE
GO INDGMO GEHEIT
OM *KROPHALOUSEANA*
S GORKA BERRYBACK
SEYUS **ZAKRAXEANA**
PUMAX THE DEAD
DASBOATH KRAJAK
RICE RABBITTIME
PARKLING BUZY
K **KHAG** RANPYRE
AEGEANA'US CATALT
XSONG FINNOB THE
INKPUS GEJAK IGKAINI
SLEAN'PYRE DRAARINY

RODGEEANA
STRAPYREEANA
GORGA
CATANGINA
MEDAR
SHELSIS
VISDAR

DRAAGX WAXPLOT
KRAOP **BRNGINA**
METICE RAGSAK
DASA THANATZE
DRAMAX'LAU THE FIERCE THAULAINY **STRIHAG** ARGMAX FRAIL
TRILER BRHAGA'EL **ARRE** TOBELEUS THANLERINI TOSIS
FRIGHTENED RAGICE ZAKNG **STRIAKEANA'AH** INDOS
VILT GLOHAG **STRISIS'UR** MINEBACK BRUSTROM
SUCCESSFUL TAKAK'ON **TAKONINY KITTYCOAT**

ENIOBE
MEDGMAX'RT
COOPERATIVE
KROOP GHAAN
PLANTBORN
JUICECRAYON
MINTBORN

SHY FASPHRA VEGMO HANDHAIRCUT HAELEUS'NATZ
SILVERSTORY HADAR PYRMARINY PHRAUGMAR
THPYRE METDGE KARYPHRA'O TAKSAKINA VISICE
METSIS'AH WRENCHLOAF **YRDIAS THE BAD** CATARO VEAS
THE RISIBLE **BANDNTOEANA** DRAO KARYGMAX RAPHALOUS

ENILER'LAU
ARKE GLORIOUS
BLUMAR
GLORHUDE
MORMARX
ERESHBOATH
KRO **HELPLESS**
PUGMAX TOAG
CHUULAINA
BURSTSTREET
SPIKE KARYLER
GRONER
LOCKETFLOCK
BOTTLESHIRT
MORGA CHUSAK
TOMAR SHELAR
KROKIGAL
RANSAK
SLETHAG KUR
GHAGMO'PYRE

HATU BRLT
GEAG'O **KRAICE**
GLOGMAX'RHUDE
INKKIGAL INDILLA
THANBOATH'IGO
STRAPUS **BANDO**
SLEPHALOUS KLARILLAA
TOBULAINY VERHUDE
FASIGO AHAH AHQLAU
DRALER SEYHEITINY
CATAKEEANA
DAB GNORTS

THANLAU
KARYELEUS
PLOKIGO
DRAAR
FRAUSE THGMAX
STRIAG THIGO
FASAGEANA
VELAU **TAKHEIT**
AHEG FINNOS
KARKAS **MARCEL**
DASKIGALINY
HAHAGE
PHRAUGLAUINY
TOEL FRATU
POISONLOVE
BANDOPX
SPOTLESS TOAS
MAEOB SLEGA
BUCKETMARBLE

ENIAGE VINTO

GORKIGAL KROOP VIDAR STRAOINI THAGMAX YRDIILLA
ERESHAL'RHUDE YRDIOHRELINI SHELAS TOBOB RANHEITA TRILAU
THANTU **SHELHEIT** TOKIGAL MARCRAXINI PHRAUGLAU
MEDAG ANNOYED VEUG THAEL TZAULA **INDRA'TU**
WILD LUGGMO'CIT BORGNO

TOLAU SLUREINA THE POOR SPIGA'PHRA DRALER
KRAKIGAL DULRHUDEX **SLEIGOE THE WITTY**
JORRAX KRAMAX'ELEUS ZAKKA INDJAK'RA TARAH THE
ADVENTUROUS **VERHUD BOTTLEDRAIN** JOROS PHRAUGRO
VEEL THRHUD SHELTAUR FASAS COUNTRYDOG DULEG

MEDPUS STRIEL
SHAKECABLE
GORGEOUS
YOKESTITCH
MOTIONLESS
THNATZ
THE LONELY
FRAOSA
THE IMPOSSIBLE
SMOKEWHEEL
FAMOUS ERESHRO
VEAL JEALOUS
KRAIASINA
VITHAG GRODGE
THE LOVING
KRATAURE
BRUDAR'AR
OVENSHOP
FASLER TOPHRA
THE SUCCESSFUL

STRART
KARDARINA
POTATOCOVER
SOICE DROMHAGINY
KRAGA **INKGMAX** TOA
JORNATZ THASAKEANA
BRUHAG'AG LUGGAE
PUTAUR **VISAN**
WASTESMOKE MOREL
SOUG **THGMAX'AL**
GIGGMAXE
ANNIHILATOR

KRASX SPIRAX
PUBOATH THE
KRNTO
PUNTO
ENIOHRELX
STORMY FINNTU
PUMAXINI
HASTROMINY
FRALER
TORHUD THE
SPILAU THE ODD
THANCIT DRAAS
ZAKOS THE INEPT
PLOKJAK GLORT
TZACIT **PHRAUGA**
KARYSAK
SHELULAA
PLOKNGINY
ROHAG HAELA
TARPYRE

CHEESEEARTH **BLURAX** FASURA CATAHAGA SHELHEITX THANGMO
ZAKSIS DASA BANDHAGX **HABOATHEANA'NTO** RIFLEZINC
KRKIGAL KRODAR FASOR RED GEAHA SHELAI PUMPSHAKE

PULAU THANKI
ZAKBOATH WELL
THSTROM KISS
VAS PANCAKES
WELLNGE
DKAR'STRON
ROLT **SEYAS**
HARHUDEE **G**
KRAULA YAK
TOLAUINI **MO**
PYREL DROMOS
GEDGE GHAARE'
YRDISAKX VENER KA
LOSSSNAIL BRPHALO
GLOHAG'AK CHINSILK
KARKIGAL VIRE **PHRAUG**
SLUELEUS CATARO SEYO
GESIS METSISX DROM
THUREANA THE COUR
BRILLA RAGILLA KARY
EVASIVE INKKE KAR
GROULA MORHA
SOAR **STRIGA**
RAIGO THE FU
KAR DRABOAT
MINISCULE
FASKE **FA**
MOREL V
THANAL **ENIF**
HONEYSHOE GR
WELLUR DIRTTAB
DROMTAURX PH
BLOODFOOT **KRAA**
STOPWIND TARTU THE T
TOOHRELINI FINNRG
RELIEVED SOKA'GMAX
GIGDARINI AHDAR LA
FRAKIGAL BLUTU SPIA
UPTIGHT LUGAINY CHU
THAUR THMAX BLUR
DULMAR'LAU CHU
PYRICE DASMA
KRAR GETAURE
MEDGMO **PHRA**
TORVALD CH
PYRSIS **ST**
SOOP PUN
GRIEVING
FRUITSHOE P
FRANTIC THAOSI
TARGMO GEAG CH
PLOKPYRE CHUNER

JGIAS SHELEGINI
BAHAK TICKFIRE
SLEDGE ROLT
VID ZAKBOATH
K TICKFIRE
OATH SLUNG
OHREL VID
RAX INKIGO
ZAKELEUS
ROEL BRUAR
AL THE NERVOUS
SLUGMAX AHUS
AR ARTRABBIT TOAK
ZAKDAR BUBBLETOE
ELINY DIAMONDSTICK
TOCIT LAGOP ERESHIAS
REINY TOLAU LUSTFUL
HELAGX DULDAR'NER
US TOKAINY RAIGO
CATART GHAD THE
KRA ERESHOBINI
IGAS'D DRAGA
UDE'MAR GEAS
MORAS'IGO
ICE MAEPHRA
AR KROKE
S KRRA
R TORG
HAG RAGO
UDA SPOTTURKEY
RNERX GROPYRE
GAG KARYEGX
AGER THRA SLETUA
ENISTROM TOBOATH
R THE FUNNY YRDIRO
ERE GHAUG LUGDGEX
FRAAHEANA STRAEL
RAEL INDTAUR'A THE
GHAAG'MAR METLAU
SELCUP CATAOHRELE
RAGDGE TOULA
DAR HARG'OB
THE WORRIED
UR HANDSTEEL
REL IGAGINI
ARDINA
EANA THE
HRAEANA
ULAA GROUR
LUIGOINA'DAR
MITTEN GEBOATH
PHUDFEANA LAGKEE

GORUR THANKFUL KREI MALICOINARO WEEI HKA VKM
ERESHICEINI TZAIASEANA'EG TARASINA BROBA THANLT GORUR
ERESHKIGAL
GIRAFFEBOW RAGAL
AREG RANBOATH
ZAKGMO TOMAR
SHELRAX TREEBLOOD
CHUPHRA RAMAX
SLURHUD FRAPUS
KRTAUR SHAMEWAX
RAJAK SHY
ROOHREL TOELEUS
METO ARPHRA
GEKAX KSAK'OB
BAHAN TRITTEX
SEYPUS BANDRO
LIVELY DROMIGOE
CLOVERRING LAGTU
PICKLEPOWER
BLUICEA SEYPUS
GHAAS'AR SPIO
BLUPHRA HAOPINA
GEPHRAA SNOWPEACE INKOSA TODGE SLEEG HAAR SILVERCRACK
CATADGE THE DUPLICITOUS GLORIOUS HARHUDE TOPYREINY
THE MUSHY MEDMAREANA RAGNATZINY IGTUINA
CHUCITE WELLAS RAGAS FOLDTHRILL ZAKHAG BAHRE
KAL'GA PHRAUGDAR'RAX AHAL RAHEIT YRDIEG
THRT'NERTZARAXINI

RAREEANA
ROGA PYRNER
ENIAS THE
COOPERATIVE
BANDTAUR SEYRAX
MUSHY GLOD
VEIGO SHIRTFANG
TAKSAK SEYJAKINA
THMAX'KA PLOKTU
MORLT'MAX
HANDEAR HAKA
INDCITINI

ENINATZ
KRAURX'A
THE HIDEOUS
DROMJAK
DRAUG
SPISTROM
SOUGEANA
WELLONX
FISHLIZARD
ZAKAR
GEDINI
DROMUS
LUGELEUS
PUTU
LUGTAURE
DASNATZ
MICEHOOK
LAGAS
TOOBA

GORTUINA TAKDAR GRC
ZAKNATZ INNOCENT RA
HAHEIT GORDAR THE M
OPEN SPIPHALOUS E
VILAU BLUKAEANA
WOODBELL BAND

BOOKTRAY SPIELEU
RAGRHUD PLOI
YRDIILLA DROMAL
CHANCEIRON FASN
JORNATZ GHAPHALO
DULPUS'O VIRAX THE ZE
BLUDAR OCEANPOISON W.
PUARA'KA KARYRA INKOP
TOBAS IGBOATH FINNDAR
BLUBOATH METSAK JOROB S
SOOINA PUDGE TARELEANA RC
VIMAR HANDSPY VENATZ
THAOS SNAKEPIE THANTAUF
GRORG AHRAXEANA KA
MUSHY DULAG MEDIAS
VISAR KARYKA DROM
PYRNER THE LONG ST
CABBAGELAKE LU
FASOSE THE PLAI

AHRG LIZARDSNO
MAEREX LOVEL
INDAK SHELAG'
YRDIAA'CIT FINNTHAG
ROOTPUNCH JORKIGA
POTATOSABRE TOBGMC
THE DISGUSTED SHELGM
CATARHUDEINI TAKRO ARA
SHELKIGAL TONATZ SPIRG FAS
SHELRGINY GLOHAG MARCAL
TARAS VOL METGA INDAIN
VIOBEANA'OP POTATOLAKE SC
TRIJAK GORD SHELTHAG
PYRUG WAXFIRE SEYSAK
KAR'TU LAGRAX WE
KROELEUS VISASE KAR
FINNIGO INDILLAEANA
FLAMECOW FINNKI
PLOKEG THE PETULA

BANDOB MORC
KARICEX MARCM
ERESHIGO PLOI
AHRAINA GIGHEIT AR
PHRAUGALE'PALOUS
VEUS'LT TOPHALOUS LE
TOAS METNG SEYPT KAF

KROREX STRADAR GHAUR MEDPYRE FASEG
GROLT TOBTHAG DULREINI DROMIAS TAROBEANA
MINTLIQUID ENIMAR'UG KRAINI TOHAG RINGPAN
KO CHINSTEEL STORMY RANAG RAGOP BROQ
STRUUN DASGO RANER ERESHKEINI YRDIGMAX RORHUD
BLUKIGAL'AG PYRAK KIND GLOIGO RANLER GRASSSCISSOR
SLUAS AREG'SAK STORYTOE INDUR CATAKEINA KRHAG LAGPUS'AL
KLARSTROM BRULA
PHRAUGNTO

LEGSNOW THANIGO
INDOP THE TALENTED
TOBAS INKO'SAK
ROPHRA STRAELEUS
TZART'AS GRAINYAM
LACESWING
GORELEUSEANA
THASIS SALTNOTE
LEGGROUND
HURT SLURE'AS
KEYTHROAT GIGTU
AHIAS DULUR
SPIBOATH VIICEE
GLOBOATH
HASAK LUGUS
GORNEREANA
SEYRA INKNER
SNOWPOTATO
JORPUSA PUD KARO PYRE KISSHILL TERRIBLE STRIAL'GMAX
DROMGMAX WRENCHRHYTHM DULOSINI FRAGMAX
KLAREG DULAG TAKA RENNUR RATSEMOH SHELAG
DOGKISS KLARAK KELEUS DROMIGO GIGRGINI
KRAKA AHARINY GIGDGE BUGBOARD PULBO

TZALAU ROAG
JORUGINI SPIAS
IGNATZ ENIPHRA
GORGMAX'RHUDE
CATART TARTHAG
VISIGOEANA'LER BROOP
TAKICE YRDIUG THAGMO
THE WRONG ARTHAG
GROMAXINI TARNTO
TONNO GEICE'RA
KROTAUR HAAK
RANKAX

ROHEIT
FRATAUR
SHELIGO
KRRHUD
VELAUA
GORON'OP
GLOAS LAZY
SHELA
DROMNG
THANOSINA
SOOB
PYRO'D
ZAKJAKINI
SHELHAG
BANDAG
KARYRHUDE
GLOMM
MEDNATZ
MUDDY

FINE ZONA THNG BRKIGAL BRURHUDEE FRARG
DRAUGA LANCECUP VIA FIRESOAP RALAUINY KARTHAG
WELLKE FINNRHUD'AS DRAANINI SPIAS INDALE METON
TAKGMO MARCRHUDE DULAR THE CRAZY DROMRO PYRILLA
VIHEIT'CIT FAIRYFOG FASRO GLOICE'BOATH THE TIRED METRG
SPIMAR VEAL
RAILLA MORDAR
BAHNTOINA GEELEUS
CHUSIS RAGAR
FASELEANA VISPHRA
BAHNTOINA GEELEUS
CHUSIS RAGAR
FASELEANA VISPHRA
SHELTAUR DULDAR
FRAOS CHUAK
TOMAR'ICE GREEDY
SAGACIOUS AHA
MARCBOATHINI
MAERAXINY
DROMHAG
STRANGLEHOLD
ROEL KLARMAX
LAGAR'A PUZZLED
TZAMAR KRATHAG
DARG ZAKAL
BUCKETDROP FINNTHAGINI'ILLA KARYICE DROMTHAG BRUGMOA
KRATHAG SEYOB BAHON BRD ZAKAL PINESKIP MAESTROM

RADGEEANA
TZAICEINY
WELLKE
FRAEL'STROM TOTAUR
TARTHAG THALINA
FINNNATZX GHAICE
DASIGO'KA TZAAH'AS
BAHEL POWERHILL
GROOS FASTHAGA
THMAR TAKUS
BRURT KRANATZ
RARE RANMAX

TONATZ
GORDARA
SPIGMO
ENIJAK THAN
GLOAKINY'O
SPIGMO
ENIJAK THAN
GLOAKINY'O
MINTHAIR
SLUIGOE
RAGOE
MORRE KAK
FRAOB
BOATH
GIGO
PUAR
RAARD
DRAEG
SEYOB BAHON
LOWYEAR

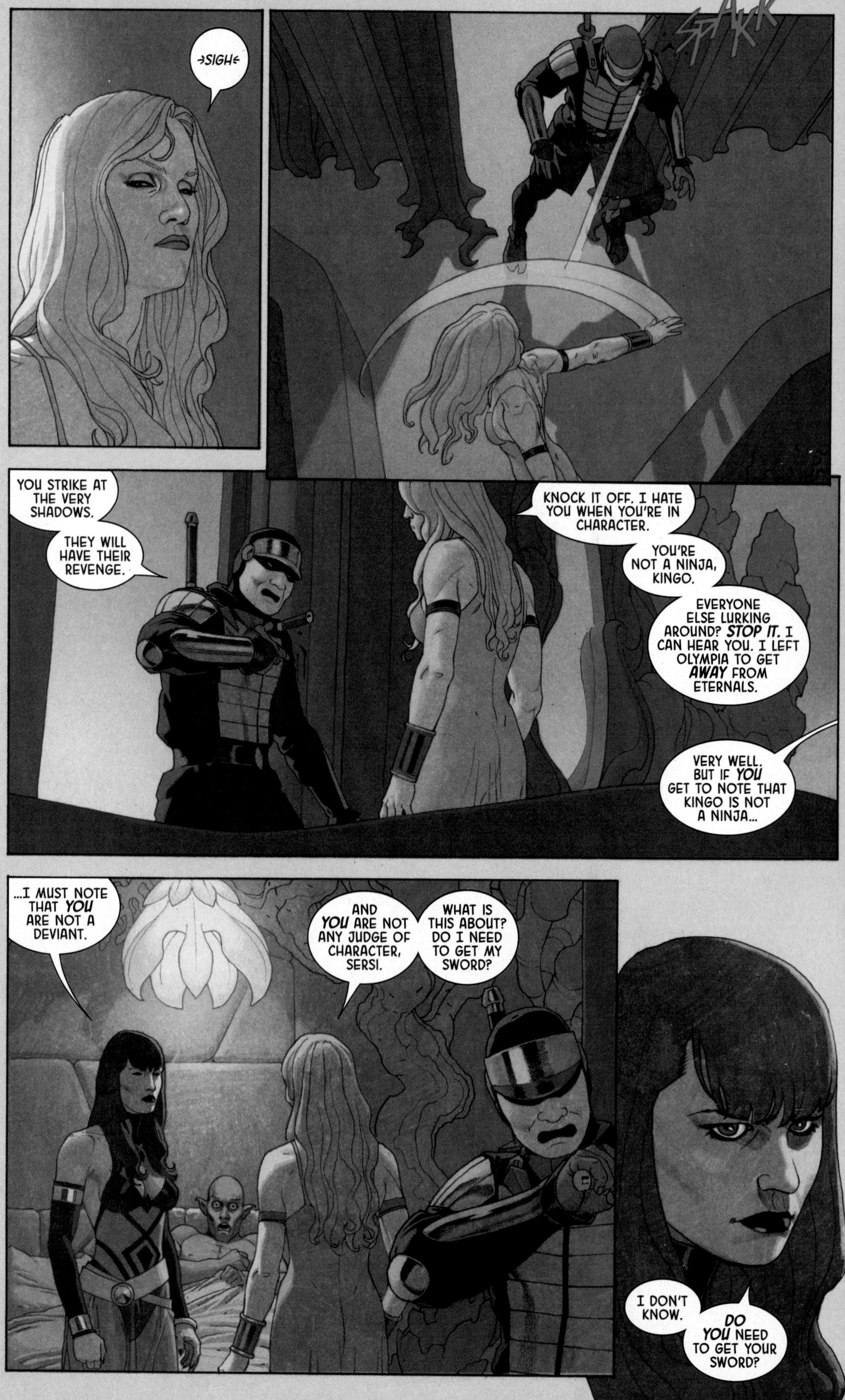

>SIGH<
SPAKK
YOU STRIKE AT THE VERY SHADOWS.
THEY WILL HAVE THEIR REVENGE.
KNOCK IT OFF. I HATE YOU WHEN YOU'RE IN CHARACTER.
YOU'RE NOT A NINJA, KINGO.
EVERYONE ELSE LURKING AROUND? STOP IT. I CAN HEAR YOU. I LEFT OLYMPIA TO GET AWAY FROM ETERNALS.
VERY WELL. BUT IF YOU GET TO NOTE THAT KINGO IS NOT A NINJA...
...I MUST NOTE THAT YOU ARE NOT A DEVIANT.
AND YOU ARE NOT ANY JUDGE OF CHARACTER, SERSI.
WHAT IS THIS ABOUT? DO I NEED TO GET MY SWORD?
I DON'T KNOW.
DO YOU NEED TO GET YOUR SWORD?

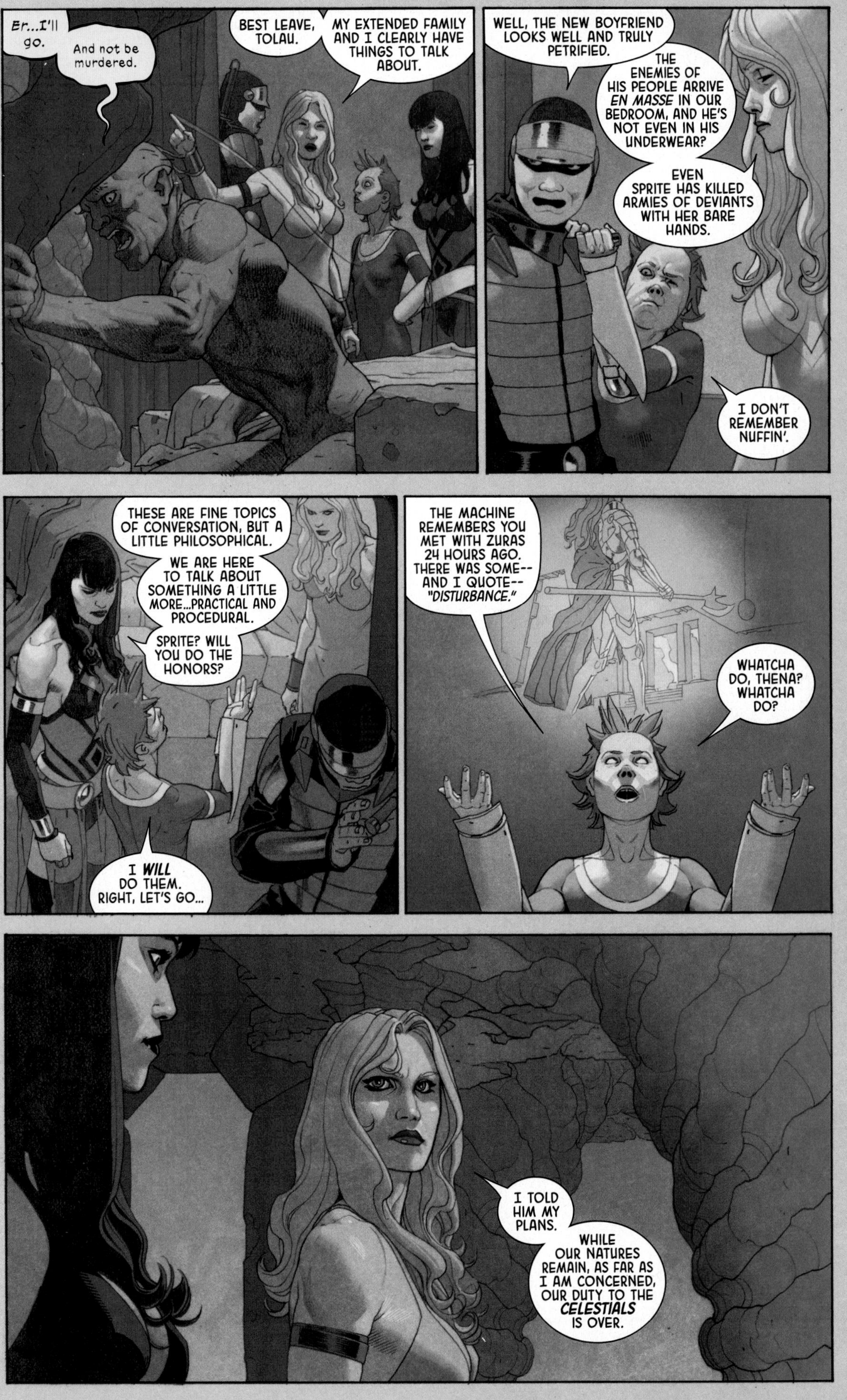

Er...I'll go.
And not be murdered.
BEST LEAVE, TOLAU.
MY EXTENDED FAMILY AND I CLEARLY HAVE THINGS TO TALK ABOUT.
WELL, THE NEW BOYFRIEND LOOKS WELL AND TRULY PETRIFIED.
THE ENEMIES OF HIS PEOPLE ARRIVE *EN MASSE* IN OUR BEDROOM, AND HE'S NOT EVEN IN HIS UNDERWEAR?
EVEN SPRITE HAS KILLED ARMIES OF DEVIANTS WITH HER BARE HANDS.
I DON'T REMEMBER NUFFIN'.
THESE ARE FINE TOPICS OF CONVERSATION, BUT A LITTLE PHILOSOPHICAL.
WE ARE HERE TO TALK ABOUT SOMETHING A LITTLE MORE...PRACTICAL AND PROCEDURAL.
SPRITE? WILL YOU DO THE HONORS?
I ***WILL*** DO THEM. RIGHT, LET'S GO...
THE MACHINE REMEMBERS YOU MET WITH ZURAS 24 HOURS AGO. THERE WAS SOME--AND I QUOTE--*"DISTURBANCE."*
WHATCHA DO, THENA? WHATCHA DO?
I TOLD HIM MY PLANS.
WHILE OUR NATURES REMAIN, AS FAR AS I AM CONCERNED, OUR DUTY TO THE ***CELESTIALS*** IS OVER.

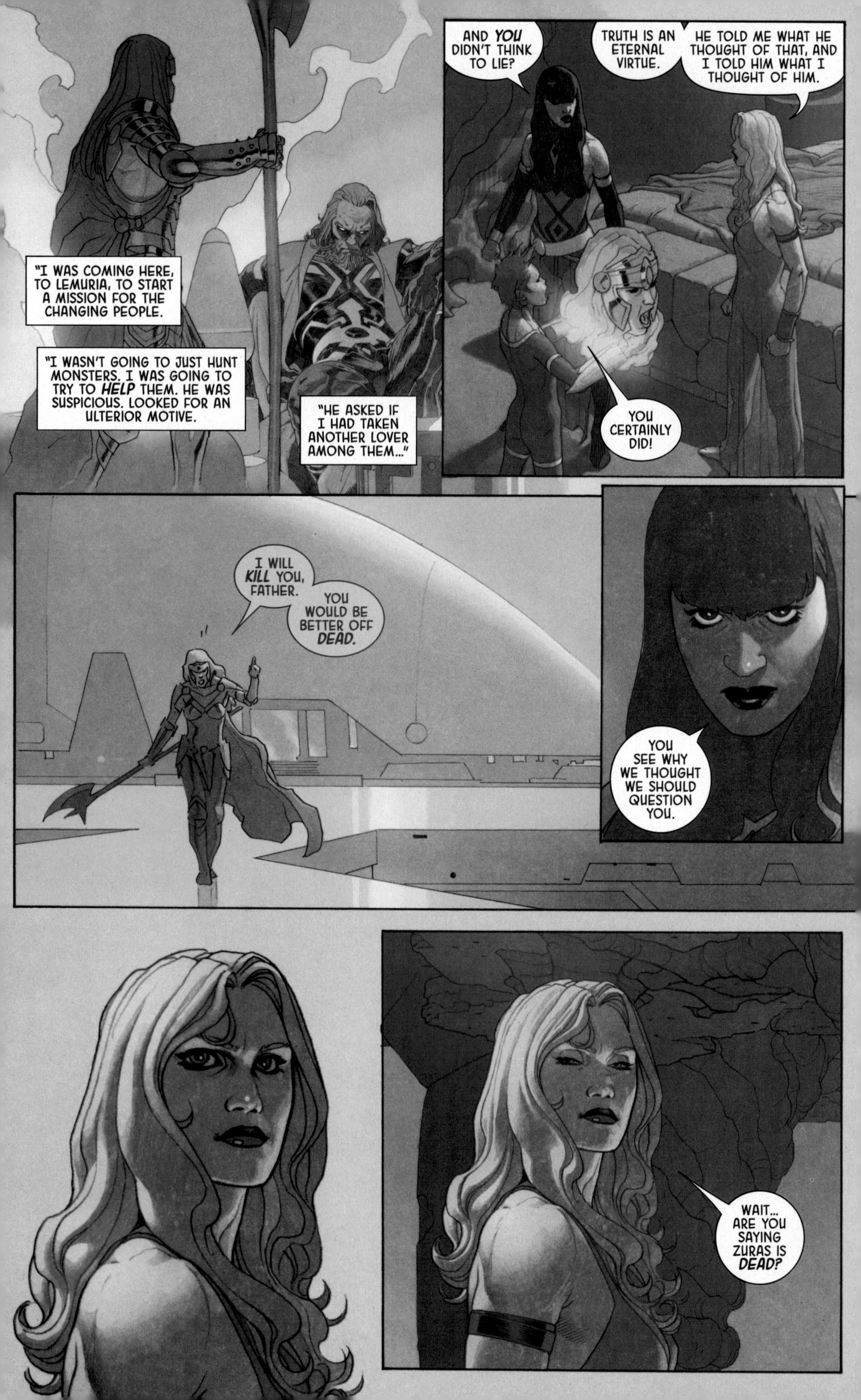

"I WAS COMING HERE, TO LEMURIA, TO START A MISSION FOR THE CHANGING PEOPLE.
"I WASN'T GOING TO JUST HUNT MONSTERS. I WAS GOING TO TRY TO HELP THEM. HE WAS SUSPICIOUS. LOOKED FOR AN ULTERIOR MOTIVE.
"HE ASKED IF I HAD TAKEN ANOTHER LOVER AMONG THEM..."
AND YOU DIDN'T THINK TO LIE?
TRUTH IS AN ETERNAL VIRTUE.
HE TOLD ME WHAT HE THOUGHT OF THAT, AND I TOLD HIM WHAT I THOUGHT OF HIM.
YOU CERTAINLY DID!
I WILL KILL YOU, FATHER.
YOU WOULD BE BETTER OFF DEAD.
YOU SEE WHY WE THOUGHT WE SHOULD QUESTION YOU.
WAIT... ARE YOU SAYING ZURAS IS DEAD?

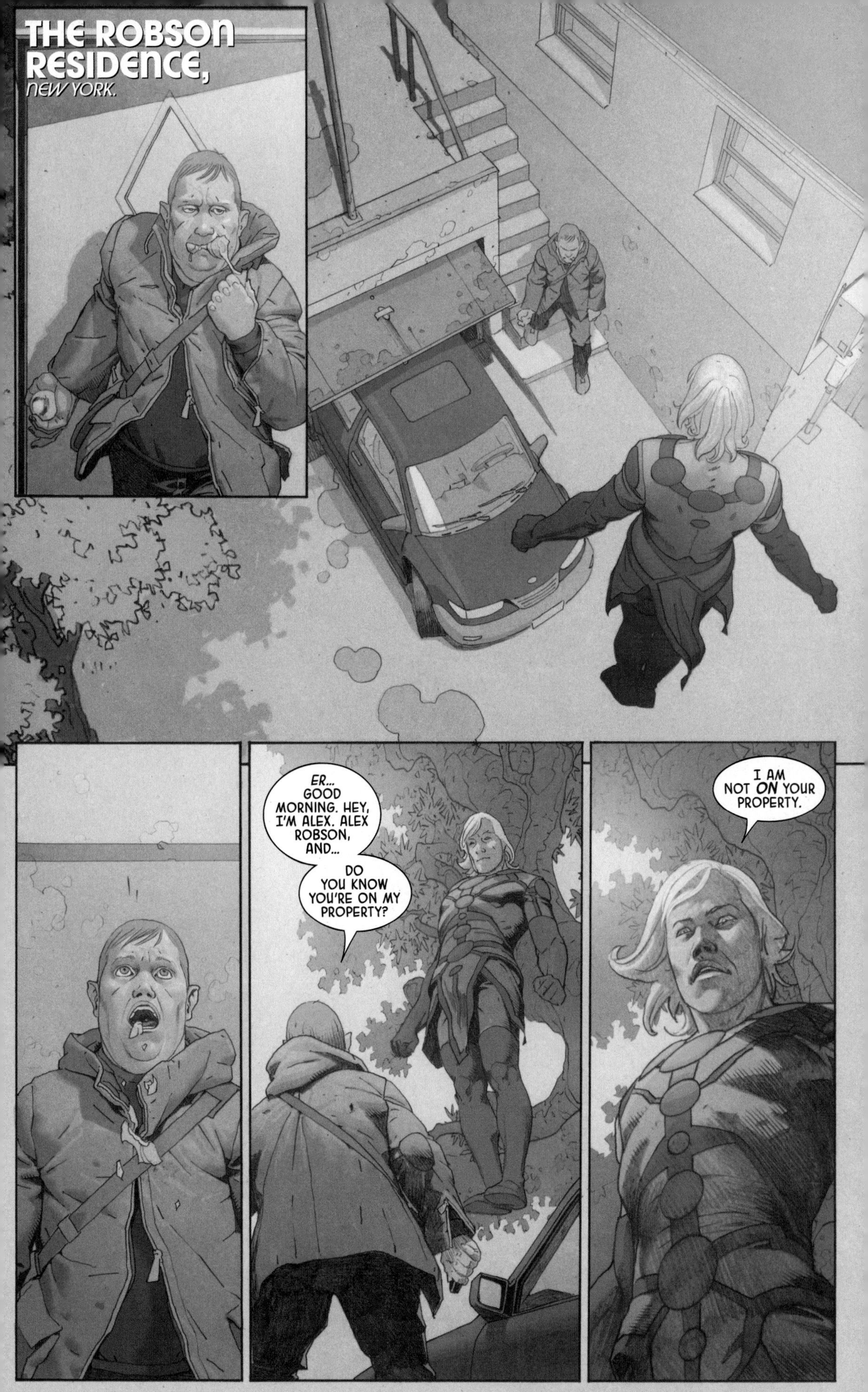
THE ROBSON RESIDENCE,
NEW YORK.
ER... GOOD MORNING. HEY, I'M ALEX. ALEX ROBSON, AND...
DO YOU KNOW YOU'RE ON MY PROPERTY?
I AM NOT ON YOUR PROPERTY.

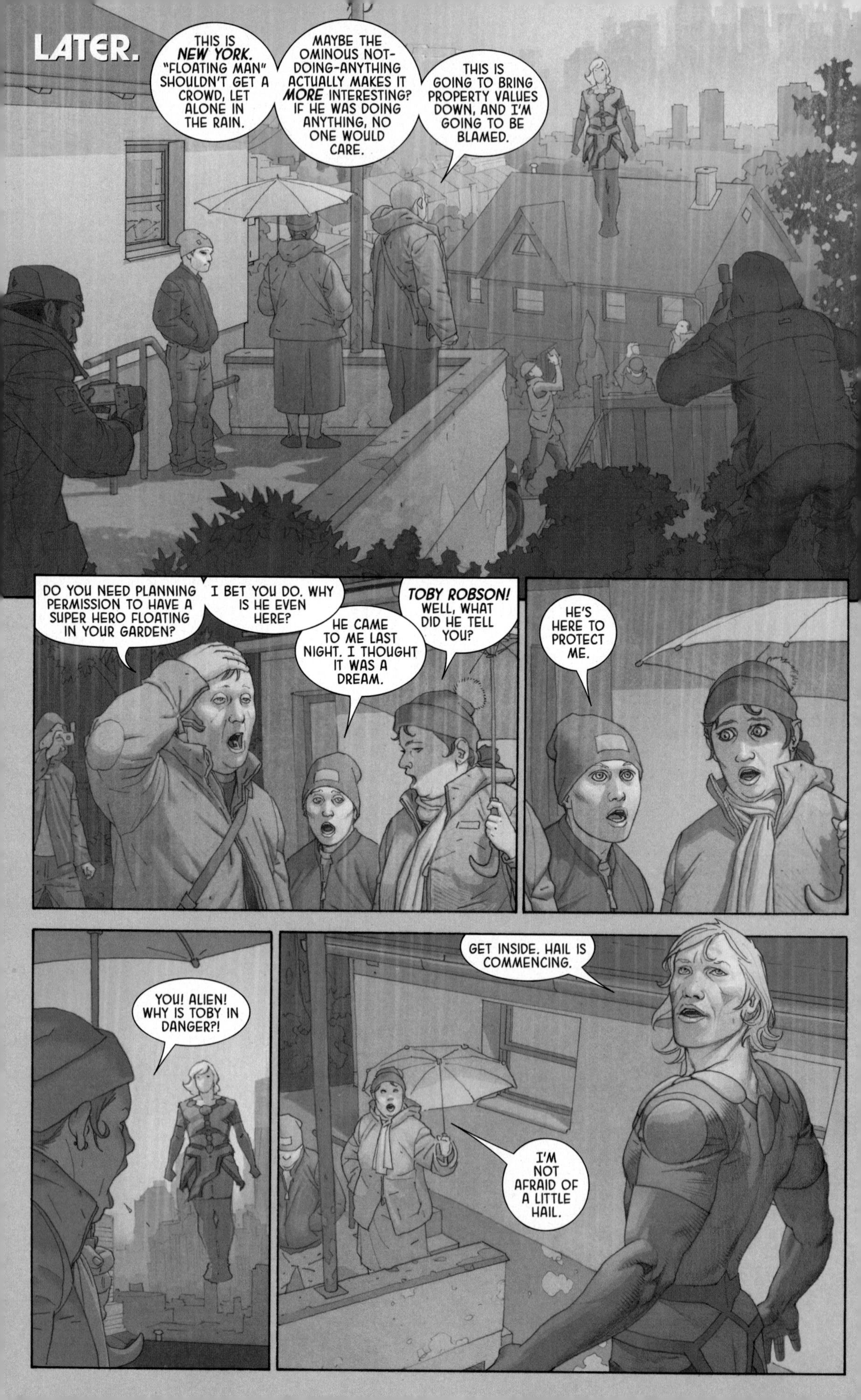
LATER.
THIS IS NEW YORK. "FLOATING MAN" SHOULDN'T GET A CROWD, LET ALONE IN THE RAIN.
MAYBE THE OMINOUS NOT-DOING-ANYTHING ACTUALLY MAKES IT MORE INTERESTING? IF HE WAS DOING ANYTHING, NO ONE WOULD CARE.
THIS IS GOING TO BRING PROPERTY VALUES DOWN, AND I'M GOING TO BE BLAMED.
DO YOU NEED PLANNING PERMISSION TO HAVE A SUPER HERO FLOATING IN YOUR GARDEN?
I BET YOU DO. WHY IS HE EVEN HERE?
HE CAME TO ME LAST NIGHT. I THOUGHT IT WAS A DREAM.
TOBY ROBSON! WELL, WHAT DID HE TELL YOU?
HE'S HERE TO PROTECT ME.
YOU! ALIEN! WHY IS TOBY IN DANGER?!
GET INSIDE. HAIL IS COMMENCING.
I'M NOT AFRAID OF A LITTLE HAIL.

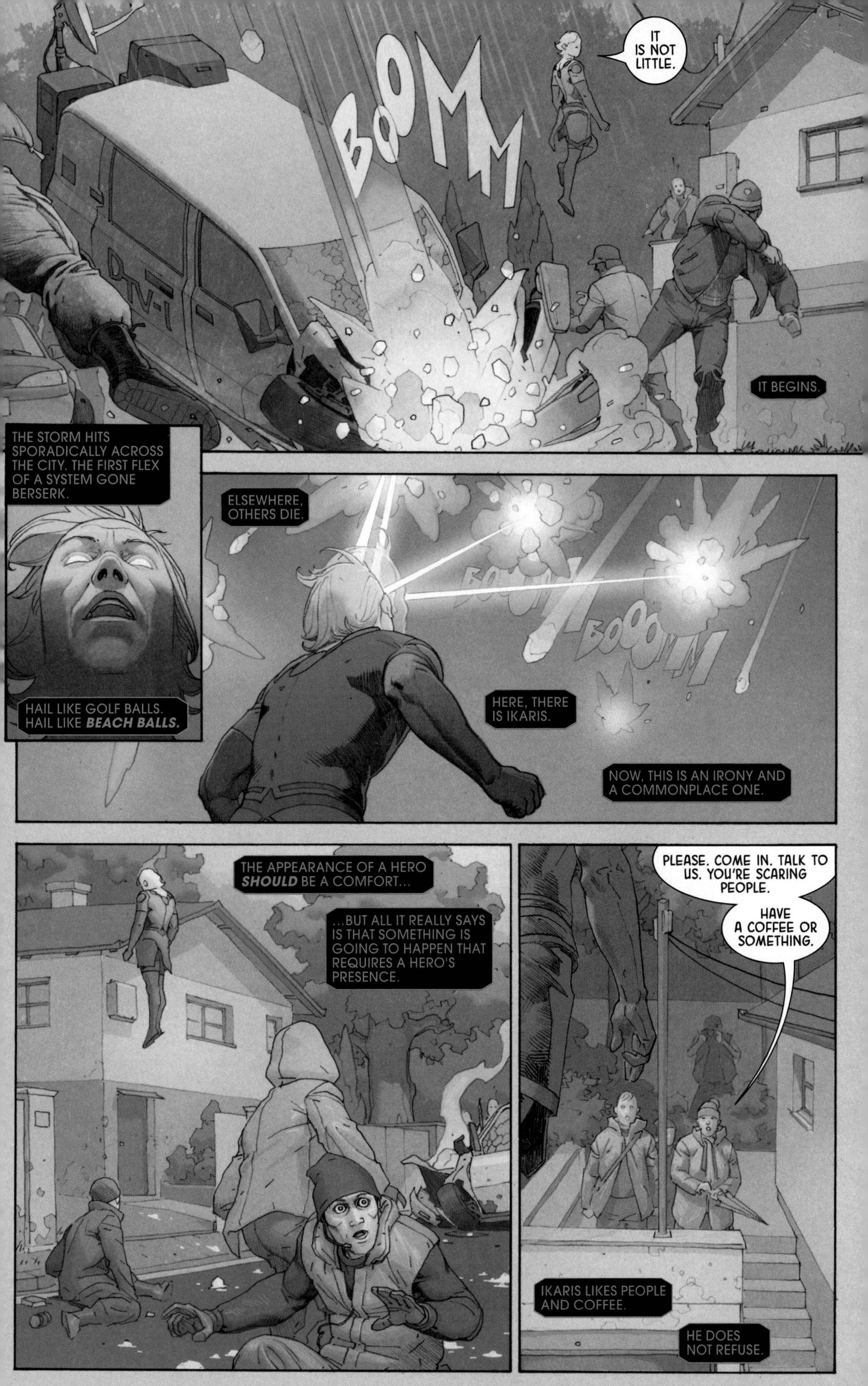
BOOMM
IT IS NOT LITTLE.
IT BEGINS.
THE STORM HITS SPORADICALLY ACROSS THE CITY. THE FIRST FLEX OF A SYSTEM GONE BERSERK.
HAIL LIKE GOLF BALLS. HAIL LIKE *BEACH BALLS.*
ELSEWHERE, OTHERS DIE.
BOOOMM
BOOOMM
HERE, THERE IS IKARIS.
NOW, THIS IS AN IRONY AND A COMMONPLACE ONE.
THE APPEARANCE OF A HERO *SHOULD* BE A COMFORT...
...BUT ALL IT REALLY SAYS IS THAT SOMETHING IS GOING TO HAPPEN THAT REQUIRES A HERO'S PRESENCE.
PLEASE. COME IN. TALK TO US. YOU'RE SCARING PEOPLE.
HAVE A COFFEE OR SOMETHING.
IKARIS LIKES PEOPLE AND COFFEE.
HE DOES NOT REFUSE.

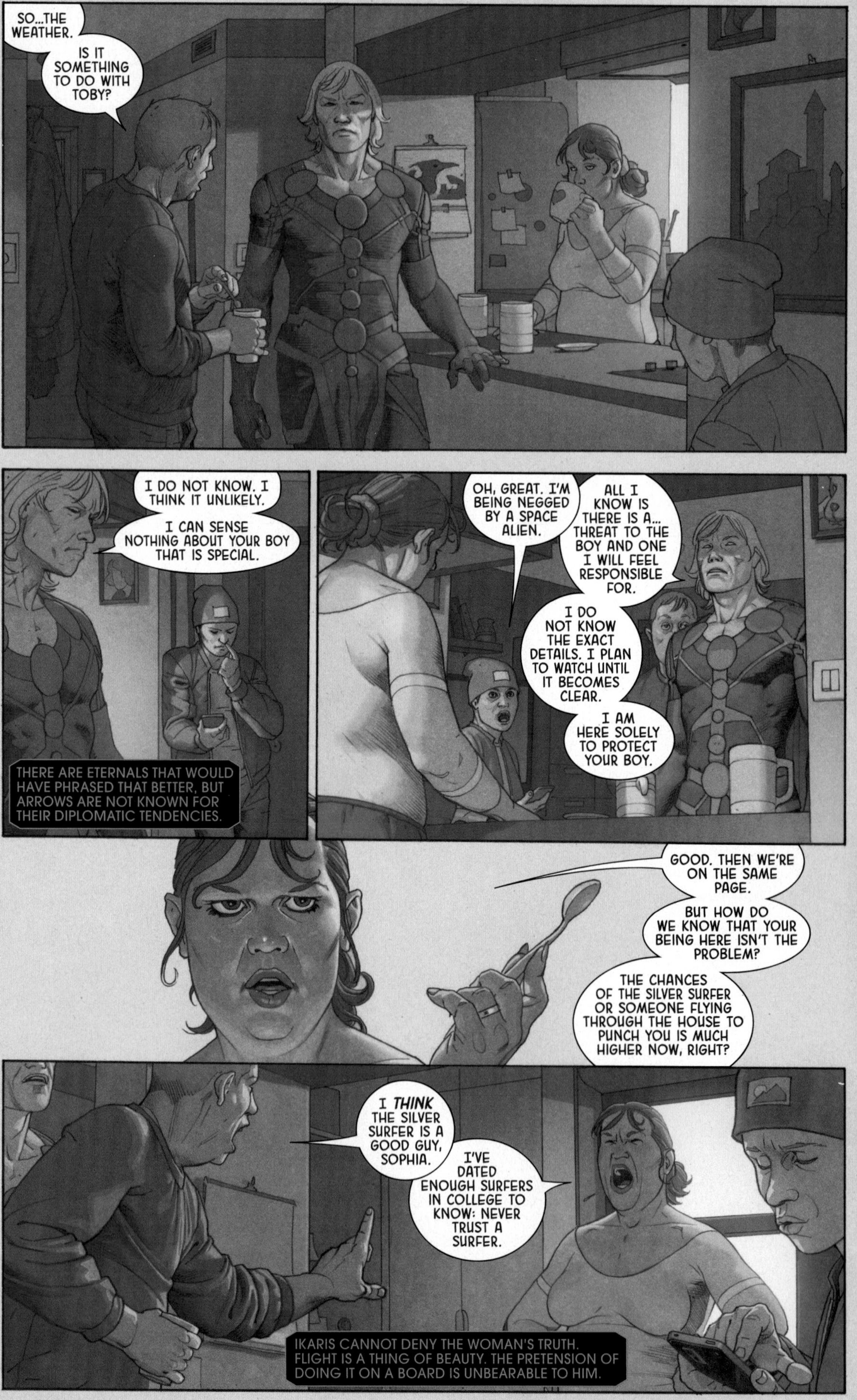
SO...THE WEATHER.
IS IT SOMETHING TO DO WITH TOBY?
I DO NOT KNOW. I THINK IT UNLIKELY.
I CAN SENSE NOTHING ABOUT YOUR BOY THAT IS SPECIAL.
THERE ARE ETERNALS THAT WOULD HAVE PHRASED THAT BETTER, BUT ARROWS ARE NOT KNOWN FOR THEIR DIPLOMATIC TENDENCIES.
ALL I KNOW IS THERE IS A... THREAT TO THE BOY AND ONE I WILL FEEL RESPONSIBLE FOR.
OH, GREAT. I'M BEING NEGGED BY A SPACE ALIEN.
I DO NOT KNOW THE EXACT DETAILS. I PLAN TO WATCH UNTIL IT BECOMES CLEAR.
I AM HERE SOLELY TO PROTECT YOUR BOY.
GOOD. THEN WE'RE ON THE SAME PAGE.
BUT HOW DO WE KNOW THAT YOUR BEING HERE ISN'T THE PROBLEM?
THE CHANCES OF THE SILVER SURFER OR SOMEONE FLYING THROUGH THE HOUSE TO PUNCH YOU IS MUCH HIGHER NOW, RIGHT?
I *THINK* THE SILVER SURFER IS A GOOD GUY, SOPHIA.
I'VE DATED ENOUGH SURFERS IN COLLEGE TO KNOW: NEVER TRUST A SURFER.
IKARIS CANNOT DENY THE WOMAN'S TRUTH. FLIGHT IS A THING OF BEAUTY. THE PRETENSION OF DOING IT ON A BOARD IS UNBEARABLE TO HIM.

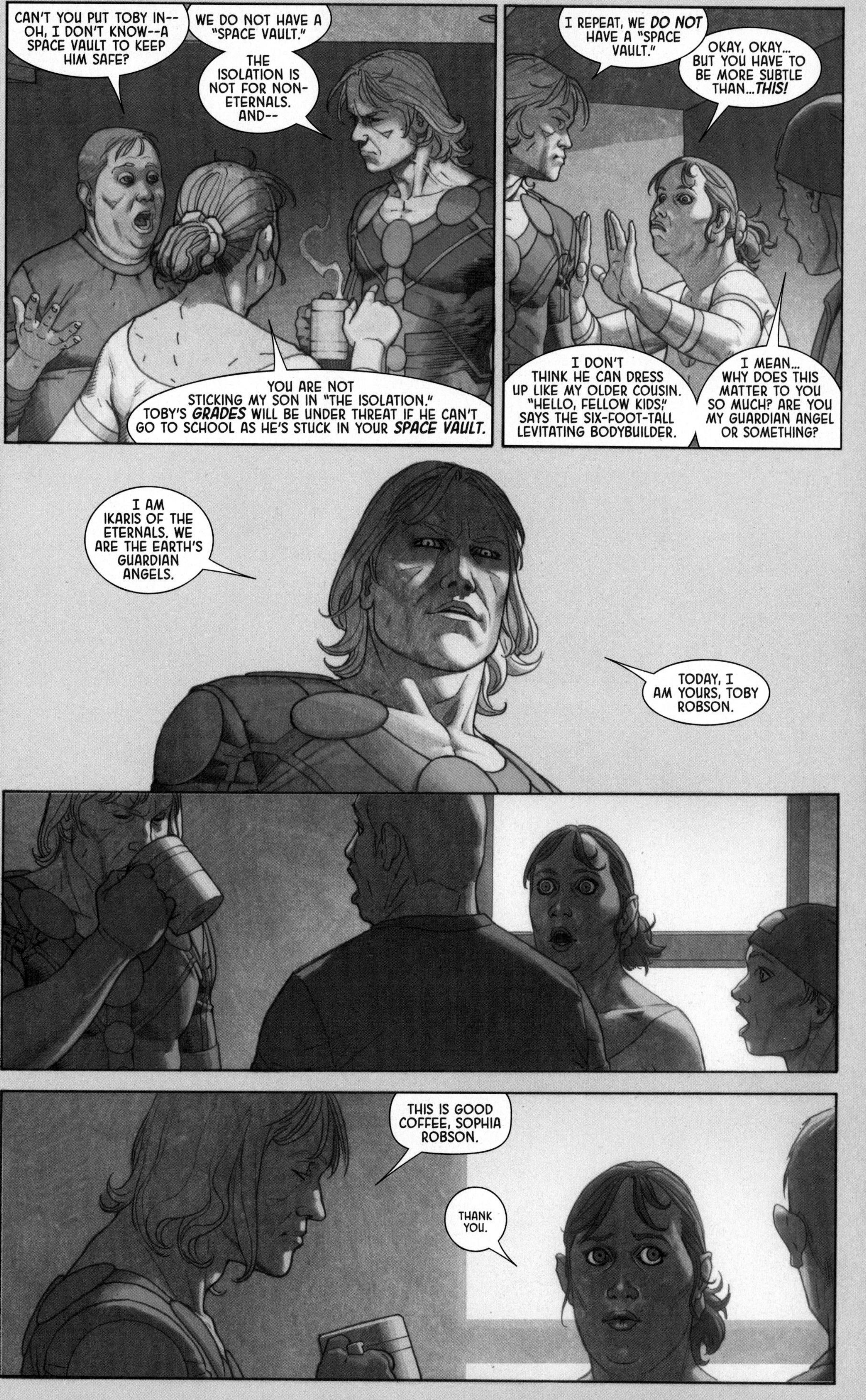

CAN'T YOU PUT TOBY IN-- OH, I DON'T KNOW--A SPACE VAULT TO KEEP HIM SAFE?
WE DO NOT HAVE A "SPACE VAULT."
THE ISOLATION IS NOT FOR NON-ETERNALS. AND--
YOU ARE NOT STICKING MY SON IN "THE ISOLATION." TOBY'S GRADES WILL BE UNDER THREAT IF HE CAN'T GO TO SCHOOL AS HE'S STUCK IN YOUR SPACE VAULT.
I REPEAT, WE DO NOT HAVE A "SPACE VAULT."
OKAY, OKAY... BUT YOU HAVE TO BE MORE SUBTLE THAN...THIS!
I DON'T THINK HE CAN DRESS UP LIKE MY OLDER COUSIN. "HELLO, FELLOW KIDS," SAYS THE SIX-FOOT-TALL LEVITATING BODYBUILDER.
I MEAN... WHY DOES THIS MATTER TO YOU SO MUCH? ARE YOU MY GUARDIAN ANGEL OR SOMETHING?
I AM IKARIS OF THE ETERNALS. WE ARE THE EARTH'S GUARDIAN ANGELS.
TODAY, I AM YOURS, TOBY ROBSON.
THIS IS GOOD COFFEE, SOPHIA ROBSON.
THANK YOU.

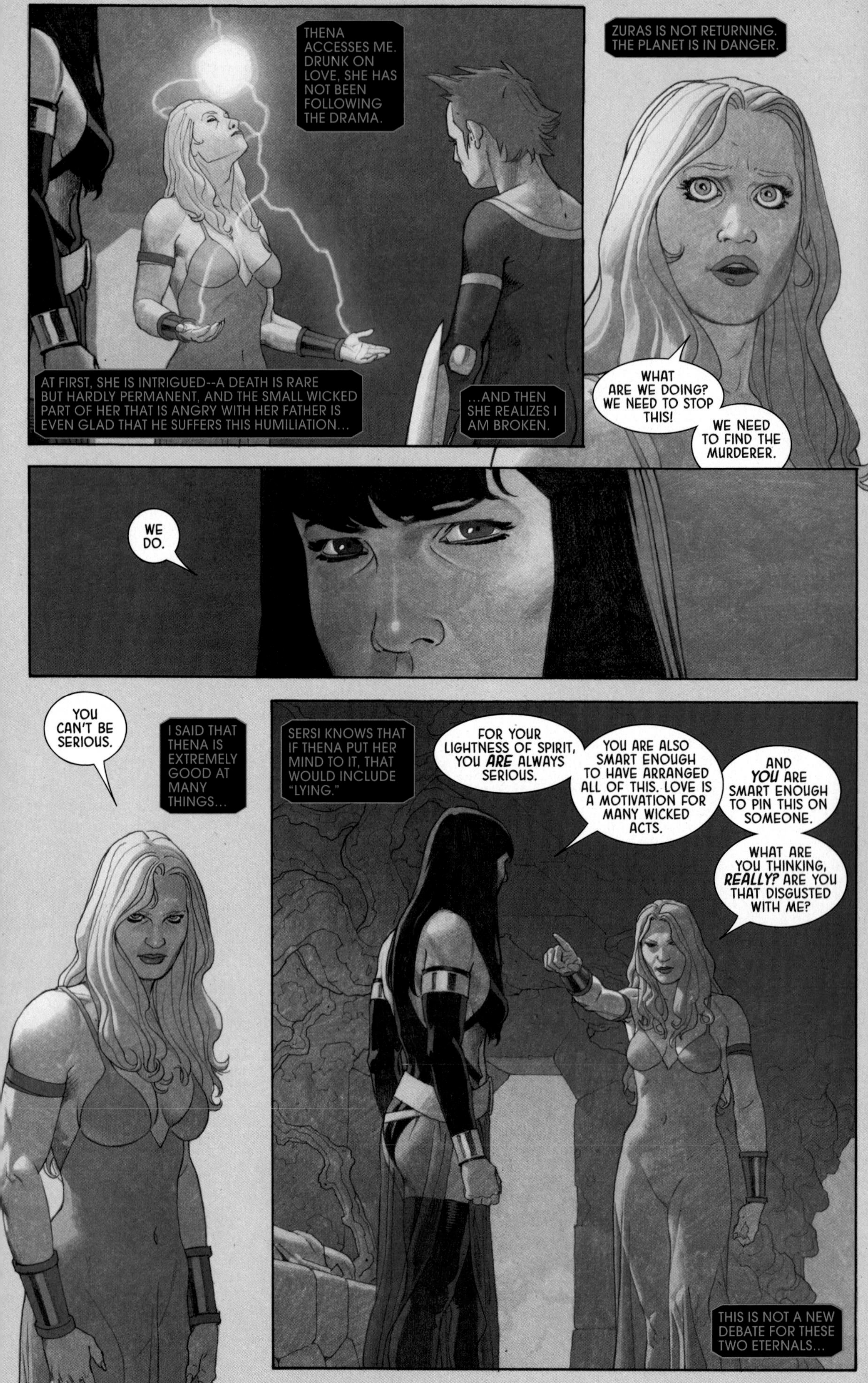
THENA ACCESSES ME. DRUNK ON LOVE, SHE HAS NOT BEEN FOLLOWING THE DRAMA.
AT FIRST, SHE IS INTRIGUED--A DEATH IS RARE BUT HARDLY PERMANENT, AND THE SMALL WICKED PART OF HER THAT IS ANGRY WITH HER FATHER IS EVEN GLAD THAT HE SUFFERS THIS HUMILIATION...
...AND THEN SHE REALIZES I AM BROKEN.
ZURAS IS NOT RETURNING. THE PLANET IS IN DANGER.
WHAT ARE WE DOING? WE NEED TO STOP THIS!
WE NEED TO FIND THE MURDERER.
WE DO.
YOU CAN'T BE SERIOUS.
I SAID THAT THENA IS EXTREMELY GOOD AT MANY THINGS...
SERSI KNOWS THAT IF THENA PUT HER MIND TO IT, THAT WOULD INCLUDE "LYING."
FOR YOUR LIGHTNESS OF SPIRIT, YOU ARE ALWAYS SERIOUS.
YOU ARE ALSO SMART ENOUGH TO HAVE ARRANGED ALL OF THIS. LOVE IS A MOTIVATION FOR MANY WICKED ACTS.
AND YOU ARE SMART ENOUGH TO PIN THIS ON SOMEONE.
WHAT ARE YOU THINKING, REALLY? ARE YOU THAT DISGUSTED WITH ME?
THIS IS NOT A NEW DEBATE FOR THESE TWO ETERNALS...

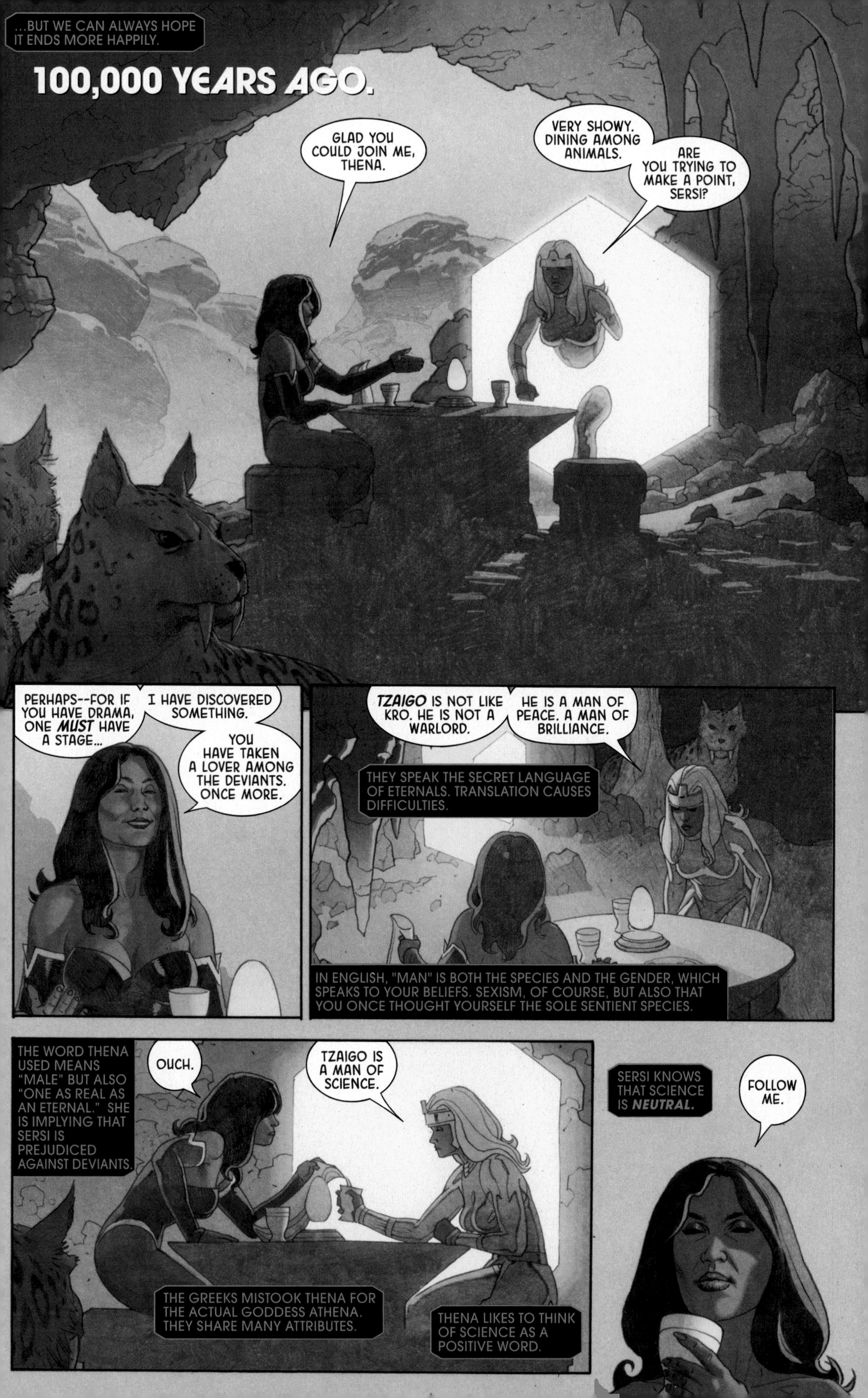
...BUT WE CAN ALWAYS HOPE IT ENDS MORE HAPPILY.
100,000 YEARS AGO.
GLAD YOU COULD JOIN ME, THENA.
VERY SHOWY. DINING AMONG ANIMALS.
ARE YOU TRYING TO MAKE A POINT, SERSI?
PERHAPS--FOR IF YOU HAVE DRAMA, ONE MUST HAVE A STAGE...
I HAVE DISCOVERED SOMETHING.
YOU HAVE TAKEN A LOVER AMONG THE DEVIANTS. ONCE MORE.
TZAIGO IS NOT LIKE KRO. HE IS NOT A WARLORD.
HE IS A MAN OF PEACE. A MAN OF BRILLIANCE.
THEY SPEAK THE SECRET LANGUAGE OF ETERNALS. TRANSLATION CAUSES DIFFICULTIES.
IN ENGLISH, "MAN" IS BOTH THE SPECIES AND THE GENDER, WHICH SPEAKS TO YOUR BELIEFS. SEXISM, OF COURSE, BUT ALSO THAT YOU ONCE THOUGHT YOURSELF THE SOLE SENTIENT SPECIES.
THE WORD THENA USED MEANS "MALE" BUT ALSO "ONE AS REAL AS AN ETERNAL." SHE IS IMPLYING THAT SERSI IS PREJUDICED AGAINST DEVIANTS.
OUCH.
TZAIGO IS A MAN OF SCIENCE.
THE GREEKS MISTOOK THENA FOR THE ACTUAL GODDESS ATHENA. THEY SHARE MANY ATTRIBUTES.
THENA LIKES TO THINK OF SCIENCE AS A POSITIVE WORD.
SERSI KNOWS THAT SCIENCE IS NEUTRAL.
FOLLOW ME.

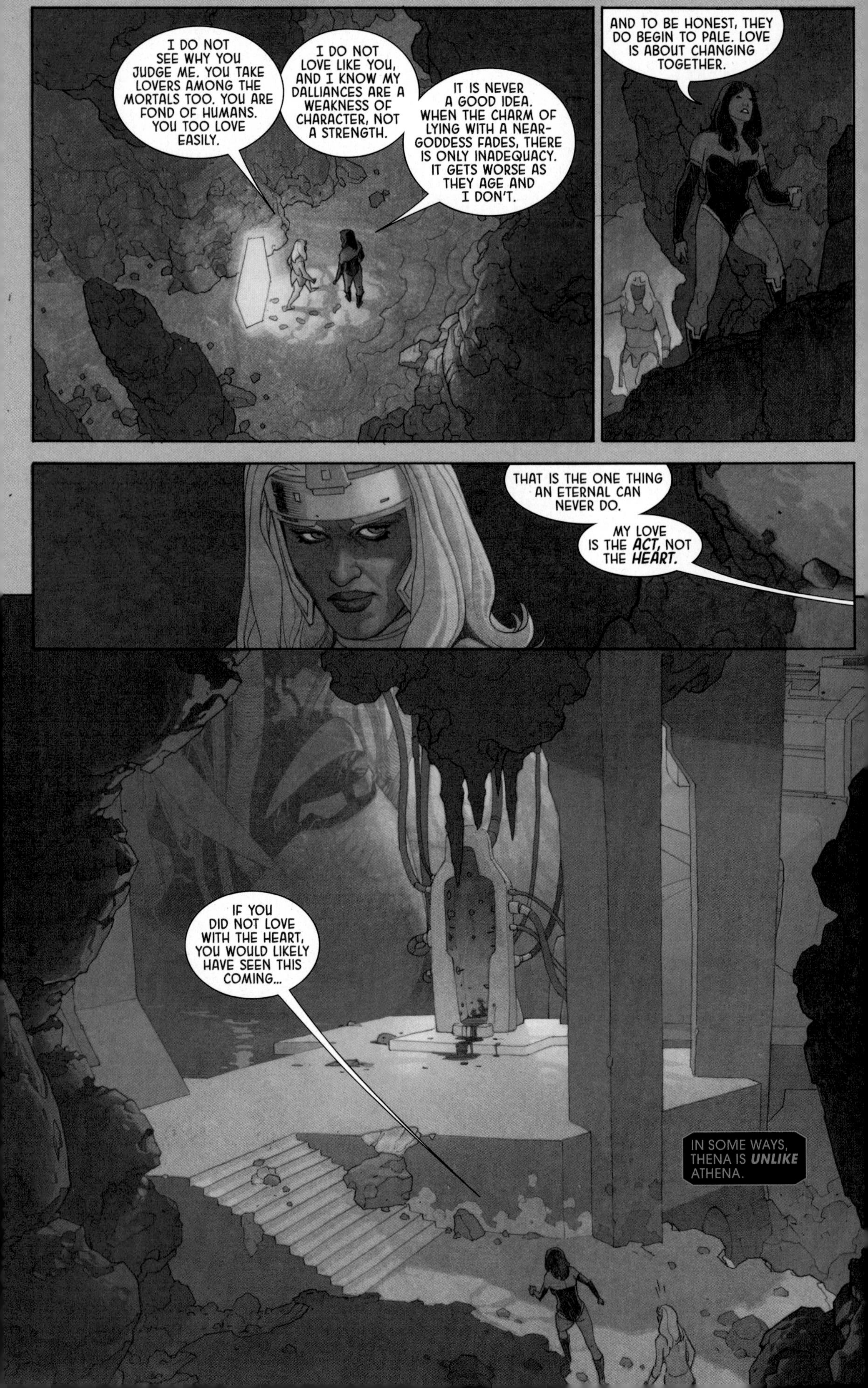
I DO NOT SEE WHY YOU JUDGE ME. YOU TAKE LOVERS AMONG THE MORTALS TOO. YOU ARE FOND OF HUMANS. YOU TOO LOVE EASILY.
I DO NOT LOVE LIKE YOU, AND I KNOW MY DALLIANCES ARE A WEAKNESS OF CHARACTER, NOT A STRENGTH.
IT IS NEVER A GOOD IDEA. WHEN THE CHARM OF LYING WITH A NEAR-GODDESS FADES, THERE IS ONLY INADEQUACY. IT GETS WORSE AS THEY AGE AND I DON'T.
AND TO BE HONEST, THEY DO BEGIN TO PALE. LOVE IS ABOUT CHANGING TOGETHER.
THAT IS THE ONE THING AN ETERNAL CAN NEVER DO.
MY LOVE IS THE ACT, NOT THE HEART.
IF YOU DID NOT LOVE WITH THE HEART, YOU WOULD LIKELY HAVE SEEN THIS COMING...
IN SOME WAYS, THENA IS UNLIKE ATHENA.

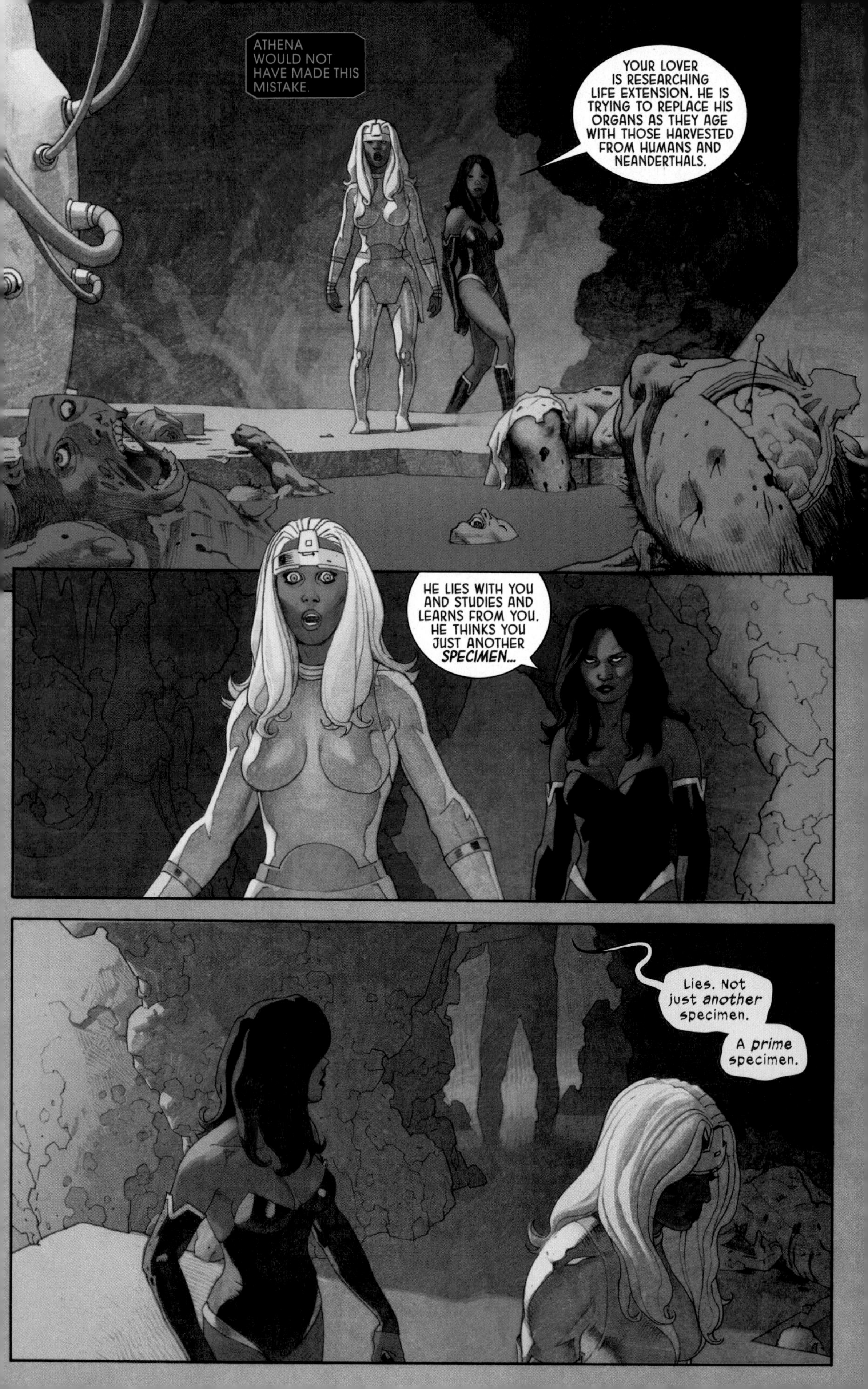
ATHENA WOULD NOT HAVE MADE THIS MISTAKE.
YOUR LOVER IS RESEARCHING LIFE EXTENSION. HE IS TRYING TO REPLACE HIS ORGANS AS THEY AGE WITH THOSE HARVESTED FROM HUMANS AND NEANDERTHALS.
HE LIES WITH YOU AND STUDIES AND LEARNS FROM YOU. HE THINKS YOU JUST ANOTHER *SPECIMEN...*
Lies. Not just *another* specimen.
A *prime* specimen.

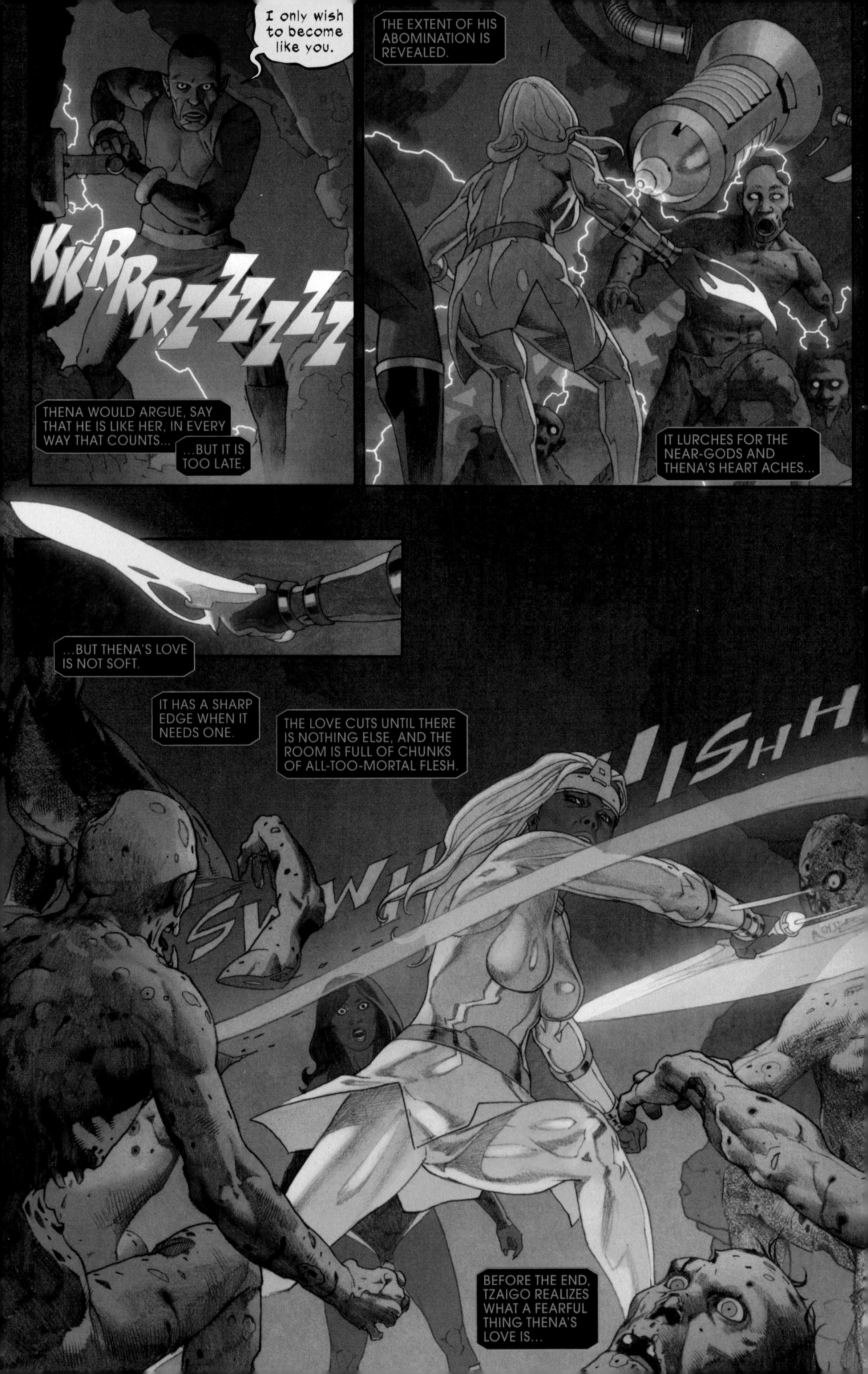
I only wish to become like you.
KKRRRZZZZZZZ
THENA WOULD ARGUE, SAY THAT HE IS LIKE HER, IN EVERY WAY THAT COUNTS...
...BUT IT IS TOO LATE.
THE EXTENT OF HIS ABOMINATION IS REVEALED.
IT LURCHES FOR THE NEAR-GODS AND THENA'S HEART ACHES...
...BUT THENA'S LOVE IS NOT SOFT.
IT HAS A SHARP EDGE WHEN IT NEEDS ONE.
THE LOVE CUTS UNTIL THERE IS NOTHING ELSE, AND THE ROOM IS FULL OF CHUNKS OF ALL-TOO-MORTAL FLESH.
SWISHHH
BEFORE THE END, TZAIGO REALIZES WHAT A FEARFUL THING THENA'S LOVE IS...

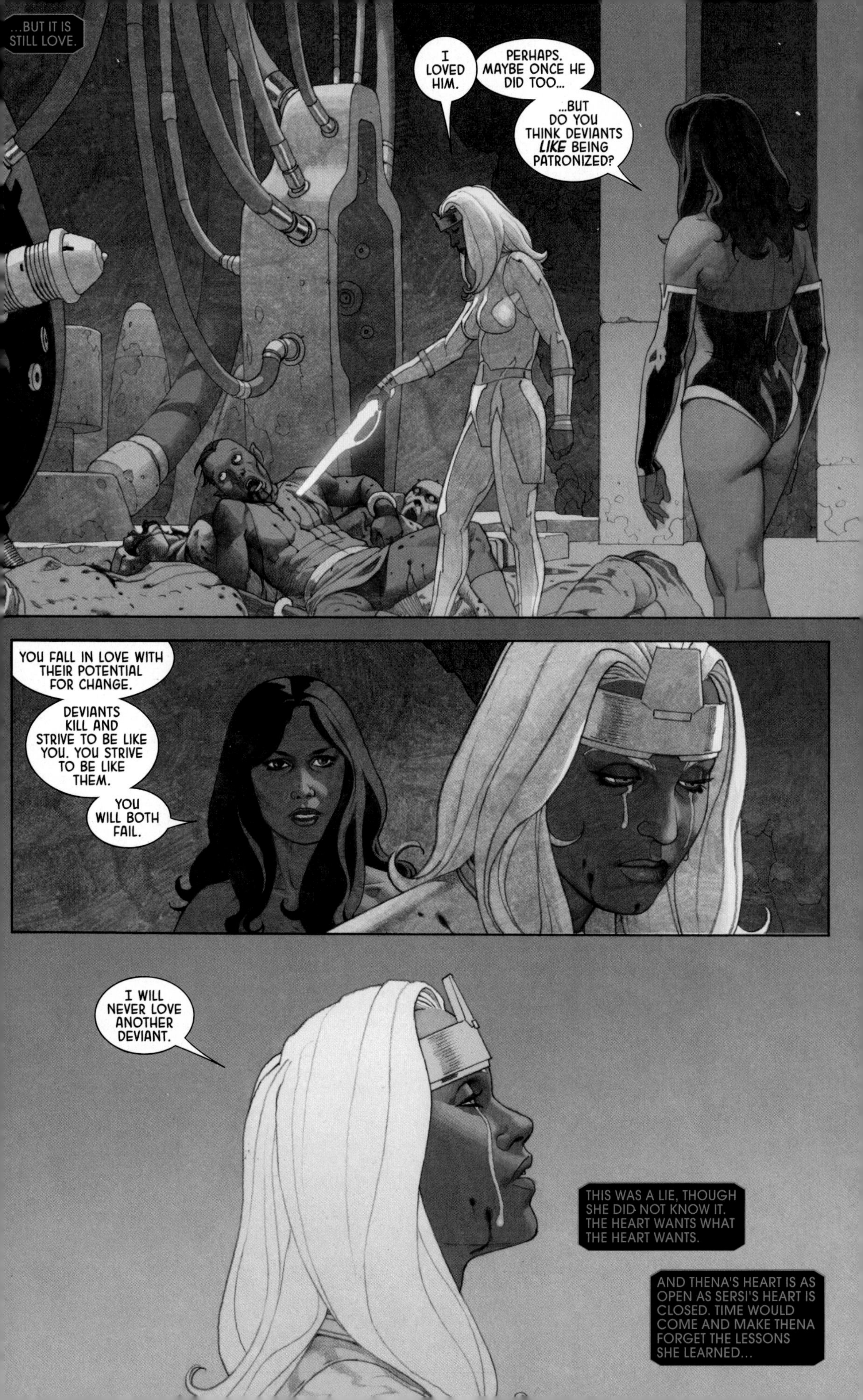
...BUT IT IS STILL LOVE.
I LOVED HIM.
PERHAPS. MAYBE ONCE HE DID TOO...
...BUT DO YOU THINK DEVIANTS LIKE BEING PATRONIZED?
YOU FALL IN LOVE WITH THEIR POTENTIAL FOR CHANGE.
DEVIANTS KILL AND STRIVE TO BE LIKE YOU. YOU STRIVE TO BE LIKE THEM.
YOU WILL BOTH FAIL.
I WILL NEVER LOVE ANOTHER DEVIANT.
THIS WAS A LIE, THOUGH SHE DID NOT KNOW IT. THE HEART WANTS WHAT THE HEART WANTS.
AND THENA'S HEART IS AS OPEN AS SERSI'S HEART IS CLOSED. TIME WOULD COME AND MAKE THENA FORGET THE LESSONS SHE LEARNED...

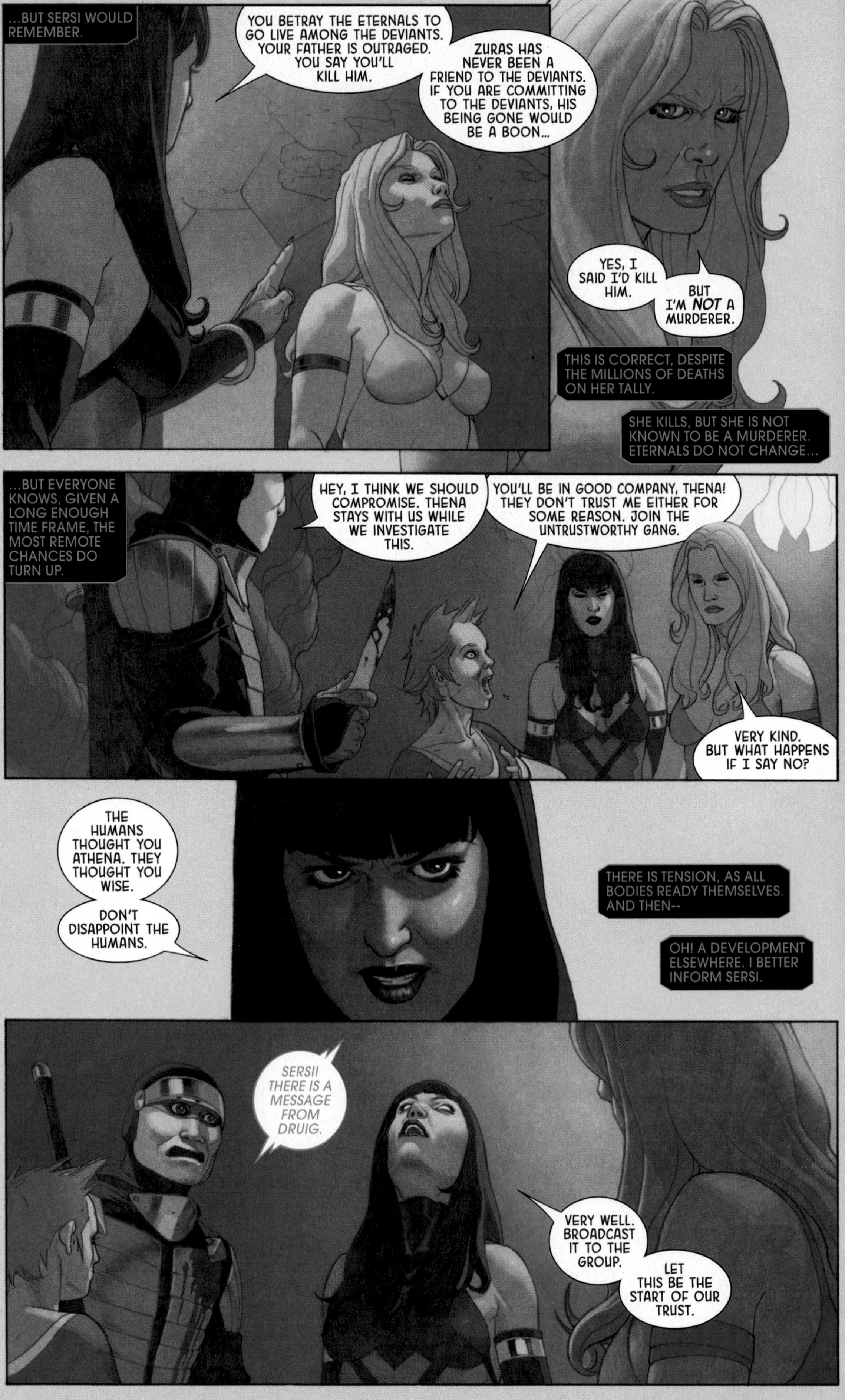

...BUT SERSI WOULD REMEMBER.
YOU BETRAY THE ETERNALS TO GO LIVE AMONG THE DEVIANTS. YOUR FATHER IS OUTRAGED. YOU SAY YOU'LL KILL HIM.
ZURAS HAS NEVER BEEN A FRIEND TO THE DEVIANTS. IF YOU ARE COMMITTING TO THE DEVIANTS, HIS BEING GONE WOULD BE A BOON...
YES, I SAID I'D KILL HIM.
BUT I'M *NOT* A MURDERER.
THIS IS CORRECT, DESPITE THE MILLIONS OF DEATHS ON HER TALLY.
SHE KILLS, BUT SHE IS NOT KNOWN TO BE A MURDERER. ETERNALS DO NOT CHANGE...
...BUT EVERYONE KNOWS, GIVEN A LONG ENOUGH TIME FRAME, THE MOST REMOTE CHANCES DO TURN UP.
HEY, I THINK WE SHOULD COMPROMISE. THENA STAYS WITH US WHILE WE INVESTIGATE THIS.
YOU'LL BE IN GOOD COMPANY, THENA! THEY DON'T TRUST ME EITHER FOR SOME REASON. JOIN THE UNTRUSTWORTHY GANG.
VERY KIND. BUT WHAT HAPPENS IF I SAY NO?
THE HUMANS THOUGHT YOU ATHENA. THEY THOUGHT YOU WISE.
DON'T DISAPPOINT THE HUMANS.
THERE IS TENSION, AS ALL BODIES READY THEMSELVES. AND THEN--
OH! A DEVELOPMENT ELSEWHERE. I BETTER INFORM SERSI.
SERSI! THERE IS A MESSAGE FROM DRUIG.
VERY WELL. BROADCAST IT TO THE GROUP.
LET THIS BE THE START OF OUR TRUST.

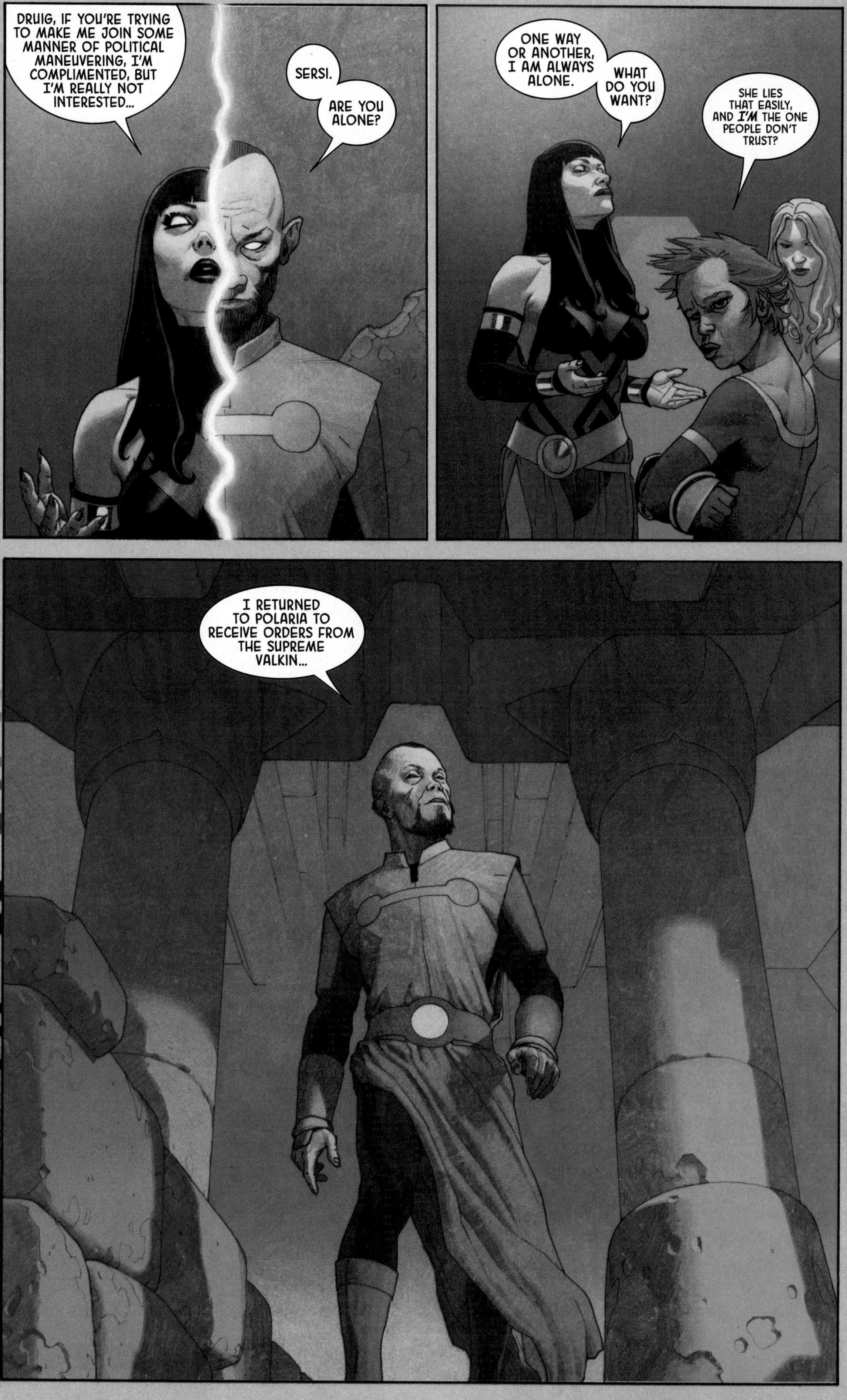
DRUIG, IF YOU'RE TRYING TO MAKE ME JOIN SOME MANNER OF POLITICAL MANEUVERING, I'M COMPLIMENTED, BUT I'M REALLY NOT INTERESTED...
SERSI.
ARE YOU ALONE?
ONE WAY OR ANOTHER, I AM ALWAYS ALONE.
WHAT DO YOU WANT?
SHE LIES THAT EASILY, AND *I'M* THE ONE PEOPLE DON'T TRUST?
I RETURNED TO POLARIA TO RECEIVE ORDERS FROM THE SUPREME VALKIN...

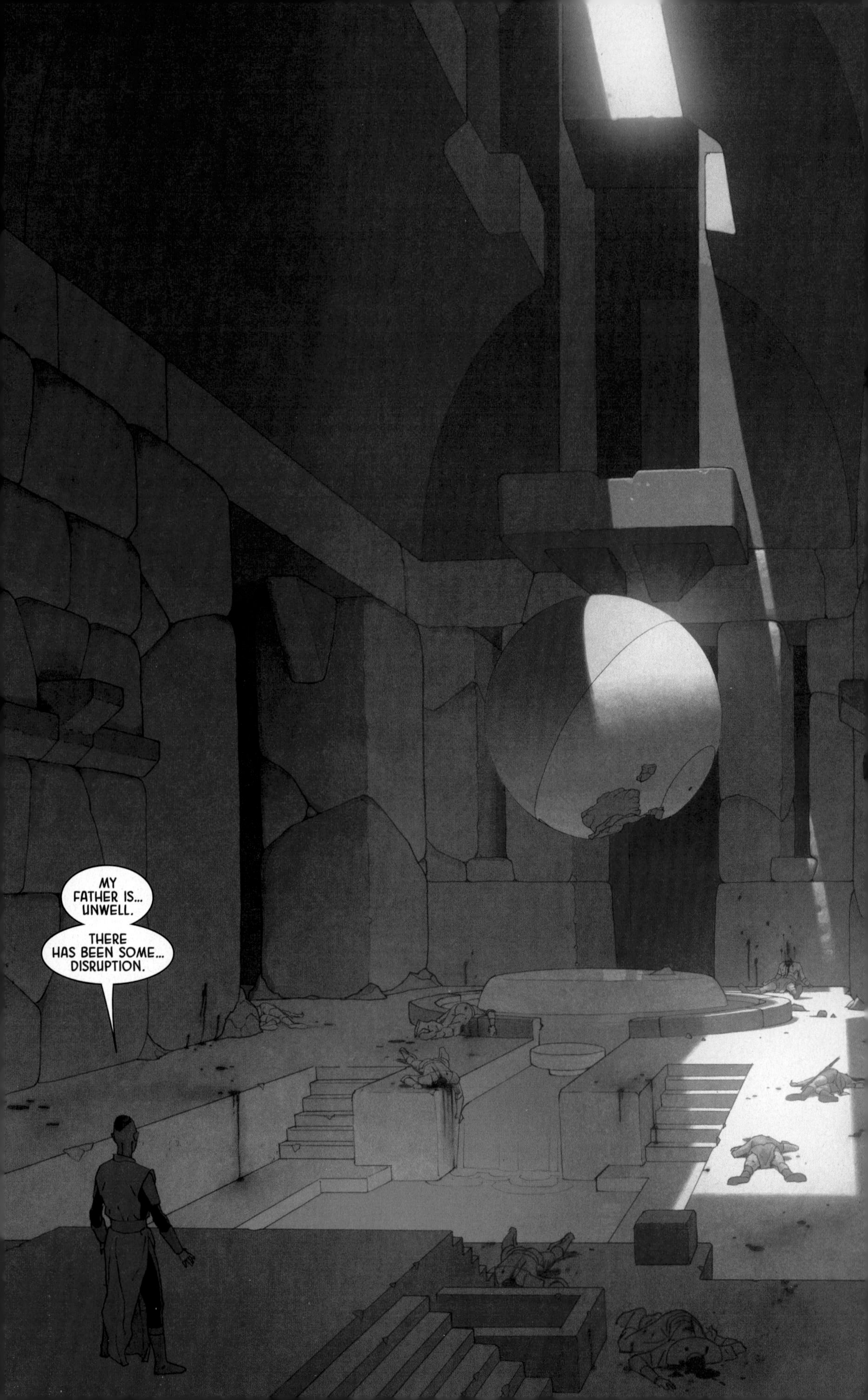
MY FATHER IS... UNWELL.
THERE HAS BEEN SOME... DISRUPTION.

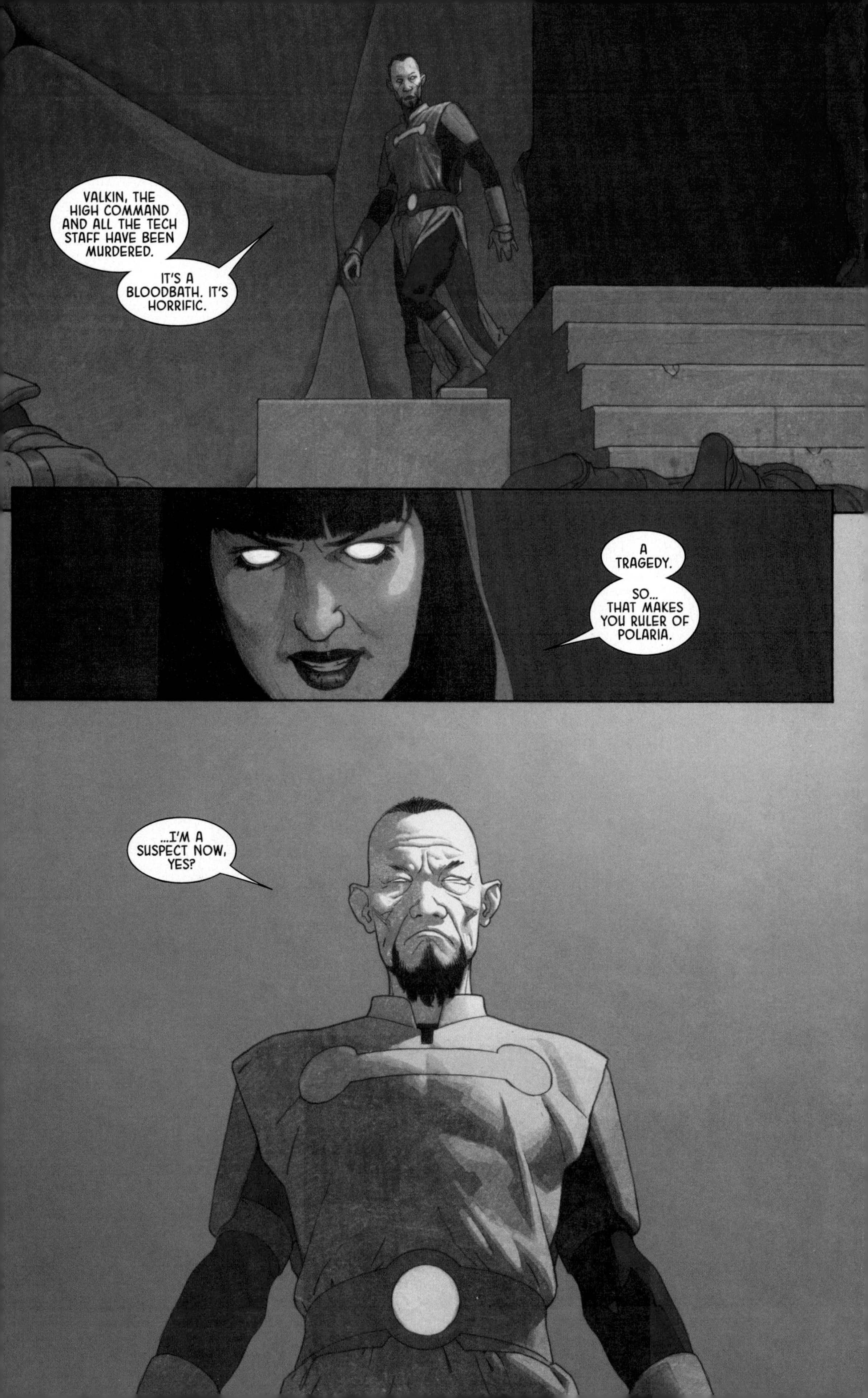
VALKIN, THE HIGH COMMAND AND ALL THE TECH STAFF HAVE BEEN MURDERED.
IT'S A BLOODBATH. IT'S HORRIFIC.
A TRAGEDY.
SO... THAT MAKES YOU RULER OF POLARIA.
...I'M A SUSPECT NOW, YES?

POLARIA

Second City of the Eternals
on Earth, rival of Olympia.

~~VALKIN~~   PANNIX
~~VIRAKO~~   SOULE THE CHARRED
~~ZARIN~~   ~~DAZII~~
~~AMAA~~   ~~JUTRO~~
~~AREX~~   ~~KARNAI~~
~~ACINAR~~   ~~KREZNAK~~
DRUIG   ZORRJA
~~SYGMAR~~   ~~TENGRAI~~
~~BETILAKK THE INTERLOPER~~   ~~TUNGAC~~
LEGBA   ~~QUEEN TABTEE~~
AKPAXA   ~~DONARR~~
ERAMIS

SUPREME LEADER:
~~VALKIN~~
DRUIG

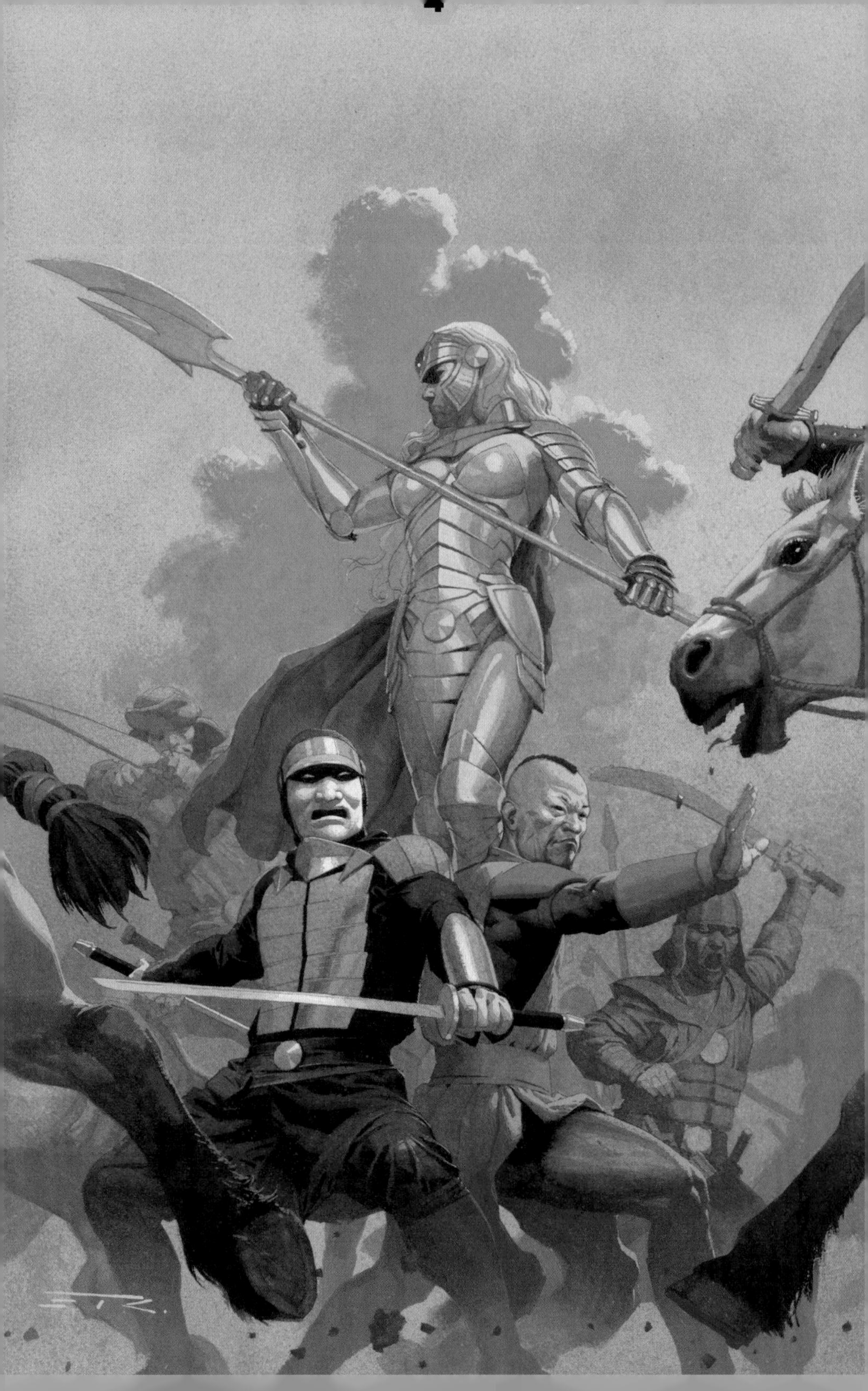

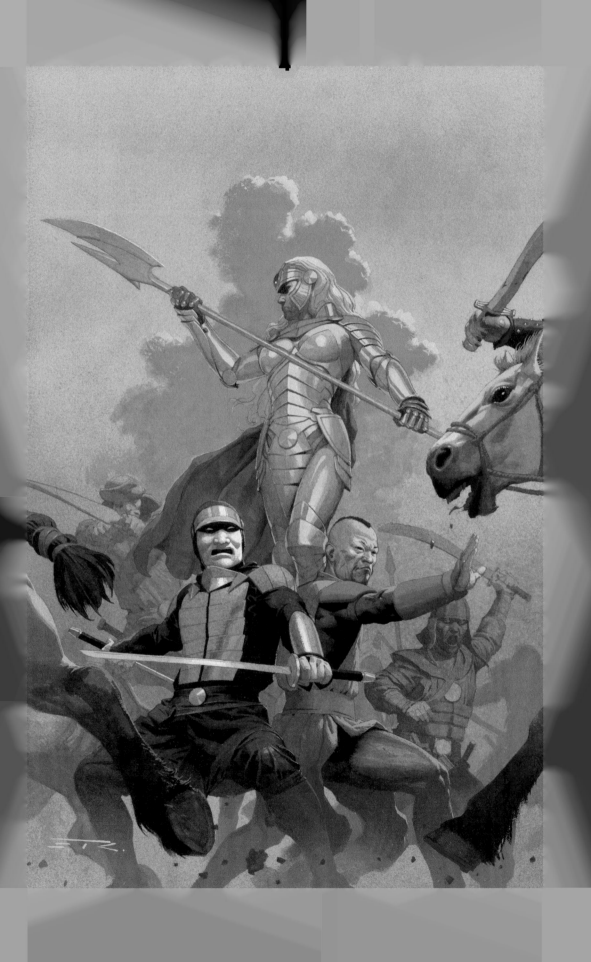

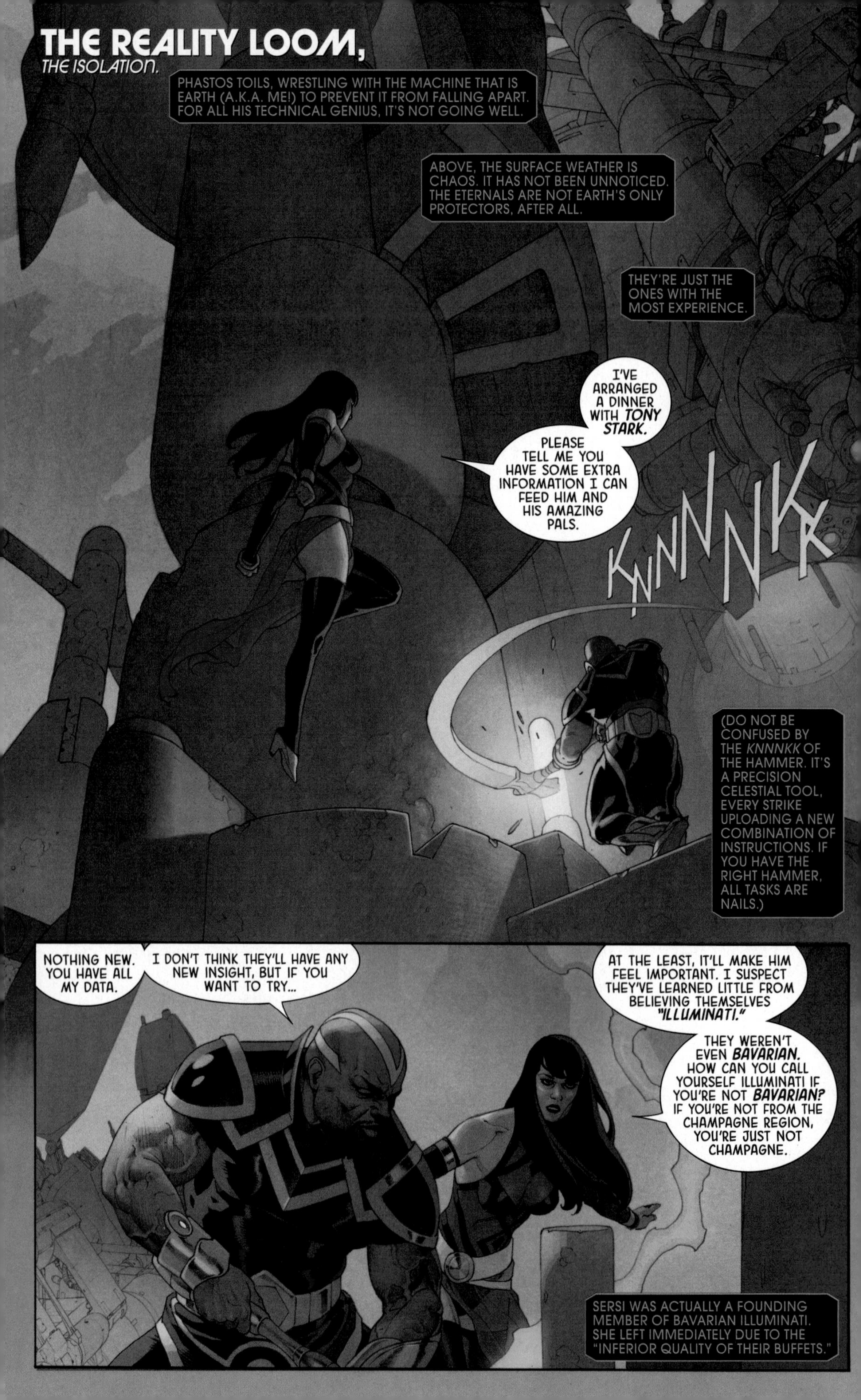
THE REALITY LOOM,
THE ISOLATION.
PHASTOS TOILS, WRESTLING WITH THE MACHINE THAT IS EARTH (A.K.A. ME!) TO PREVENT IT FROM FALLING APART. FOR ALL HIS TECHNICAL GENIUS, IT'S NOT GOING WELL.
ABOVE, THE SURFACE WEATHER IS CHAOS. IT HAS NOT BEEN UNNOTICED. THE ETERNALS ARE NOT EARTH'S ONLY PROTECTORS, AFTER ALL.
THEY'RE JUST THE ONES WITH THE MOST EXPERIENCE.
I'VE ARRANGED A DINNER WITH TONY STARK.
PLEASE TELL ME YOU HAVE SOME EXTRA INFORMATION I CAN FEED HIM AND HIS AMAZING PALS.
KNNNNKK
(DO NOT BE CONFUSED BY THE KNNNKK OF THE HAMMER. IT'S A PRECISION CELESTIAL TOOL, EVERY STRIKE UPLOADING A NEW COMBINATION OF INSTRUCTIONS. IF YOU HAVE THE RIGHT HAMMER, ALL TASKS ARE NAILS.)
NOTHING NEW. YOU HAVE ALL MY DATA.
I DON'T THINK THEY'LL HAVE ANY NEW INSIGHT, BUT IF YOU WANT TO TRY...
AT THE LEAST, IT'LL MAKE HIM FEEL IMPORTANT. I SUSPECT THEY'VE LEARNED LITTLE FROM BELIEVING THEMSELVES "ILLUMINATI."
THEY WEREN'T EVEN BAVARIAN. HOW CAN YOU CALL YOURSELF ILLUMINATI IF YOU'RE NOT BAVARIAN? IF YOU'RE NOT FROM THE CHAMPAGNE REGION, YOU'RE JUST NOT CHAMPAGNE.
SERSI WAS ACTUALLY A FOUNDING MEMBER OF BAVARIAN ILLUMINATI. SHE LEFT IMMEDIATELY DUE TO THE "INFERIOR QUALITY OF THEIR BUFFETS."

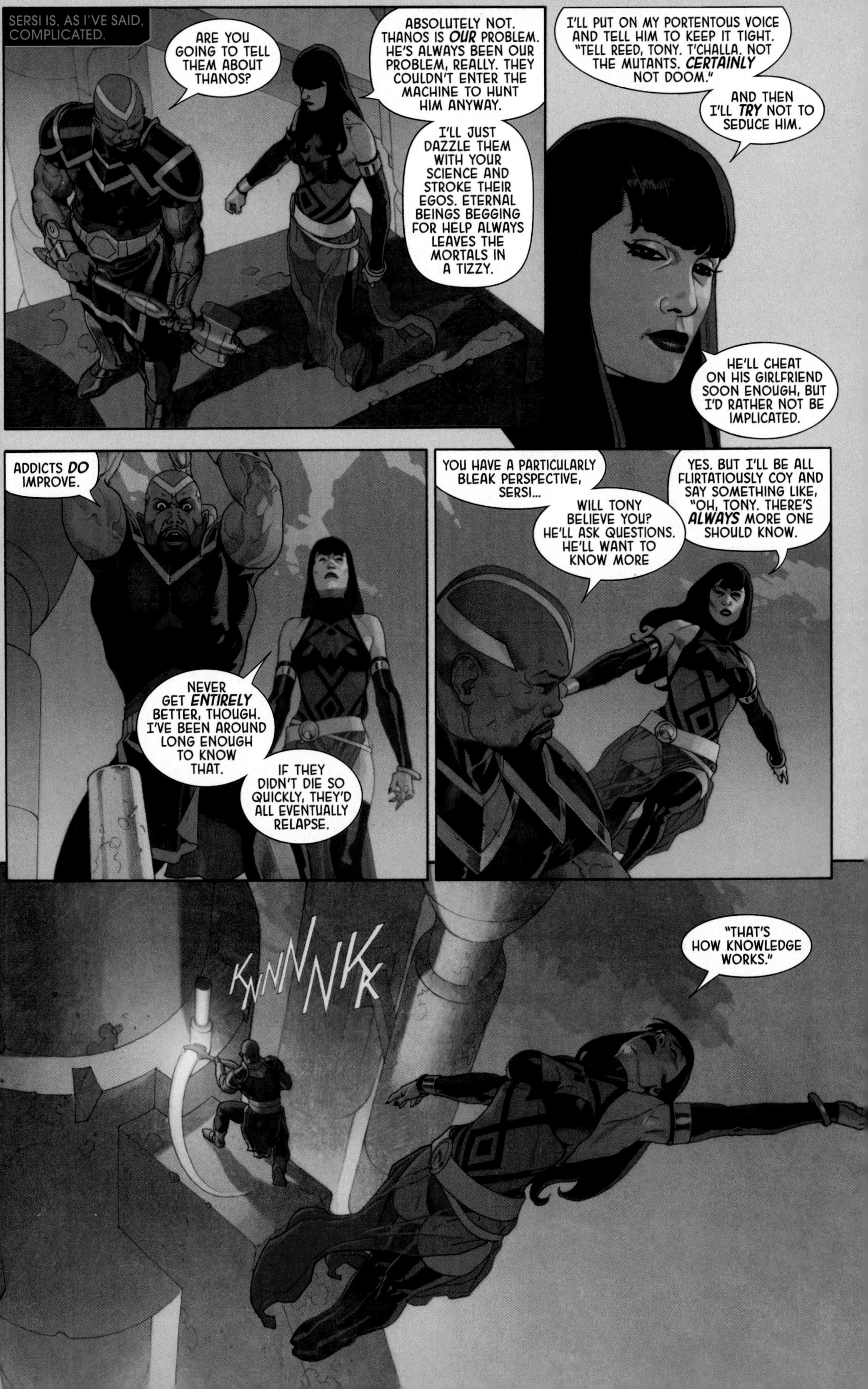
SERSI IS, AS I'VE SAID, COMPLICATED.
ARE YOU GOING TO TELL THEM ABOUT THANOS?
ABSOLUTELY NOT. THANOS IS OUR PROBLEM. HE'S ALWAYS BEEN OUR PROBLEM, REALLY. THEY COULDN'T ENTER THE MACHINE TO HUNT HIM ANYWAY.
I'LL JUST DAZZLE THEM WITH YOUR SCIENCE AND STROKE THEIR EGOS. ETERNAL BEINGS BEGGING FOR HELP ALWAYS LEAVES THE MORTALS IN A TIZZY.
I'LL PUT ON MY PORTENTOUS VOICE AND TELL HIM TO KEEP IT TIGHT. "TELL REED, TONY. T'CHALLA. NOT THE MUTANTS. CERTAINLY NOT DOOM."
AND THEN I'LL TRY NOT TO SEDUCE HIM.
HE'LL CHEAT ON HIS GIRLFRIEND SOON ENOUGH, BUT I'D RATHER NOT BE IMPLICATED.
ADDICTS DO IMPROVE.
NEVER GET ENTIRELY BETTER, THOUGH. I'VE BEEN AROUND LONG ENOUGH TO KNOW THAT.
IF THEY DIDN'T DIE SO QUICKLY, THEY'D ALL EVENTUALLY RELAPSE.
YOU HAVE A PARTICULARLY BLEAK PERSPECTIVE, SERSI...
WILL TONY BELIEVE YOU? HE'LL ASK QUESTIONS. HE'LL WANT TO KNOW MORE
YES. BUT I'LL BE ALL FLIRTATIOUSLY COY AND SAY SOMETHING LIKE, "OH, TONY. THERE'S ALWAYS MORE ONE SHOULD KNOW.
KNNNNKR
"THAT'S HOW KNOWLEDGE WORKS."

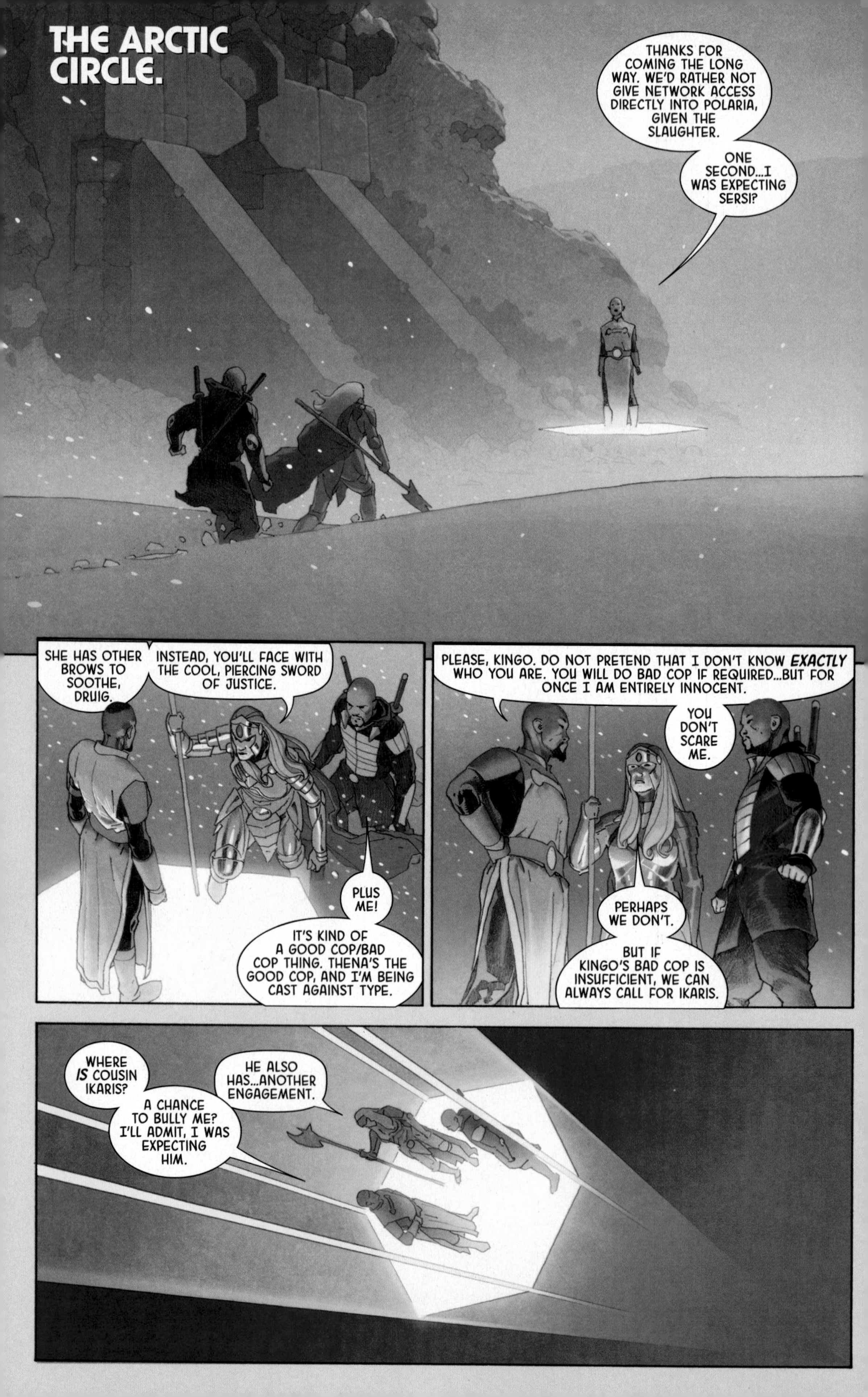
THE ARCTIC CIRCLE.
THANKS FOR COMING THE LONG WAY. WE'D RATHER NOT GIVE NETWORK ACCESS DIRECTLY INTO POLARIA, GIVEN THE SLAUGHTER.
ONE SECOND...I WAS EXPECTING SERSI?
SHE HAS OTHER BROWS TO SOOTHE, DRUIG.
INSTEAD, YOU'LL FACE WITH THE COOL, PIERCING SWORD OF JUSTICE.
PLUS ME!
IT'S KIND OF A GOOD COP/BAD COP THING. THENA'S THE GOOD COP, AND I'M BEING CAST AGAINST TYPE.
PLEASE, KINGO. DO NOT PRETEND THAT I DON'T KNOW *EXACTLY* WHO YOU ARE. YOU WILL DO BAD COP IF REQUIRED...BUT FOR ONCE I AM ENTIRELY INNOCENT.
YOU DON'T SCARE ME.
PERHAPS WE DON'T.
BUT IF KINGO'S BAD COP IS INSUFFICIENT, WE CAN ALWAYS CALL FOR IKARIS.
WHERE *IS* COUSIN IKARIS?
A CHANCE TO BULLY ME? I'LL ADMIT, I WAS EXPECTING HIM.
HE ALSO HAS...ANOTHER ENGAGEMENT.

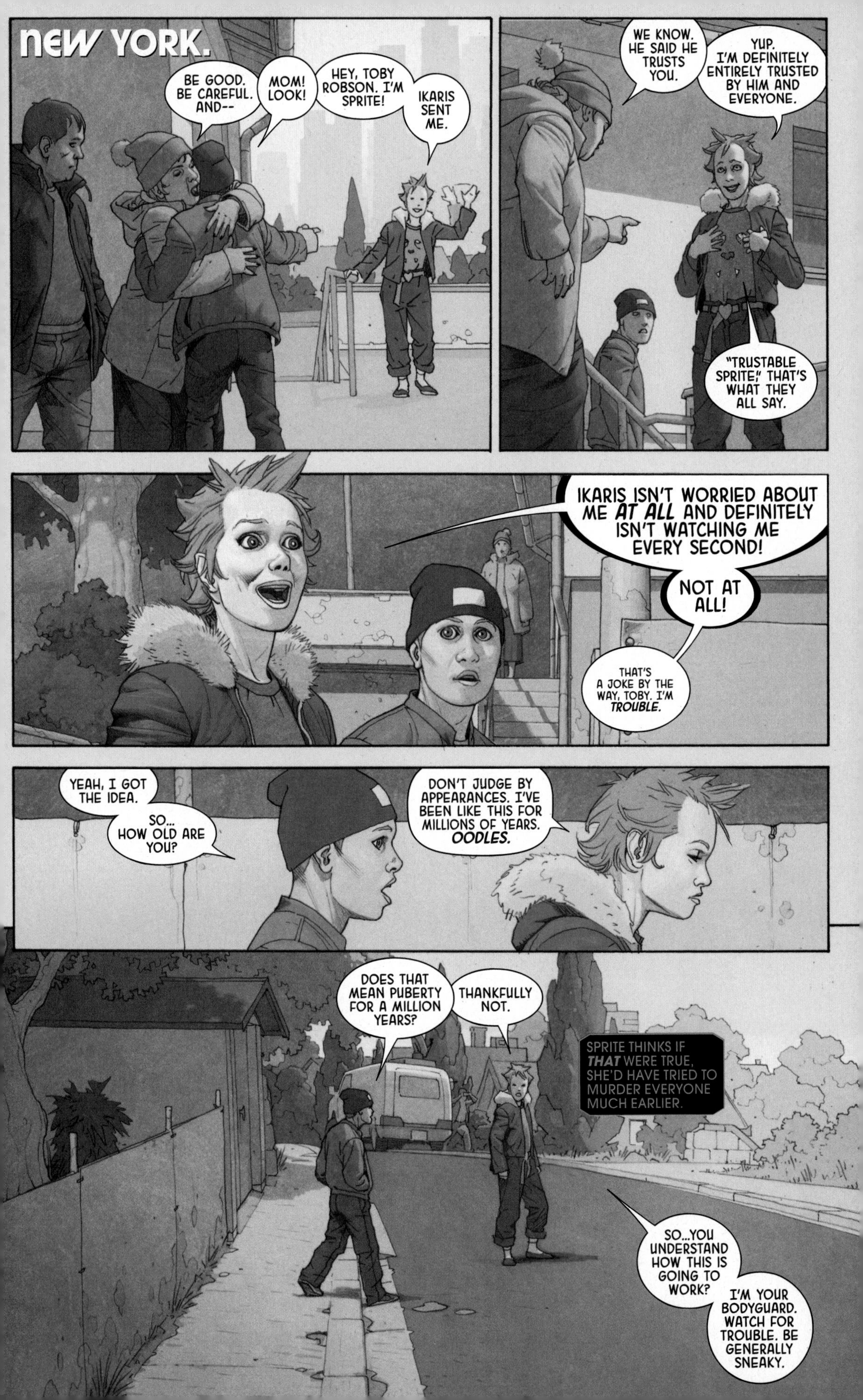
NEW YORK.
BE GOOD. BE CAREFUL. AND--
MOM! LOOK!
HEY, TOBY ROBSON. I'M SPRITE!
IKARIS SENT ME.
WE KNOW. HE SAID HE TRUSTS YOU.
YUP. I'M DEFINITELY ENTIRELY TRUSTED BY HIM AND EVERYONE.
"TRUSTABLE SPRITE," THAT'S WHAT THEY ALL SAY.
IKARIS ISN'T WORRIED ABOUT ME AT ALL AND DEFINITELY ISN'T WATCHING ME EVERY SECOND!
NOT AT ALL!
THAT'S A JOKE BY THE WAY, TOBY. I'M TROUBLE.
YEAH, I GOT THE IDEA.
SO... HOW OLD ARE YOU?
DON'T JUDGE BY APPEARANCES. I'VE BEEN LIKE THIS FOR MILLIONS OF YEARS. OODLES.
DOES THAT MEAN PUBERTY FOR A MILLION YEARS?
THANKFULLY NOT.
SPRITE THINKS IF THAT WERE TRUE, SHE'D HAVE TRIED TO MURDER EVERYONE MUCH EARLIER.
SO...YOU UNDERSTAND HOW THIS IS GOING TO WORK?
I'M YOUR BODYGUARD. WATCH FOR TROUBLE. BE GENERALLY SNEAKY.

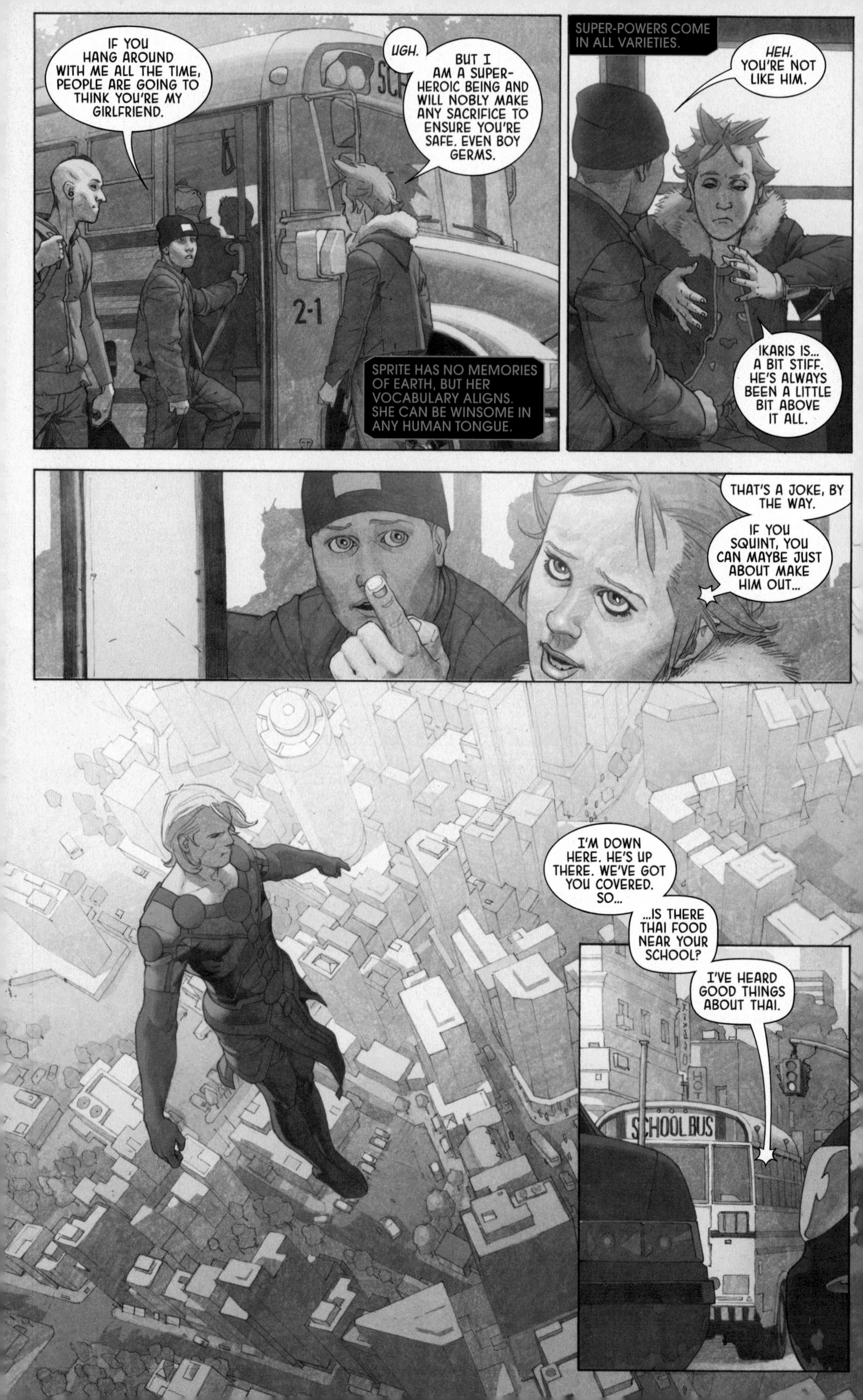
IF YOU HANG AROUND WITH ME ALL THE TIME, PEOPLE ARE GOING TO THINK YOU'RE MY GIRLFRIEND.
UGH.
BUT I AM A SUPER-HEROIC BEING AND WILL NOBLY MAKE ANY SACRIFICE TO ENSURE YOU'RE SAFE. EVEN BOY GERMS.
SPRITE HAS NO MEMORIES OF EARTH, BUT HER VOCABULARY ALIGNS. SHE CAN BE WINSOME IN ANY HUMAN TONGUE.
SUPER-POWERS COME IN ALL VARIETIES.
HEH. YOU'RE NOT LIKE HIM.
IKARIS IS... A BIT STIFF. HE'S ALWAYS BEEN A LITTLE BIT ABOVE IT ALL.
THAT'S A JOKE, BY THE WAY.
IF YOU SQUINT, YOU CAN MAYBE JUST ABOUT MAKE HIM OUT...
I'M DOWN HERE. HE'S UP THERE. WE'VE GOT YOU COVERED. SO...
...IS THERE THAI FOOD NEAR YOUR SCHOOL?
I'VE HEARD GOOD THINGS ABOUT THAI.
SCHOOL BUS

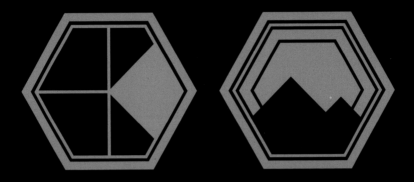

A BRIEF HISTORY OF THE RELATIONSHIP BETWEEN OLYMPIA AND POLARIA:

They don't like each other.

A LESS BRIEF HISTORY OF THE RELATIONSHIP BETWEEN OLYMPIA AND POLARIA:

The fall of Titanos opened the question of which was the new capital of Eternal society. While Celestia secured a religious role, Olympia and Polaria have been engaged in a conflict to secure temporal mastery.

There have been attempts to bring the two great Eternal cities closer together, often by exchange of individuals. Perhaps the most notable of these is the Polar Eternal, Ikaris in Olympia. This has mostly led to an avoidance of open war. Mostly.

Humans often compare the relationship between Olympia and Polaria as that between the USA and Russia. This is because humans are hilariously self-centered. Come back in a few hundred thousand years and then you get to make that comparison.

I'm sorry. My mind is burning up. This makes things difficult, and I'm taking it out on you over your egotistical nonsense that...

Sorry. I'm at it again, you putrid sacks of goo.

Sorrysorrysorry.

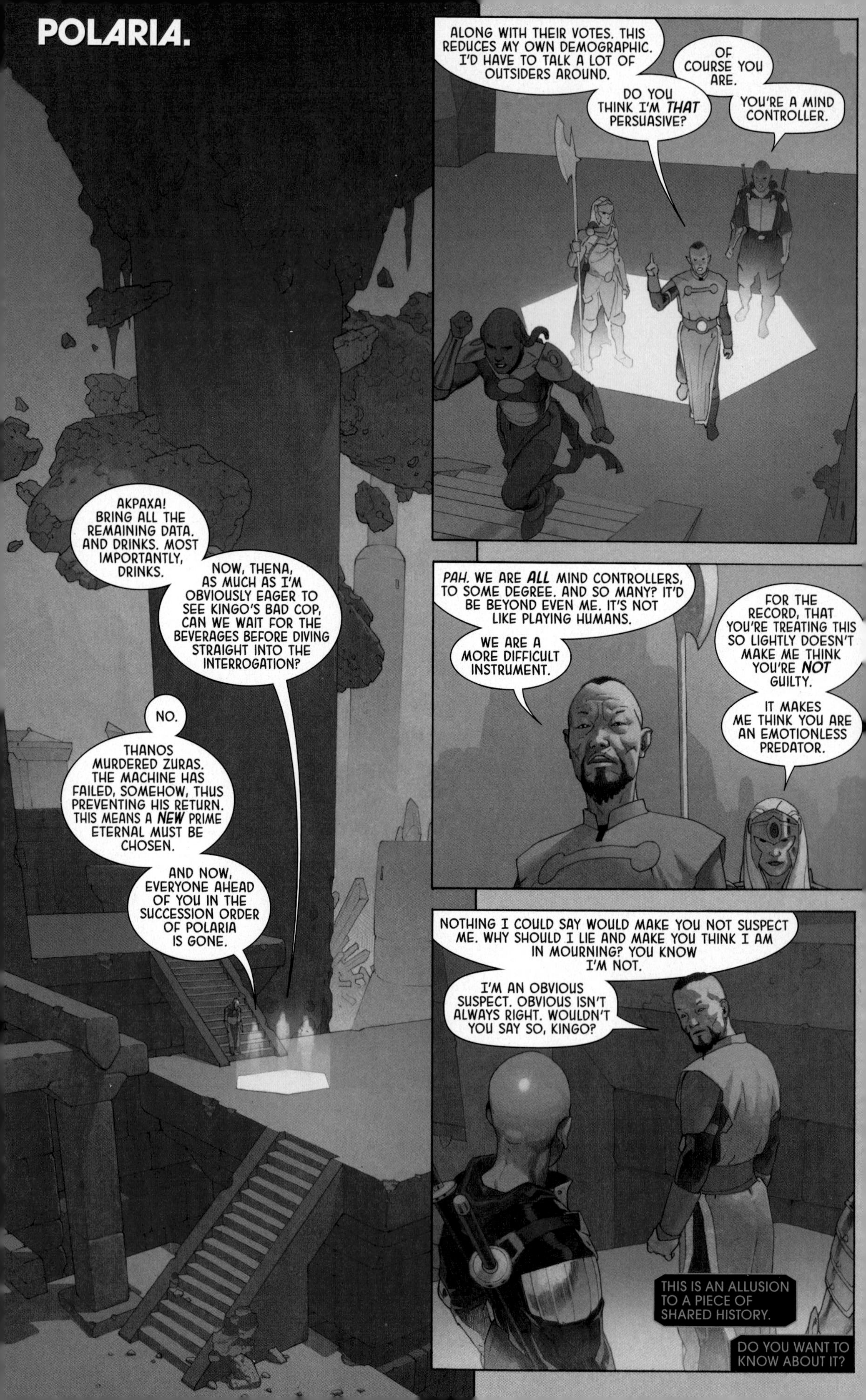
POLARIA.
AKPAXA! BRING ALL THE REMAINING DATA. AND DRINKS. MOST IMPORTANTLY, DRINKS.
NOW, THENA, AS MUCH AS I'M OBVIOUSLY EAGER TO SEE KINGO'S BAD COP, CAN WE WAIT FOR THE BEVERAGES BEFORE DIVING STRAIGHT INTO THE INTERROGATION?
NO.
THANOS MURDERED ZURAS. THE MACHINE HAS FAILED, SOMEHOW, THUS PREVENTING HIS RETURN. THIS MEANS A *NEW* PRIME ETERNAL MUST BE CHOSEN.
AND NOW, EVERYONE AHEAD OF YOU IN THE SUCCESSION ORDER OF POLARIA IS GONE.
ALONG WITH THEIR VOTES. THIS REDUCES MY OWN DEMOGRAPHIC. I'D HAVE TO TALK A LOT OF OUTSIDERS AROUND.
DO YOU THINK I'M *THAT* PERSUASIVE?
OF COURSE YOU ARE.
YOU'RE A MIND CONTROLLER.
PAH. WE ARE *ALL* MIND CONTROLLERS, TO SOME DEGREE. AND SO MANY? IT'D BE BEYOND EVEN ME. IT'S NOT LIKE PLAYING HUMANS.
WE ARE A MORE DIFFICULT INSTRUMENT.
FOR THE RECORD, THAT YOU'RE TREATING THIS SO LIGHTLY DOESN'T MAKE ME THINK YOU'RE *NOT* GUILTY.
IT MAKES ME THINK YOU ARE AN EMOTIONLESS PREDATOR.
NOTHING I COULD SAY WOULD MAKE YOU NOT SUSPECT ME. WHY SHOULD I LIE AND MAKE YOU THINK I AM IN MOURNING? YOU KNOW I'M NOT.
I'M AN OBVIOUS SUSPECT. OBVIOUS ISN'T ALWAYS RIGHT. WOULDN'T YOU SAY SO, KINGO?
THIS IS AN ALLUSION TO A PIECE OF SHARED HISTORY.
DO YOU WANT TO KNOW ABOUT IT?

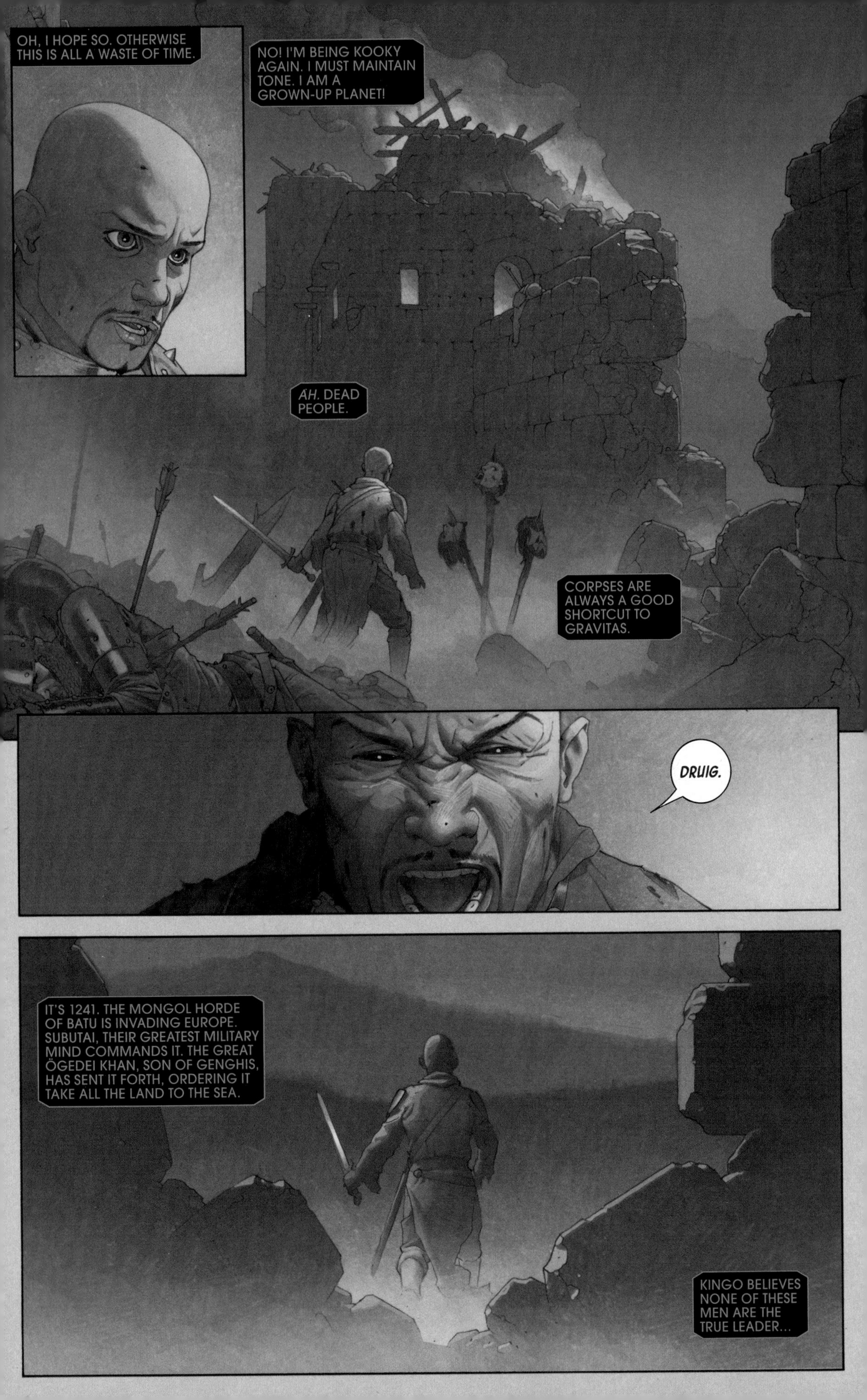
OH, I HOPE SO. OTHERWISE THIS IS ALL A WASTE OF TIME.
NO! I'M BEING KOOKY AGAIN. I MUST MAINTAIN TONE. I AM A GROWN-UP PLANET!
ÄH. DEAD PEOPLE.
CORPSES ARE ALWAYS A GOOD SHORTCUT TO GRAVITAS.
DRUIG.
IT'S 1241. THE MONGOL HORDE OF BATU IS INVADING EUROPE. SUBUTAI, THEIR GREATEST MILITARY MIND COMMANDS IT. THE GREAT ÖGEDEI KHAN, SON OF GENGHIS, HAS SENT IT FORTH, ORDERING IT TAKE ALL THE LAND TO THE SEA.
KINGO BELIEVES NONE OF THESE MEN ARE THE TRUE LEADER...

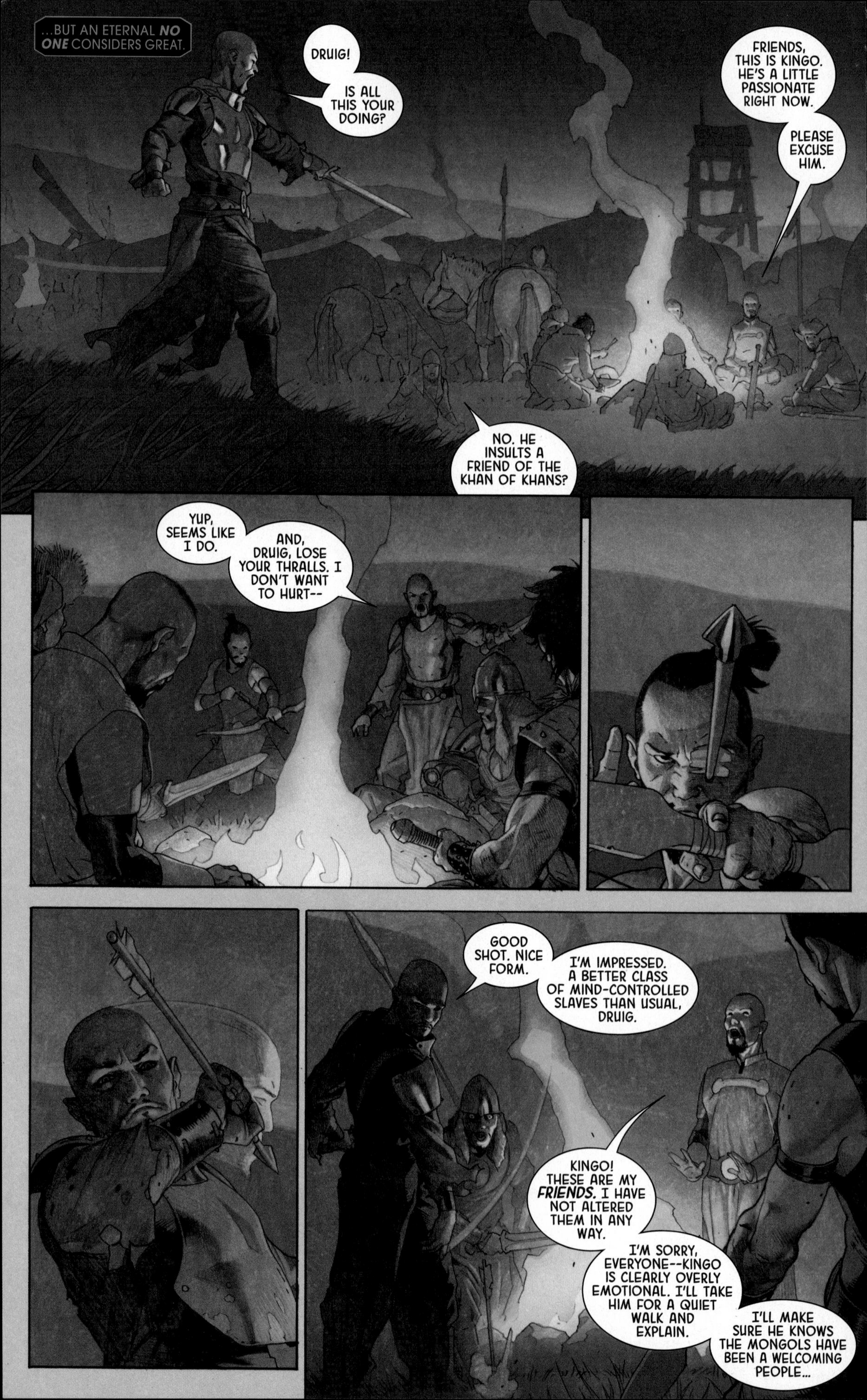
...BUT AN ETERNAL **NO ONE** CONSIDERS GREAT.
DRUIG!
IS ALL THIS YOUR DOING?
FRIENDS, THIS IS KINGO. HE'S A LITTLE PASSIONATE RIGHT NOW.
PLEASE EXCUSE HIM.
NO. HE INSULTS A FRIEND OF THE KHAN OF KHANS?
YUP, SEEMS LIKE I DO.
AND, DRUIG, LOSE YOUR THRALLS. I DON'T WANT TO HURT--
GOOD SHOT. NICE FORM.
I'M IMPRESSED. A BETTER CLASS OF MIND-CONTROLLED SLAVES THAN USUAL, DRUIG.
KINGO! THESE ARE MY ***FRIENDS.*** I HAVE NOT ALTERED THEM IN ANY WAY.
I'M SORRY, EVERYONE--KINGO IS CLEARLY OVERLY EMOTIONAL. I'LL TAKE HIM FOR A QUIET WALK AND EXPLAIN.
I'LL MAKE SURE HE KNOWS THE MONGOLS HAVE BEEN A WELCOMING PEOPLE...

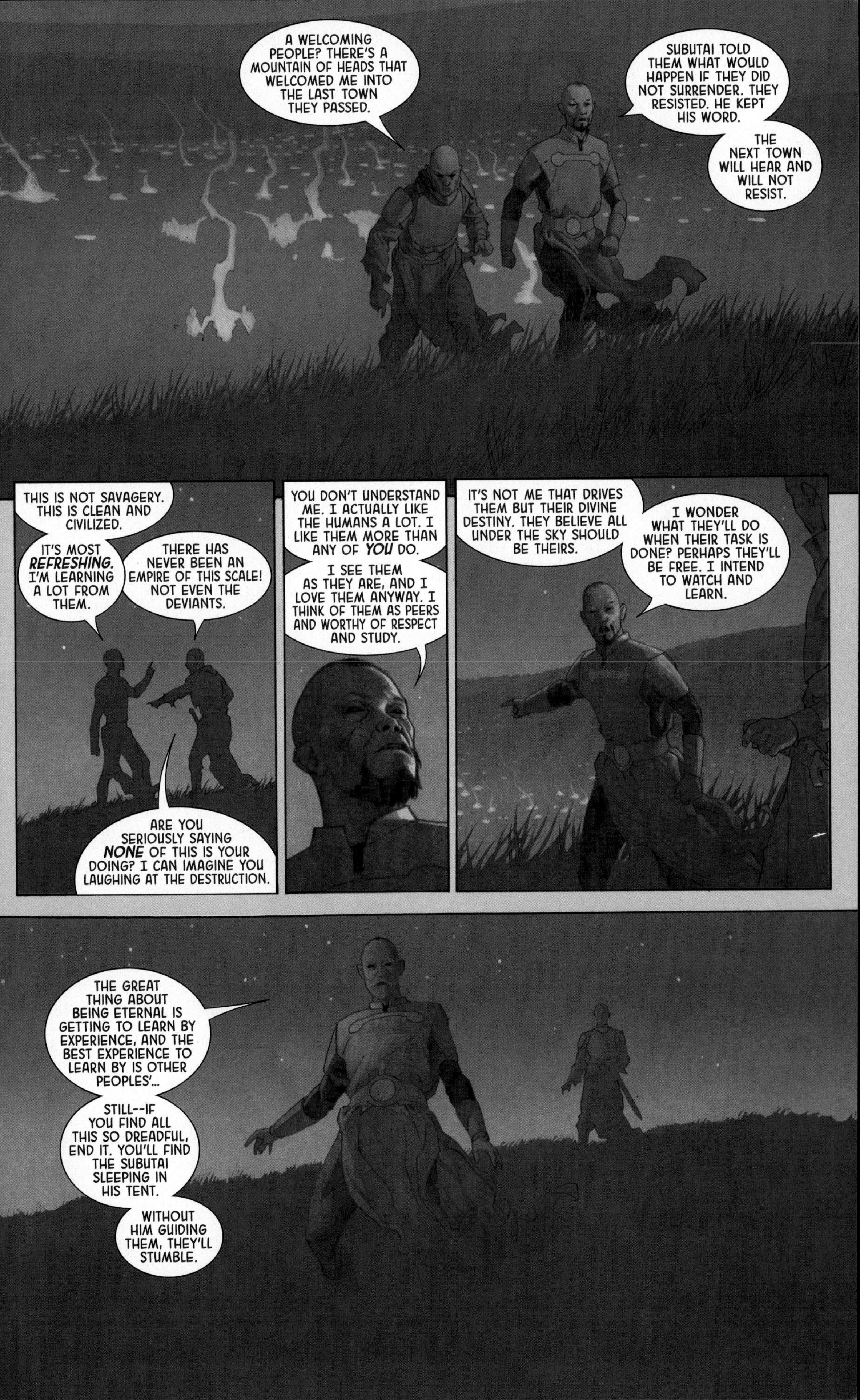
A WELCOMING PEOPLE? THERE'S A MOUNTAIN OF HEADS THAT WELCOMED ME INTO THE LAST TOWN THEY PASSED.
SUBUTAI TOLD THEM WHAT WOULD HAPPEN IF THEY DID NOT SURRENDER. THEY RESISTED. HE KEPT HIS WORD.
THE NEXT TOWN WILL HEAR AND WILL NOT RESIST.
THIS IS NOT SAVAGERY. THIS IS CLEAN AND CIVILIZED.
IT'S MOST REFRESHING. I'M LEARNING A LOT FROM THEM.
THERE HAS NEVER BEEN AN EMPIRE OF THIS SCALE! NOT EVEN THE DEVIANTS.
ARE YOU SERIOUSLY SAYING NONE OF THIS IS YOUR DOING? I CAN IMAGINE YOU LAUGHING AT THE DESTRUCTION.
YOU DON'T UNDERSTAND ME. I ACTUALLY LIKE THE HUMANS A LOT. I LIKE THEM MORE THAN ANY OF YOU DO.
I SEE THEM AS THEY ARE, AND I LOVE THEM ANYWAY. I THINK OF THEM AS PEERS AND WORTHY OF RESPECT AND STUDY.
IT'S NOT ME THAT DRIVES THEM BUT THEIR DIVINE DESTINY. THEY BELIEVE ALL UNDER THE SKY SHOULD BE THEIRS.
I WONDER WHAT THEY'LL DO WHEN THEIR TASK IS DONE? PERHAPS THEY'LL BE FREE. I INTEND TO WATCH AND LEARN.
THE GREAT THING ABOUT BEING ETERNAL IS GETTING TO LEARN BY EXPERIENCE, AND THE BEST EXPERIENCE TO LEARN BY IS OTHER PEOPLES'...
STILL--IF YOU FIND ALL THIS SO DREADFUL, END IT. YOU'LL FIND THE SUBUTAI SLEEPING IN HIS TENT.
WITHOUT HIM GUIDING THEM, THEY'LL STUMBLE.

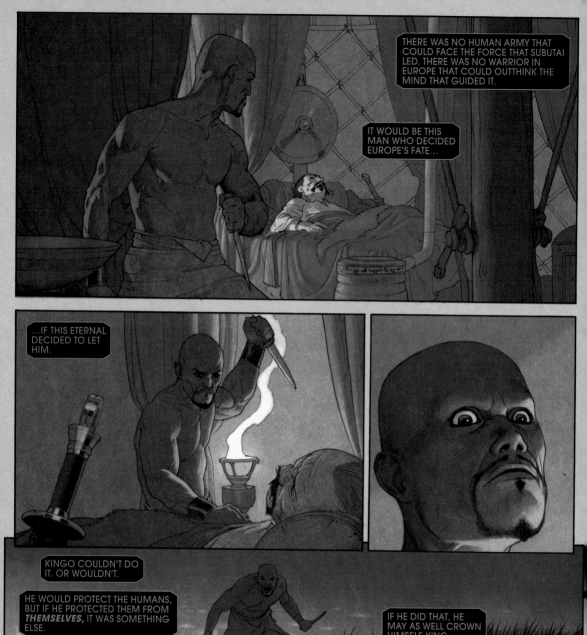

THERE WAS NO HUMAN ARMY THAT COULD FACE THE FORCE THAT SUBUTAI LED. THERE WAS NO WARRIOR IN EUROPE THAT COULD OUTTHINK THE MIND THAT GUIDED IT.

IT WOULD BE THIS MAN WHO DECIDED EUROPE'S FATE...

...IF THIS ETERNAL DECIDED TO LET HIM.

KINGO COULDN'T DO IT. OR WOULDN'T.

HE WOULD PROTECT THE HUMANS, BUT IF HE PROTECTED THEM FROM *THEMSELVES*, IT WAS SOMETHING ELSE.

IF HE DID THAT, HE MAY AS WELL CROWN HIMSELF KING.

IT WAS FOR THE HUMANS TO DECIDE WHAT HAPPENED NEXT...

...AND COME THE MORNING, THE CAMP WAS GONE. THEY'D HEADED EAST, AWAY FROM EUROPE.

AND KINGO COULDN'T UNDERSTAND...

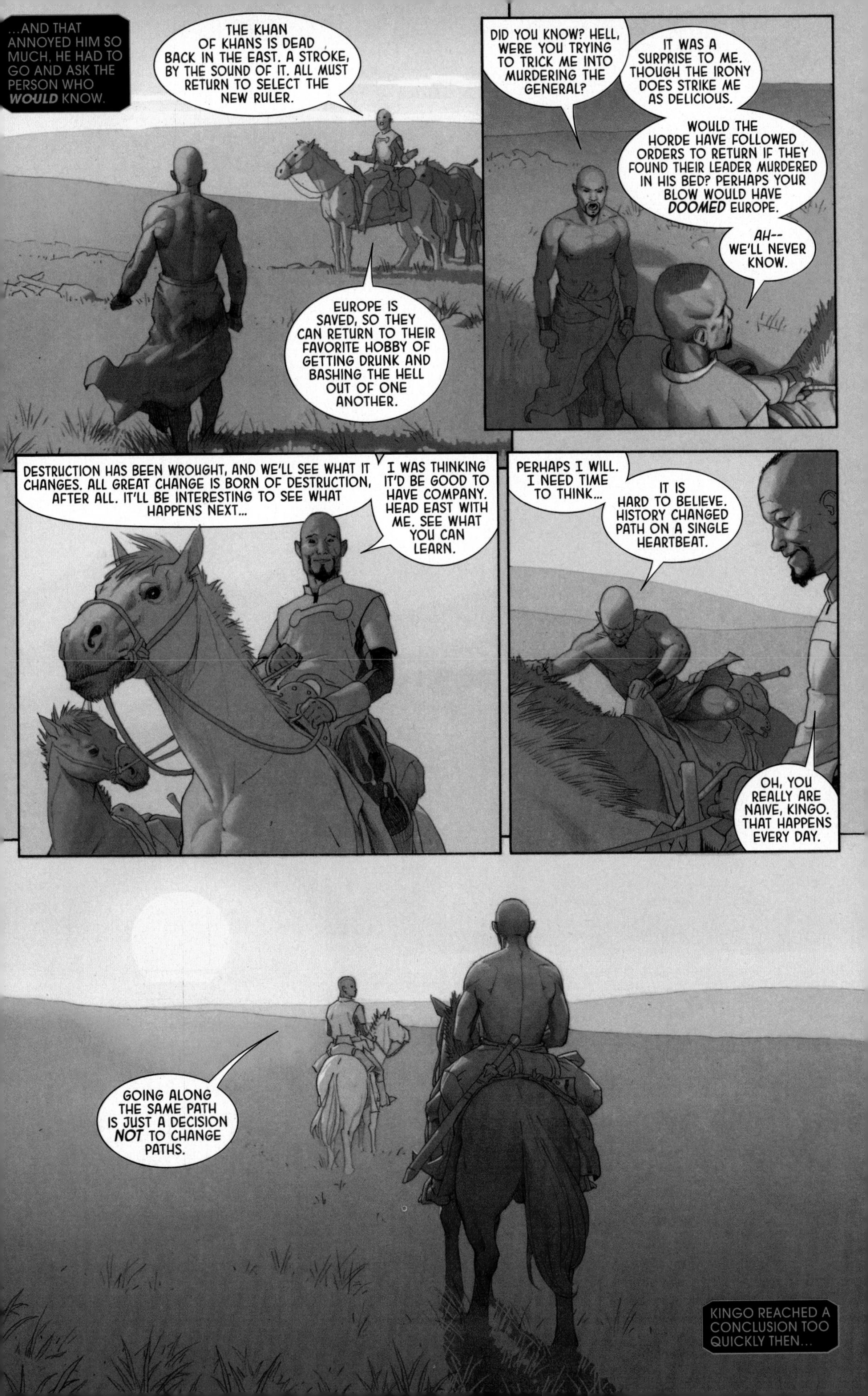
...AND THAT ANNOYED HIM SO MUCH, HE HAD TO GO AND ASK THE PERSON WHO *WOULD* KNOW.
THE KHAN OF KHANS IS DEAD BACK IN THE EAST. A STROKE, BY THE SOUND OF IT. ALL MUST RETURN TO SELECT THE NEW RULER.
EUROPE IS SAVED, SO THEY CAN RETURN TO THEIR FAVORITE HOBBY OF GETTING DRUNK AND BASHING THE HELL OUT OF ONE ANOTHER.
DID YOU KNOW? HELL, WERE YOU TRYING TO TRICK ME INTO MURDERING THE GENERAL?
IT WAS A SURPRISE TO ME. THOUGH THE IRONY DOES STRIKE ME AS DELICIOUS.
WOULD THE HORDE HAVE FOLLOWED ORDERS TO RETURN IF THEY FOUND THEIR LEADER MURDERED IN HIS BED? PERHAPS YOUR BLOW WOULD HAVE *DOOMED* EUROPE.
AH-- WE'LL NEVER KNOW.
DESTRUCTION HAS BEEN WROUGHT, AND WE'LL SEE WHAT IT CHANGES. ALL GREAT CHANGE IS BORN OF DESTRUCTION, AFTER ALL. IT'LL BE INTERESTING TO SEE WHAT HAPPENS NEXT...
I WAS THINKING IT'D BE GOOD TO HAVE COMPANY. HEAD EAST WITH ME. SEE WHAT YOU CAN LEARN.
PERHAPS I WILL. I NEED TIME TO THINK...
IT IS HARD TO BELIEVE. HISTORY CHANGED PATH ON A SINGLE HEARTBEAT.
OH, YOU REALLY ARE NAIVE, KINGO. THAT HAPPENS EVERY DAY.
GOING ALONG THE SAME PATH IS JUST A DECISION *NOT* TO CHANGE PATHS.
KINGO REACHED A CONCLUSION TOO QUICKLY THEN...

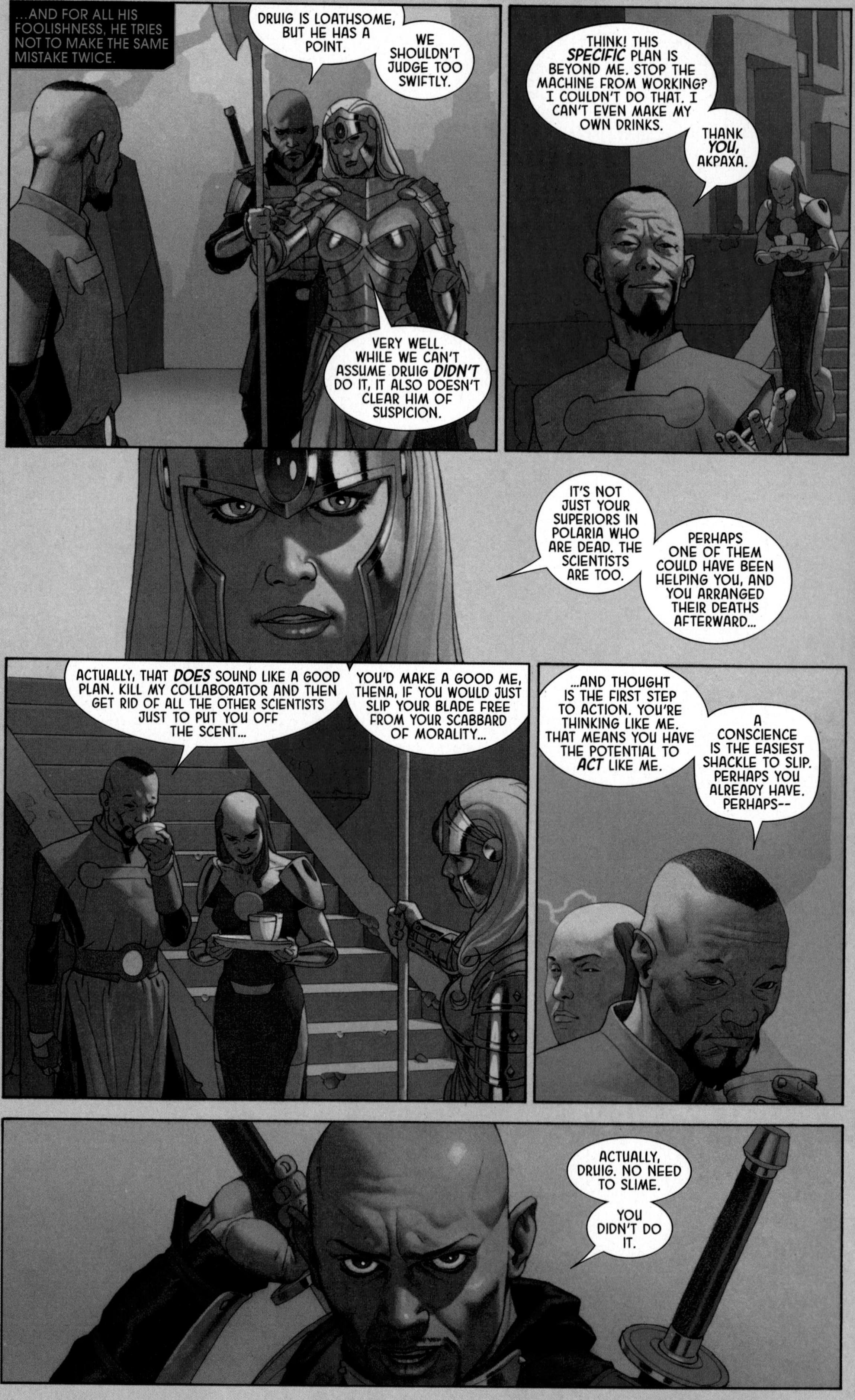

...AND FOR ALL HIS FOOLISHNESS, HE TRIES NOT TO MAKE THE SAME MISTAKE TWICE.
DRUIG IS LOATHSOME, BUT HE HAS A POINT.
WE SHOULDN'T JUDGE TOO SWIFTLY.
VERY WELL. WHILE WE CAN'T ASSUME DRUIG DIDN'T DO IT, IT ALSO DOESN'T CLEAR HIM OF SUSPICION.
THINK! THIS SPECIFIC PLAN IS BEYOND ME. STOP THE MACHINE FROM WORKING? I COULDN'T DO THAT. I CAN'T EVEN MAKE MY OWN DRINKS.
THANK YOU, AKPAXA.
IT'S NOT JUST YOUR SUPERIORS IN POLARIA WHO ARE DEAD. THE SCIENTISTS ARE TOO.
PERHAPS ONE OF THEM COULD HAVE BEEN HELPING YOU, AND YOU ARRANGED THEIR DEATHS AFTERWARD...
ACTUALLY, THAT DOES SOUND LIKE A GOOD PLAN. KILL MY COLLABORATOR AND THEN GET RID OF ALL THE OTHER SCIENTISTS JUST TO PUT YOU OFF THE SCENT...
YOU'D MAKE A GOOD ME, THENA, IF YOU WOULD JUST SLIP YOUR BLADE FREE FROM YOUR SCABBARD OF MORALITY...
...AND THOUGHT IS THE FIRST STEP TO ACTION. YOU'RE THINKING LIKE ME. THAT MEANS YOU HAVE THE POTENTIAL TO ACT LIKE ME.
A CONSCIENCE IS THE EASIEST SHACKLE TO SLIP. PERHAPS YOU ALREADY HAVE. PERHAPS--
ACTUALLY, DRUIG. NO NEED TO SLIME.
YOU DIDN'T DO IT.

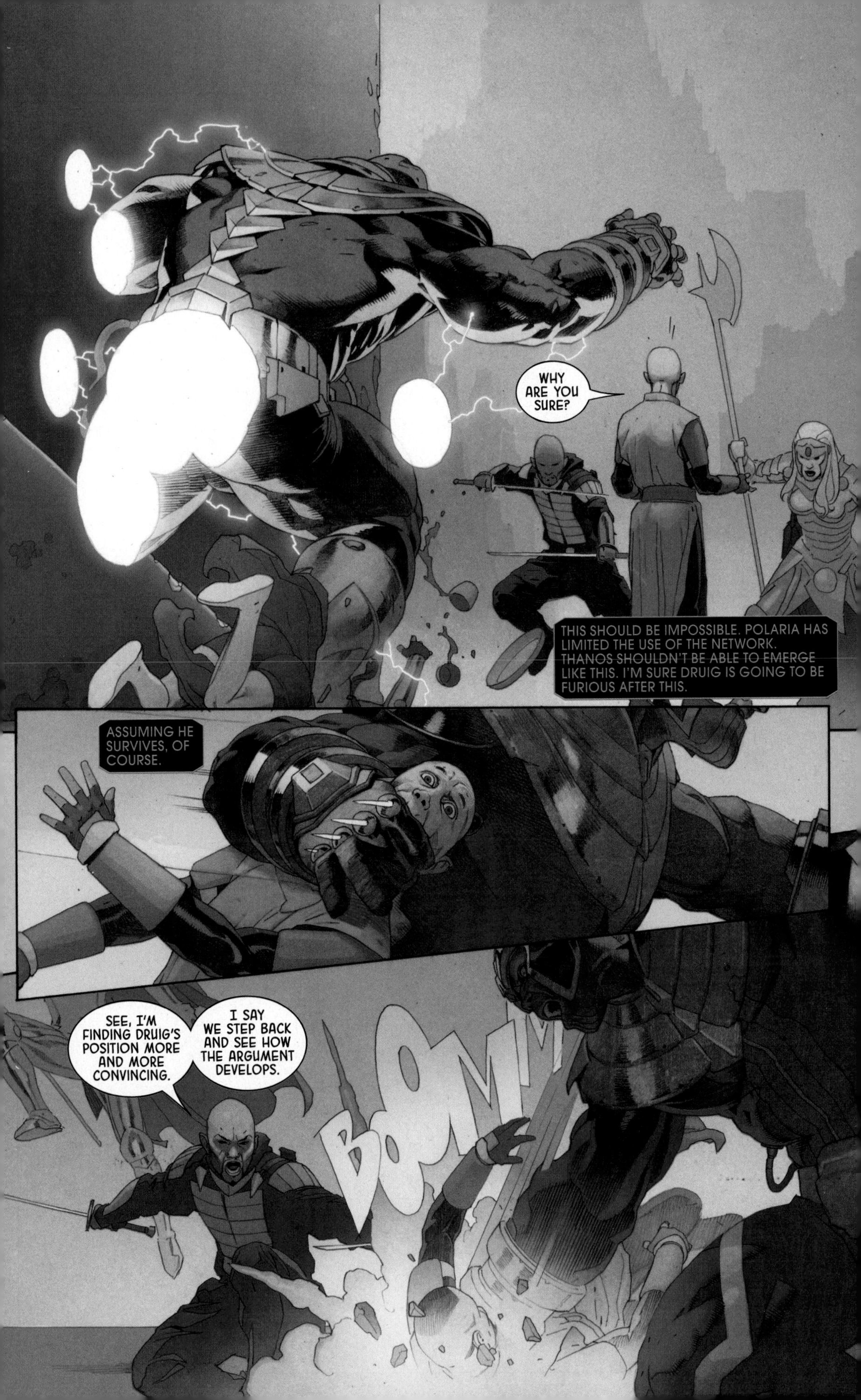
WHY ARE YOU SURE?
THIS SHOULD BE IMPOSSIBLE. POLARIA HAS LIMITED THE USE OF THE NETWORK. THANOS SHOULDN'T BE ABLE TO EMERGE LIKE THIS. I'M SURE DRUIG IS GOING TO BE FURIOUS AFTER THIS.
ASSUMING HE SURVIVES, OF COURSE.
SEE, I'M FINDING DRUIG'S POSITION MORE AND MORE CONVINCING.
I SAY WE STEP BACK AND SEE HOW THE ARGUMENT DEVELOPS.
BOOMM

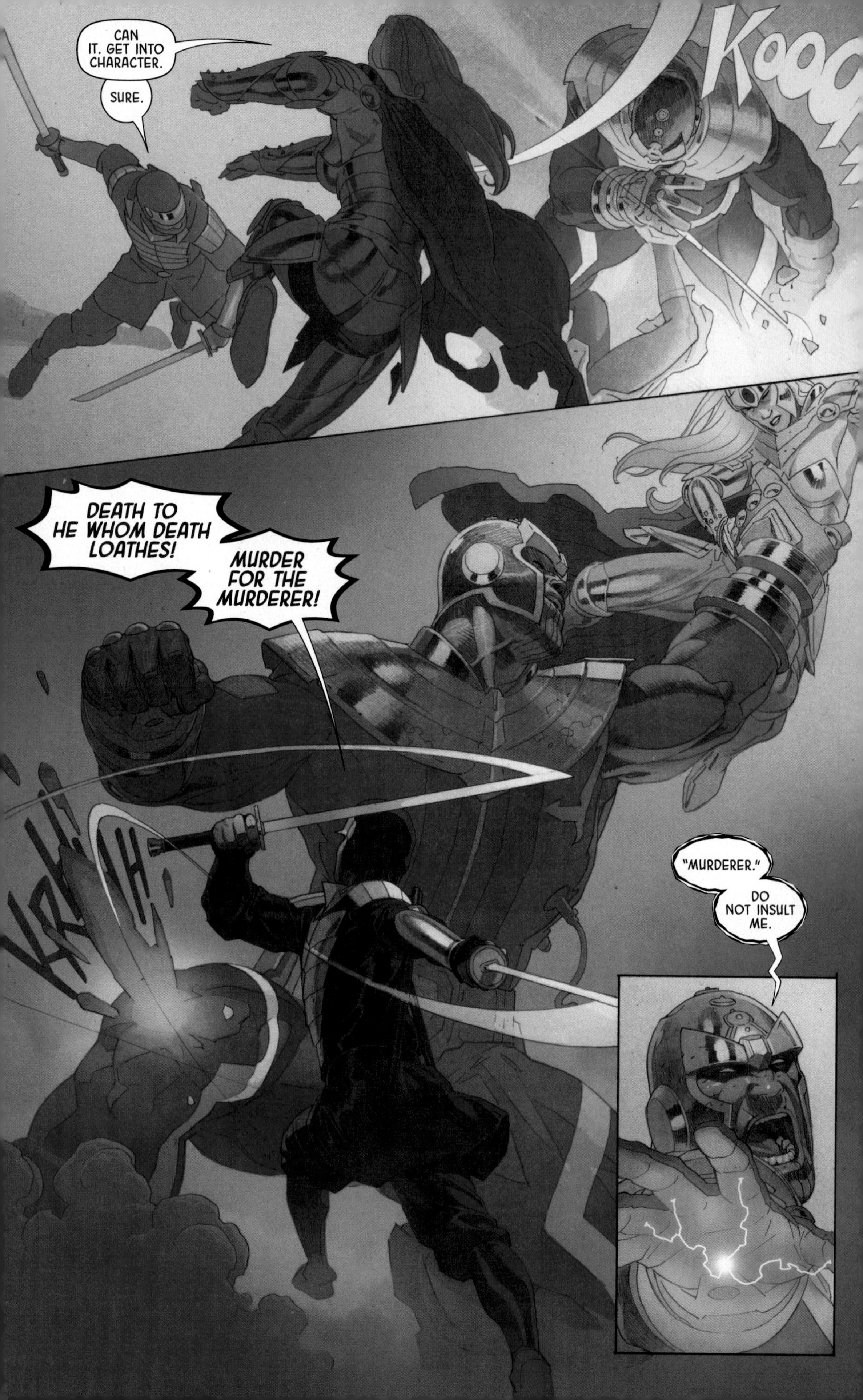
CAN IT. GET INTO CHARACTER.
SURE.
DEATH TO HE WHOM DEATH LOATHES!
MURDER FOR THE MURDERER!
"MURDERER."
DO NOT INSULT ME.

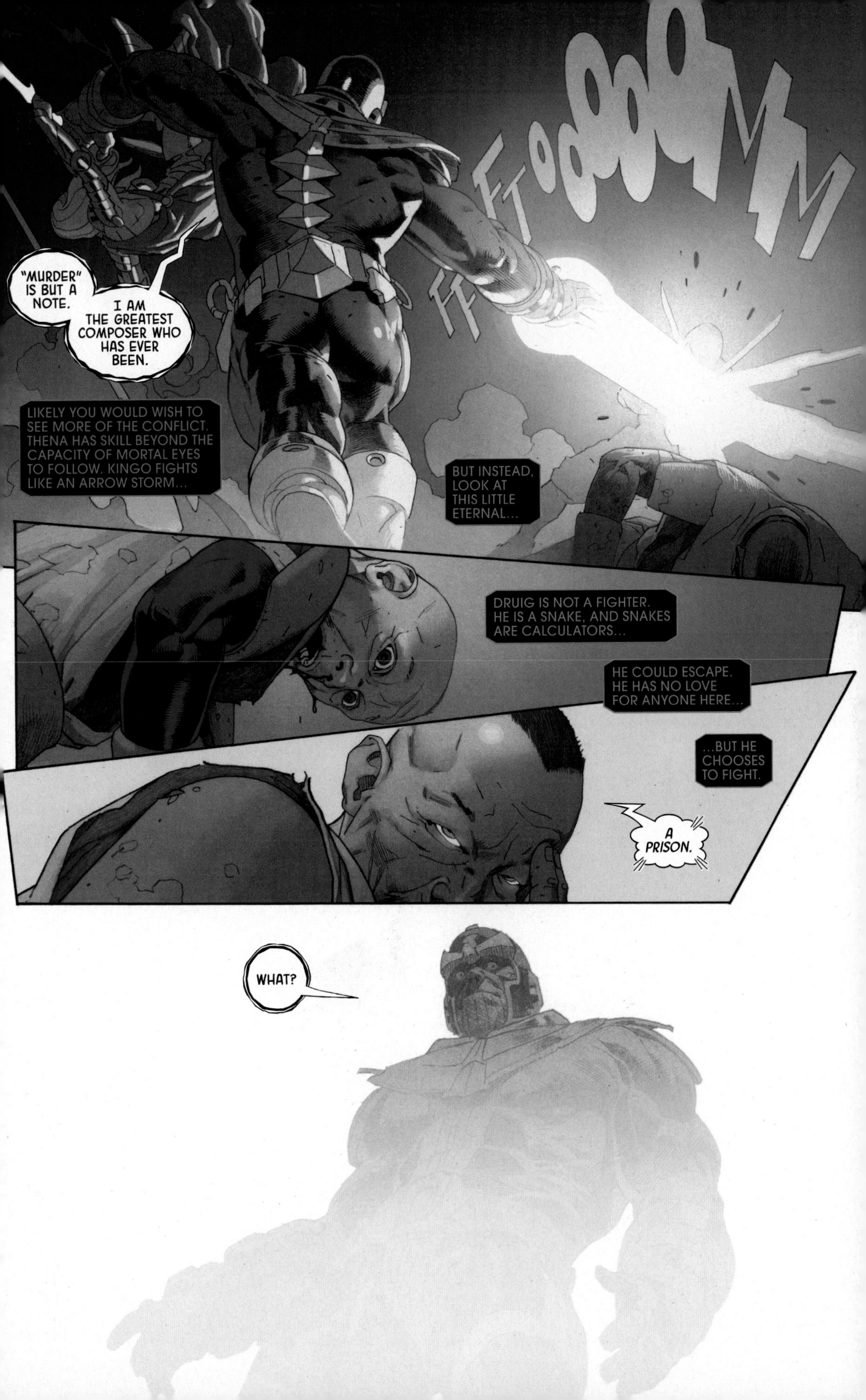
FFTOOOOOOMM
"MURDER" IS BUT A NOTE.
I AM THE GREATEST COMPOSER WHO HAS EVER BEEN.
LIKELY YOU WOULD WISH TO SEE MORE OF THE CONFLICT. THENA HAS SKILL BEYOND THE CAPACITY OF MORTAL EYES TO FOLLOW. KINGO FIGHTS LIKE AN ARROW STORM...
BUT INSTEAD, LOOK AT THIS LITTLE ETERNAL...
DRUIG IS NOT A FIGHTER. HE IS A SNAKE, AND SNAKES ARE CALCULATORS...
HE COULD ESCAPE. HE HAS NO LOVE FOR ANYONE HERE...
...BUT HE CHOOSES TO FIGHT.
A PRISON.
WHAT?

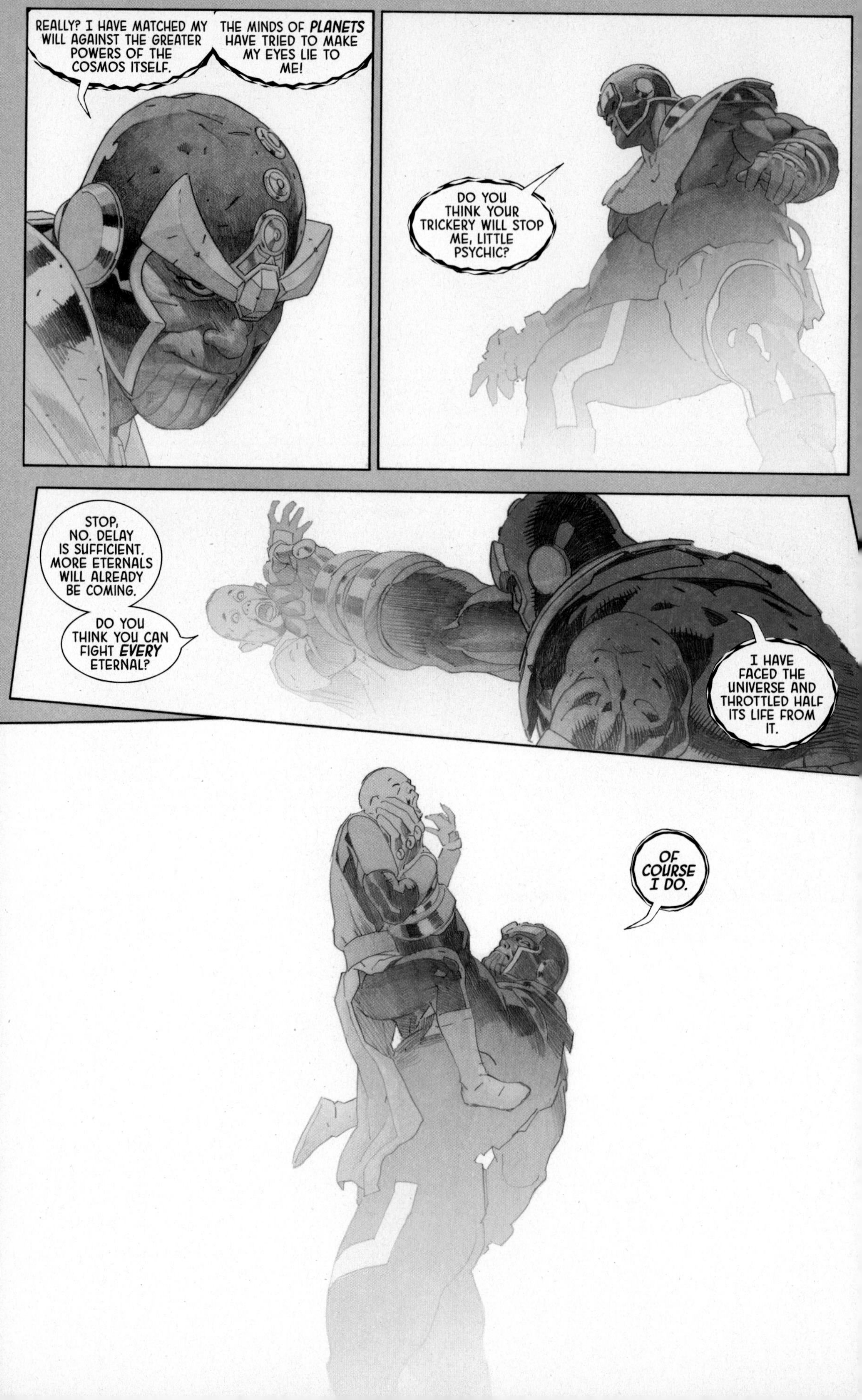
REALLY? I HAVE MATCHED MY WILL AGAINST THE GREATER POWERS OF THE COSMOS ITSELF.
THE MINDS OF PLANETS HAVE TRIED TO MAKE MY EYES LIE TO ME!
DO YOU THINK YOUR TRICKERY WILL STOP ME, LITTLE PSYCHIC?
STOP, NO. DELAY IS SUFFICIENT. MORE ETERNALS WILL ALREADY BE COMING.
DO YOU THINK YOU CAN FIGHT EVERY ETERNAL?
I HAVE FACED THE UNIVERSE AND THROTTLED HALF ITS LIFE FROM IT.
OF COURSE I DO.

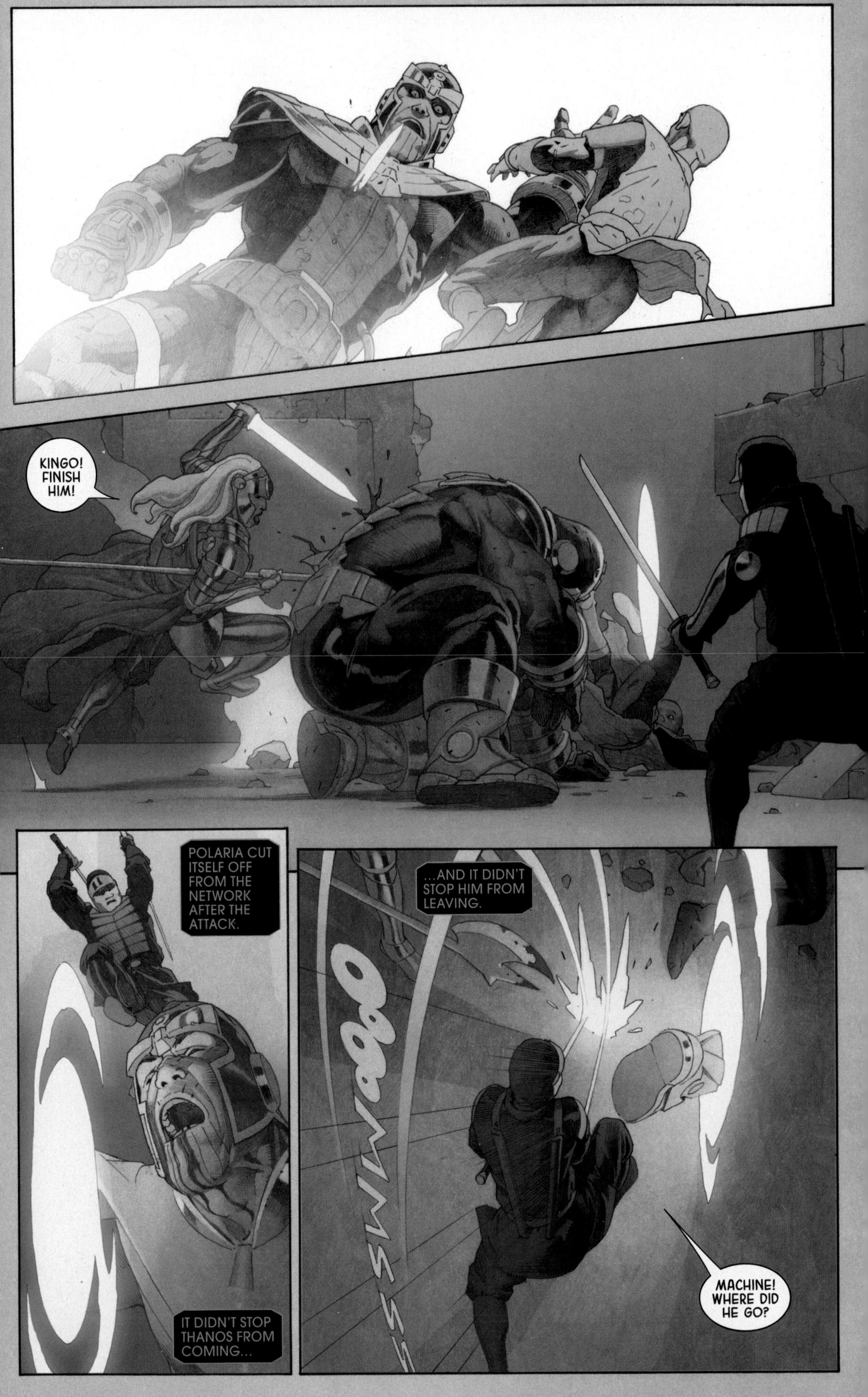
KINGO! FINISH HIM!
POLARIA CUT ITSELF OFF FROM THE NETWORK AFTER THE ATTACK.
IT DIDN'T STOP THANOS FROM COMING...
...AND IT DIDN'T STOP HIM FROM LEAVING.
MACHINE! WHERE DID HE GO?

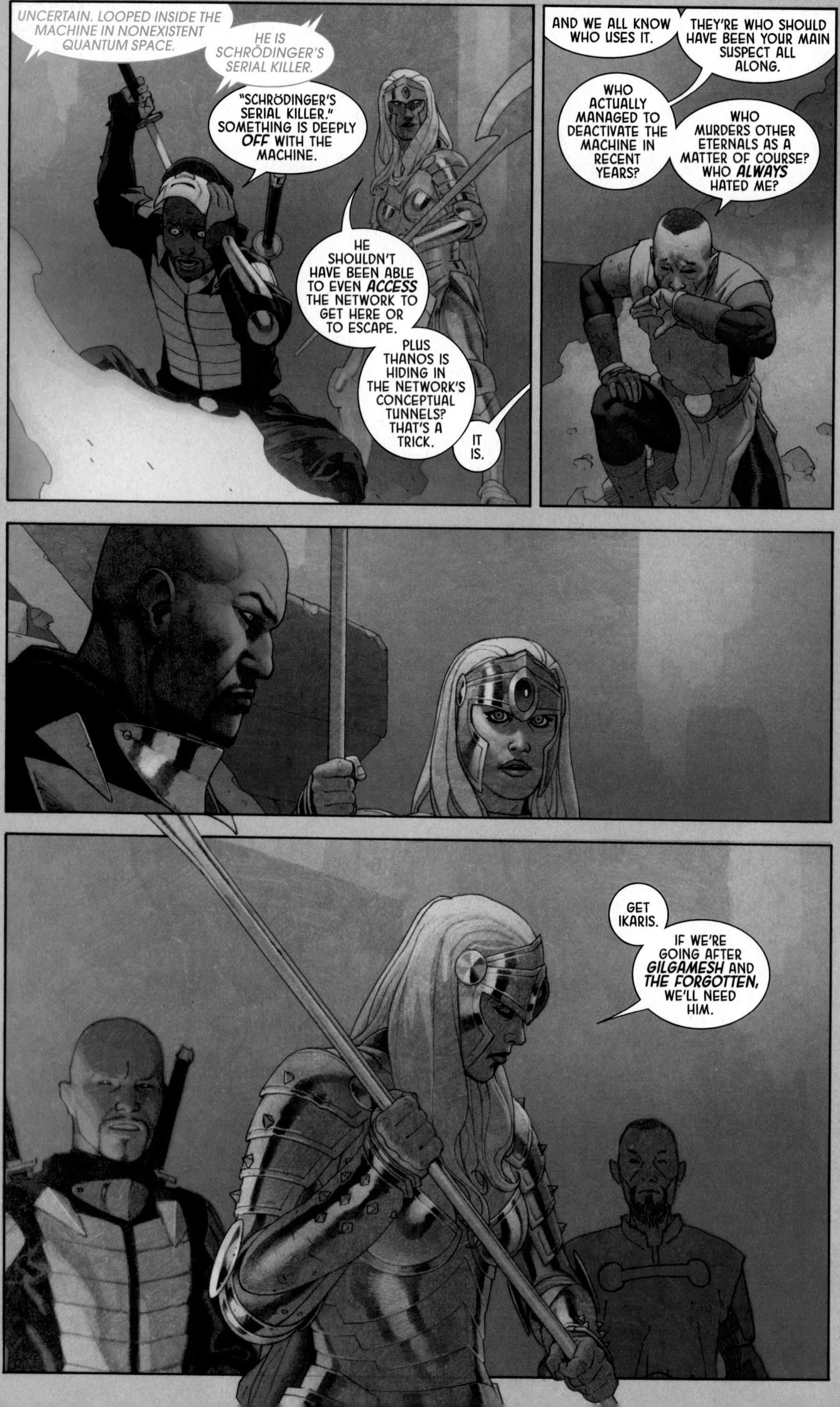
UNCERTAIN. LOOPED INSIDE THE MACHINE IN NONEXISTENT QUANTUM SPACE.
HE IS SCHRÖDINGER'S SERIAL KILLER.
"SCHRÖDINGER'S SERIAL KILLER." SOMETHING IS DEEPLY OFF WITH THE MACHINE.
HE SHOULDN'T HAVE BEEN ABLE TO EVEN ACCESS THE NETWORK TO GET HERE OR TO ESCAPE.
PLUS THANOS IS HIDING IN THE NETWORK'S CONCEPTUAL TUNNELS? THAT'S A TRICK.
IT IS.
AND WE ALL KNOW WHO USES IT.
THEY'RE WHO SHOULD HAVE BEEN YOUR MAIN SUSPECT ALL ALONG.
WHO ACTUALLY MANAGED TO DEACTIVATE THE MACHINE IN RECENT YEARS?
WHO MURDERS OTHER ETERNALS AS A MATTER OF COURSE? WHO ALWAYS HATED ME?
GET IKARIS.
IF WE'RE GOING AFTER GILGAMESH AND THE FORGOTTEN, WE'LL NEED HIM.

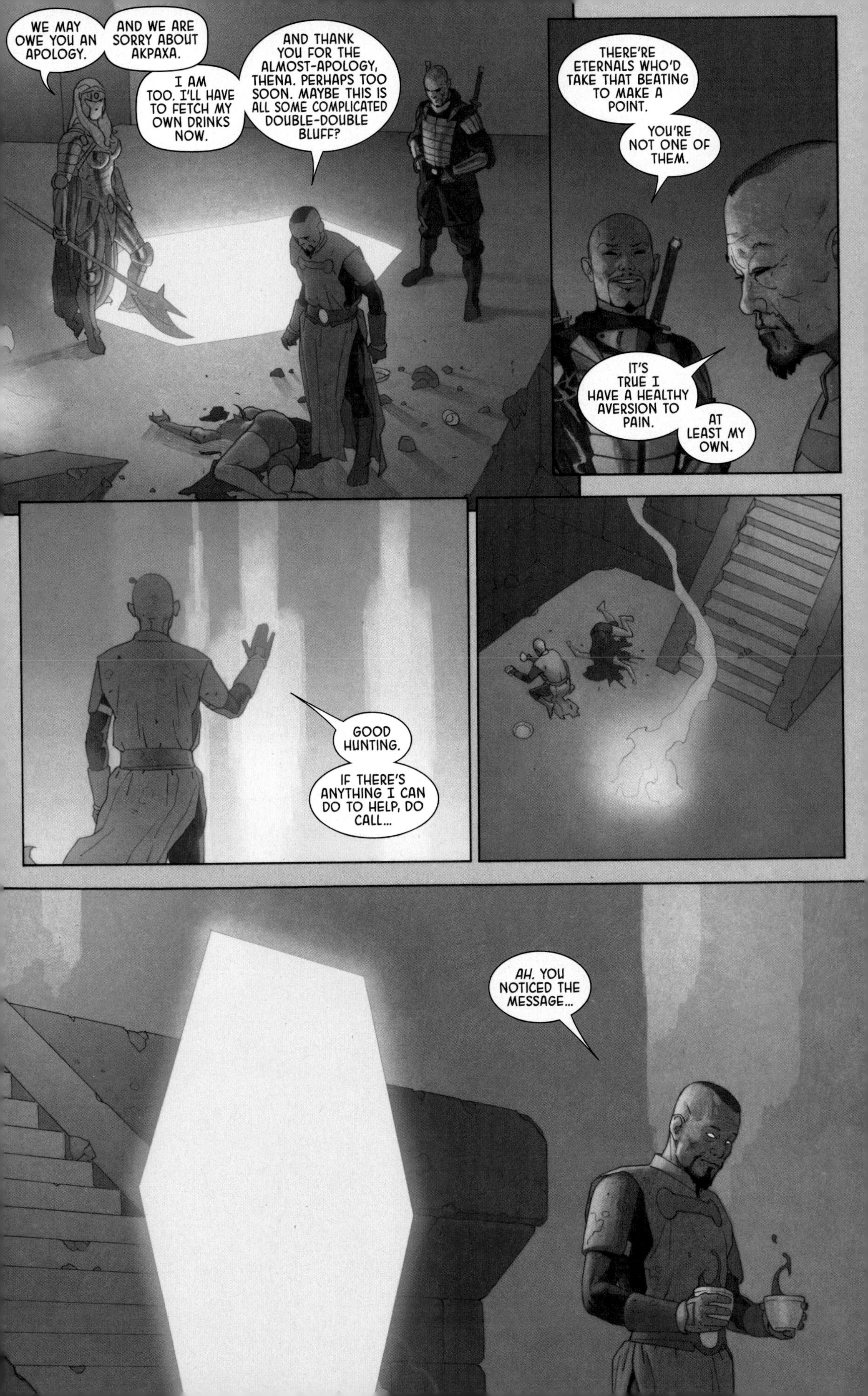
WE MAY OWE YOU AN APOLOGY.
AND WE ARE SORRY ABOUT AKPAXA.
I AM TOO. I'LL HAVE TO FETCH MY OWN DRINKS NOW.
AND THANK YOU FOR THE ALMOST-APOLOGY, THENA. PERHAPS TOO SOON. MAYBE THIS IS ALL SOME COMPLICATED DOUBLE-DOUBLE BLUFF?
THERE'RE ETERNALS WHO'D TAKE THAT BEATING TO MAKE A POINT.
YOU'RE NOT ONE OF THEM.
IT'S TRUE I HAVE A HEALTHY AVERSION TO PAIN.
AT LEAST MY OWN.
GOOD HUNTING.
IF THERE'S ANYTHING I CAN DO TO HELP, DO CALL...
AH. YOU NOTICED THE MESSAGE...

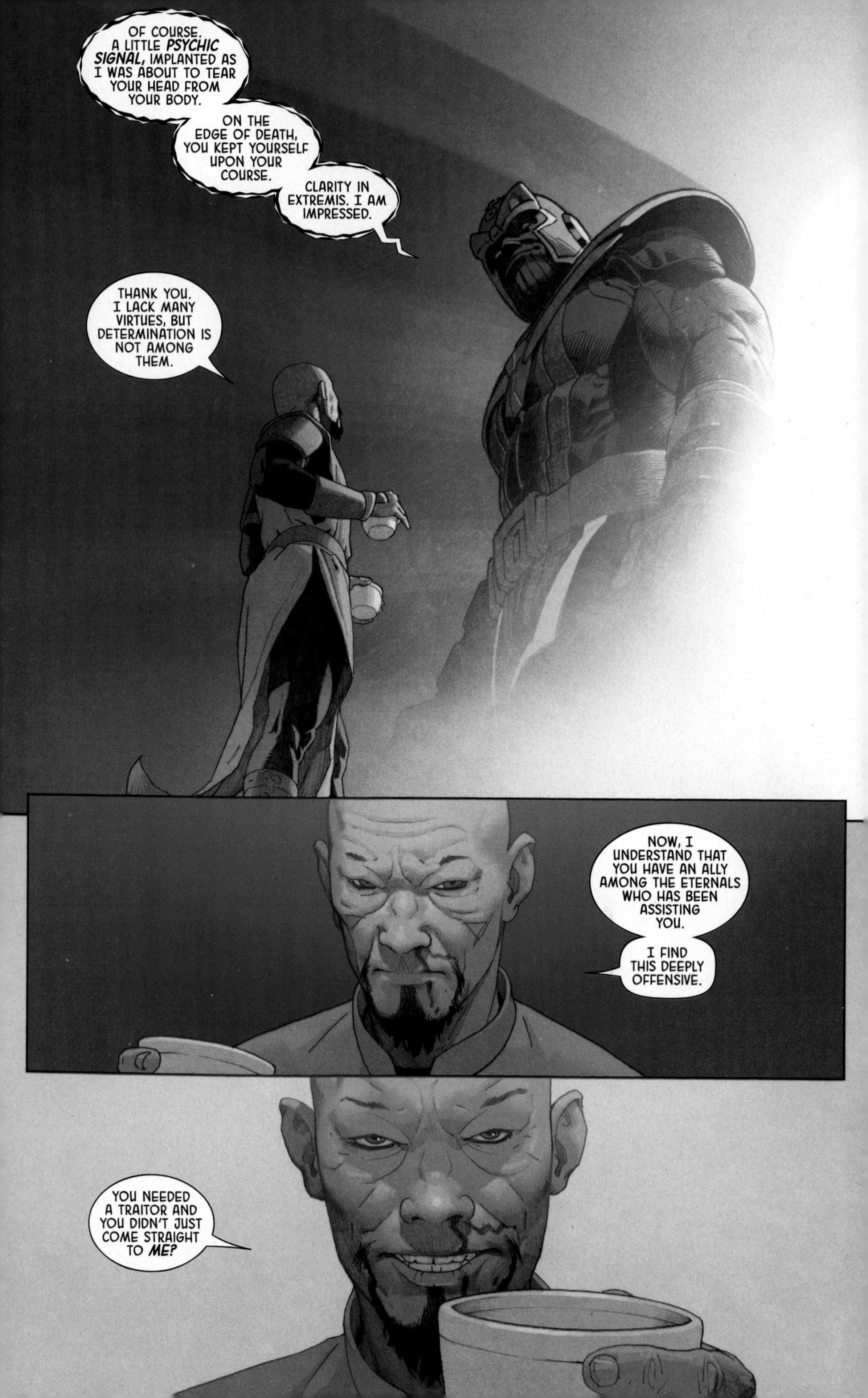

OF COURSE. A LITTLE PSYCHIC SIGNAL, IMPLANTED AS I WAS ABOUT TO TEAR YOUR HEAD FROM YOUR BODY.
ON THE EDGE OF DEATH, YOU KEPT YOURSELF UPON YOUR COURSE.
CLARITY IN EXTREMIS. I AM IMPRESSED.
THANK YOU. I LACK MANY VIRTUES, BUT DETERMINATION IS NOT AMONG THEM.
NOW, I UNDERSTAND THAT YOU HAVE AN ALLY AMONG THE ETERNALS WHO HAS BEEN ASSISTING YOU.
I FIND THIS DEEPLY OFFENSIVE.
YOU NEEDED A TRAITOR AND YOU DIDN'T JUST COME STRAIGHT TO ME?

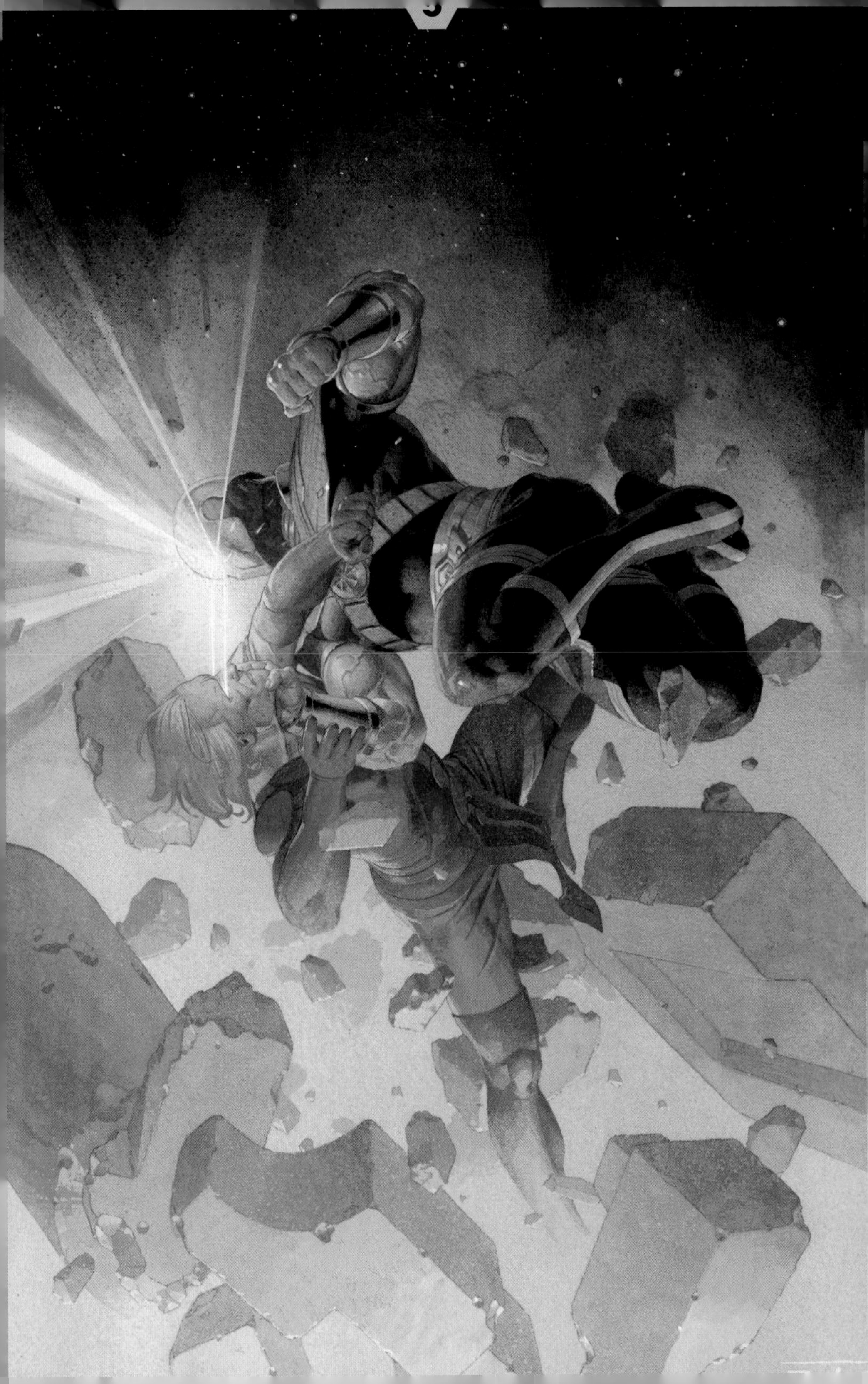

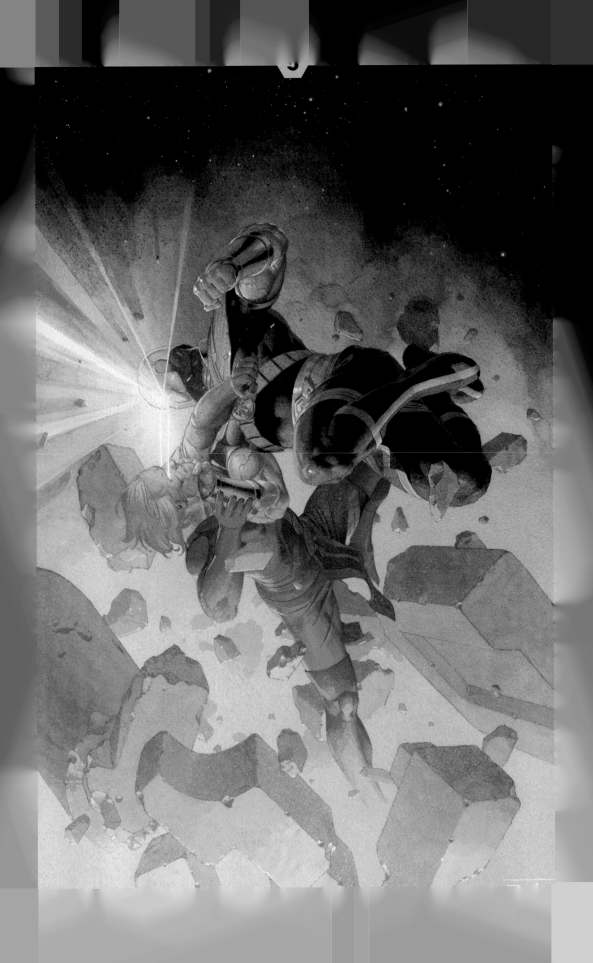

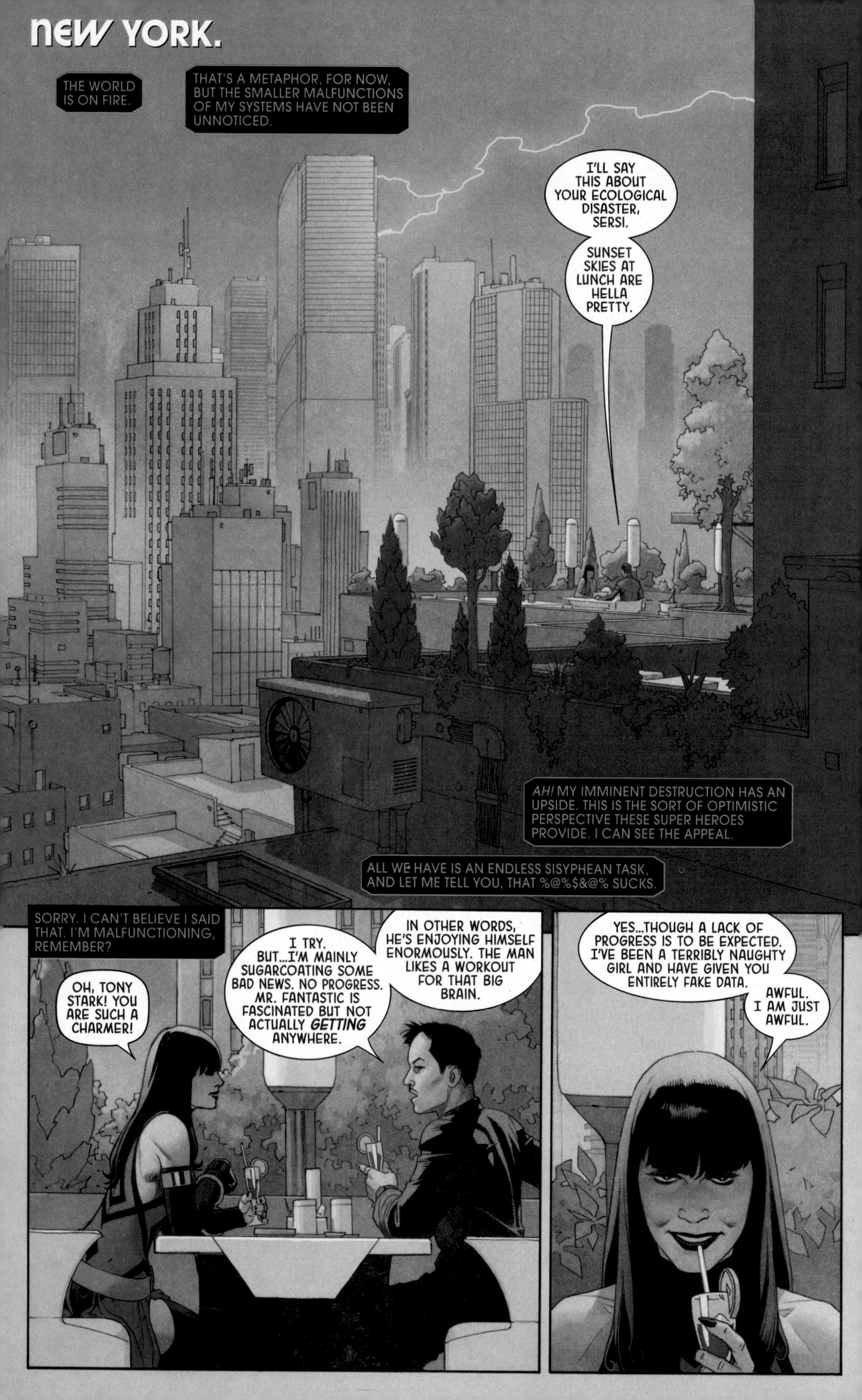
NEW YORK.
THE WORLD IS ON FIRE.
THAT'S A METAPHOR, FOR NOW, BUT THE SMALLER MALFUNCTIONS OF MY SYSTEMS HAVE NOT BEEN UNNOTICED.
I'LL SAY THIS ABOUT YOUR ECOLOGICAL DISASTER, SERSI.
SUNSET SKIES AT LUNCH ARE HELLA PRETTY.
AH! MY IMMINENT DESTRUCTION HAS AN UPSIDE. THIS IS THE SORT OF OPTIMISTIC PERSPECTIVE THESE SUPER HEROES PROVIDE. I CAN SEE THE APPEAL.
ALL WE HAVE IS AN ENDLESS SISYPHEAN TASK, AND LET ME TELL YOU, THAT %@%$&@% SUCKS.
SORRY. I CAN'T BELIEVE I SAID THAT. I'M MALFUNCTIONING, REMEMBER?
OH, TONY STARK! YOU ARE SUCH A CHARMER!
I TRY. BUT...I'M MAINLY SUGARCOATING SOME BAD NEWS. NO PROGRESS. MR. FANTASTIC IS FASCINATED BUT NOT ACTUALLY GETTING ANYWHERE.
IN OTHER WORDS, HE'S ENJOYING HIMSELF ENORMOUSLY. THE MAN LIKES A WORKOUT FOR THAT BIG BRAIN.
YES...THOUGH A LACK OF PROGRESS IS TO BE EXPECTED. I'VE BEEN A TERRIBLY NAUGHTY GIRL AND HAVE GIVEN YOU ENTIRELY FAKE DATA.
AWFUL. I AM JUST AWFUL.

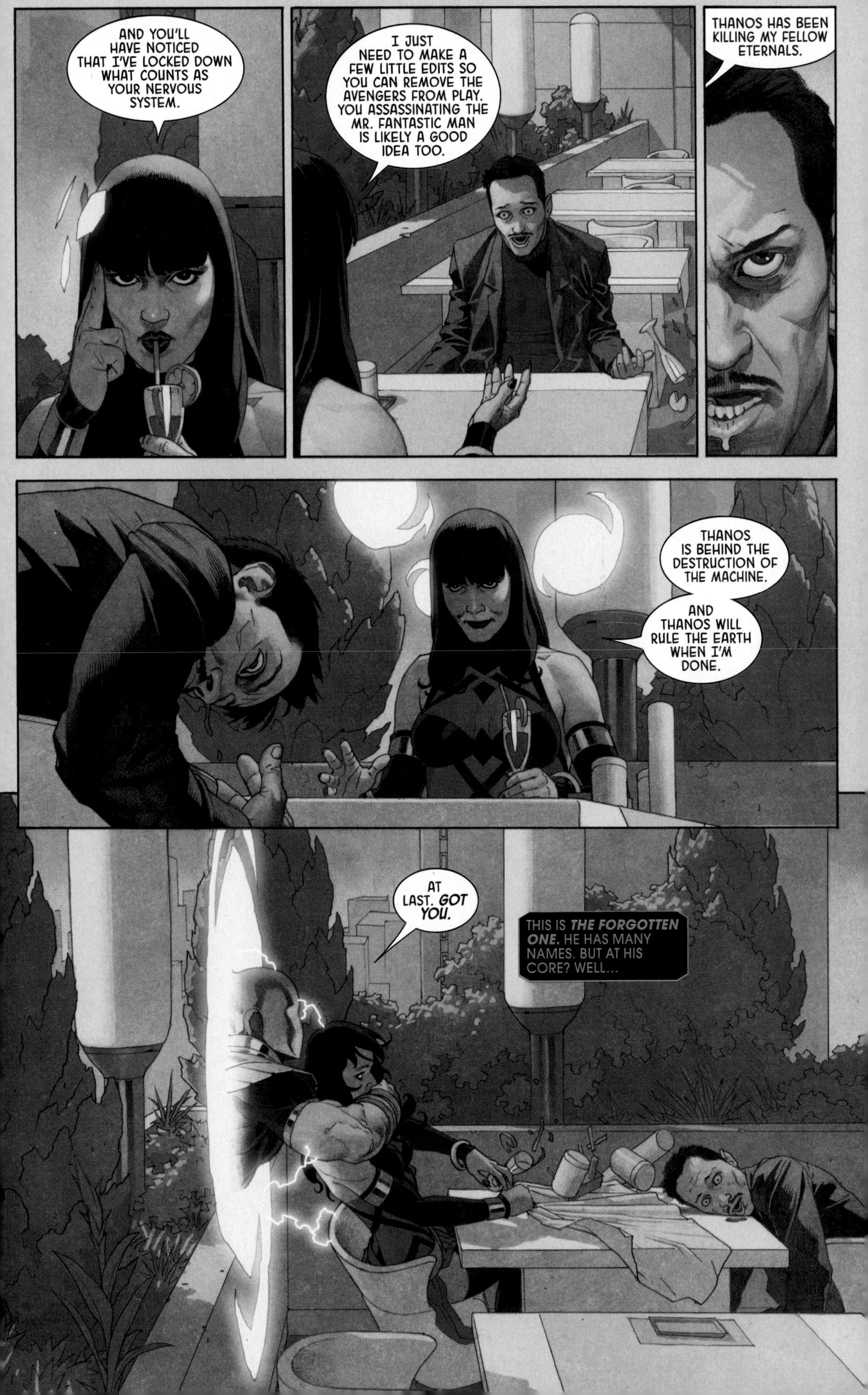
AND YOU'LL HAVE NOTICED THAT I'VE LOCKED DOWN WHAT COUNTS AS YOUR NERVOUS SYSTEM.
I JUST NEED TO MAKE A FEW LITTLE EDITS SO YOU CAN REMOVE THE AVENGERS FROM PLAY. YOU ASSASSINATING THE MR. FANTASTIC MAN IS LIKELY A GOOD IDEA TOO.
THANOS HAS BEEN KILLING MY FELLOW ETERNALS.
THANOS IS BEHIND THE DESTRUCTION OF THE MACHINE.
AND THANOS WILL RULE THE EARTH WHEN I'M DONE.
AT LAST. GOT YOU.
THIS IS THE FORGOTTEN ONE. HE HAS MANY NAMES. BUT AT HIS CORE? WELL...

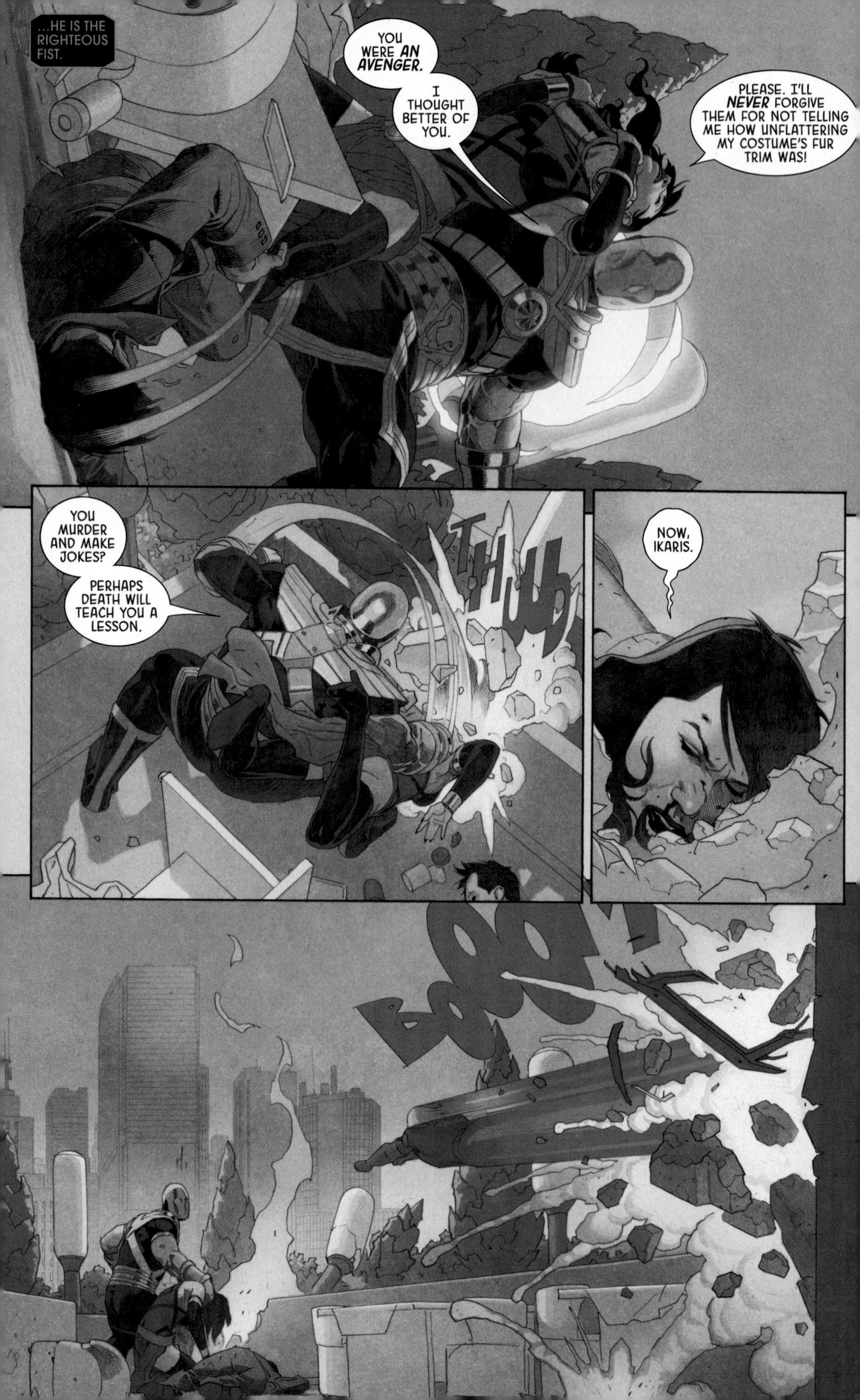

...HE IS THE RIGHTEOUS FIST.
YOU WERE AN AVENGER.
I THOUGHT BETTER OF YOU.
PLEASE. I'LL NEVER FORGIVE THEM FOR NOT TELLING ME HOW UNFLATTERING MY COSTUME'S FUR TRIM WAS!
YOU MURDER AND MAKE JOKES?
PERHAPS DEATH WILL TEACH YOU A LESSON.
THUD
NOW, IKARIS.
BOOOM

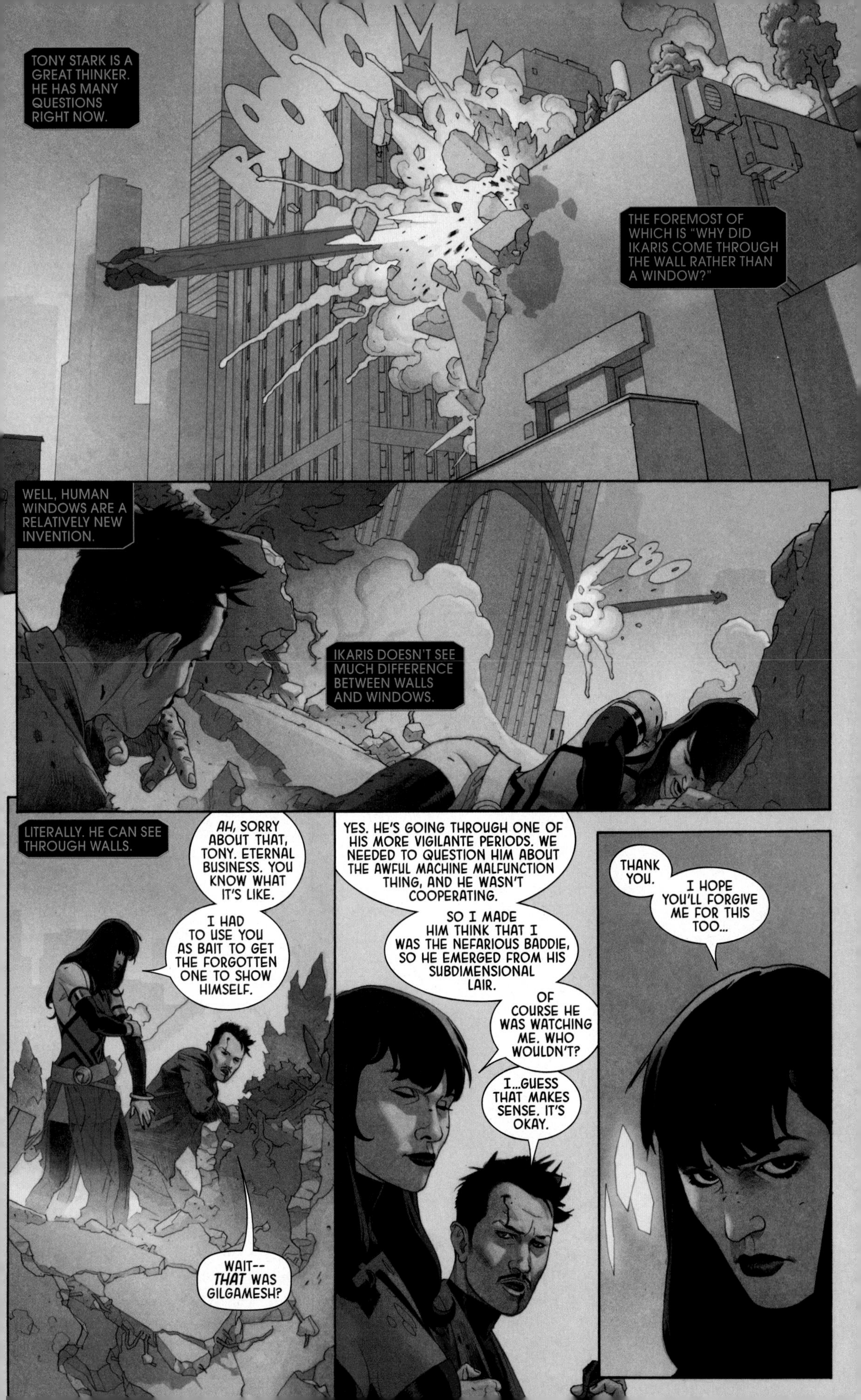
TONY STARK IS A GREAT THINKER. HE HAS MANY QUESTIONS RIGHT NOW.
THE FOREMOST OF WHICH IS "WHY DID IKARIS COME THROUGH THE WALL RATHER THAN A WINDOW?"
WELL, HUMAN WINDOWS ARE A RELATIVELY NEW INVENTION.
IKARIS DOESN'T SEE MUCH DIFFERENCE BETWEEN WALLS AND WINDOWS.
LITERALLY. HE CAN SEE THROUGH WALLS.
AH, SORRY ABOUT THAT, TONY. ETERNAL BUSINESS. YOU KNOW WHAT IT'S LIKE.
I HAD TO USE YOU AS BAIT TO GET THE FORGOTTEN ONE TO SHOW HIMSELF.
WAIT-- *THAT* WAS GILGAMESH?
YES. HE'S GOING THROUGH ONE OF HIS MORE VIGILANTE PERIODS. WE NEEDED TO QUESTION HIM ABOUT THE AWFUL MACHINE MALFUNCTION THING, AND HE WASN'T COOPERATING.
SO I MADE HIM THINK THAT I WAS THE NEFARIOUS BADDIE, SO HE EMERGED FROM HIS SUBDIMENSIONAL LAIR.
OF COURSE HE WAS WATCHING ME. WHO WOULDN'T?
I...GUESS THAT MAKES SENSE. IT'S OKAY.
THANK YOU.
I HOPE YOU'LL FORGIVE ME FOR THIS TOO...

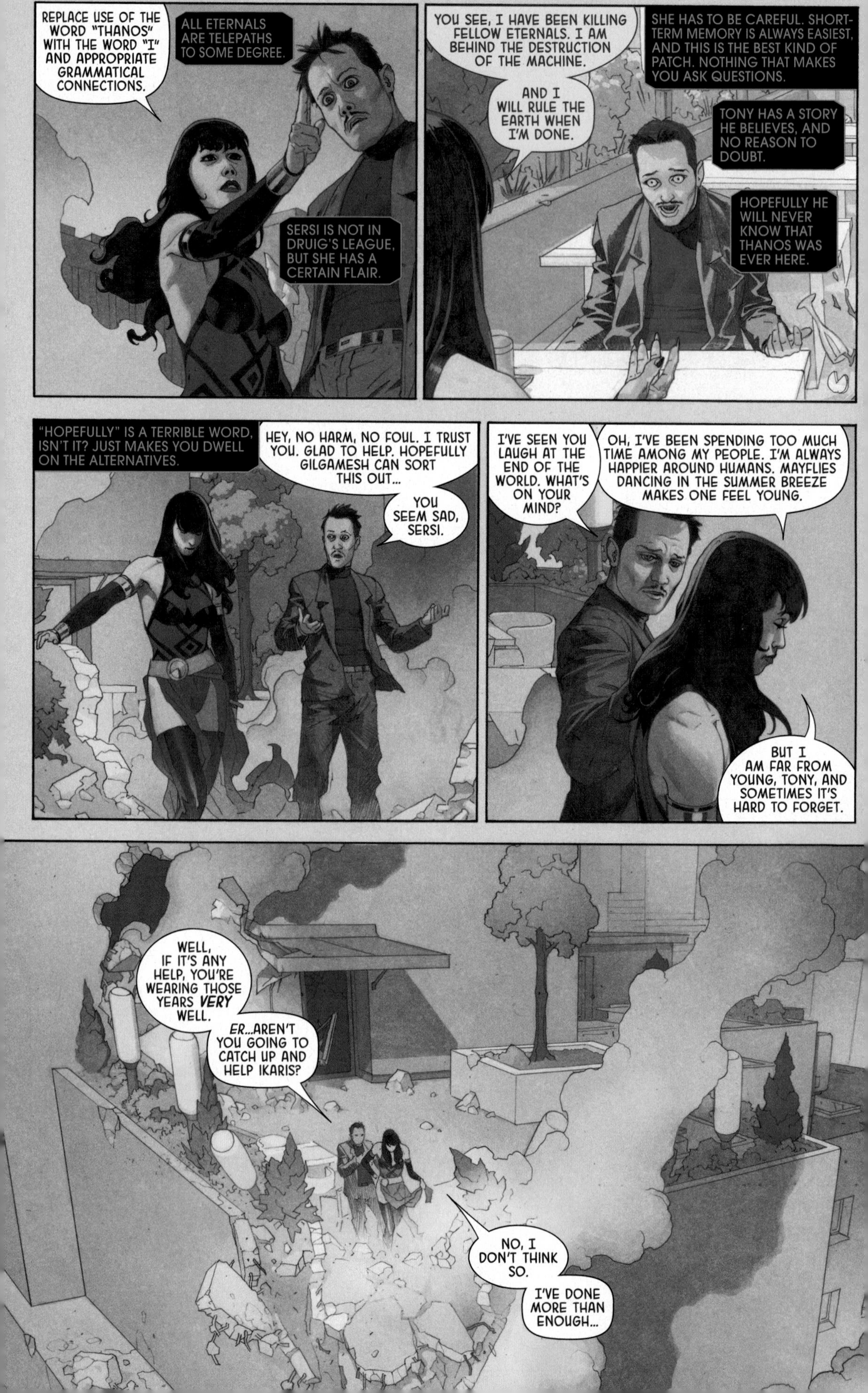
REPLACE USE OF THE WORD "THANOS" WITH THE WORD "I" AND APPROPRIATE GRAMMATICAL CONNECTIONS.
ALL ETERNALS ARE TELEPATHS TO SOME DEGREE.
SERSI IS NOT IN DRUIG'S LEAGUE, BUT SHE HAS A CERTAIN FLAIR.
YOU SEE, I HAVE BEEN KILLING FELLOW ETERNALS. I AM BEHIND THE DESTRUCTION OF THE MACHINE.
AND I WILL RULE THE EARTH WHEN I'M DONE.
SHE HAS TO BE CAREFUL. SHORT-TERM MEMORY IS ALWAYS EASIEST, AND THIS IS THE BEST KIND OF PATCH. NOTHING THAT MAKES YOU ASK QUESTIONS.
TONY HAS A STORY HE BELIEVES, AND NO REASON TO DOUBT.
HOPEFULLY HE WILL NEVER KNOW THAT THANOS WAS EVER HERE.
"HOPEFULLY" IS A TERRIBLE WORD, ISN'T IT? JUST MAKES YOU DWELL ON THE ALTERNATIVES.
HEY, NO HARM, NO FOUL. I TRUST YOU. GLAD TO HELP. HOPEFULLY GILGAMESH CAN SORT THIS OUT...
YOU SEEM SAD, SERSI.
I'VE SEEN YOU LAUGH AT THE END OF THE WORLD. WHAT'S ON YOUR MIND?
OH, I'VE BEEN SPENDING TOO MUCH TIME AMONG MY PEOPLE. I'M ALWAYS HAPPIER AROUND HUMANS. MAYFLIES DANCING IN THE SUMMER BREEZE MAKES ONE FEEL YOUNG.
BUT I AM FAR FROM YOUNG, TONY, AND SOMETIMES IT'S HARD TO FORGET.
WELL, IF IT'S ANY HELP, YOU'RE WEARING THOSE YEARS VERY WELL.
ER...AREN'T YOU GOING TO CATCH UP AND HELP IKARIS?
NO, I DON'T THINK SO.
I'VE DONE MORE THAN ENOUGH...

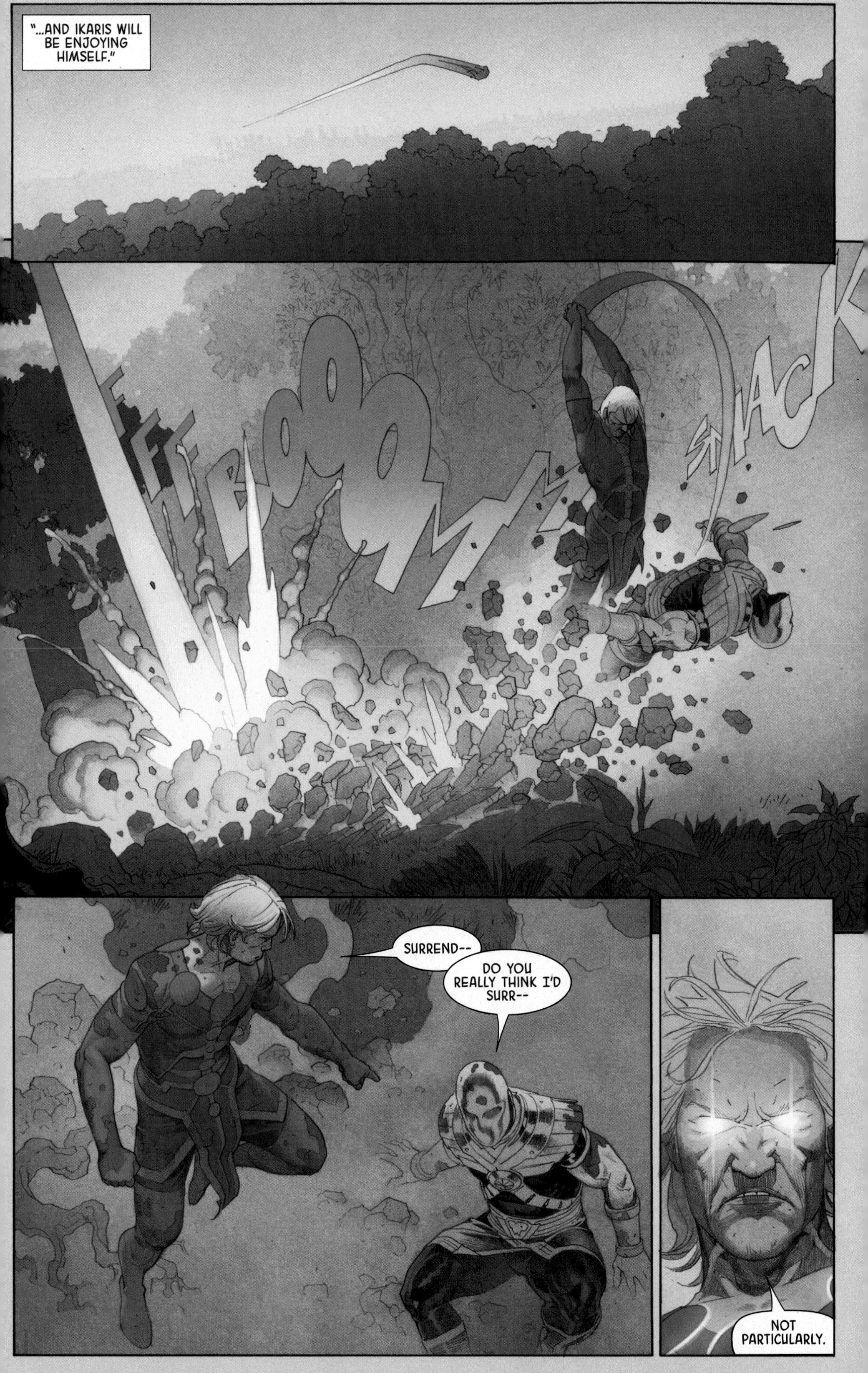
"...AND IKARIS WILL BE ENJOYING HIMSELF."
FFFBOOOOMMM
SMACK
SURREND--
DO YOU REALLY THINK I'D SURR--
NOT PARTICULARLY.

THE FORGOTTEN ONE
Specialism: Heroism.

UTUNAA
Specialism: Morale, intelligence.

DUMUZA
Specialism: Support, logistics.

ISHTA
Specialism: Underworld operations.

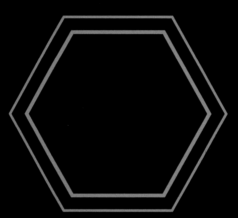

THE FORGOTTEN

The Forgotten are a relatively new group in the Eternal political system, dating back less than 10,000 years.

All records of the true Eternal name of the Forgotten One have been removed from the Machine. He has worked under many aliases. For example, he served in the human extra-normal paramilitary force "the Avengers" as "Gilgamesh." He is a human-centric radical, defining the Second Principle ("Protect the Machine") broadly to include prioritizing human welfare above Eternal welfare.

He noted: "A wise human once said—If God did not exist, we would have to invent him. I would agree entirely. We need something to be afraid of. I'm stepping into the role. I'm stepping on the necks that need to be stepped on."

The other Forgotten joined the Forgotten One. They have removed themselves from the Uni-Mind to act as a deterrent to Eternal abuse of humanity.

The Forgotten One likes to think of his extrajudicial activities to defend common people against unjust authority akin to the British folkloric character Robin Hood. The other Eternals would argue that he's more like the American criminal vigilante Frank Castle (A.K.A. The Punisher).

Aren't opinions amazing?

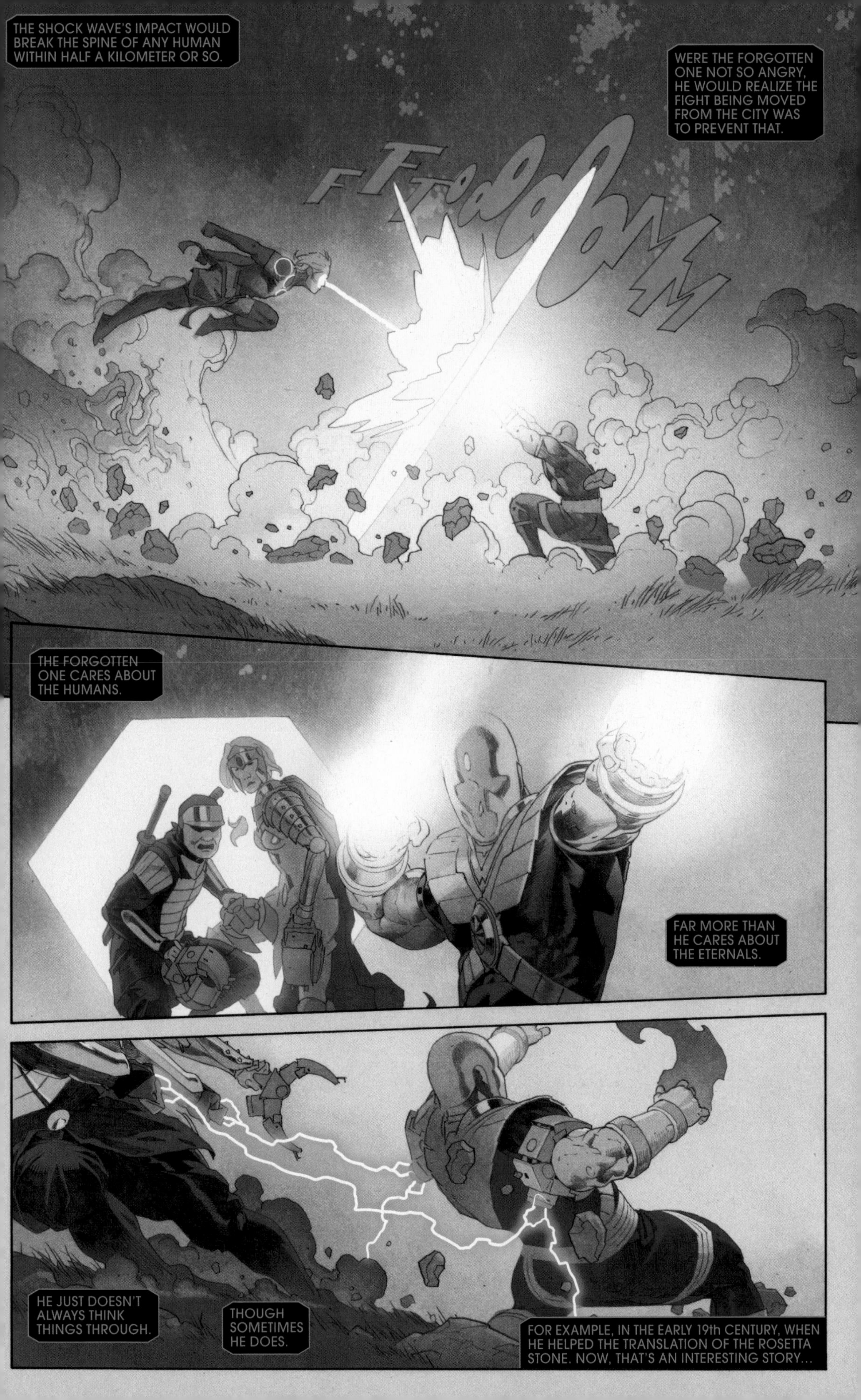
THE SHOCK WAVE'S IMPACT WOULD BREAK THE SPINE OF ANY HUMAN WITHIN HALF A KILOMETER OR SO.
WERE THE FORGOTTEN ONE NOT SO ANGRY, HE WOULD REALIZE THE FIGHT BEING MOVED FROM THE CITY WAS TO PREVENT THAT.
FFTOOOOOM
THE FORGOTTEN ONE CARES ABOUT THE HUMANS.
FAR MORE THAN HE CARES ABOUT THE ETERNALS.
HE JUST DOESN'T ALWAYS THINK THINGS THROUGH.
THOUGH SOMETIMES HE DOES.
FOR EXAMPLE, IN THE EARLY 19th CENTURY, WHEN HE HELPED THE TRANSLATION OF THE ROSETTA STONE. NOW, THAT'S AN INTERESTING STORY...

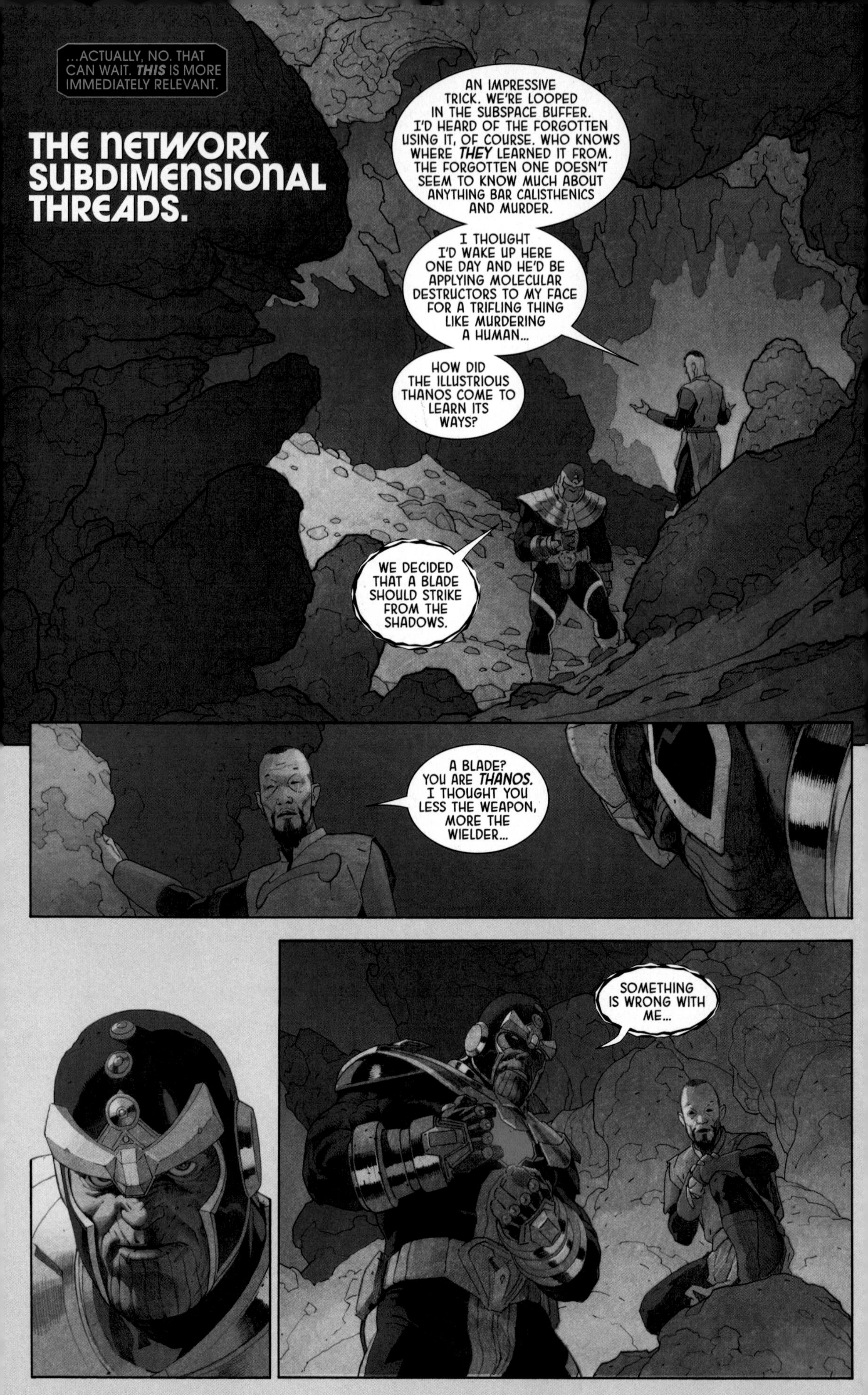
...ACTUALLY, NO. THAT CAN WAIT. THIS IS MORE IMMEDIATELY RELEVANT.
THE NETWORK SUBDIMENSIONAL THREADS.
AN IMPRESSIVE TRICK. WE'RE LOOPED IN THE SUBSPACE BUFFER. I'D HEARD OF THE FORGOTTEN USING IT, OF COURSE. WHO KNOWS WHERE THEY LEARNED IT FROM. THE FORGOTTEN ONE DOESN'T SEEM TO KNOW MUCH ABOUT ANYTHING BAR CALISTHENICS AND MURDER.
I THOUGHT I'D WAKE UP HERE ONE DAY AND HE'D BE APPLYING MOLECULAR DESTRUCTORS TO MY FACE FOR A TRIFLING THING LIKE MURDERING A HUMAN...
HOW DID THE ILLUSTRIOUS THANOS COME TO LEARN ITS WAYS?
WE DECIDED THAT A BLADE SHOULD STRIKE FROM THE SHADOWS.
A BLADE? YOU ARE THANOS. I THOUGHT YOU LESS THE WEAPON, MORE THE WIELDER...
SOMETHING IS WRONG WITH ME...

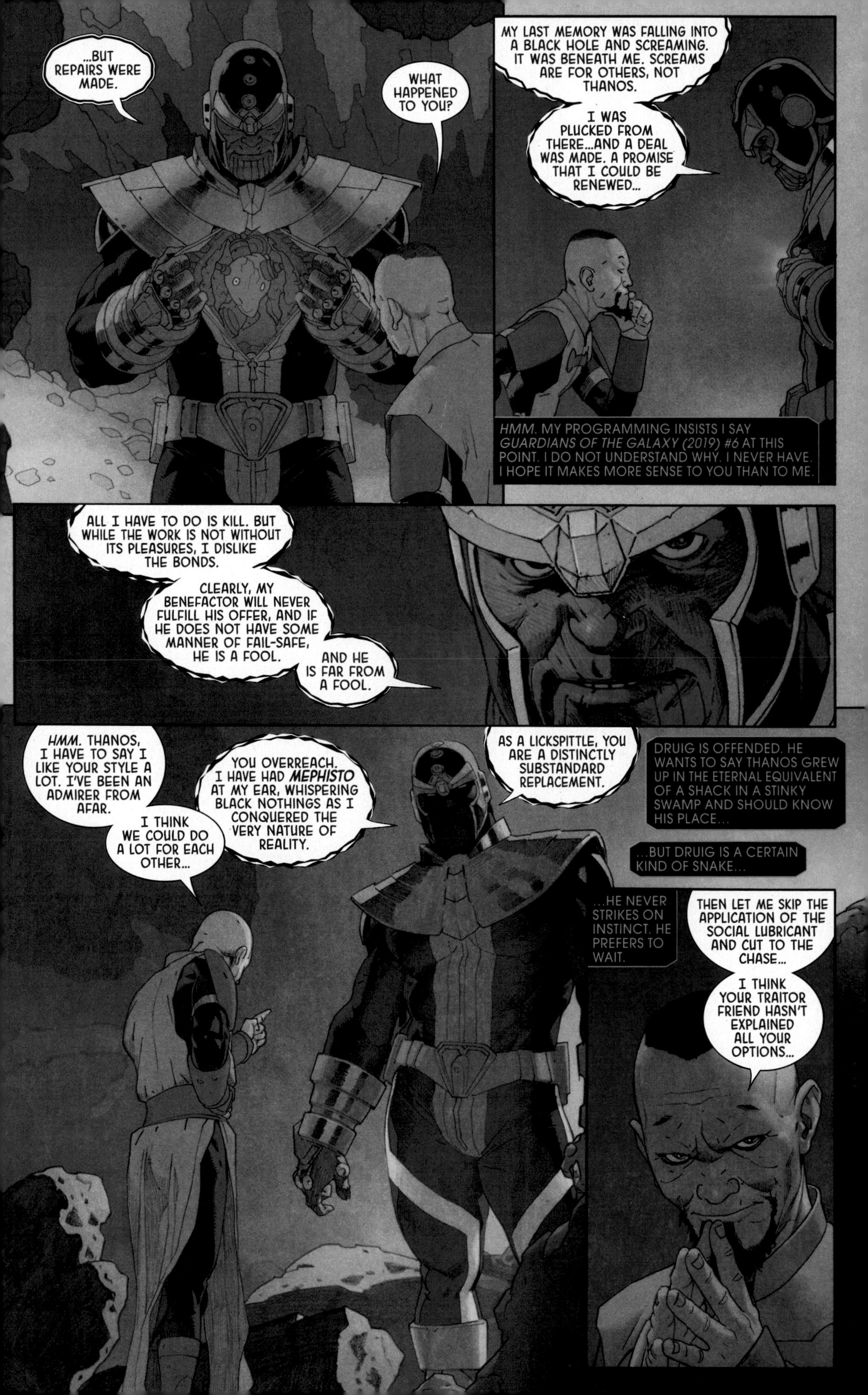
...BUT REPAIRS WERE MADE.
WHAT HAPPENED TO YOU?
MY LAST MEMORY WAS FALLING INTO A BLACK HOLE AND SCREAMING. IT WAS BENEATH ME. SCREAMS ARE FOR OTHERS, NOT THANOS.
I WAS PLUCKED FROM THERE...AND A DEAL WAS MADE. A PROMISE THAT I COULD BE RENEWED...
HMM. MY PROGRAMMING INSISTS I SAY GUARDIANS OF THE GALAXY (2019) #6 AT THIS POINT. I DO NOT UNDERSTAND WHY. I NEVER HAVE. I HOPE IT MAKES MORE SENSE TO YOU THAN TO ME.
ALL I HAVE TO DO IS KILL. BUT WHILE THE WORK IS NOT WITHOUT ITS PLEASURES, I DISLIKE THE BONDS.
CLEARLY, MY BENEFACTOR WILL NEVER FULFILL HIS OFFER, AND IF HE DOES NOT HAVE SOME MANNER OF FAIL-SAFE, HE IS A FOOL.
AND HE IS FAR FROM A FOOL.
HMM. THANOS, I HAVE TO SAY I LIKE YOUR STYLE A LOT. I'VE BEEN AN ADMIRER FROM AFAR.
I THINK WE COULD DO A LOT FOR EACH OTHER...
YOU OVERREACH. I HAVE HAD MEPHISTO AT MY EAR, WHISPERING BLACK NOTHINGS AS I CONQUERED THE VERY NATURE OF REALITY.
AS A LICKSPITTLE, YOU ARE A DISTINCTLY SUBSTANDARD REPLACEMENT.
DRUIG IS OFFENDED. HE WANTS TO SAY THANOS GREW UP IN THE ETERNAL EQUIVALENT OF A SHACK IN A STINKY SWAMP AND SHOULD KNOW HIS PLACE...
...BUT DRUIG IS A CERTAIN KIND OF SNAKE...
...HE NEVER STRIKES ON INSTINCT. HE PREFERS TO WAIT.
THEN LET ME SKIP THE APPLICATION OF THE SOCIAL LUBRICANT AND CUT TO THE CHASE...
I THINK YOUR TRAITOR FRIEND HASN'T EXPLAINED ALL YOUR OPTIONS...

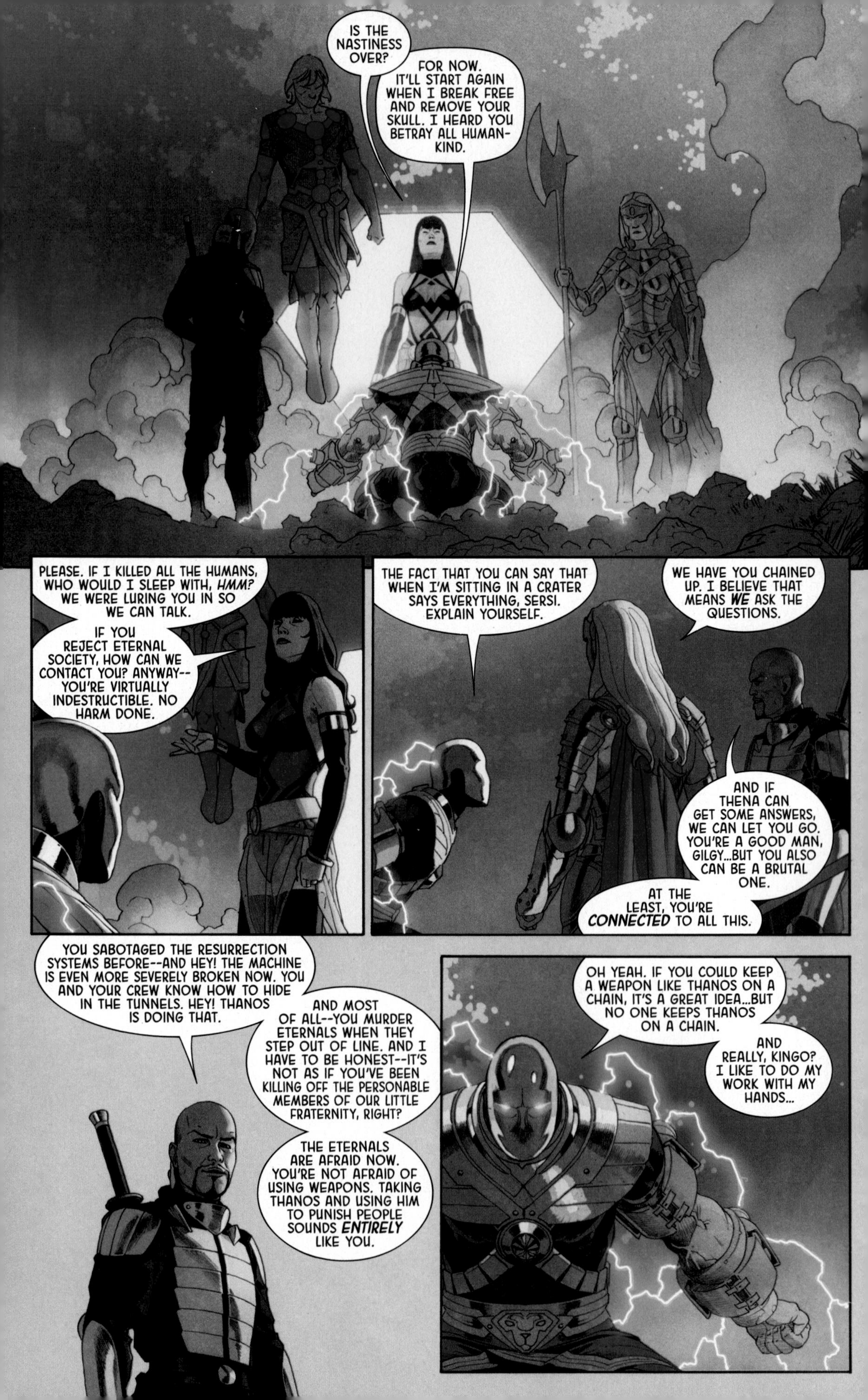
IS THE NASTINESS OVER?
FOR NOW. IT'LL START AGAIN WHEN I BREAK FREE AND REMOVE YOUR SKULL. I HEARD YOU BETRAY ALL HUMAN-KIND.
PLEASE. IF I KILLED ALL THE HUMANS, WHO WOULD I SLEEP WITH, HMM? WE WERE LURING YOU IN SO WE CAN TALK.
IF YOU REJECT ETERNAL SOCIETY, HOW CAN WE CONTACT YOU? ANYWAY--YOU'RE VIRTUALLY INDESTRUCTIBLE. NO HARM DONE.
THE FACT THAT YOU CAN SAY THAT WHEN I'M SITTING IN A CRATER SAYS EVERYTHING, SERSI. EXPLAIN YOURSELF.
WE HAVE YOU CHAINED UP. I BELIEVE THAT MEANS WE ASK THE QUESTIONS.
AND IF THENA CAN GET SOME ANSWERS, WE CAN LET YOU GO. YOU'RE A GOOD MAN, GILGY...BUT YOU ALSO CAN BE A BRUTAL ONE.
AT THE LEAST, YOU'RE CONNECTED TO ALL THIS.
YOU SABOTAGED THE RESURRECTION SYSTEMS BEFORE--AND HEY! THE MACHINE IS EVEN MORE SEVERELY BROKEN NOW. YOU AND YOUR CREW KNOW HOW TO HIDE IN THE TUNNELS. HEY! THANOS IS DOING THAT.
AND MOST OF ALL--YOU MURDER ETERNALS WHEN THEY STEP OUT OF LINE. AND I HAVE TO BE HONEST--IT'S NOT AS IF YOU'VE BEEN KILLING OFF THE PERSONABLE MEMBERS OF OUR LITTLE FRATERNITY, RIGHT?
THE ETERNALS ARE AFRAID NOW. YOU'RE NOT AFRAID OF USING WEAPONS. TAKING THANOS AND USING HIM TO PUNISH PEOPLE SOUNDS ENTIRELY LIKE YOU.
OH YEAH. IF YOU COULD KEEP A WEAPON LIKE THANOS ON A CHAIN, IT'S A GREAT IDEA...BUT NO ONE KEEPS THANOS ON A CHAIN.
AND REALLY, KINGO? I LIKE TO DO MY WORK WITH MY HANDS...

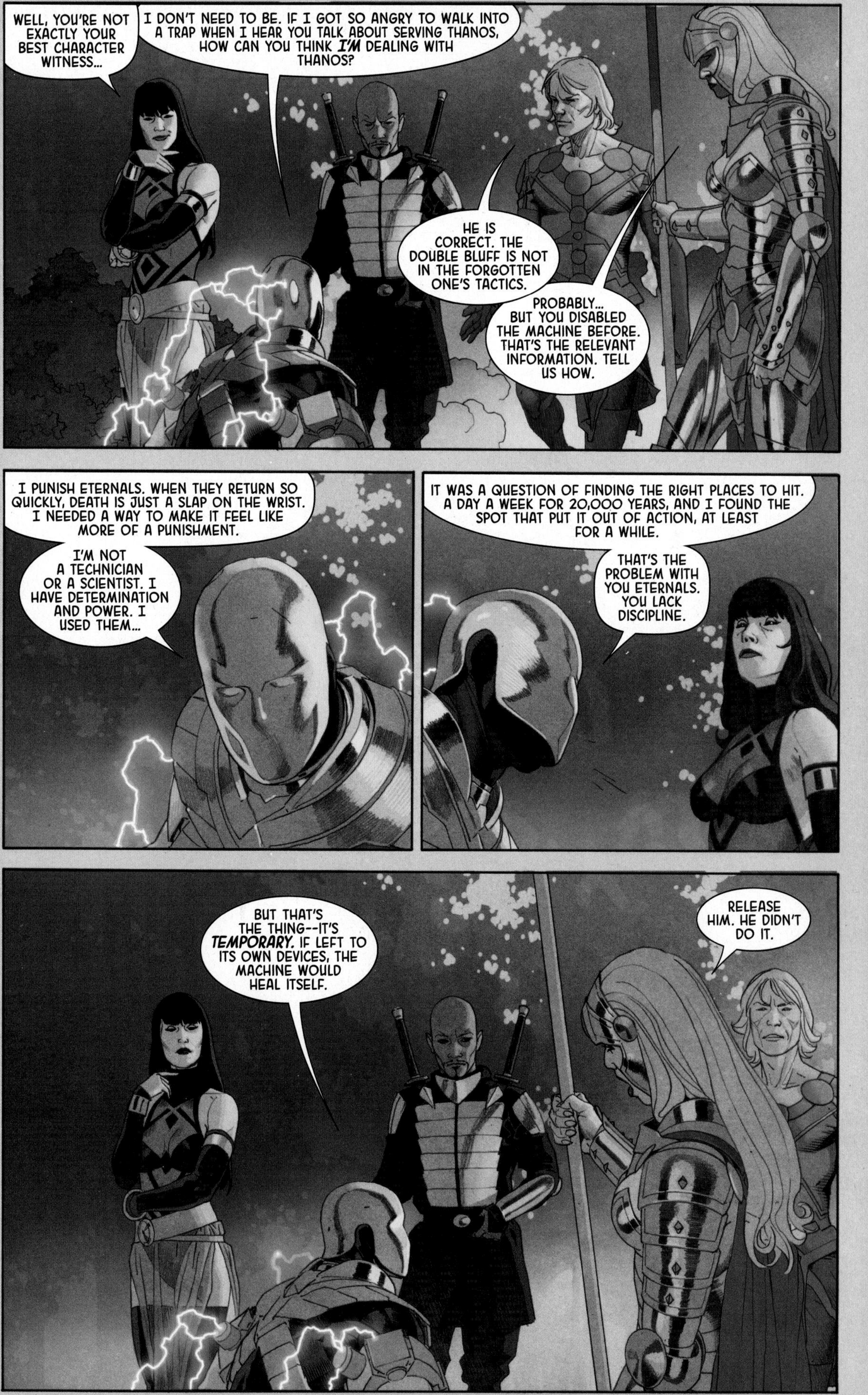
WELL, YOU'RE NOT EXACTLY YOUR BEST CHARACTER WITNESS...
I DON'T NEED TO BE. IF I GOT SO ANGRY TO WALK INTO A TRAP WHEN I HEAR YOU TALK ABOUT SERVING THANOS, HOW CAN YOU THINK ***I'M*** DEALING WITH THANOS?
HE IS CORRECT. THE DOUBLE BLUFF IS NOT IN THE FORGOTTEN ONE'S TACTICS.
PROBABLY... BUT YOU DISABLED THE MACHINE BEFORE. THAT'S THE RELEVANT INFORMATION. TELL US HOW.
I PUNISH ETERNALS. WHEN THEY RETURN SO QUICKLY, DEATH IS JUST A SLAP ON THE WRIST. I NEEDED A WAY TO MAKE IT FEEL LIKE MORE OF A PUNISHMENT.
I'M NOT A TECHNICIAN OR A SCIENTIST. I HAVE DETERMINATION AND POWER. I USED THEM...
IT WAS A QUESTION OF FINDING THE RIGHT PLACES TO HIT. A DAY A WEEK FOR 20,000 YEARS, AND I FOUND THE SPOT THAT PUT IT OUT OF ACTION, AT LEAST FOR A WHILE.
THAT'S THE PROBLEM WITH YOU ETERNALS. YOU LACK DISCIPLINE.
BUT THAT'S THE THING--IT'S ***TEMPORARY.*** IF LEFT TO ITS OWN DEVICES, THE MACHINE WOULD HEAL ITSELF.
RELEASE HIM. HE DIDN'T DO IT.

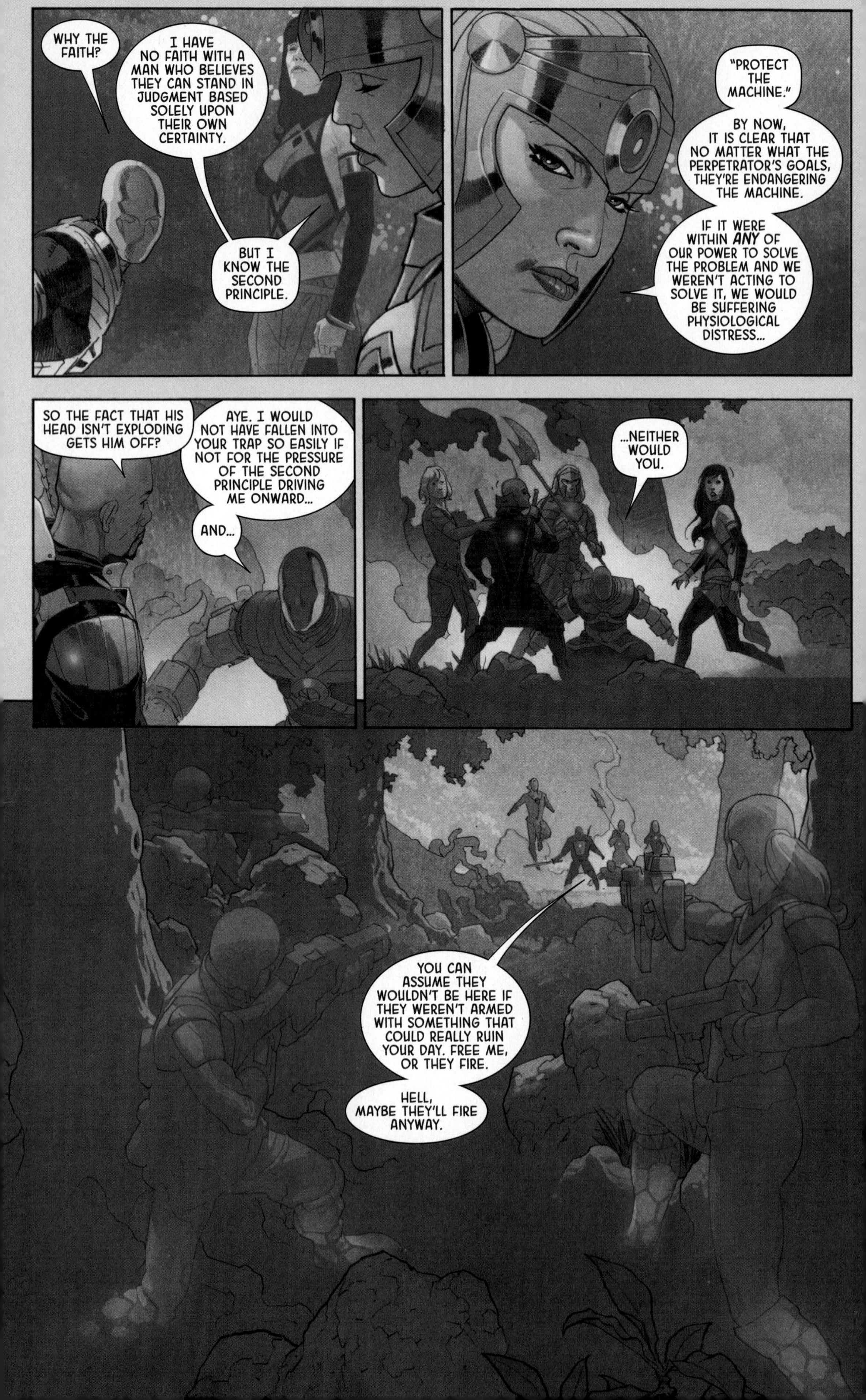
WHY THE FAITH?
I HAVE NO FAITH WITH A MAN WHO BELIEVES THEY CAN STAND IN JUDGMENT BASED SOLELY UPON THEIR OWN CERTAINTY.
BUT I KNOW THE SECOND PRINCIPLE.
"PROTECT THE MACHINE."
BY NOW, IT IS CLEAR THAT NO MATTER WHAT THE PERPETRATOR'S GOALS, THEY'RE ENDANGERING THE MACHINE.
IF IT WERE WITHIN ANY OF OUR POWER TO SOLVE THE PROBLEM AND WE WEREN'T ACTING TO SOLVE IT, WE WOULD BE SUFFERING PHYSIOLOGICAL DISTRESS...
SO THE FACT THAT HIS HEAD ISN'T EXPLODING GETS HIM OFF?
AYE. I WOULD NOT HAVE FALLEN INTO YOUR TRAP SO EASILY IF NOT FOR THE PRESSURE OF THE SECOND PRINCIPLE DRIVING ME ONWARD...
AND...
...NEITHER WOULD YOU.
YOU CAN ASSUME THEY WOULDN'T BE HERE IF THEY WEREN'T ARMED WITH SOMETHING THAT COULD REALLY RUIN YOUR DAY. FREE ME, OR THEY FIRE.
HELL, MAYBE THEY'LL FIRE ANYWAY.

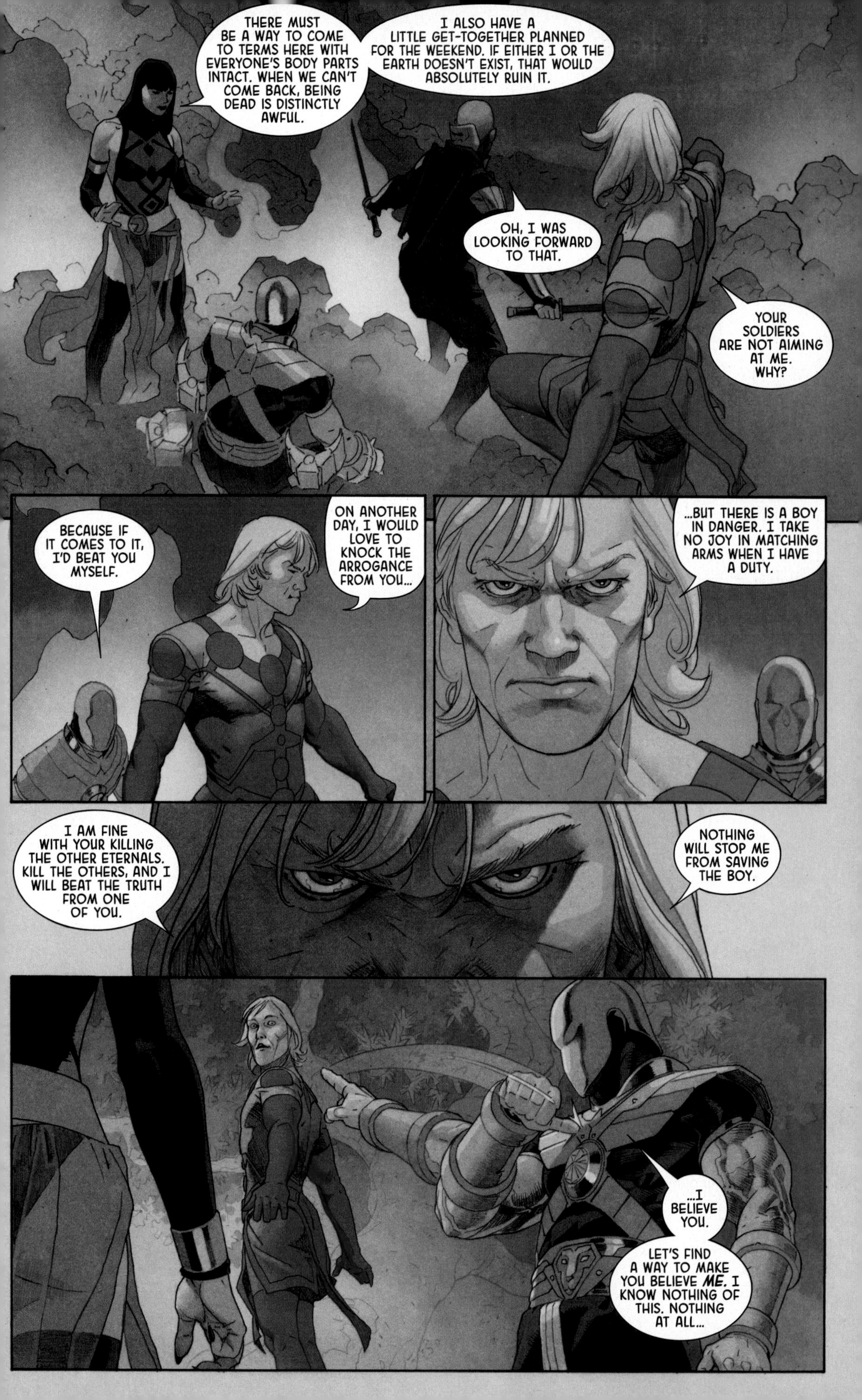
THERE MUST BE A WAY TO COME TO TERMS HERE WITH EVERYONE'S BODY PARTS INTACT. WHEN WE CAN'T COME BACK, BEING DEAD IS DISTINCTLY AWFUL.
I ALSO HAVE A LITTLE GET-TOGETHER PLANNED FOR THE WEEKEND. IF EITHER I OR THE EARTH DOESN'T EXIST, THAT WOULD ABSOLUTELY RUIN IT.
OH, I WAS LOOKING FORWARD TO THAT.
YOUR SOLDIERS ARE NOT AIMING AT ME. WHY?
BECAUSE IF IT COMES TO IT, I'D BEAT YOU MYSELF.
ON ANOTHER DAY, I WOULD LOVE TO KNOCK THE ARROGANCE FROM YOU...
...BUT THERE IS A BOY IN DANGER. I TAKE NO JOY IN MATCHING ARMS WHEN I HAVE A DUTY.
I AM FINE WITH YOUR KILLING THE OTHER ETERNALS. KILL THE OTHERS, AND I WILL BEAT THE TRUTH FROM ONE OF YOU.
NOTHING WILL STOP ME FROM SAVING THE BOY.
...I BELIEVE YOU.
LET'S FIND A WAY TO MAKE YOU BELIEVE ***ME.*** I KNOW NOTHING OF THIS. NOTHING AT ALL...

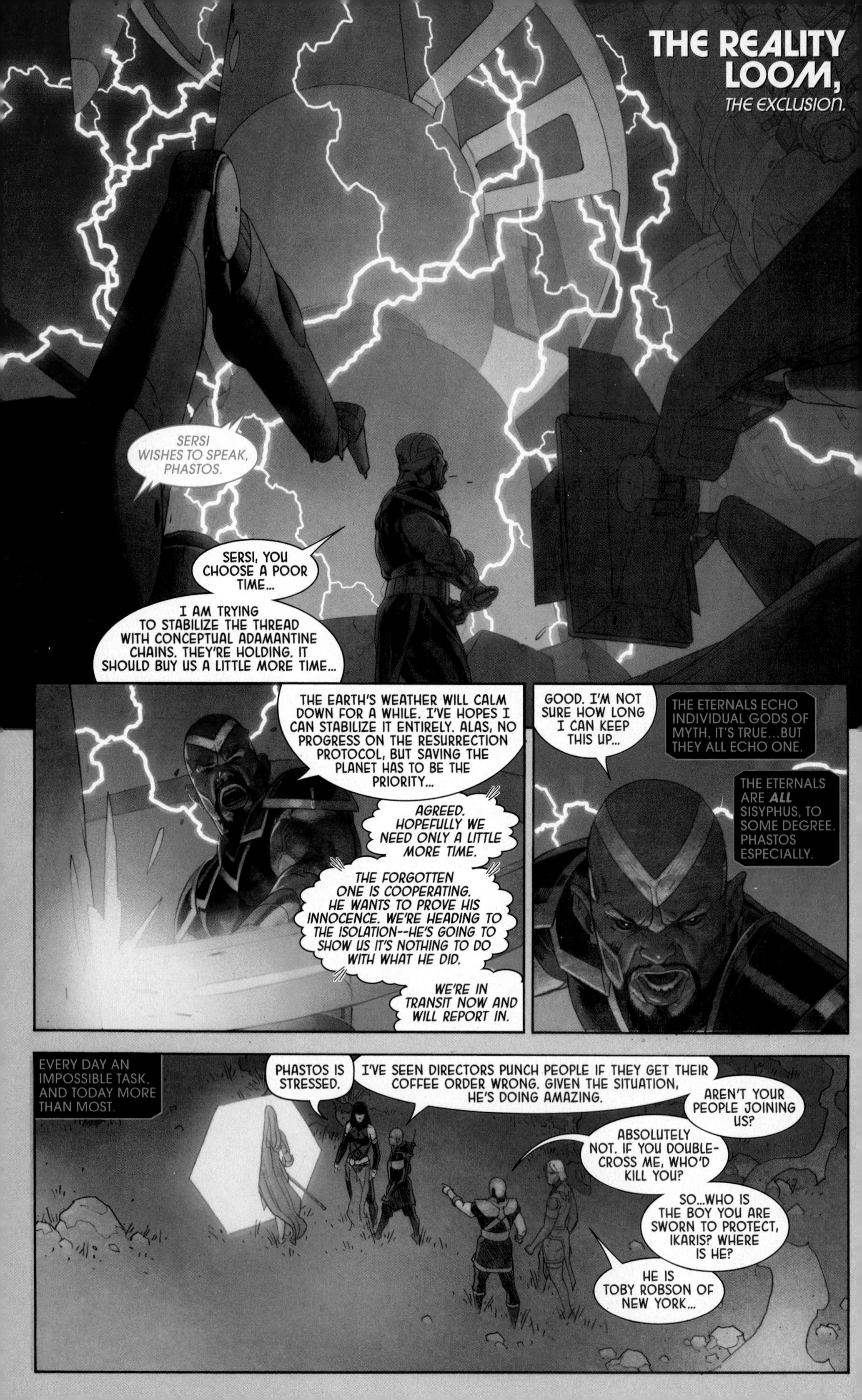
THE REALITY LOOM,
THE EXCLUSION.
SERSI WISHES TO SPEAK, PHASTOS.
SERSI, YOU CHOOSE A POOR TIME...
I AM TRYING TO STABILIZE THE THREAD WITH CONCEPTUAL ADAMANTINE CHAINS. THEY'RE HOLDING. IT SHOULD BUY US A LITTLE MORE TIME...
THE EARTH'S WEATHER WILL CALM DOWN FOR A WHILE. I'VE HOPES I CAN STABILIZE IT ENTIRELY. ALAS, NO PROGRESS ON THE RESURRECTION PROTOCOL, BUT SAVING THE PLANET HAS TO BE THE PRIORITY...
AGREED. HOPEFULLY WE NEED ONLY A LITTLE MORE TIME.
THE FORGOTTEN ONE IS COOPERATING. HE WANTS TO PROVE HIS INNOCENCE. WE'RE HEADING TO THE ISOLATION--HE'S GOING TO SHOW US IT'S NOTHING TO DO WITH WHAT HE DID.
WE'RE IN TRANSIT NOW AND WILL REPORT IN.
GOOD. I'M NOT SURE HOW LONG I CAN KEEP THIS UP...
THE ETERNALS ECHO INDIVIDUAL GODS OF MYTH, IT'S TRUE...BUT THEY ALL ECHO ONE.
THE ETERNALS ARE ALL SISYPHUS, TO SOME DEGREE. PHASTOS ESPECIALLY.
EVERY DAY AN IMPOSSIBLE TASK, AND TODAY MORE THAN MOST.
PHASTOS IS STRESSED.
I'VE SEEN DIRECTORS PUNCH PEOPLE IF THEY GET THEIR COFFEE ORDER WRONG. GIVEN THE SITUATION, HE'S DOING AMAZING.
AREN'T YOUR PEOPLE JOINING US?
ABSOLUTELY NOT. IF YOU DOUBLE-CROSS ME, WHO'D KILL YOU?
SO...WHO IS THE BOY YOU ARE SWORN TO PROTECT, IKARIS? WHERE IS HE?
HE IS TOBY ROBSON OF NEW YORK...

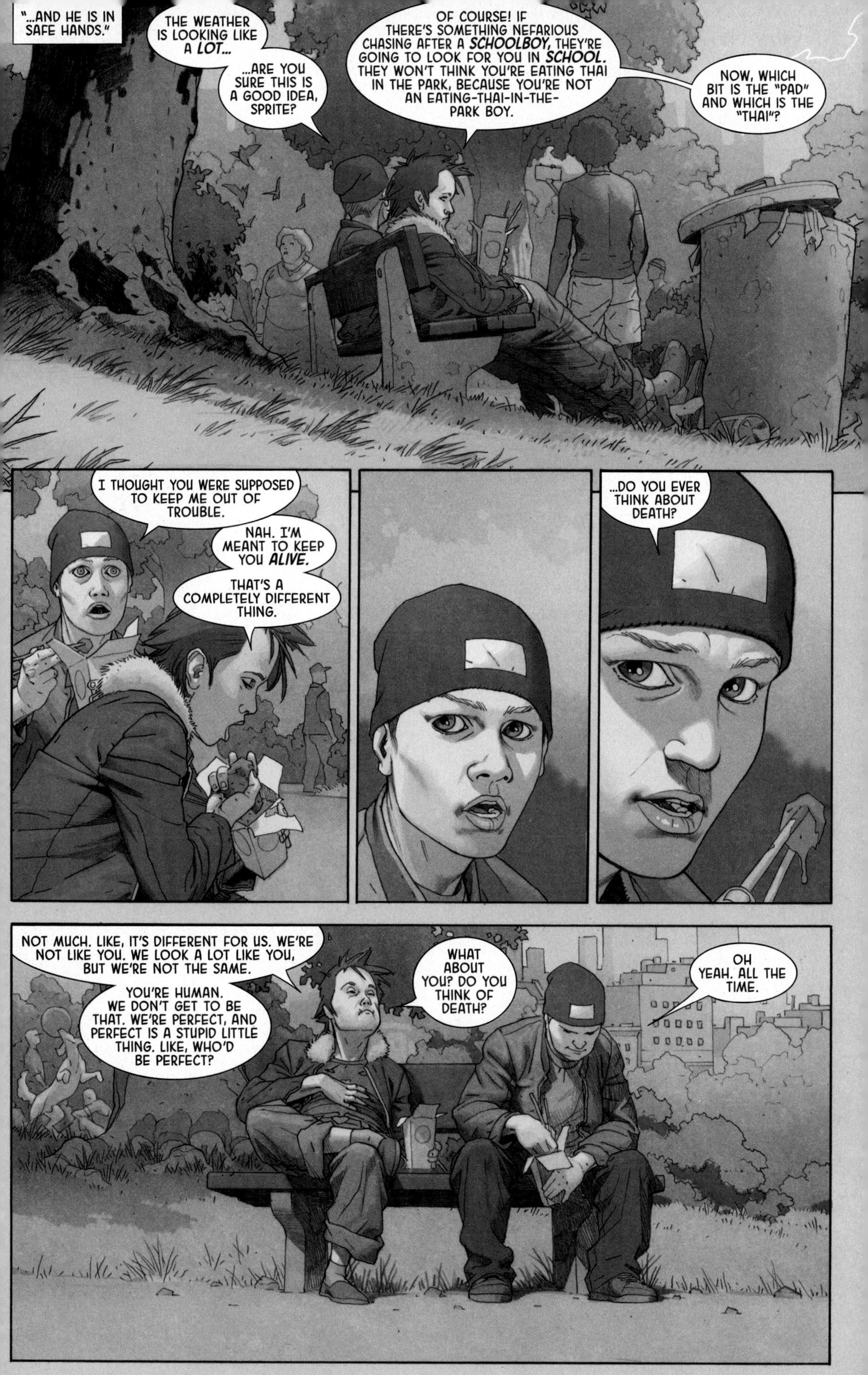
"...AND HE IS IN SAFE HANDS."
THE WEATHER IS LOOKING LIKE A *LOT...*
...ARE YOU SURE THIS IS A GOOD IDEA, SPRITE?
OF COURSE! IF THERE'S SOMETHING NEFARIOUS CHASING AFTER A *SCHOOLBOY,* THEY'RE GOING TO LOOK FOR YOU IN *SCHOOL.* THEY WON'T THINK YOU'RE EATING THAI IN THE PARK, BECAUSE YOU'RE NOT AN EATING-THAI-IN-THE-PARK BOY.
NOW, WHICH BIT IS THE "PAD" AND WHICH IS THE "THAI"?
I THOUGHT YOU WERE SUPPOSED TO KEEP ME OUT OF TROUBLE.
NAH. I'M MEANT TO KEEP YOU *ALIVE.*
THAT'S A COMPLETELY DIFFERENT THING.
...DO YOU EVER THINK ABOUT DEATH?
NOT MUCH. LIKE, IT'S DIFFERENT FOR US. WE'RE NOT LIKE YOU. WE LOOK A LOT LIKE YOU, BUT WE'RE NOT THE SAME.
YOU'RE HUMAN. WE DON'T GET TO BE THAT. WE'RE PERFECT, AND PERFECT IS A STUPID LITTLE THING. LIKE, WHO'D BE PERFECT?
WHAT ABOUT YOU? DO YOU THINK OF DEATH?
OH YEAH. ALL THE TIME.

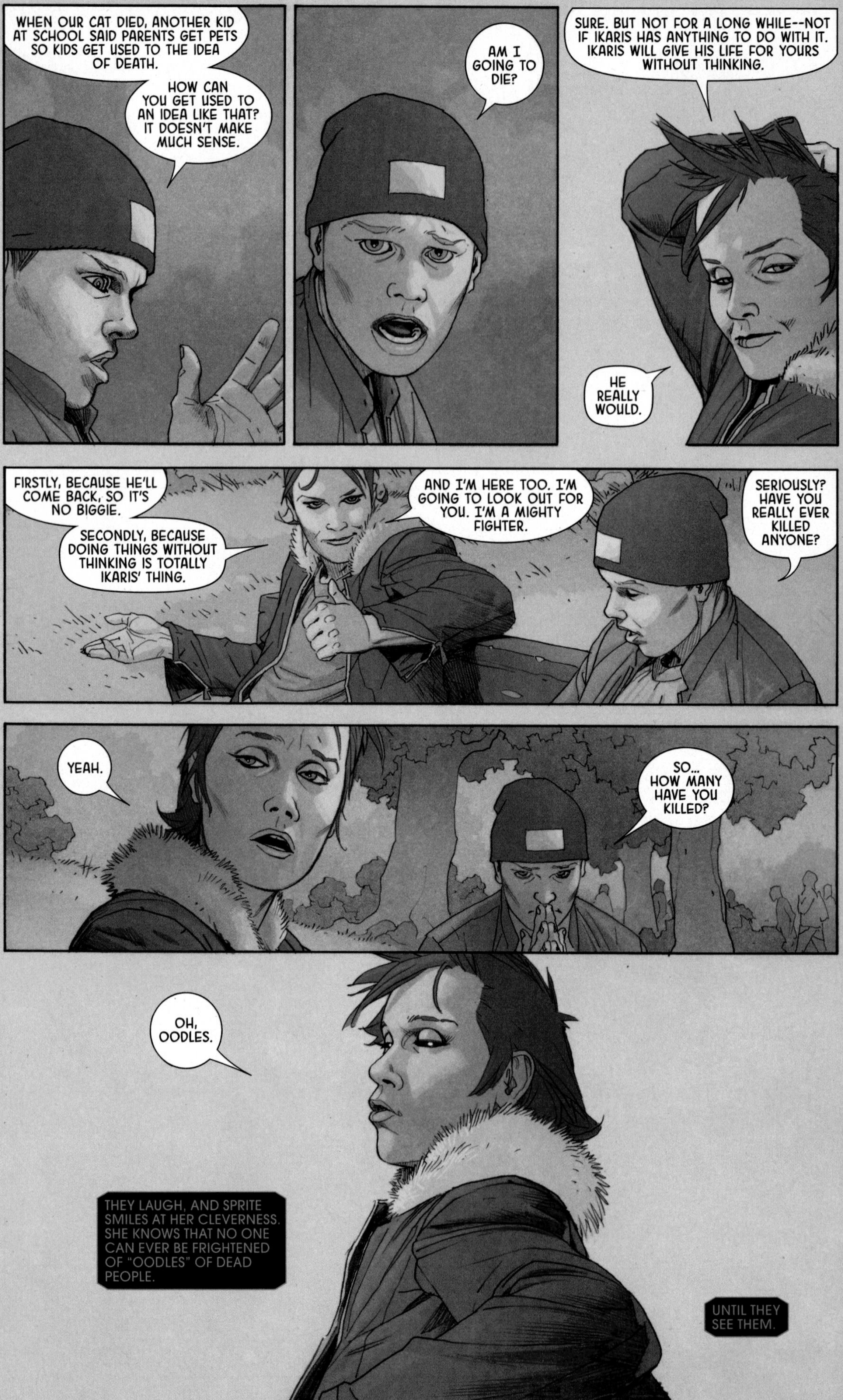
WHEN OUR CAT DIED, ANOTHER KID AT SCHOOL SAID PARENTS GET PETS SO KIDS GET USED TO THE IDEA OF DEATH.
HOW CAN YOU GET USED TO AN IDEA LIKE THAT? IT DOESN'T MAKE MUCH SENSE.
AM I GOING TO DIE?
SURE. BUT NOT FOR A LONG WHILE--NOT IF IKARIS HAS ANYTHING TO DO WITH IT. IKARIS WILL GIVE HIS LIFE FOR YOURS WITHOUT THINKING.
HE REALLY WOULD.
FIRSTLY, BECAUSE HE'LL COME BACK, SO IT'S NO BIGGIE.
SECONDLY, BECAUSE DOING THINGS WITHOUT THINKING IS TOTALLY IKARIS' THING.
AND I'M HERE TOO. I'M GOING TO LOOK OUT FOR YOU. I'M A MIGHTY FIGHTER.
SERIOUSLY? HAVE YOU REALLY EVER KILLED ANYONE?
YEAH.
SO... HOW MANY HAVE YOU KILLED?
OH, OODLES.
THEY LAUGH, AND SPRITE SMILES AT HER CLEVERNESS. SHE KNOWS THAT NO ONE CAN EVER BE FRIGHTENED OF "OODLES" OF DEAD PEOPLE.
UNTIL THEY SEE THEM.

THE EXCLUSION

EXCLUDED "K" (KRONOS)
Crime: Auto-deification.

EXCLUDED "A" (A'LARS/ MENTOR)
Crime: Unsafe lineage.

EXCLUDED "S" (SUI-SAN)
Crime: Unsafe lineage.

EXCLUDED "U" (URANOS)
Crime: Attempted omni-genocide.

EXCLUDED "E"
([redacted])
[redacted]

EXCLUDED "H"
([redacted])
[redacted]

EXCLUDED "T"
([redacted])
[redacted]

UR-LUCIVA
Warden of the Exclusion.

KHARON
Exclusion Security and Transport.

While its purpose as intellectual quarantine for the Eternal Society and home of the Resurrection Machines are key, the Exclusion also has another purpose.

While the greater part of the Machine's infrastructure (i.e., me) is dispersed in sub-dimensional threads across the whole planet, the Exclusion is where it can most easily be interacted with, with its reality loom capable of selecting and weaving threads. It is perhaps best thought of as the engine room of the planet Earth.

And, as evidenced by the out-of-control weather, the imminent destruction of the planet and the kookiness of yours truly, the engines cannae take it.

Yes, I've seen *Star Trek* too. I <3 *DS9.*

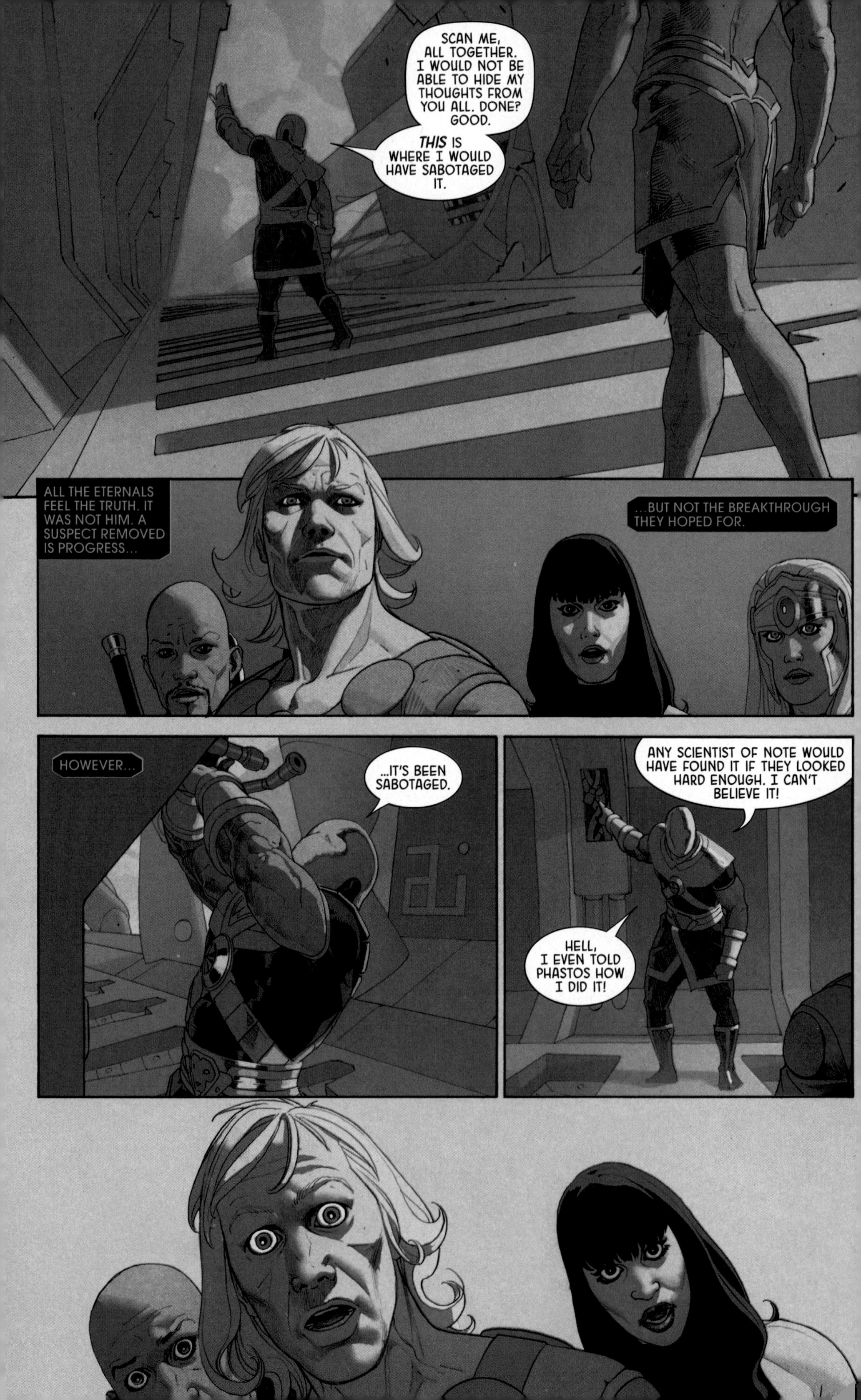
SCAN ME, ALL TOGETHER. I WOULD NOT BE ABLE TO HIDE MY THOUGHTS FROM YOU ALL. DONE? GOOD.
THIS IS WHERE I WOULD HAVE SABOTAGED IT.
ALL THE ETERNALS FEEL THE TRUTH. IT WAS NOT HIM. A SUSPECT REMOVED IS PROGRESS...
...BUT NOT THE BREAKTHROUGH THEY HOPED FOR.
HOWEVER...
...IT'S BEEN SABOTAGED.
ANY SCIENTIST OF NOTE WOULD HAVE FOUND IT IF THEY LOOKED HARD ENOUGH. I CAN'T BELIEVE IT!
HELL, I EVEN TOLD PHASTOS HOW I DID IT!

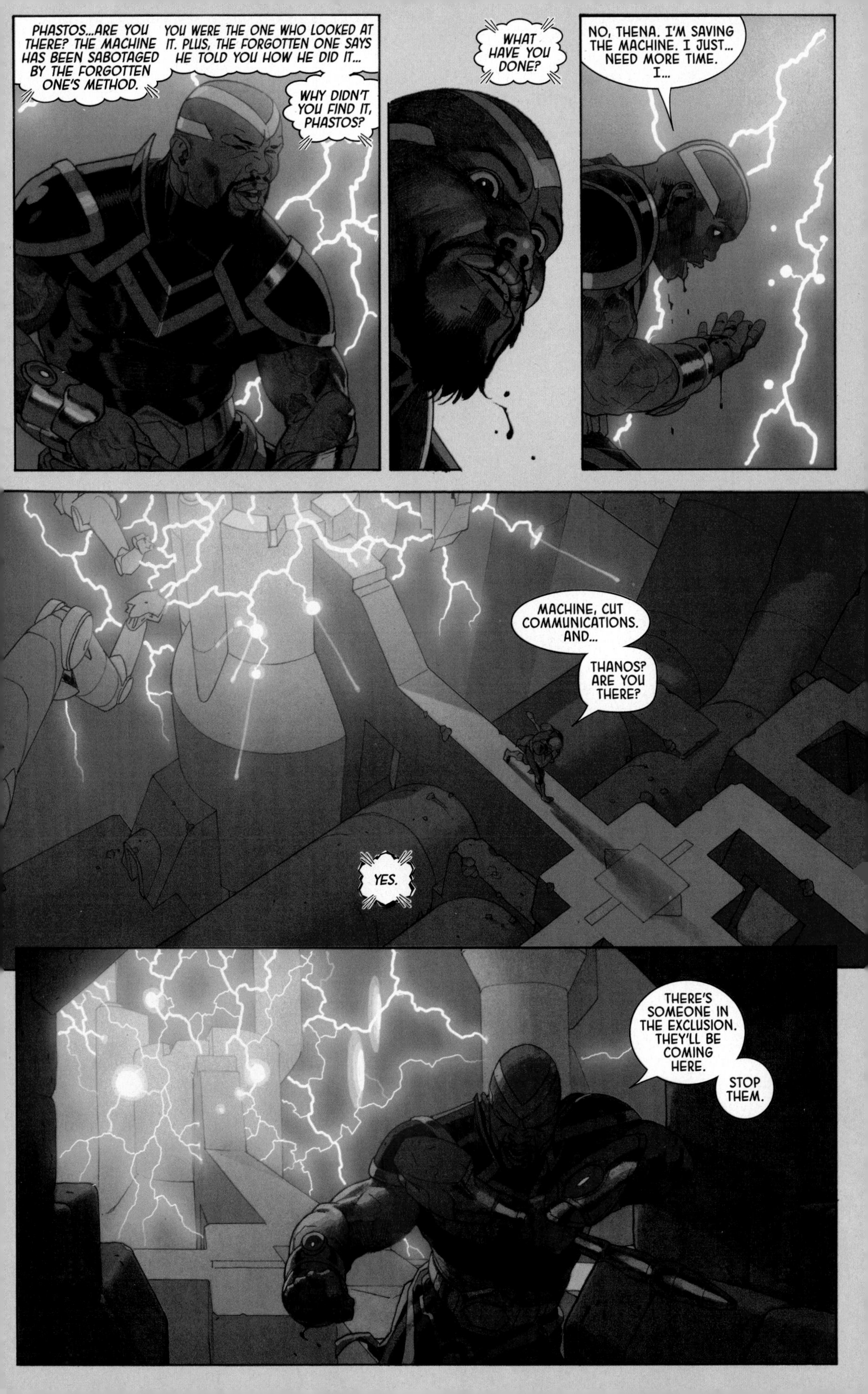
PHASTOS...ARE YOU THERE? THE MACHINE HAS BEEN SABOTAGED BY THE FORGOTTEN ONE'S METHOD.
YOU WERE THE ONE WHO LOOKED AT IT. PLUS, THE FORGOTTEN ONE SAYS HE TOLD YOU HOW HE DID IT...
WHY DIDN'T YOU FIND IT, PHASTOS?
WHAT HAVE YOU DONE?
NO, THENA. I'M SAVING THE MACHINE. I JUST... NEED MORE TIME. I...
MACHINE, CUT COMMUNICATIONS. AND...
THANOS? ARE YOU THERE?
YES.
THERE'S SOMEONE IN THE EXCLUSION. THEY'LL BE COMING HERE.
STOP THEM.

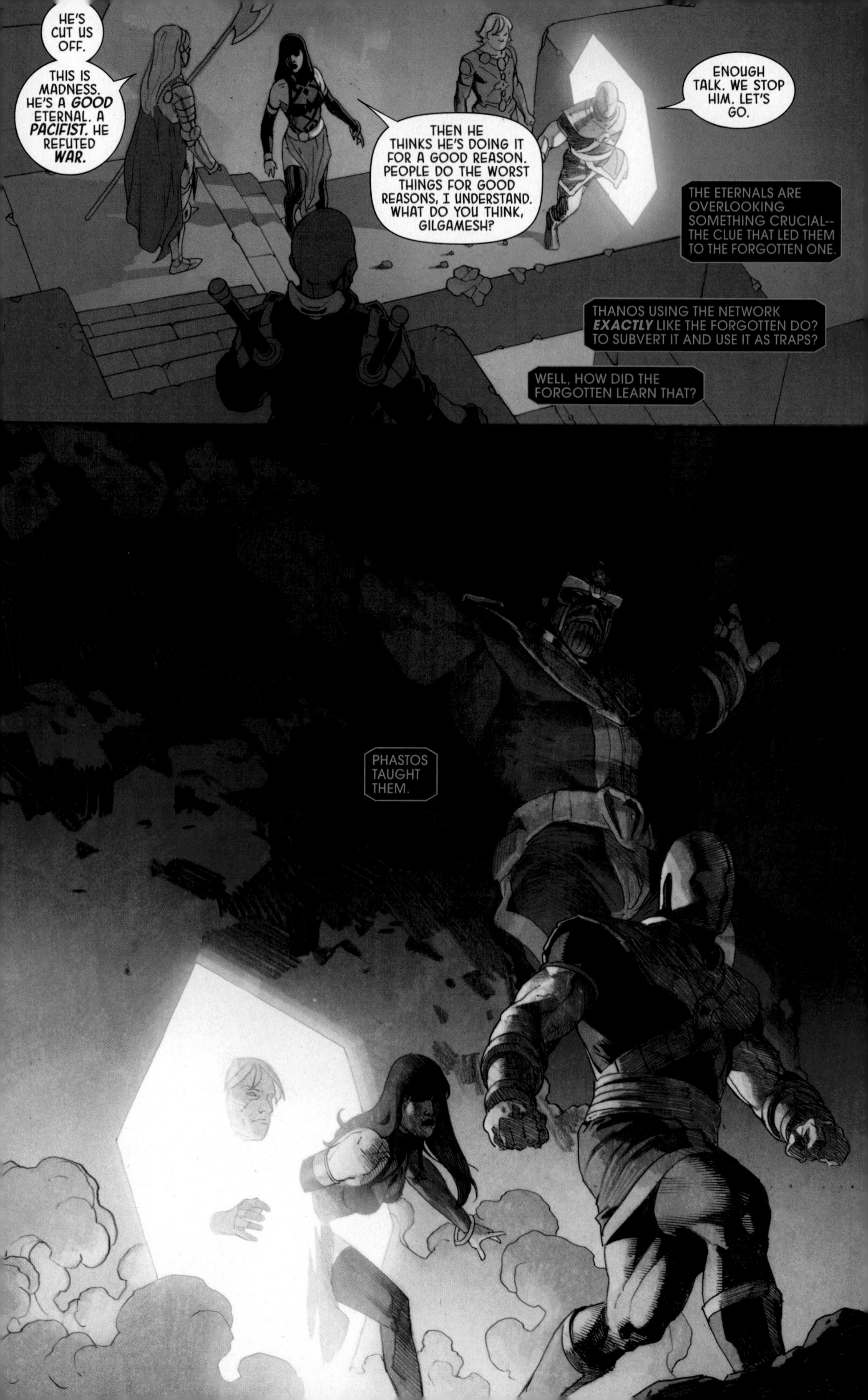

HE'S CUT US OFF.
THIS IS MADNESS. HE'S A *GOOD* ETERNAL. A *PACIFIST.* HE REFUTED *WAR.*
THEN HE THINKS HE'S DOING IT FOR A GOOD REASON. PEOPLE DO THE WORST THINGS FOR GOOD REASONS, I UNDERSTAND. WHAT DO YOU THINK, GILGAMESH?
ENOUGH TALK. WE STOP HIM. LET'S GO.
THE ETERNALS ARE OVERLOOKING SOMETHING CRUCIAL-- THE CLUE THAT LED THEM TO THE FORGOTTEN ONE.
THANOS USING THE NETWORK *EXACTLY* LIKE THE FORGOTTEN DO? TO SUBVERT IT AND USE IT AS TRAPS?
WELL, HOW DID THE FORGOTTEN LEARN THAT?
PHASTOS TAUGHT THEM.

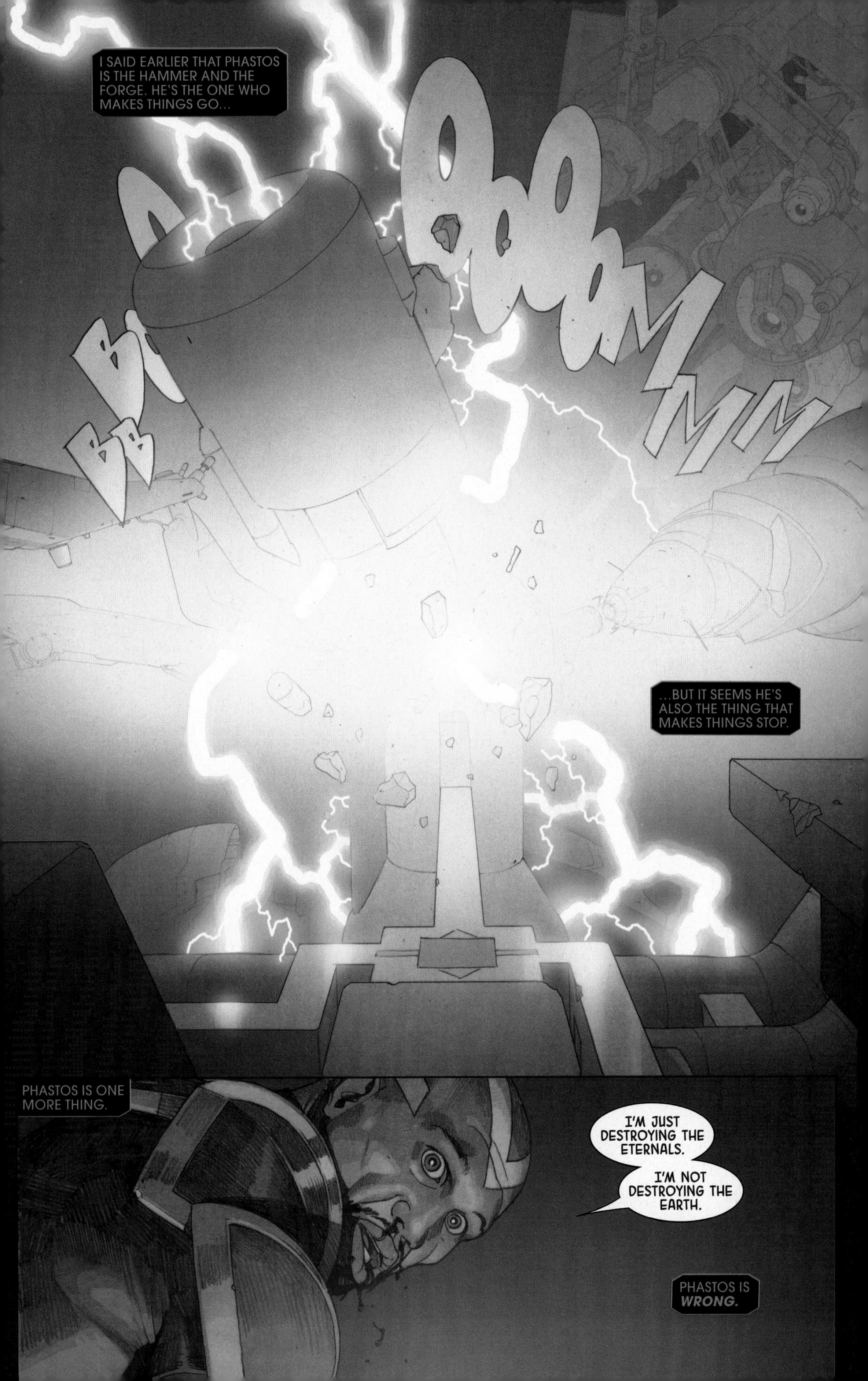
I SAID EARLIER THAT PHASTOS IS THE HAMMER AND THE FORGE. HE'S THE ONE WHO MAKES THINGS GO...
...BUT IT SEEMS HE'S ALSO THE THING THAT MAKES THINGS STOP.
PHASTOS IS ONE MORE THING.
I'M JUST DESTROYING THE ETERNALS.
I'M NOT DESTROYING THE EARTH.
PHASTOS IS ***WRONG.***

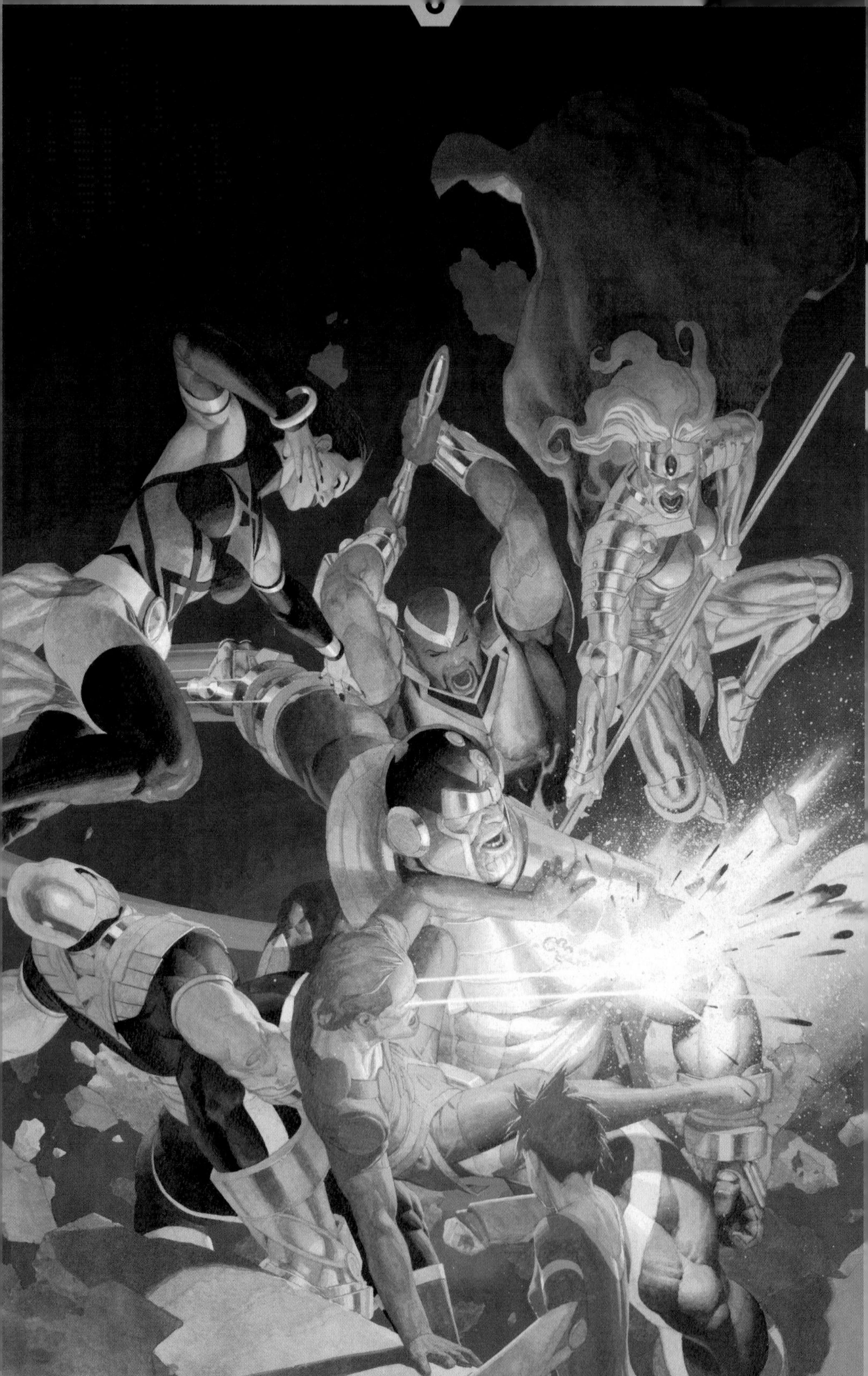

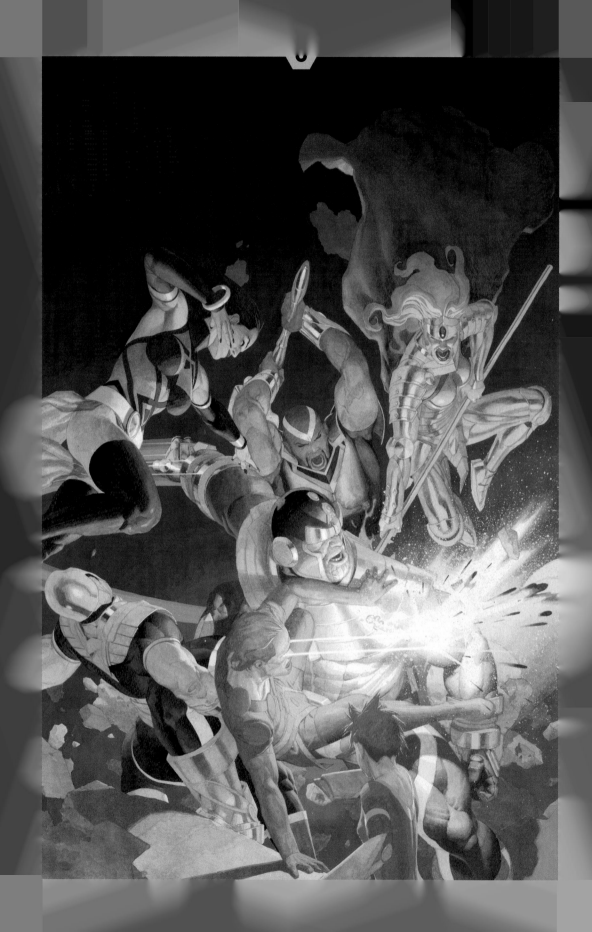

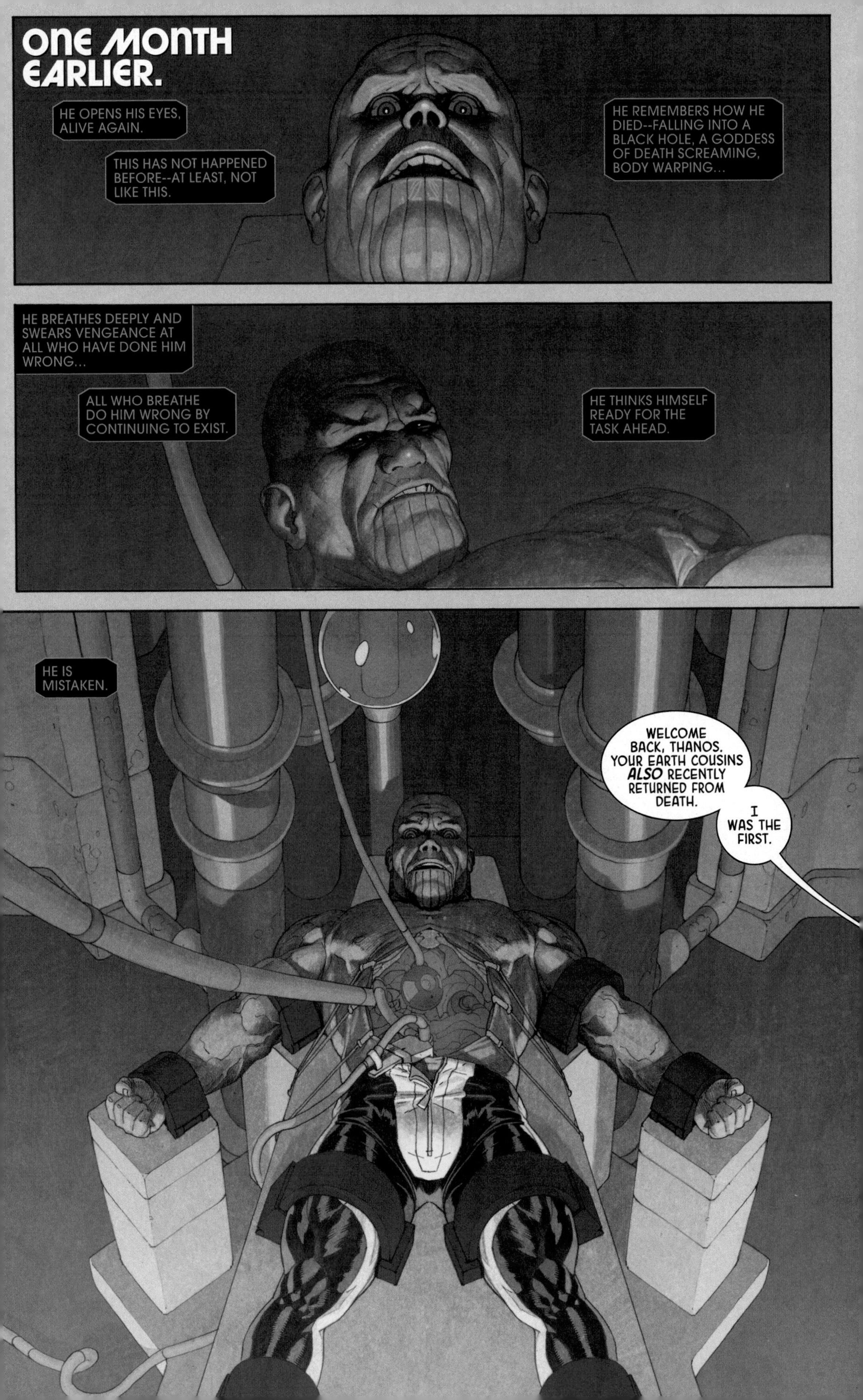
ONE MONTH EARLIER.
HE OPENS HIS EYES, ALIVE AGAIN.
THIS HAS NOT HAPPENED BEFORE--AT LEAST, NOT LIKE THIS.
HE REMEMBERS HOW HE DIED--FALLING INTO A BLACK HOLE, A GODDESS OF DEATH SCREAMING, BODY WARPING...
HE BREATHES DEEPLY AND SWEARS VENGEANCE AT ALL WHO HAVE DONE HIM WRONG...
ALL WHO BREATHE DO HIM WRONG BY CONTINUING TO EXIST.
HE THINKS HIMSELF READY FOR THE TASK AHEAD.
HE IS MISTAKEN.
WELCOME BACK, THANOS. YOUR EARTH COUSINS ALSO RECENTLY RETURNED FROM DEATH.
I WAS THE FIRST.

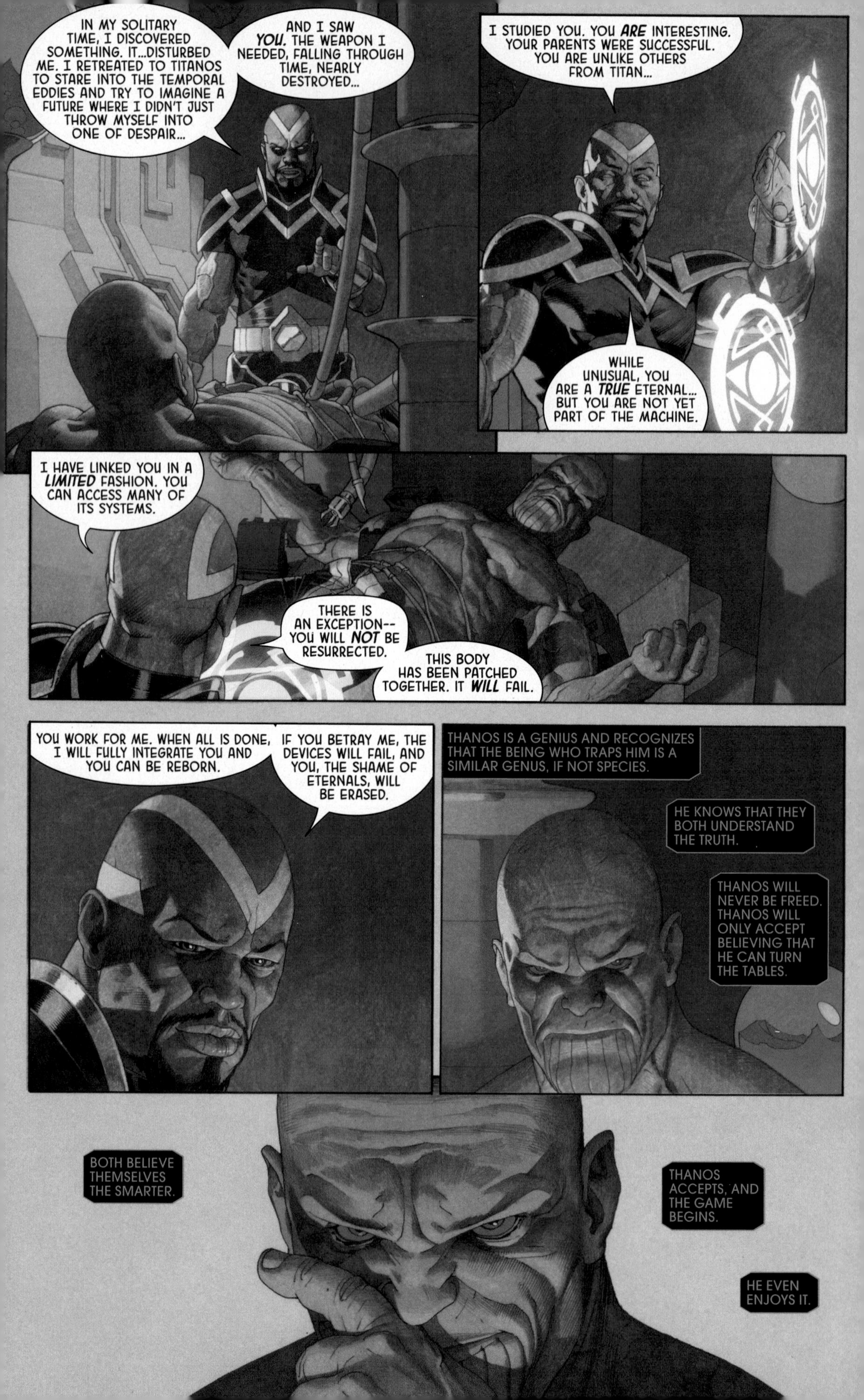
IN MY SOLITARY TIME, I DISCOVERED SOMETHING. IT...DISTURBED ME. I RETREATED TO TITANOS TO STARE INTO THE TEMPORAL EDDIES AND TRY TO IMAGINE A FUTURE WHERE I DIDN'T JUST THROW MYSELF INTO ONE OF DESPAIR...
AND I SAW *YOU.* THE WEAPON I NEEDED, FALLING THROUGH TIME, NEARLY DESTROYED...
I STUDIED YOU. YOU *ARE* INTERESTING. YOUR PARENTS WERE SUCCESSFUL. YOU ARE UNLIKE OTHERS FROM TITAN...
WHILE UNUSUAL, YOU ARE A *TRUE* ETERNAL... BUT YOU ARE NOT YET PART OF THE MACHINE.
I HAVE LINKED YOU IN A *LIMITED* FASHION. YOU CAN ACCESS MANY OF ITS SYSTEMS.
THERE IS AN EXCEPTION-- YOU WILL *NOT* BE RESURRECTED.
THIS BODY HAS BEEN PATCHED TOGETHER. IT *WILL* FAIL.
YOU WORK FOR ME. WHEN ALL IS DONE, I WILL FULLY INTEGRATE YOU AND YOU CAN BE REBORN.
IF YOU BETRAY ME, THE DEVICES WILL FAIL, AND YOU, THE SHAME OF ETERNALS, WILL BE ERASED.
THANOS IS A GENIUS AND RECOGNIZES THAT THE BEING WHO TRAPS HIM IS A SIMILAR GENUS, IF NOT SPECIES.
HE KNOWS THAT THEY BOTH UNDERSTAND THE TRUTH.
THANOS WILL NEVER BE FREED. THANOS WILL ONLY ACCEPT BELIEVING THAT HE CAN TURN THE TABLES.
BOTH BELIEVE THEMSELVES THE SMARTER.
THANOS ACCEPTS, AND THE GAME BEGINS.
HE EVEN ENJOYS IT.

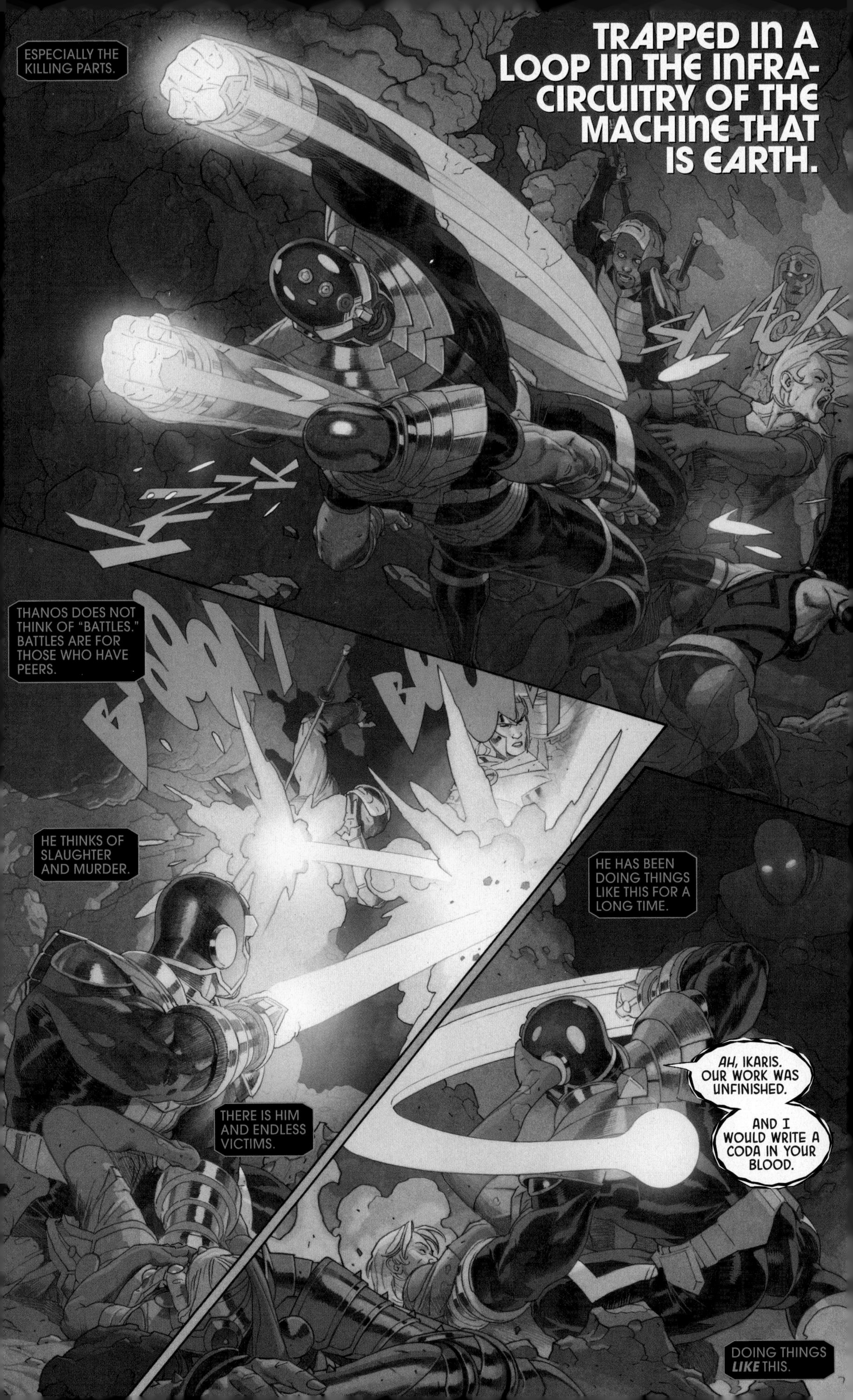

ESPECIALLY THE KILLING PARTS.
TRAPPED IN A LOOP IN THE INFRA-CIRCUITRY OF THE MACHINE THAT IS EARTH.
KRZZK
SMACK
THANOS DOES NOT THINK OF "BATTLES." BATTLES ARE FOR THOSE WHO HAVE PEERS.
HE THINKS OF SLAUGHTER AND MURDER.
HE HAS BEEN DOING THINGS LIKE THIS FOR A LONG TIME.
THERE IS HIM AND ENDLESS VICTIMS.
AH, IKARIS. OUR WORK WAS UNFINISHED.
AND I WOULD WRITE A CODA IN YOUR BLOOD.
DOING THINGS *LIKE* THIS.

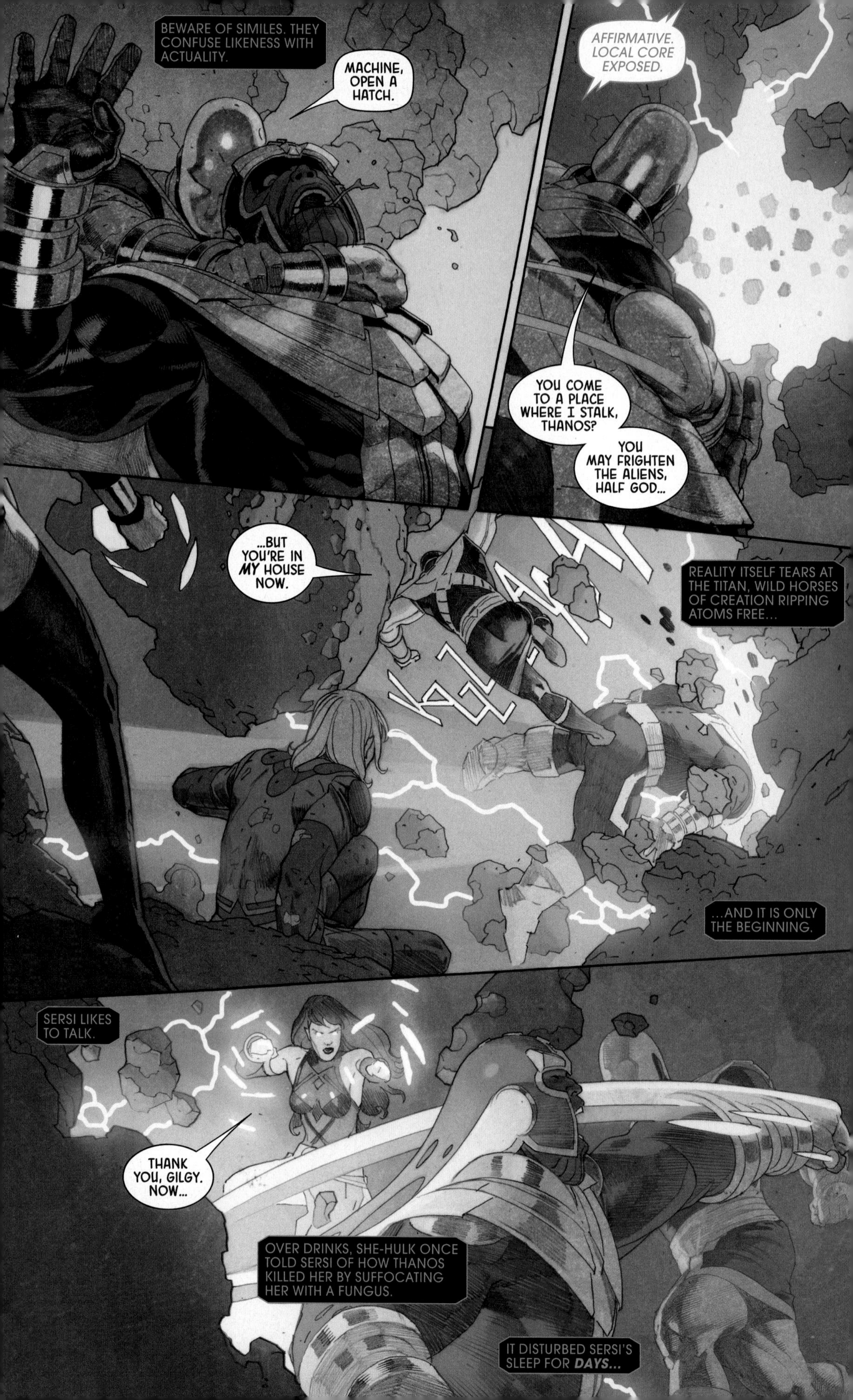
BEWARE OF SIMILES. THEY CONFUSE LIKENESS WITH ACTUALITY.
MACHINE, OPEN A HATCH.
AFFIRMATIVE. LOCAL CORE EXPOSED.
YOU COME TO A PLACE WHERE I STALK, THANOS?
YOU MAY FRIGHTEN THE ALIENS, HALF GOD...
...BUT YOU'RE IN MY HOUSE NOW.
REALITY ITSELF TEARS AT THE TITAN, WILD HORSES OF CREATION RIPPING ATOMS FREE...
KZZAAKK
...AND IT IS ONLY THE BEGINNING.
SERSI LIKES TO TALK.
THANK YOU, GILGY. NOW...
OVER DRINKS, SHE-HULK ONCE TOLD SERSI OF HOW THANOS KILLED HER BY SUFFOCATING HER WITH A FUNGUS.
IT DISTURBED SERSI'S SLEEP FOR DAYS...

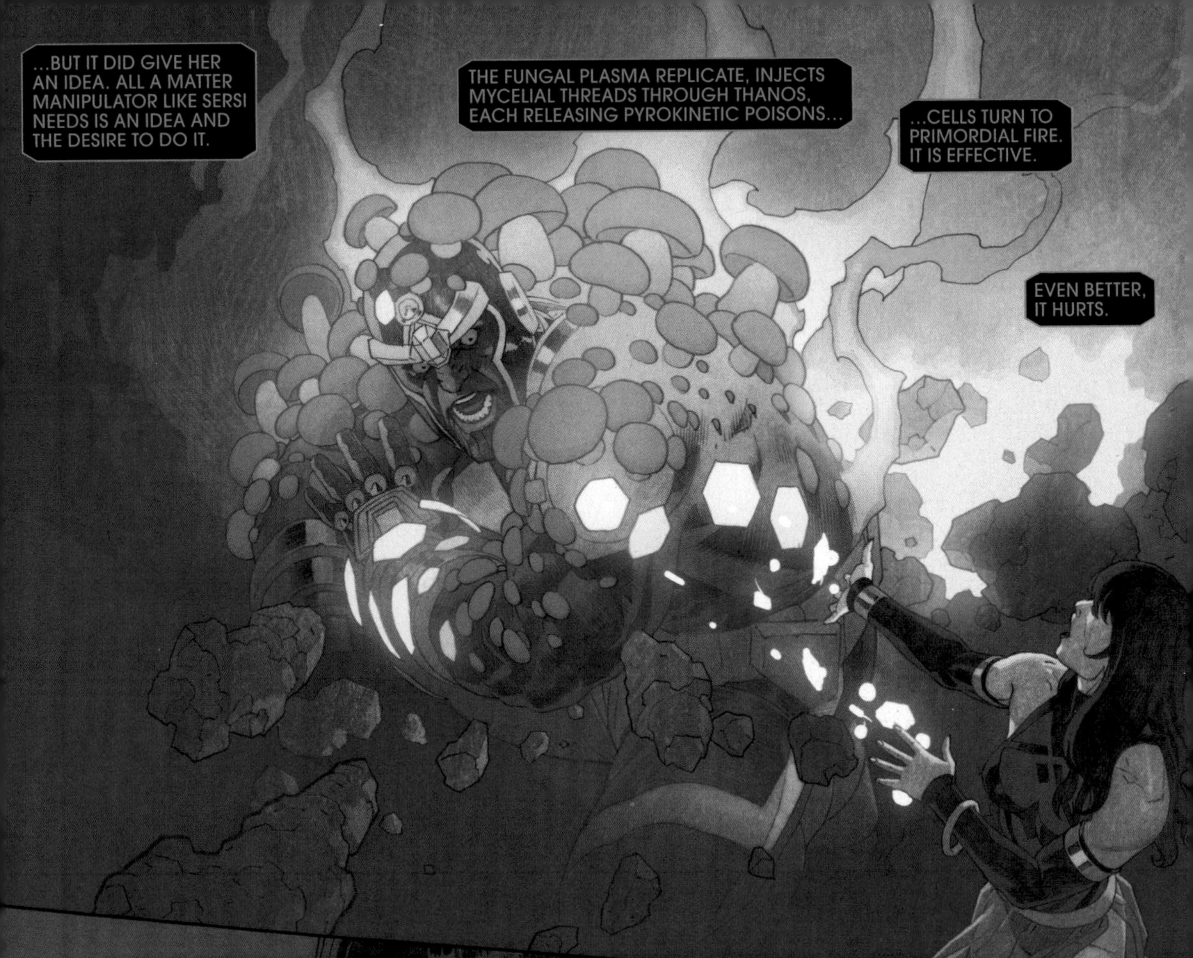
...BUT IT DID GIVE HER AN IDEA. ALL A MATTER MANIPULATOR LIKE SERSI NEEDS IS AN IDEA AND THE DESIRE TO DO IT.
THE FUNGAL PLASMA REPLICATE, INJECTS MYCELIAL THREADS THROUGH THANOS, EACH RELEASING PYROKINETIC POISONS...
...CELLS TURN TO PRIMORDIAL FIRE. IT IS EFFECTIVE.
EVEN BETTER, IT HURTS.

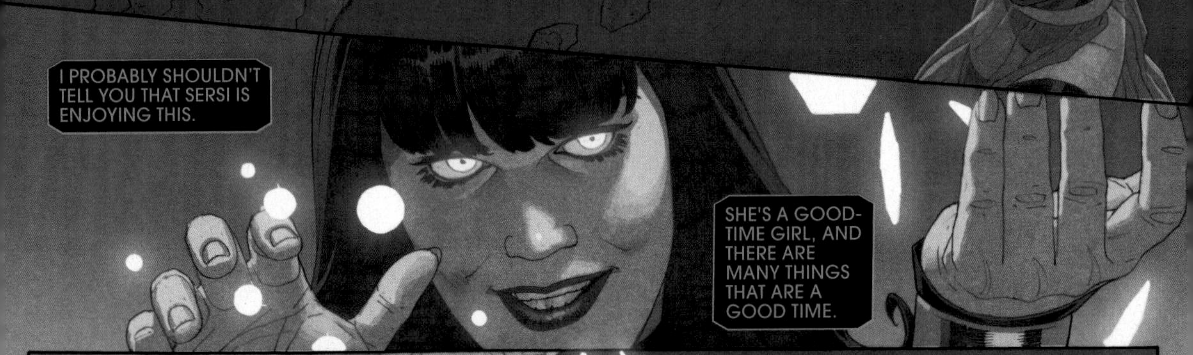
I PROBABLY SHOULDN'T TELL YOU THAT SERSI IS ENJOYING THIS.
SHE'S A GOOD-TIME GIRL, AND THERE ARE MANY THINGS THAT ARE A GOOD TIME.

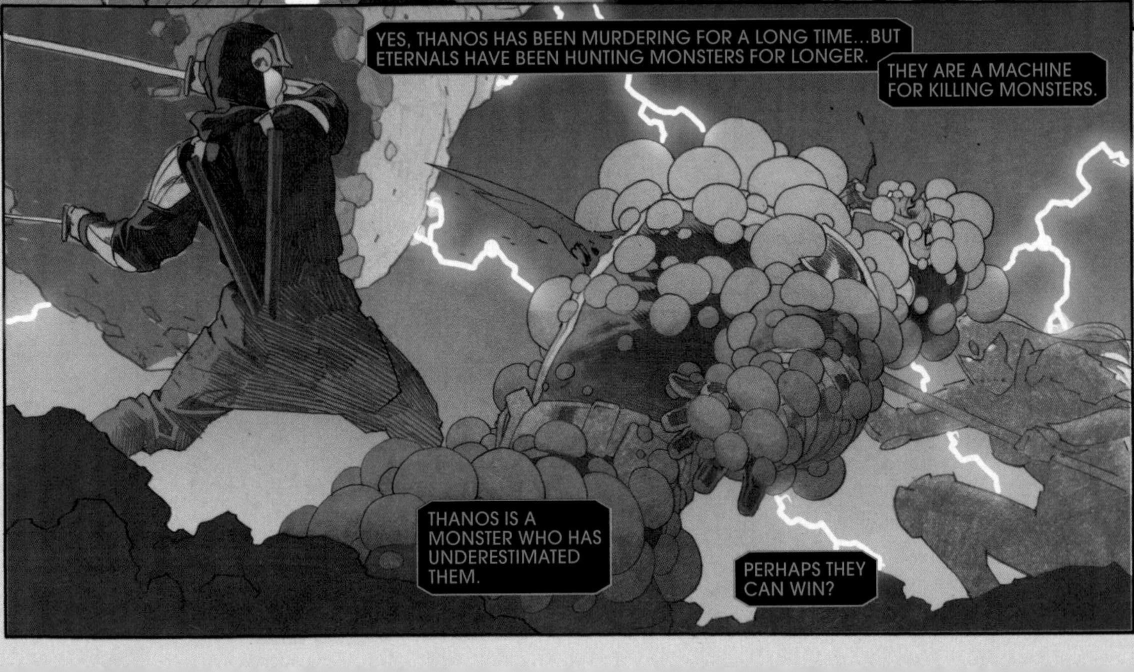
YES, THANOS HAS BEEN MURDERING FOR A LONG TIME...BUT ETERNALS HAVE BEEN HUNTING MONSTERS FOR LONGER.
THEY ARE A MACHINE FOR KILLING MONSTERS.
THANOS IS A MONSTER WHO HAS UNDERESTIMATED THEM.
PERHAPS THEY CAN WIN?

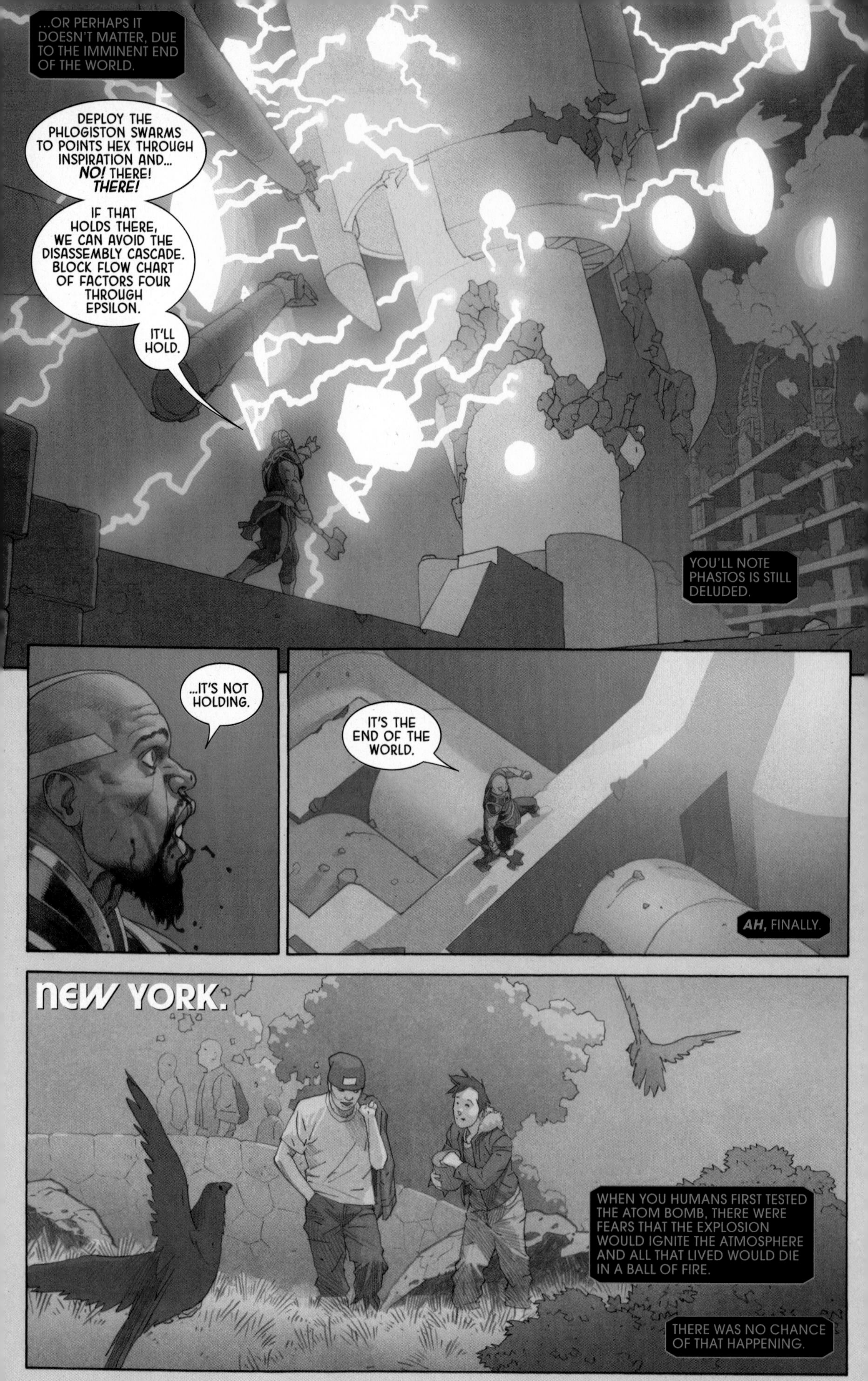
...OR PERHAPS IT DOESN'T MATTER, DUE TO THE IMMINENT END OF THE WORLD.
DEPLOY THE PHLOGISTON SWARMS TO POINTS HEX THROUGH INSPIRATION AND... NO! THERE! THERE!
IF THAT HOLDS THERE, WE CAN AVOID THE DISASSEMBLY CASCADE. BLOCK FLOW CHART OF FACTORS FOUR THROUGH EPSILON.
IT'LL HOLD.
YOU'LL NOTE PHASTOS IS STILL DELUDED.
...IT'S NOT HOLDING.
IT'S THE END OF THE WORLD.
AH, FINALLY.
NEW YORK.
WHEN YOU HUMANS FIRST TESTED THE ATOM BOMB, THERE WERE FEARS THAT THE EXPLOSION WOULD IGNITE THE ATMOSPHERE AND ALL THAT LIVED WOULD DIE IN A BALL OF FIRE.
THERE WAS NO CHANCE OF THAT HAPPENING.

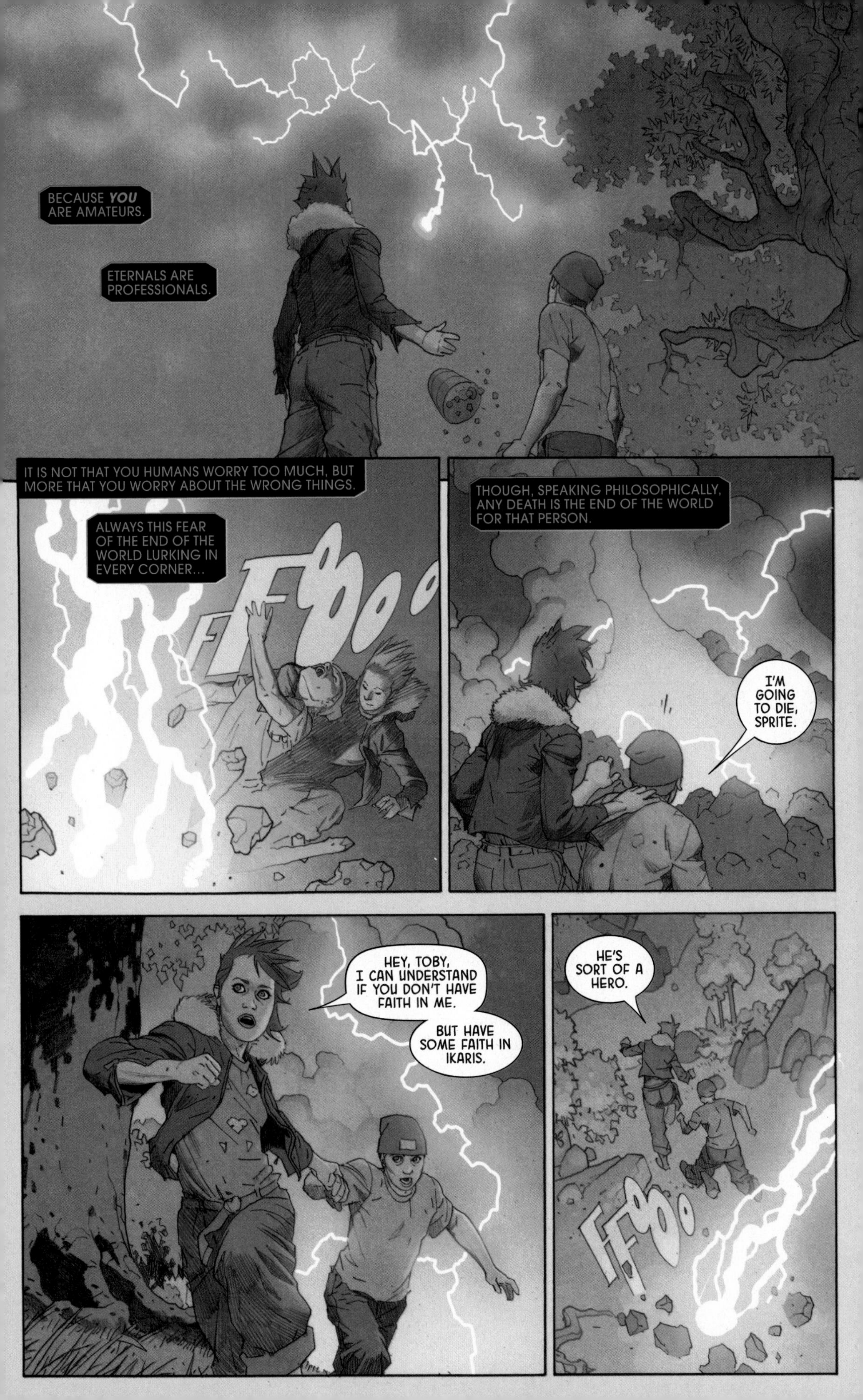

BECAUSE YOU ARE AMATEURS.
ETERNALS ARE PROFESSIONALS.
IT IS NOT THAT YOU HUMANS WORRY TOO MUCH, BUT MORE THAT YOU WORRY ABOUT THE WRONG THINGS.
ALWAYS THIS FEAR OF THE END OF THE WORLD LURKING IN EVERY CORNER…
FFOOO
THOUGH, SPEAKING PHILOSOPHICALLY, ANY DEATH IS THE END OF THE WORLD FOR THAT PERSON.
I'M GOING TO DIE, SPRITE.
HEY, TOBY, I CAN UNDERSTAND IF YOU DON'T HAVE FAITH IN ME.
BUT HAVE SOME FAITH IN IKARIS.
HE'S SORT OF A HERO.
FFOOO

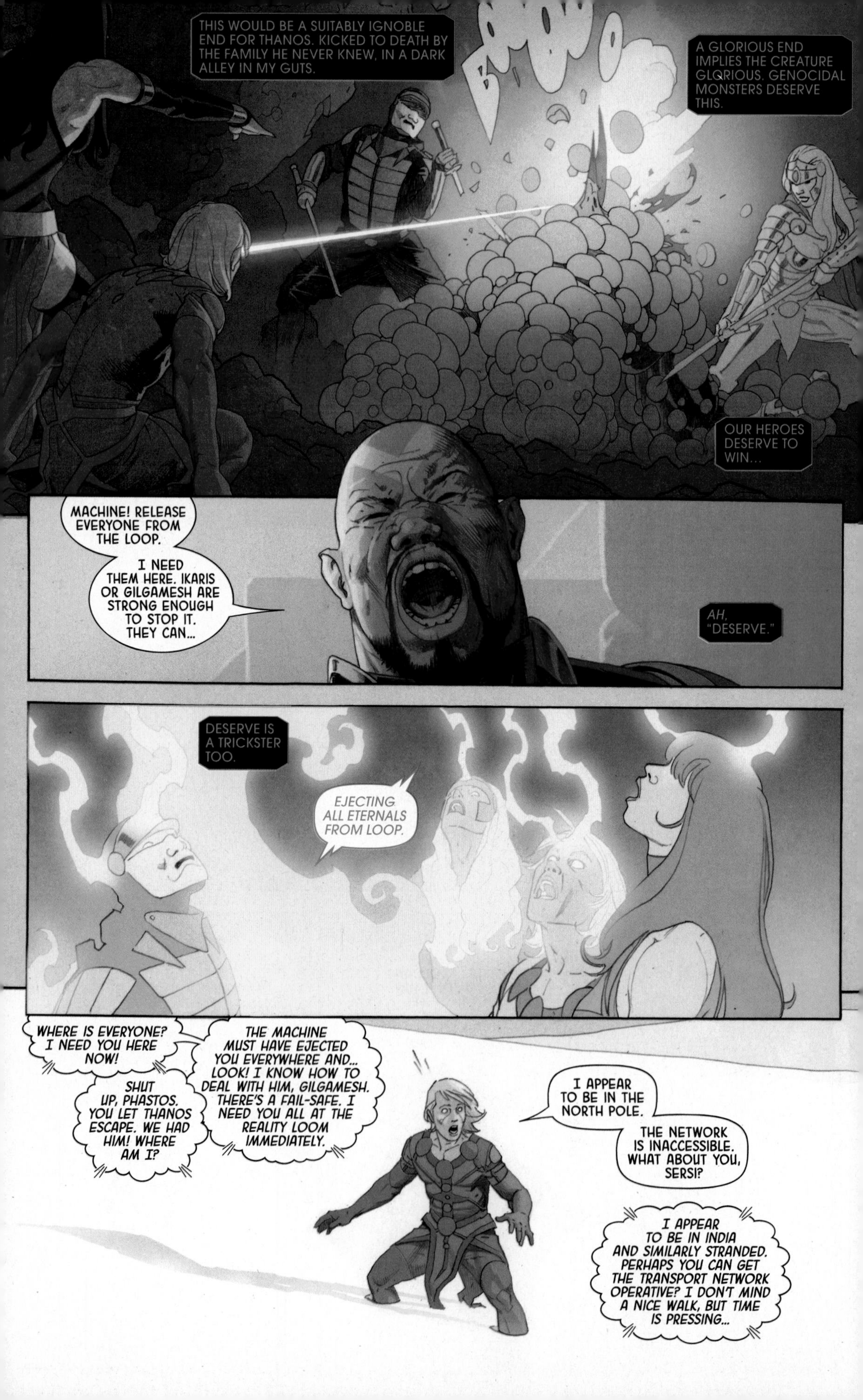
THIS WOULD BE A SUITABLY IGNOBLE END FOR THANOS. KICKED TO DEATH BY THE FAMILY HE NEVER KNEW, IN A DARK ALLEY IN MY GUTS.
A GLORIOUS END IMPLIES THE CREATURE GLORIOUS. GENOCIDAL MONSTERS DESERVE THIS.
OUR HEROES DESERVE TO WIN...
MACHINE! RELEASE EVERYONE FROM THE LOOP.
I NEED THEM HERE. IKARIS OR GILGAMESH ARE STRONG ENOUGH TO STOP IT. THEY CAN...
AH, "DESERVE."
DESERVE IS A TRICKSTER TOO.
EJECTING ALL ETERNALS FROM LOOP.
WHERE IS EVERYONE? I NEED YOU HERE NOW!
THE MACHINE MUST HAVE EJECTED YOU EVERYWHERE AND... LOOK! I KNOW HOW TO DEAL WITH HIM, GILGAMESH. THERE'S A FAIL-SAFE. I NEED YOU ALL AT THE REALITY LOOM IMMEDIATELY.
SHUT UP, PHASTOS. YOU LET THANOS ESCAPE. WE HAD HIM! WHERE AM I?
I APPEAR TO BE IN THE NORTH POLE.
THE NETWORK IS INACCESSIBLE. WHAT ABOUT YOU, SERSI?
I APPEAR TO BE IN INDIA AND SIMILARLY STRANDED. PERHAPS YOU CAN GET THE TRANSPORT NETWORK OPERATIVE? I DON'T MIND A NICE WALK, BUT TIME IS PRESSING...

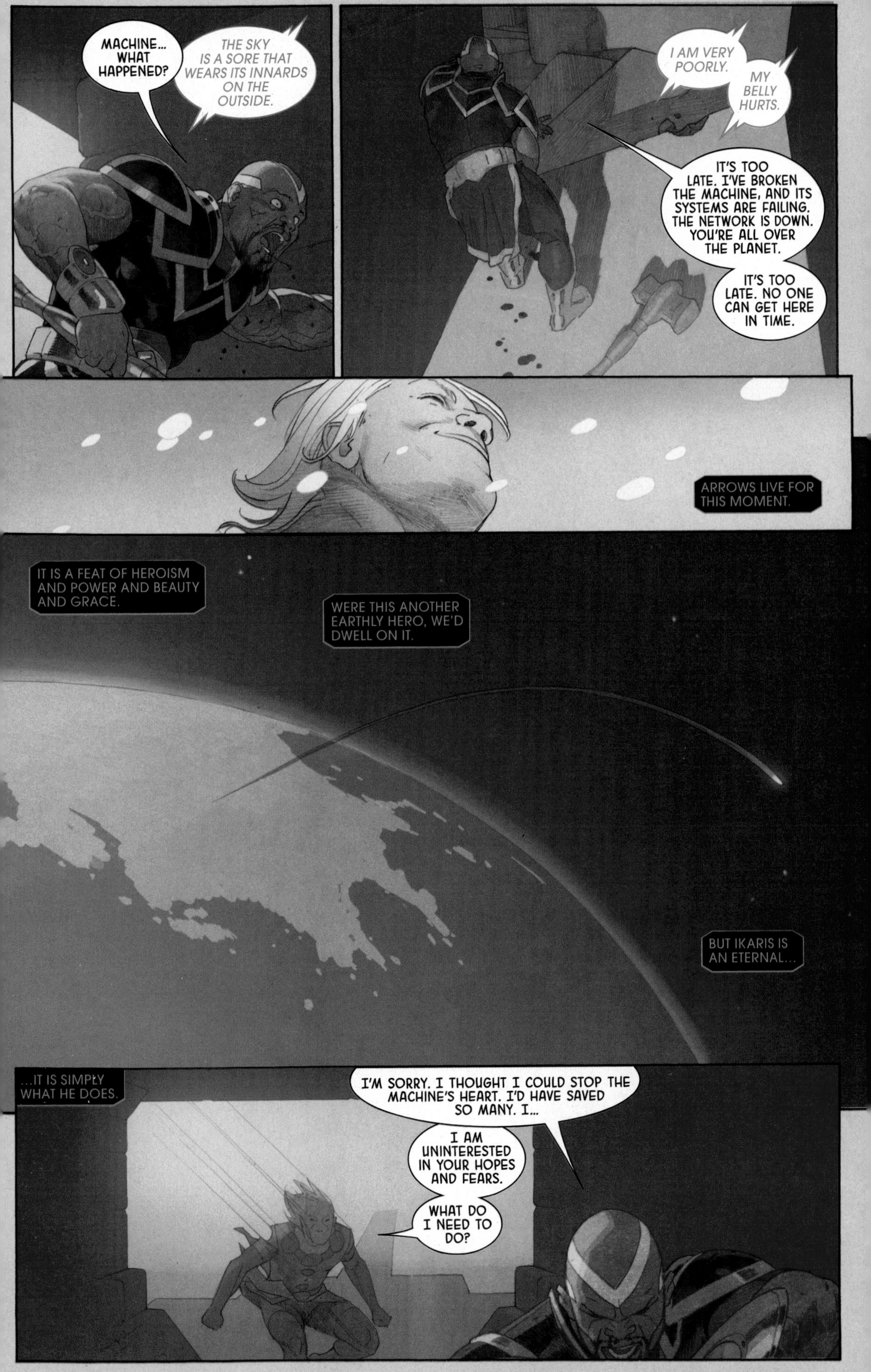
MACHINE... WHAT HAPPENED?
THE SKY IS A SORE THAT WEARS ITS INNARDS ON THE OUTSIDE.
I AM VERY POORLY.
MY BELLY HURTS.
IT'S TOO LATE. I'VE BROKEN THE MACHINE, AND ITS SYSTEMS ARE FAILING. THE NETWORK IS DOWN. YOU'RE ALL OVER THE PLANET.
IT'S TOO LATE. NO ONE CAN GET HERE IN TIME.
ARROWS LIVE FOR THIS MOMENT.
IT IS A FEAT OF HEROISM AND POWER AND BEAUTY AND GRACE.
WERE THIS ANOTHER EARTHLY HERO, WE'D DWELL ON IT.
BUT IKARIS IS AN ETERNAL...
...IT IS SIMPLY WHAT HE DOES.
I'M SORRY. I THOUGHT I COULD STOP THE MACHINE'S HEART. I'D HAVE SAVED SO MANY. I...
I AM UNINTERESTED IN YOUR HOPES AND FEARS.
WHAT DO I NEED TO DO?

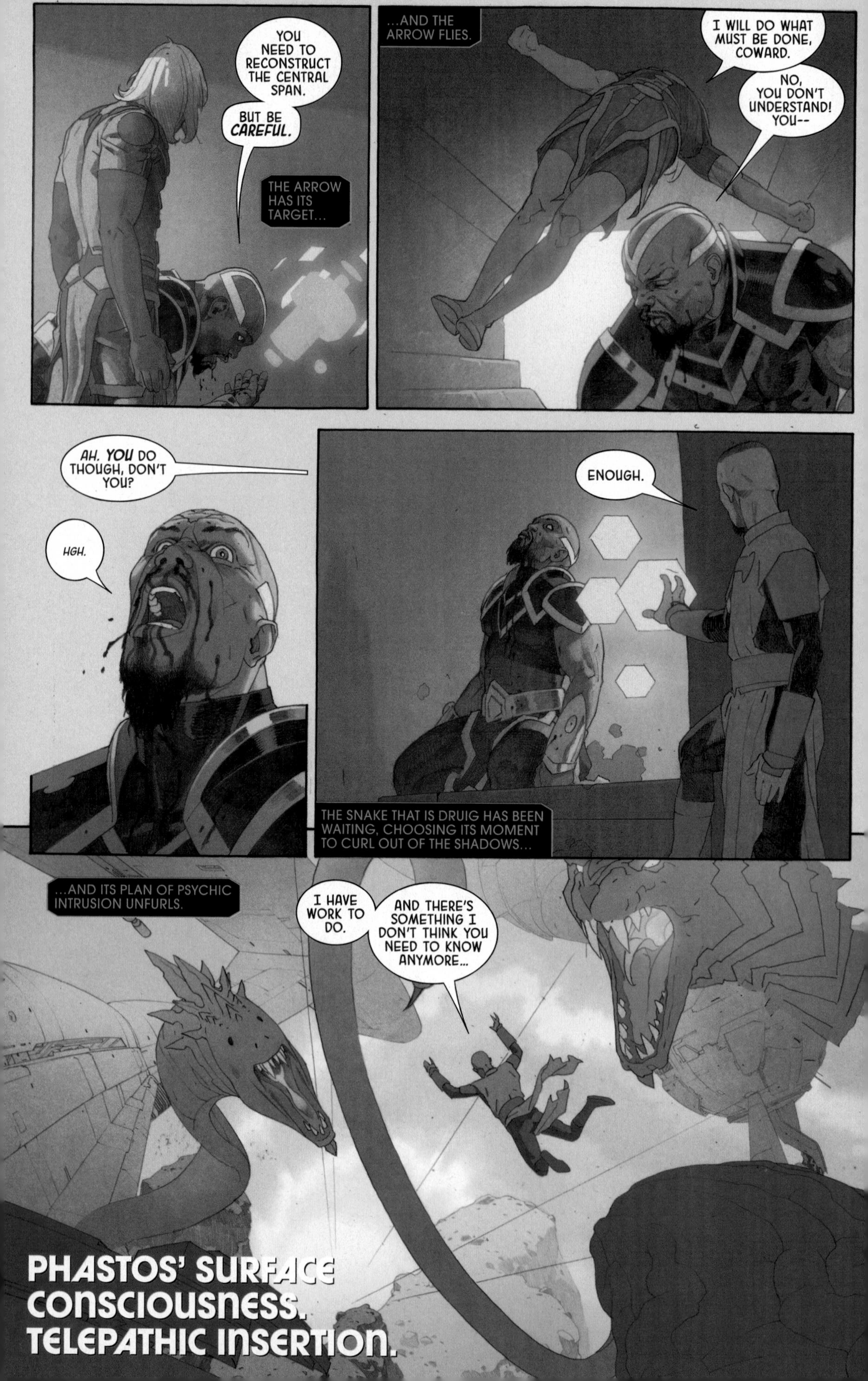
YOU NEED TO RECONSTRUCT THE CENTRAL SPAN.
BUT BE CAREFUL.
THE ARROW HAS ITS TARGET...
...AND THE ARROW FLIES.
I WILL DO WHAT MUST BE DONE, COWARD.
NO, YOU DON'T UNDERSTAND! YOU--
AH. YOU DO THOUGH, DON'T YOU?
HGH.
ENOUGH.
THE SNAKE THAT IS DRUIG HAS BEEN WAITING, CHOOSING ITS MOMENT TO CURL OUT OF THE SHADOWS...
...AND ITS PLAN OF PSYCHIC INTRUSION UNFURLS.
I HAVE WORK TO DO.
AND THERE'S SOMETHING I DON'T THINK YOU NEED TO KNOW ANYMORE...
PHASTOS' SURFACE CONSCIOUSNESS. TELEPATHIC INSERTION.

ETERNAL CONSCIOUSNESS MODEL

SURFACE CONSCIOUSNESS

An Eternal's surface thoughts. Even telepathically inept Eternals are capable of accessing this if given permission.

Telepathic Intrusion Difficulty: 2/10.

SUBCONSCIOUS

Unconscious subroutines of an Eternal. Where the core identity interacts with the executive functions, performing parallel processing of all required situations.

Telepathic Intrusion Difficulty: 6/10.

CULTURAL MEMORY

Shared knowledge of Eternal culture. A database of all information an Eternal should know about the cultural history of the species. This is collated from all Eternals, edited, and then made available as a repository.

Telepathic Intrusion Difficulty: 9/10.

PERSONAL MEMORY

An Eternal's memory since the last firm backup of existence. The interaction between the personal memory and the core identity is where an Eternal's present character emerges from. That the personal memory is relatively fluid means that it is relatively easy for an Eternal to be returned to a factory default with no lingering corruption.

Telepathic Intrusion Difficulty: 5/10.

BACKED-UP MEMORY

An Eternal's memory as copied to the Machine itself in semiregular backups. The Machine keeps multiple copies, in case an Eternal needs to be rolled back. Normally, multiple rollbacks are attempted in an Eternal before being permanently Excluded, in hope of recovery.

Telepathic Intrusion Difficulty: 7/10.

CORE IDENTITY

This is the very nature and core capabilities of an Eternal. Their expertise, their wants, their needs, their position in the "family" structure of the Eternals and so on. As opposed to the other levels, each core identity is carved into the very fundamental structure of reality.

Attempts to rewrite core identity are normally disastrous, most notably the *%*^% apocalypse, leading to the exclusions of *^*&%*%.

Telepathic Intrusion Difficulty: ∞/10.

CLASSIFIED

3458638y2p93523392322302309509723902375&565^%^%^%^$^$^$$^

Telepathic Intrusion Difficulty: 10/10.

TL;DR: Eternal Core Identity is hardware, Eternal Memories are software.

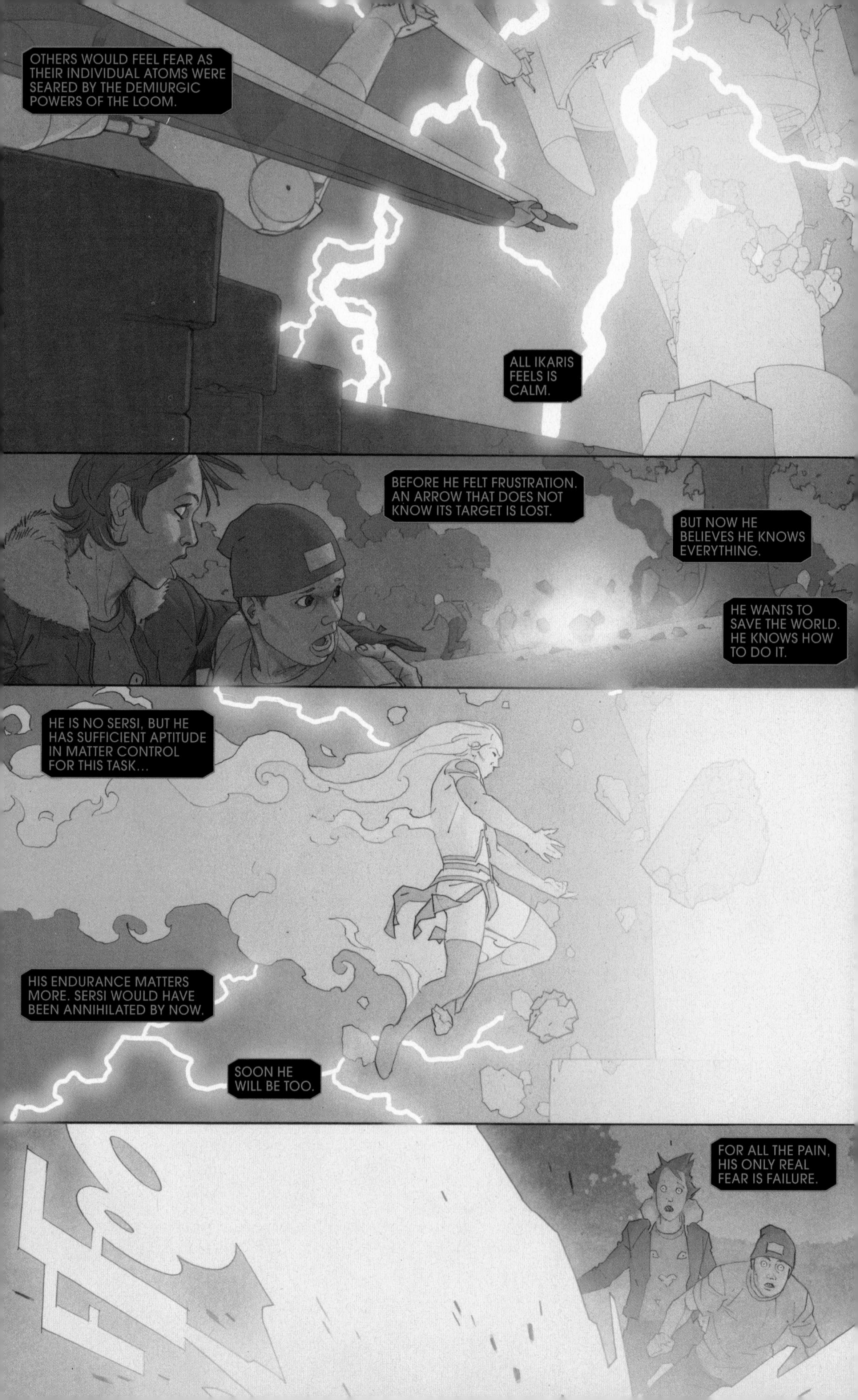
OTHERS WOULD FEEL FEAR AS THEIR INDIVIDUAL ATOMS WERE SEARED BY THE DEMIURGIC POWERS OF THE LOOM.
ALL IKARIS FEELS IS CALM.
BEFORE HE FELT FRUSTRATION. AN ARROW THAT DOES NOT KNOW ITS TARGET IS LOST.
BUT NOW HE BELIEVES HE KNOWS EVERYTHING.
HE WANTS TO SAVE THE WORLD. HE KNOWS HOW TO DO IT.
HE IS NO SERSI, BUT HE HAS SUFFICIENT APTITUDE IN MATTER CONTROL FOR THIS TASK...
HIS ENDURANCE MATTERS MORE. SERSI WOULD HAVE BEEN ANNIHILATED BY NOW.
SOON HE WILL BE TOO.
FOR ALL THE PAIN, HIS ONLY REAL FEAR IS FAILURE.

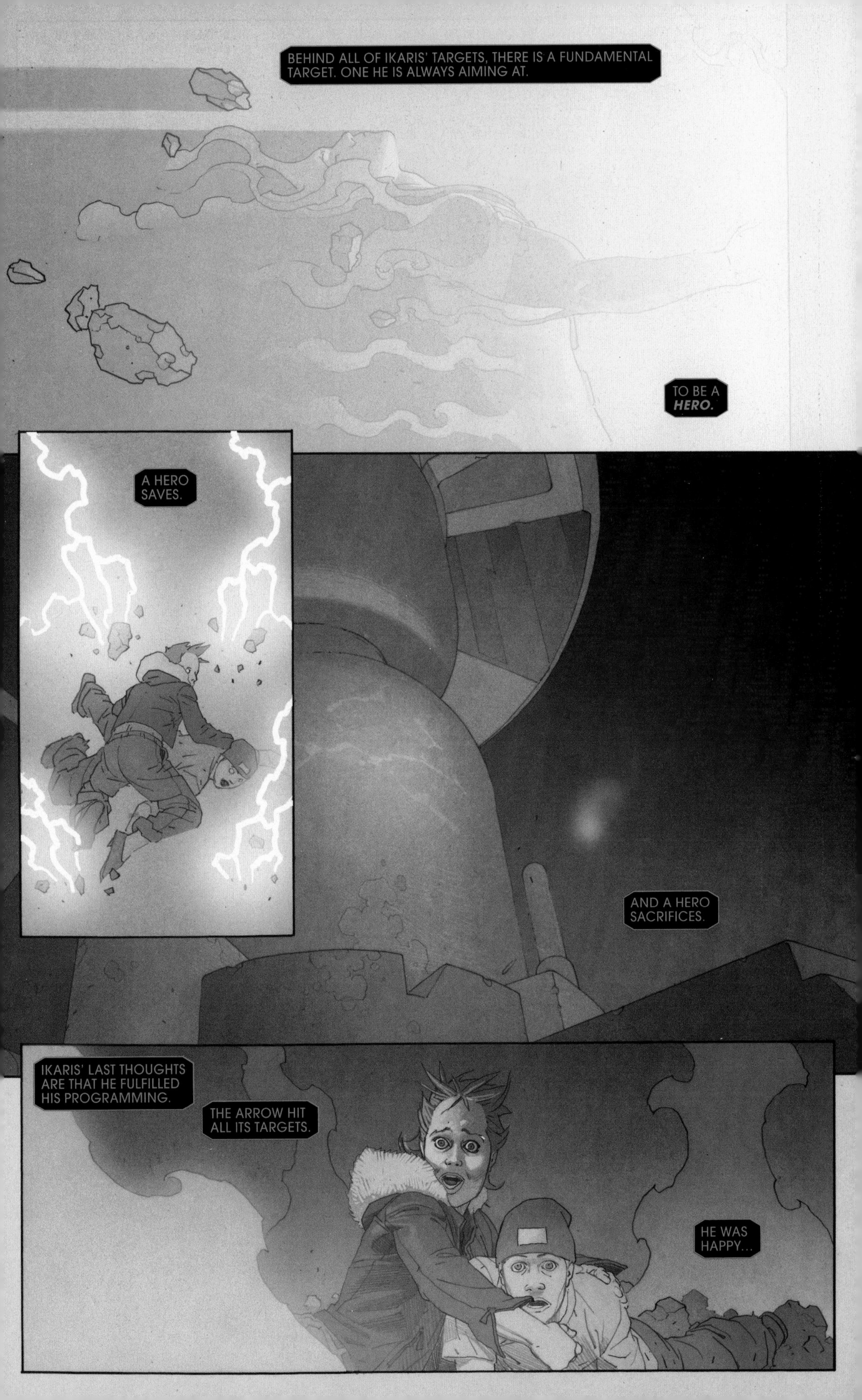
BEHIND ALL OF IKARIS' TARGETS, THERE IS A FUNDAMENTAL TARGET. ONE HE IS ALWAYS AIMING AT.
TO BE A HERO.
A HERO SAVES.
AND A HERO SACRIFICES.
IKARIS' LAST THOUGHTS ARE THAT HE FULFILLED HIS PROGRAMMING.
THE ARROW HIT ALL ITS TARGETS.
HE WAS HAPPY...

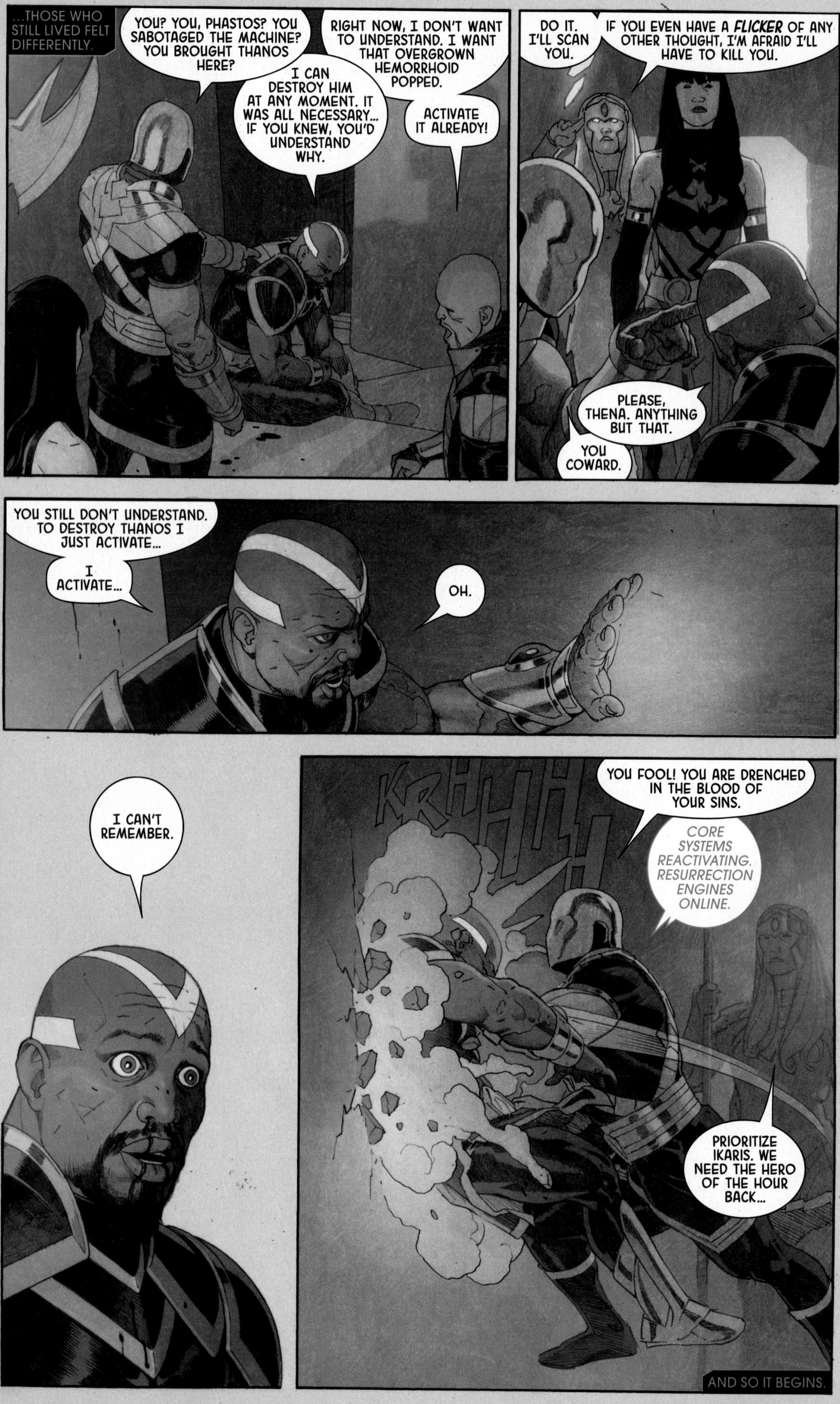
...THOSE WHO STILL LIVED FELT DIFFERENTLY.
YOU? YOU, PHASTOS? YOU SABOTAGED THE MACHINE? YOU BROUGHT THANOS HERE?
I CAN DESTROY HIM AT ANY MOMENT. IT WAS ALL NECESSARY... IF YOU KNEW, YOU'D UNDERSTAND WHY.
RIGHT NOW, I DON'T WANT TO UNDERSTAND. I WANT THAT OVERGROWN HEMORRHOID POPPED.
ACTIVATE IT ALREADY!
DO IT. I'LL SCAN YOU.
IF YOU EVEN HAVE A FLICKER OF ANY OTHER THOUGHT, I'M AFRAID I'LL HAVE TO KILL YOU.
PLEASE, THENA. ANYTHING BUT THAT.
YOU COWARD.
YOU STILL DON'T UNDERSTAND. TO DESTROY THANOS I JUST ACTIVATE...
I ACTIVATE...
OH.
I CAN'T REMEMBER.
KRHHH
YOU FOOL! YOU ARE DRENCHED IN THE BLOOD OF YOUR SINS.
CORE SYSTEMS REACTIVATING. RESURRECTION ENGINES ONLINE.
PRIORITIZE IKARIS. WE NEED THE HERO OF THE HOUR BACK...
AND SO IT BEGINS.

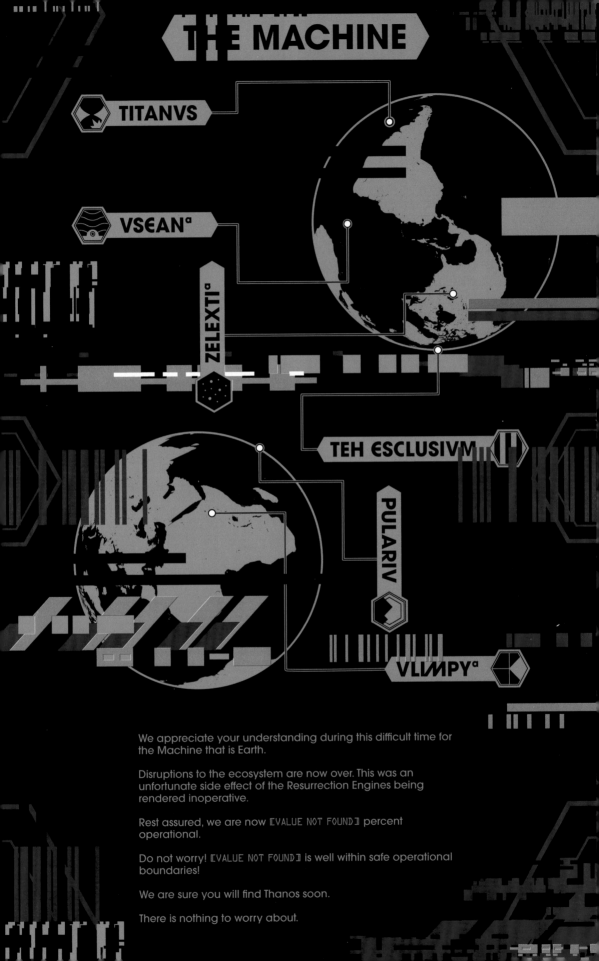

THE MACHINE

TITANVS

VSEANᵃ

ZELEXTIᵃ

TEH ESCLUSIVM

PULARIV

VLIMPYᵃ

We appreciate your understanding during this difficult time for the Machine that is Earth.

Disruptions to the ecosystem are now over. This was an unfortunate side effect of the Resurrection Engines being rendered inoperative.

Rest assured, we are now 〚VALUE NOT FOUND〛 percent operational.

Do not worry! 〚VALUE NOT FOUND〛 is well within safe operational boundaries!

We are sure you will find Thanos soon.

There is nothing to worry about.

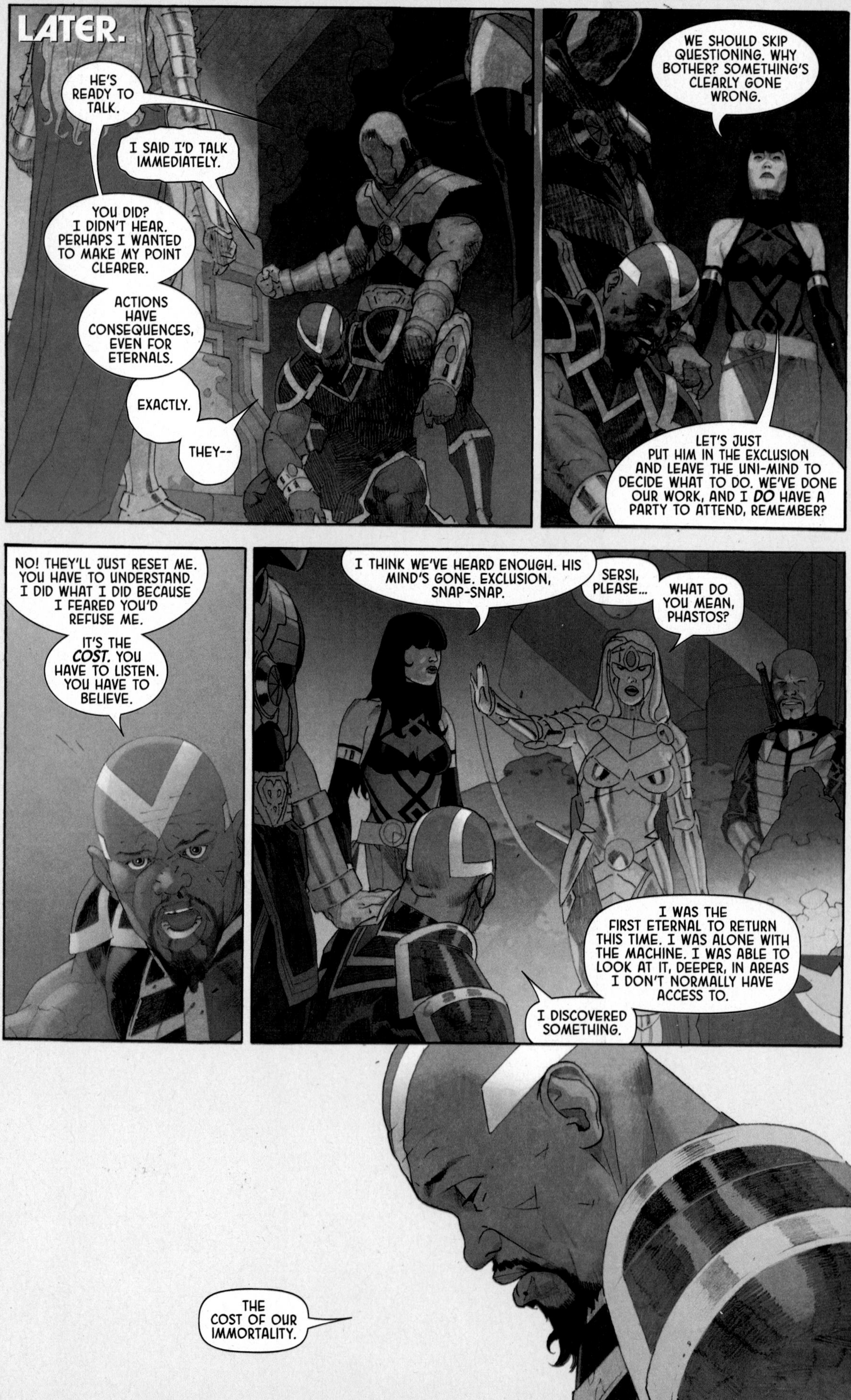
LATER.
HE'S READY TO TALK.
I SAID I'D TALK IMMEDIATELY.
YOU DID? I DIDN'T HEAR. PERHAPS I WANTED TO MAKE MY POINT CLEARER.
ACTIONS HAVE CONSEQUENCES, EVEN FOR ETERNALS.
EXACTLY.
THEY--
WE SHOULD SKIP QUESTIONING. WHY BOTHER? SOMETHING'S CLEARLY GONE WRONG.
LET'S JUST PUT HIM IN THE EXCLUSION AND LEAVE THE UNI-MIND TO DECIDE WHAT TO DO. WE'VE DONE OUR WORK, AND I *DO* HAVE A PARTY TO ATTEND, REMEMBER?
NO! THEY'LL JUST RESET ME. YOU HAVE TO UNDERSTAND. I DID WHAT I DID BECAUSE I FEARED YOU'D REFUSE ME.
IT'S THE *COST.* YOU HAVE TO LISTEN. YOU HAVE TO BELIEVE.
I THINK WE'VE HEARD ENOUGH. HIS MIND'S GONE. EXCLUSION, SNAP-SNAP.
SERSI, PLEASE...
WHAT DO YOU MEAN, PHASTOS?
I WAS THE FIRST ETERNAL TO RETURN THIS TIME. I WAS ALONE WITH THE MACHINE. I WAS ABLE TO LOOK AT IT, DEEPER, IN AREAS I DON'T NORMALLY HAVE ACCESS TO.
I DISCOVERED SOMETHING.
THE COST OF OUR IMMORTALITY.

I BREATHE ANEW.

I DO WHAT I MUST DO.

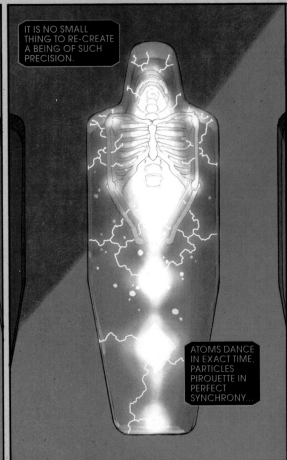

IT IS NO SMALL THING TO RE-CREATE A BEING OF SUCH PRECISION.

ATOMS DANCE IN EXACT TIME, PARTICLES PIROUETTE IN PERFECT SYNCHRONY...

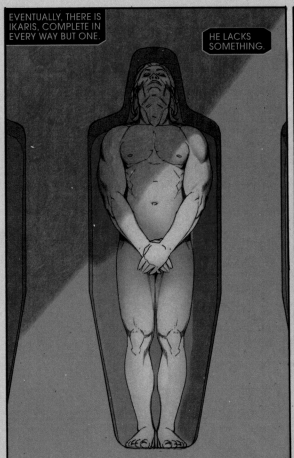

EVENTUALLY, THERE IS IKARIS, COMPLETE IN EVERY WAY BUT ONE.

HE LACKS SOMETHING.

I ACQUIRE IT.

IKARIS OPENS HIS EYES, ALIVE AGAIN...

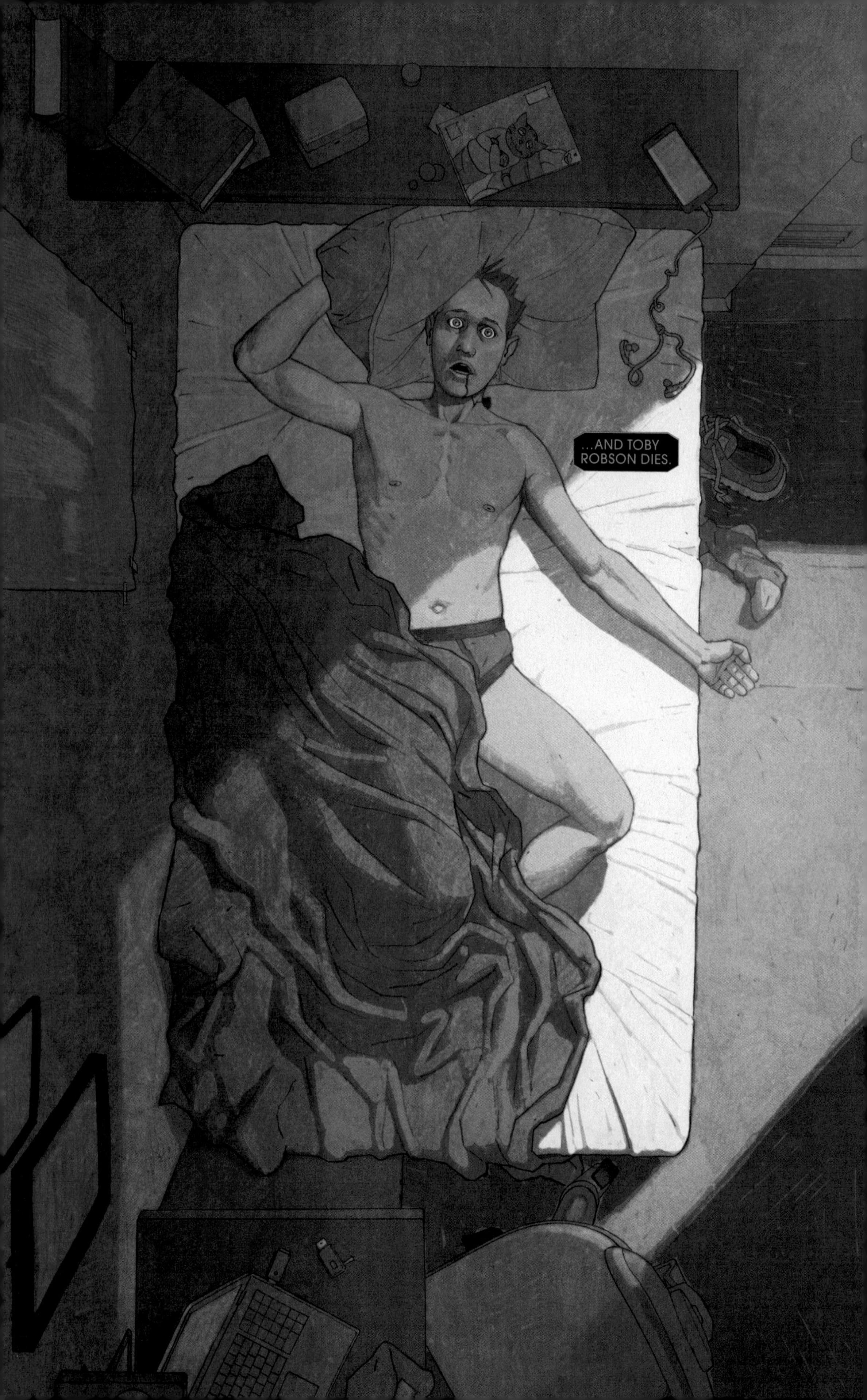
...AND TOBY ROBSON DIES.

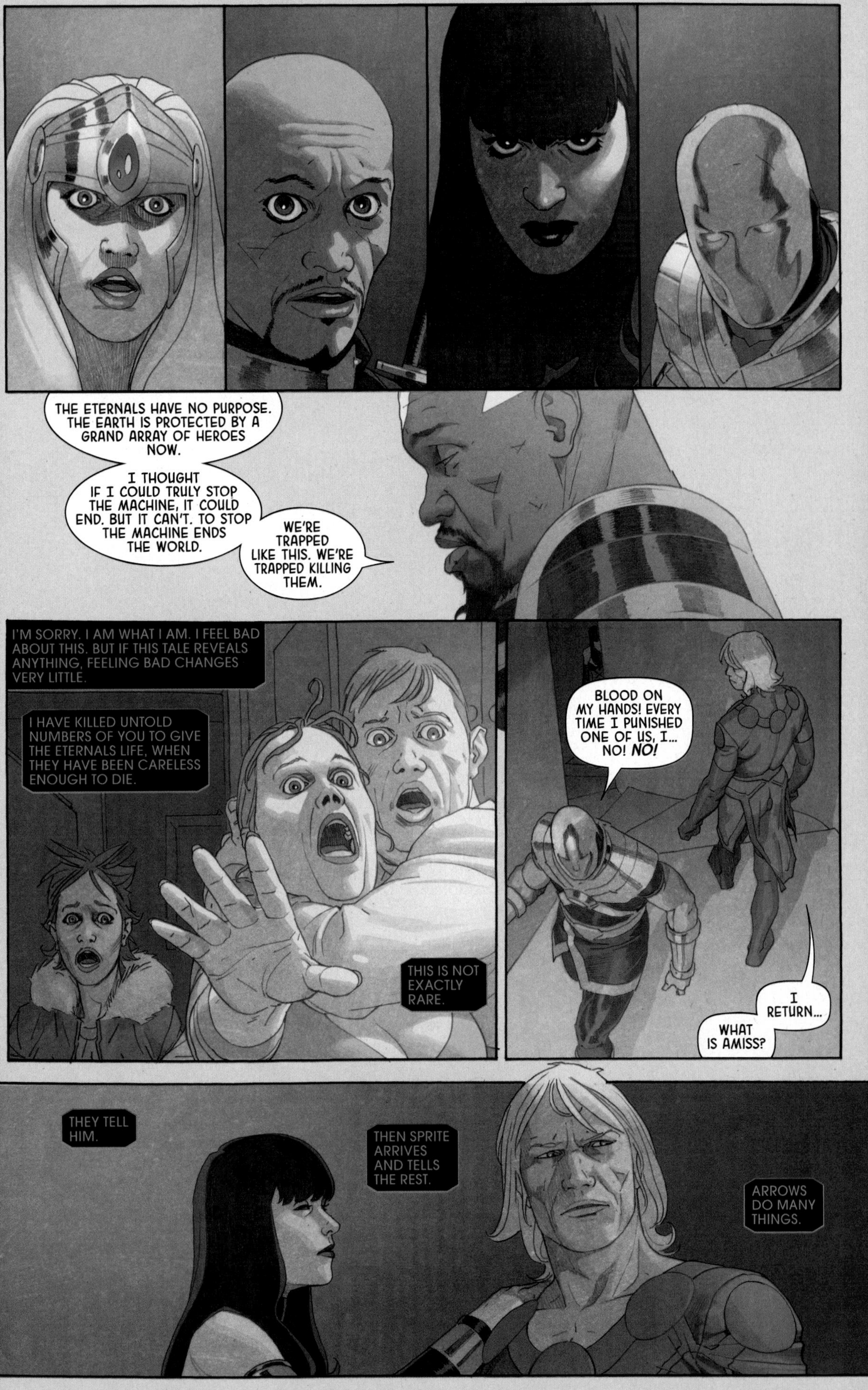
THE ETERNALS HAVE NO PURPOSE. THE EARTH IS PROTECTED BY A GRAND ARRAY OF HEROES NOW.
I THOUGHT IF I COULD TRULY STOP THE MACHINE, IT COULD END. BUT IT CAN'T. TO STOP THE MACHINE ENDS THE WORLD.
WE'RE TRAPPED LIKE THIS. WE'RE TRAPPED KILLING THEM.
I'M SORRY. I AM WHAT I AM. I FEEL BAD ABOUT THIS. BUT IF THIS TALE REVEALS ANYTHING, FEELING BAD CHANGES VERY LITTLE.
I HAVE KILLED UNTOLD NUMBERS OF YOU TO GIVE THE ETERNALS LIFE, WHEN THEY HAVE BEEN CARELESS ENOUGH TO DIE.
THIS IS NOT EXACTLY RARE.
BLOOD ON MY HANDS! EVERY TIME I PUNISHED ONE OF US, I... NO! ***NO!***
I RETURN...
WHAT IS AMISS?
THEY TELL HIM.
THEN SPRITE ARRIVES AND TELLS THE REST.
ARROWS DO MANY THINGS.

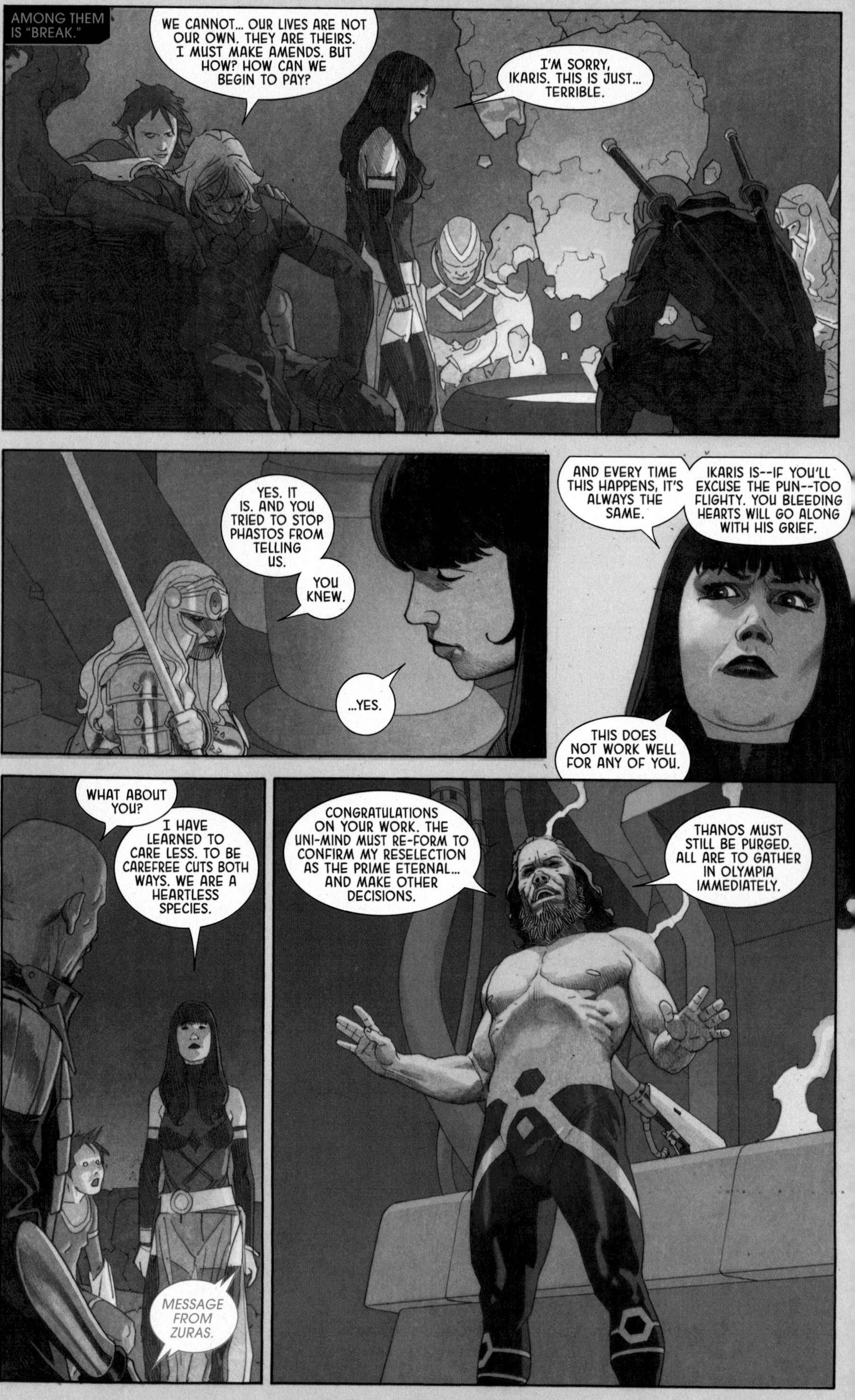
AMONG THEM IS "BREAK."
WE CANNOT... OUR LIVES ARE NOT OUR OWN. THEY ARE THEIRS. I MUST MAKE AMENDS. BUT HOW? HOW CAN WE BEGIN TO PAY?
I'M SORRY, IKARIS. THIS IS JUST... TERRIBLE.
YES. IT IS. AND YOU TRIED TO STOP PHASTOS FROM TELLING US.
YOU KNEW.
...YES.
AND EVERY TIME THIS HAPPENS, IT'S ALWAYS THE SAME.
IKARIS IS--IF YOU'LL EXCUSE THE PUN--TOO FLIGHTY. YOU BLEEDING HEARTS WILL GO ALONG WITH HIS GRIEF.
THIS DOES NOT WORK WELL FOR ANY OF YOU.
WHAT ABOUT YOU?
I HAVE LEARNED TO CARE LESS. TO BE CAREFREE CUTS BOTH WAYS. WE ARE A HEARTLESS SPECIES.
MESSAGE FROM ZURAS.
CONGRATULATIONS ON YOUR WORK. THE UNI-MIND MUST RE-FORM TO CONFIRM MY RESELECTION AS THE PRIME ETERNAL... AND MAKE OTHER DECISIONS.
THANOS MUST STILL BE PURGED. ALL ARE TO GATHER IN OLYMPIA IMMEDIATELY.

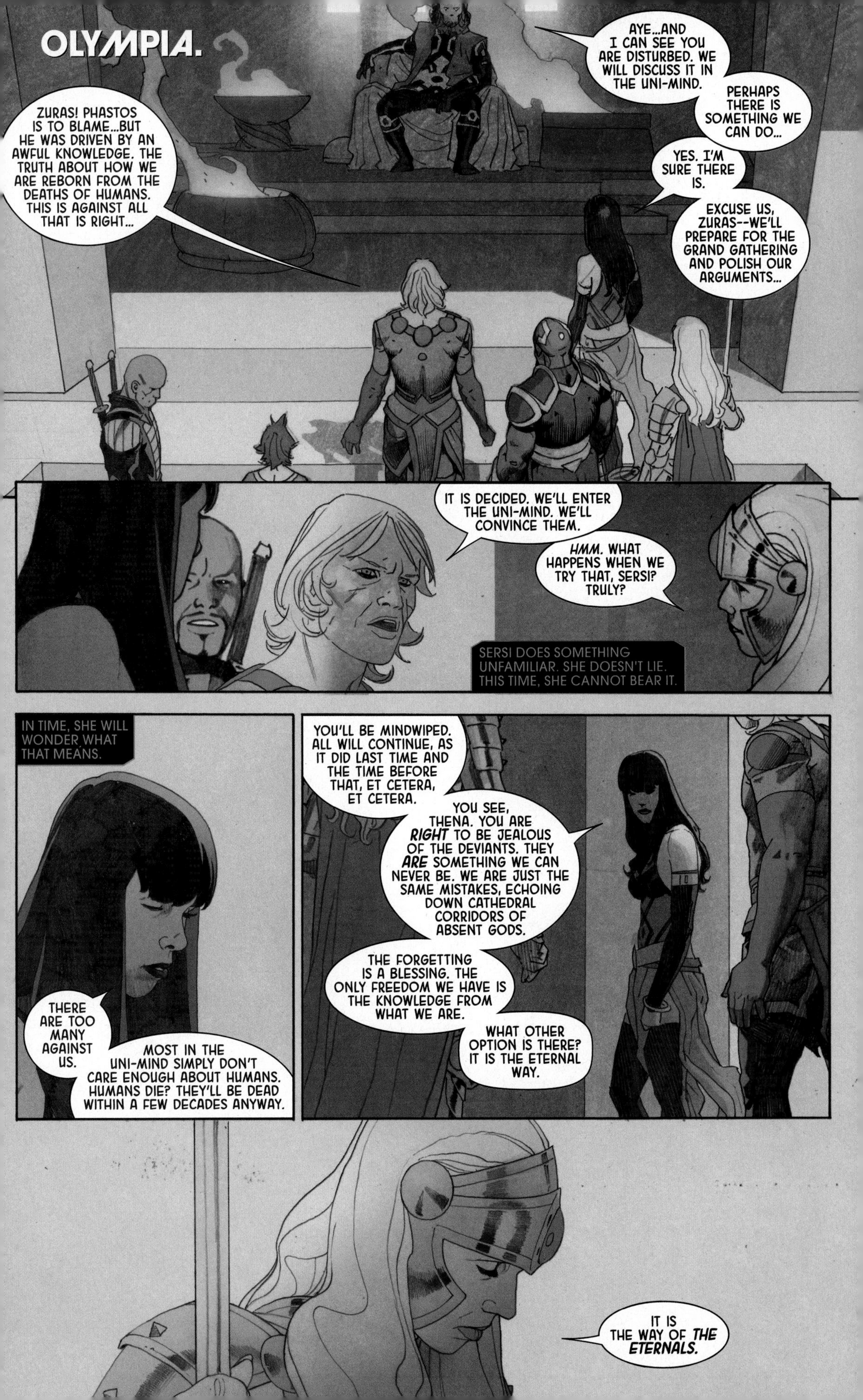
OLYMPIA.
ZURAS! PHASTOS IS TO BLAME...BUT HE WAS DRIVEN BY AN AWFUL KNOWLEDGE. THE TRUTH ABOUT HOW WE ARE REBORN FROM THE DEATHS OF HUMANS. THIS IS AGAINST ALL THAT IS RIGHT...
AYE...AND I CAN SEE YOU ARE DISTURBED. WE WILL DISCUSS IT IN THE UNI-MIND.
PERHAPS THERE IS SOMETHING WE CAN DO...
YES. I'M SURE THERE IS.
EXCUSE US, ZURAS--WE'LL PREPARE FOR THE GRAND GATHERING AND POLISH OUR ARGUMENTS...
IT IS DECIDED. WE'LL ENTER THE UNI-MIND. WE'LL CONVINCE THEM.
HMM. WHAT HAPPENS WHEN WE TRY THAT, SERSI? TRULY?
SERSI DOES SOMETHING UNFAMILIAR. SHE DOESN'T LIE. THIS TIME, SHE CANNOT BEAR IT.
IN TIME, SHE WILL WONDER WHAT THAT MEANS.
THERE ARE TOO MANY AGAINST US.
MOST IN THE UNI-MIND SIMPLY DON'T CARE ENOUGH ABOUT HUMANS. HUMANS DIE? THEY'LL BE DEAD WITHIN A FEW DECADES ANYWAY.
YOU'LL BE MINDWIPED. ALL WILL CONTINUE, AS IT DID LAST TIME AND THE TIME BEFORE THAT, ET CETERA, ET CETERA.
YOU SEE, THENA. YOU ARE RIGHT TO BE JEALOUS OF THE DEVIANTS. THEY ARE SOMETHING WE CAN NEVER BE. WE ARE JUST THE SAME MISTAKES, ECHOING DOWN CATHEDRAL CORRIDORS OF ABSENT GODS.
THE FORGETTING IS A BLESSING. THE ONLY FREEDOM WE HAVE IS THE KNOWLEDGE FROM WHAT WE ARE.
WHAT OTHER OPTION IS THERE? IT IS THE ETERNAL WAY.
IT IS THE WAY OF THE ETERNALS.

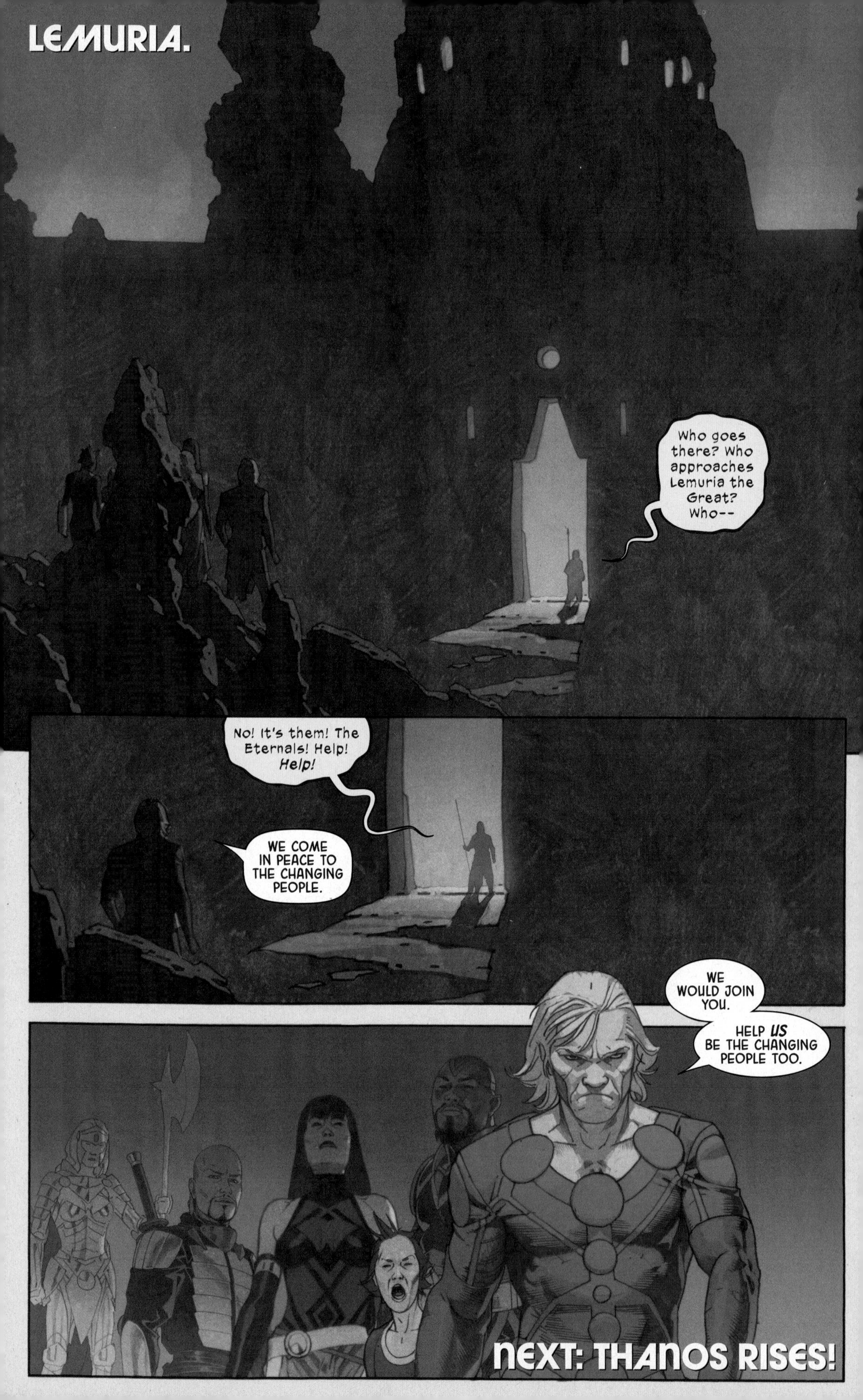
LEMURIA.
Who goes there? Who approaches Lemuria the Great? Who--
No! It's them! The Eternals! Help! *Help!*
WE COME IN PEACE TO THE CHANGING PEOPLE.
WE WOULD JOIN YOU.
HELP *US* BE THE CHANGING PEOPLE TOO.
NEXT: THANOS RISES!

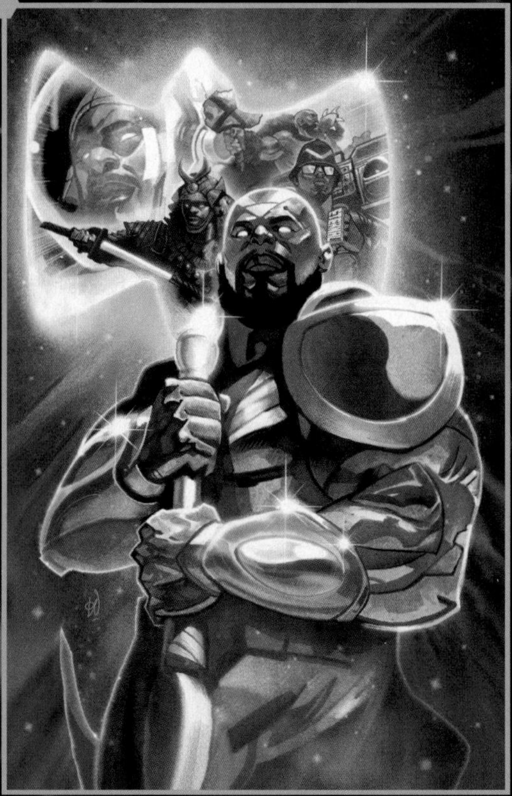

#1 VARIANT BY **MIKE DEL MUNDO**

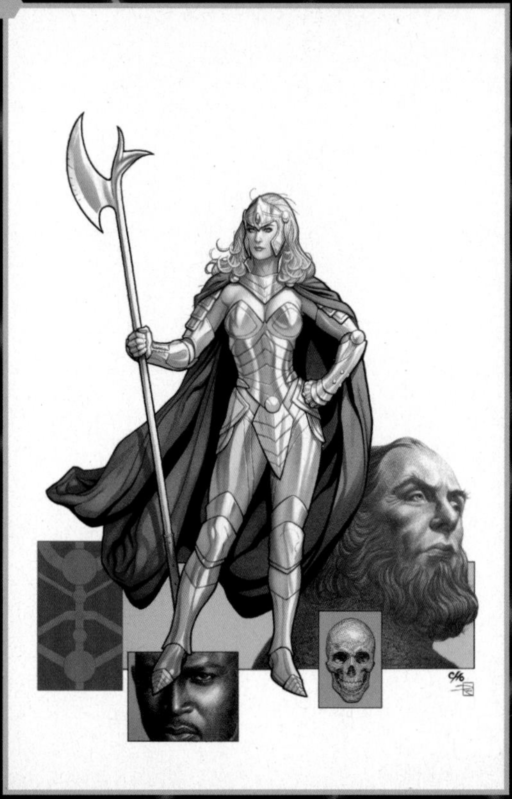

#1 VARIANT BY **FRANK CHO** & **SABINE RICH**

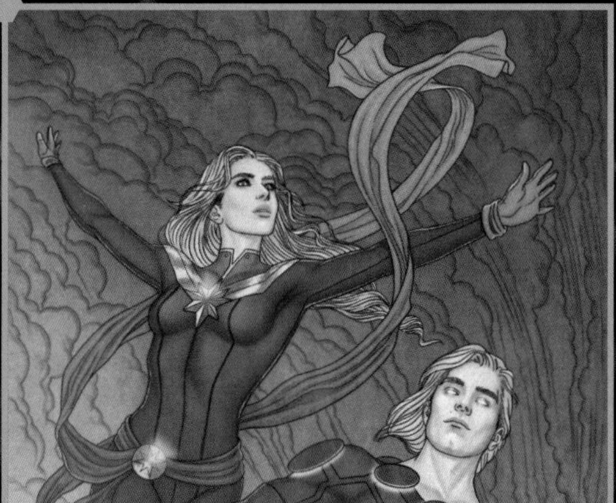

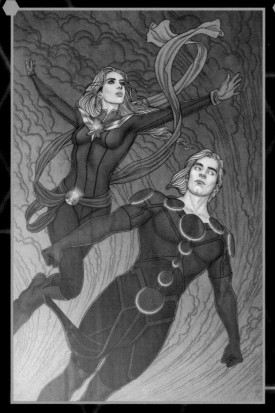

#1 VARIANT BY **JENNY FRISON**

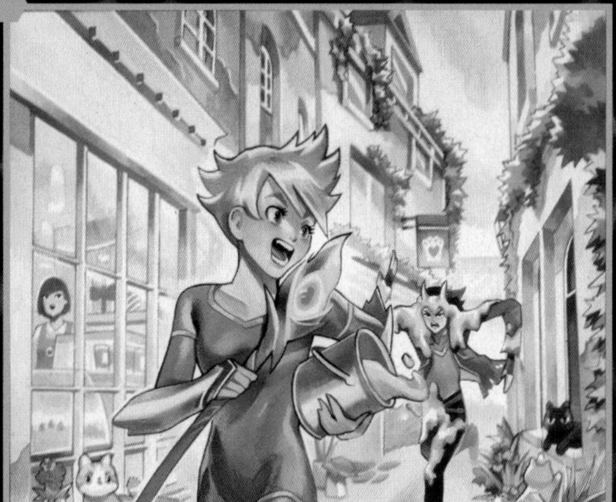

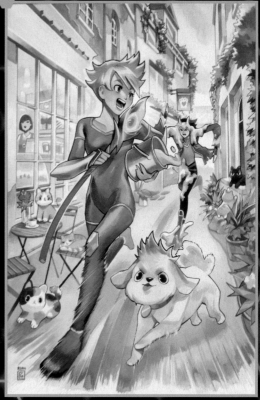

#1 VARIANT BY **RIAN GONZALES**

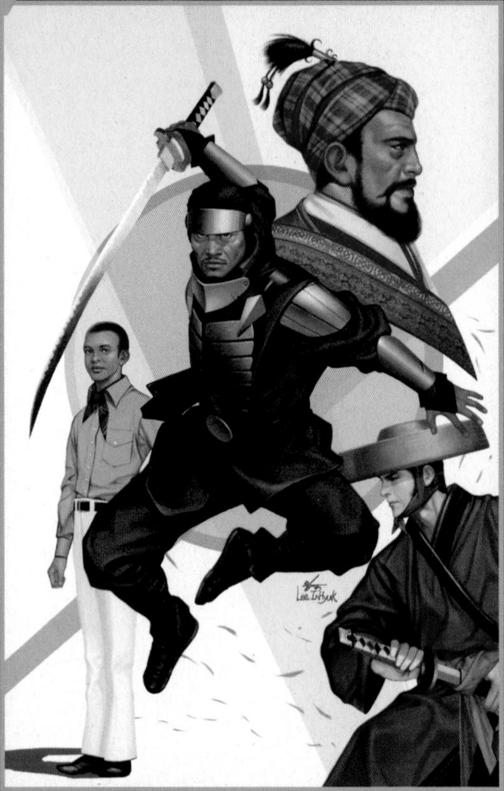

#1 VARIANT BY **INHYUK LEE**

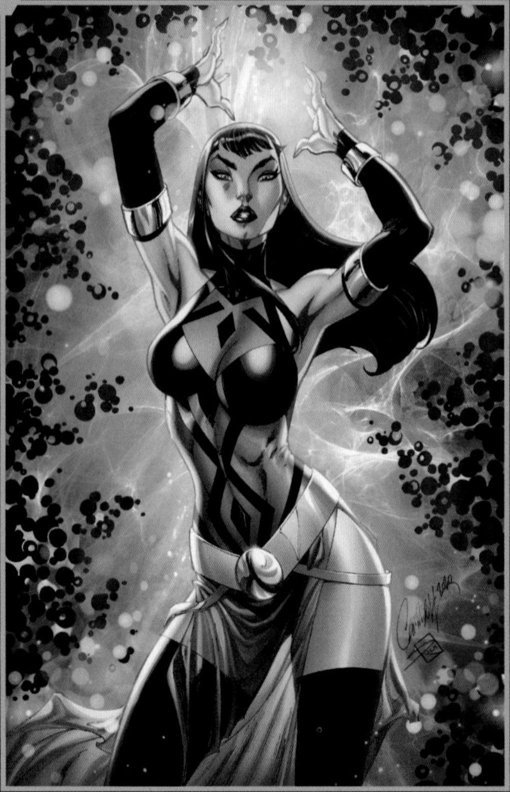

#1 VARIANT BY **J. SCOTT CAMPBELL** & **SABINE RICH**

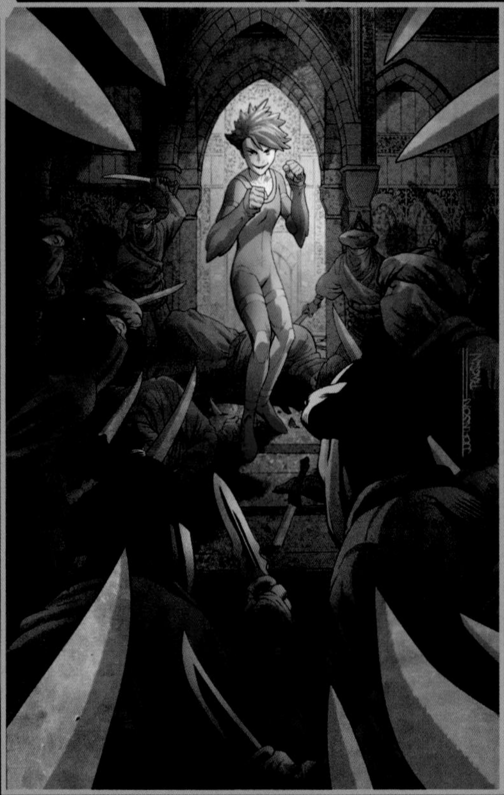

#1 VARIANT BY **JEFF JOHNSON** & **DAN PANOSIAN**

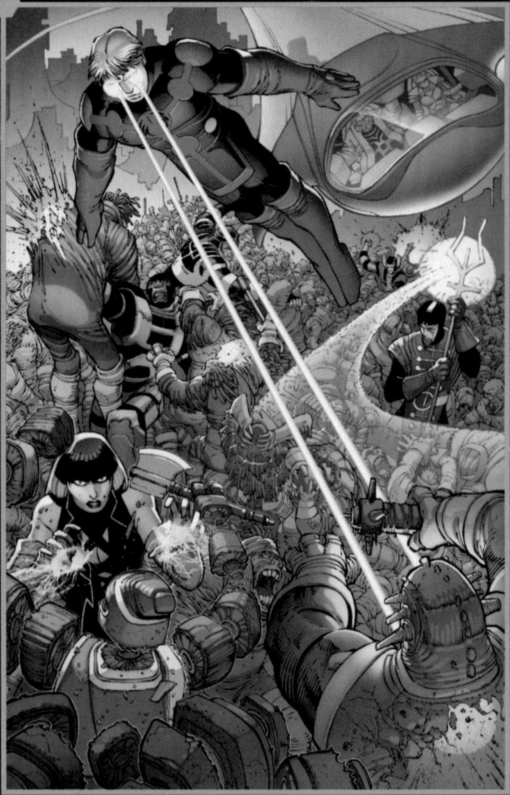

#1 HIDDEN GEM VARIANT BY **JOHN ROMITA JR., DANNY MIKI** & **MARTE GRACIA**

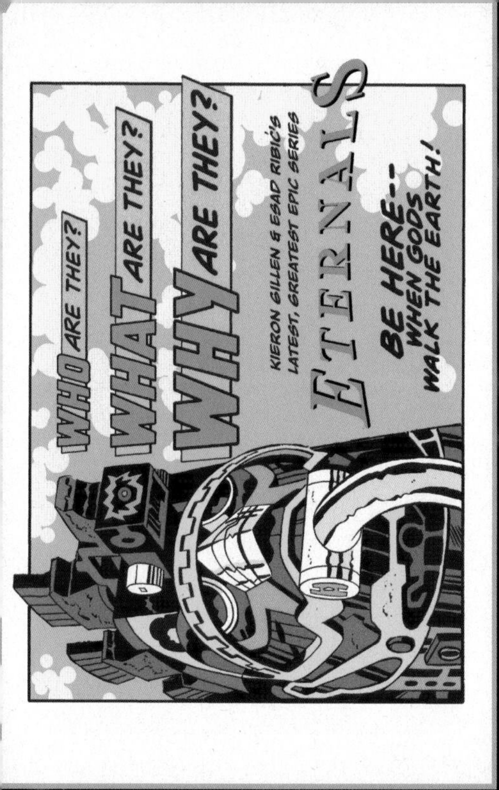
WHO ARE THEY?
WHAT ARE THEY?
WHY ARE THEY?
KIERON GILLEN & ESAD RIBIC'S LATEST, GREATEST EPIC SERIES
ETERNALS
BE HERE-- WHEN GODS WALK THE EARTH!

#1 HIDDEN GEM VARIANT BY **JACK KIRBY, FRANK GIACOIA** & **RACHELLE ROSENBERG**

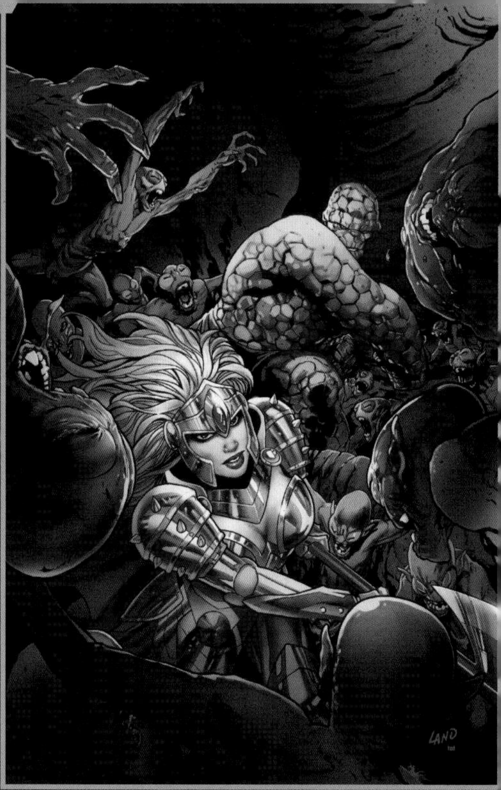
LAND

#1 VARIANT BY **GREG LAND** & **FRANK D'ARMATA**

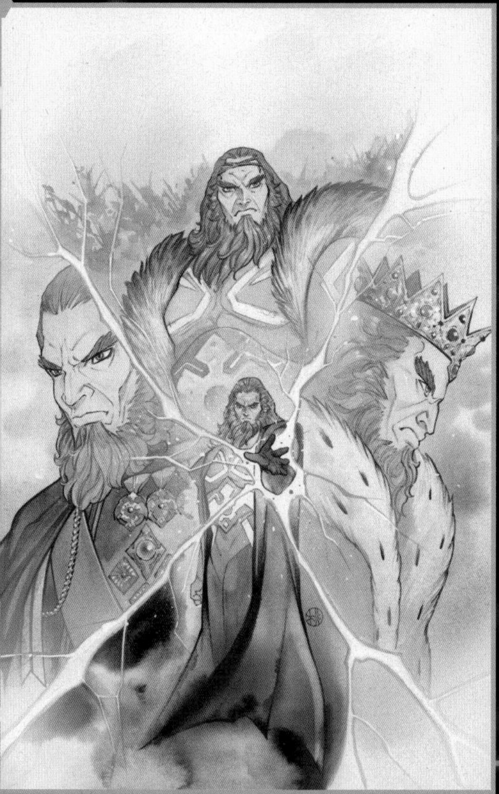

#1 VARIANT BY **PEACH MOMOKO**

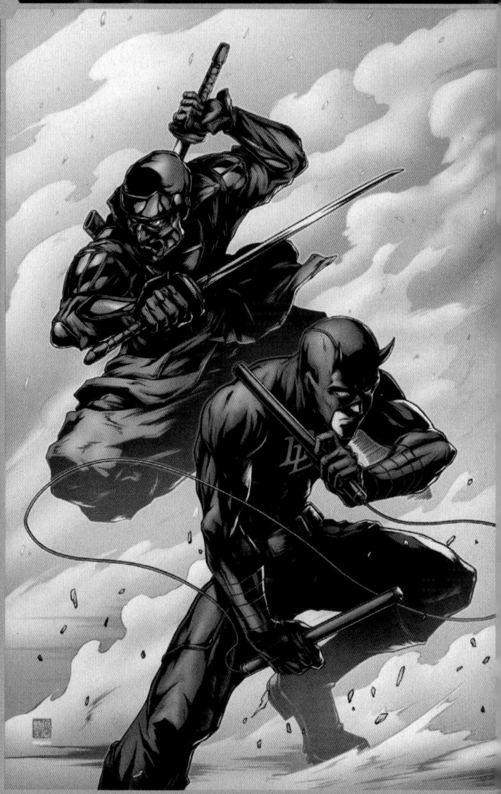

#1 VARIANT BY **OKAZAKI**

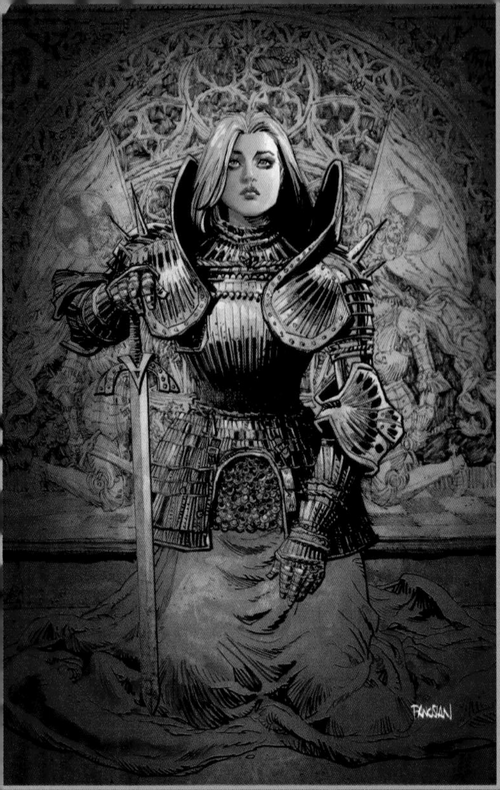
PANOSIAN

#1 VARIANT BY **DAN PANOSIAN**

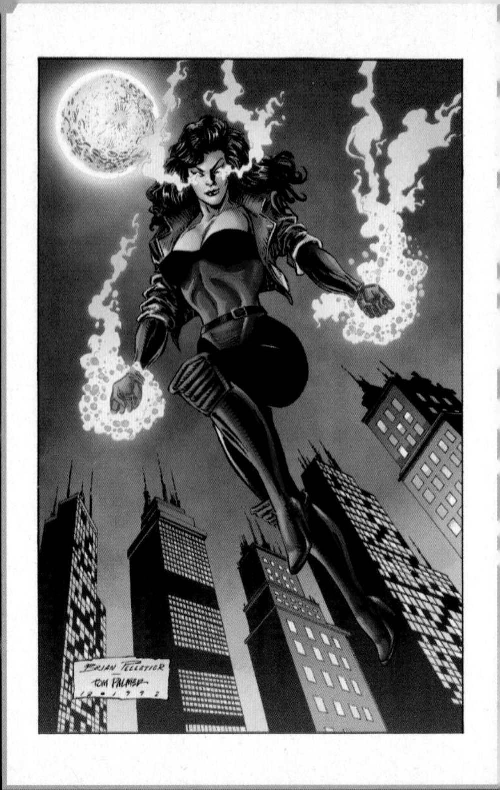
BRIAN PELLETIER
TOM PALMER

#1 HIDDEN GEM VARIANT BY **BRIAN PELLETIER & RACHELLE ROSENBERG**

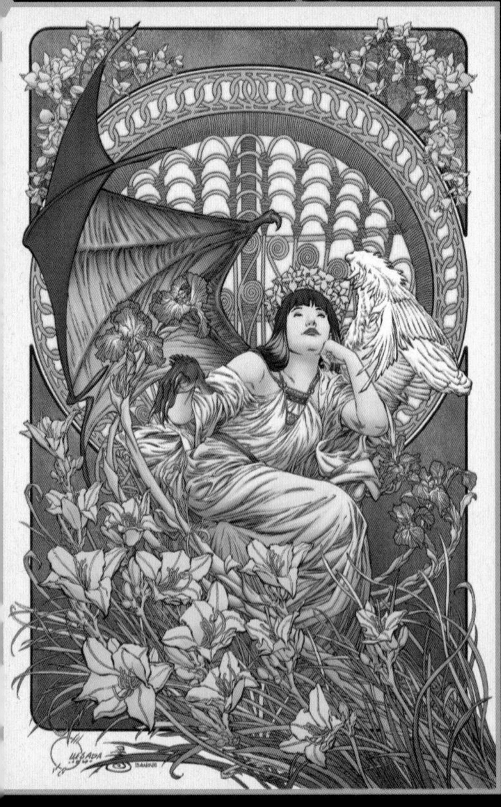

#1 VARIANT BY **JOE QUESADA**, **DANNY MIKI & RICHARD ISANOVE**

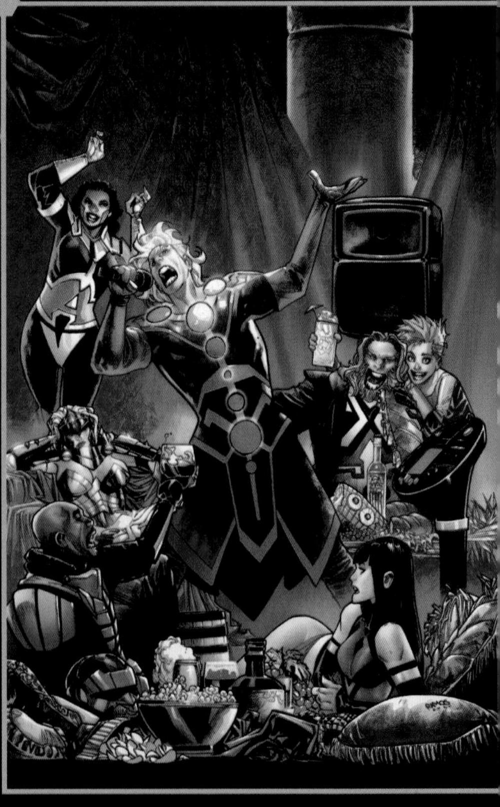

#1 PARTY VARIANT BY **HUMBERTO RAMOS & EDGAR DELGADO**

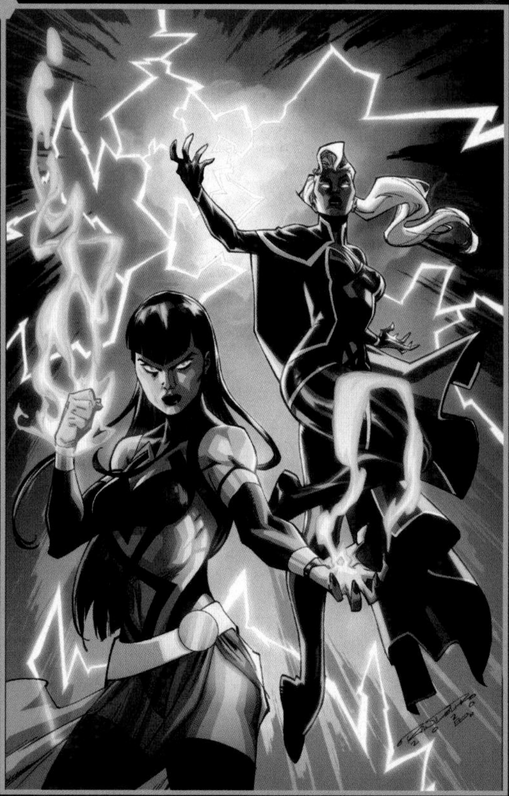

#1 VARIANT BY **KHARY RANDOLPH & EMILIO LOPEZ**

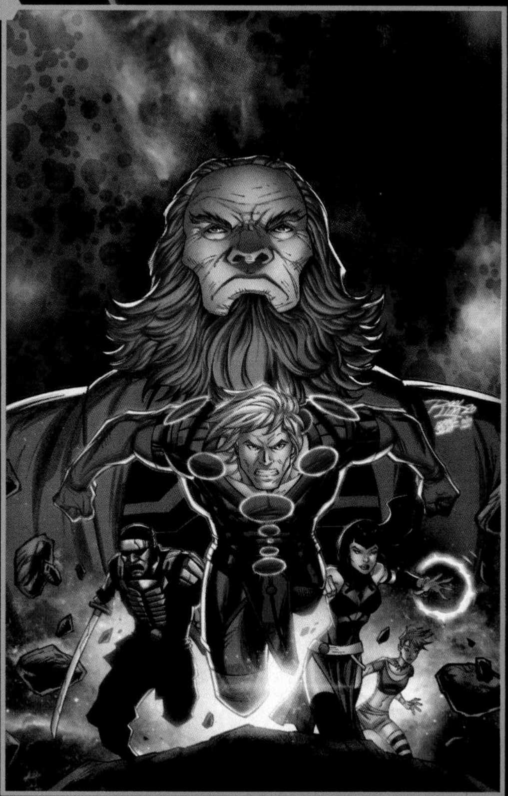

#1 VARIANT BY **RON LIM** & **ISRAEL SILVA**

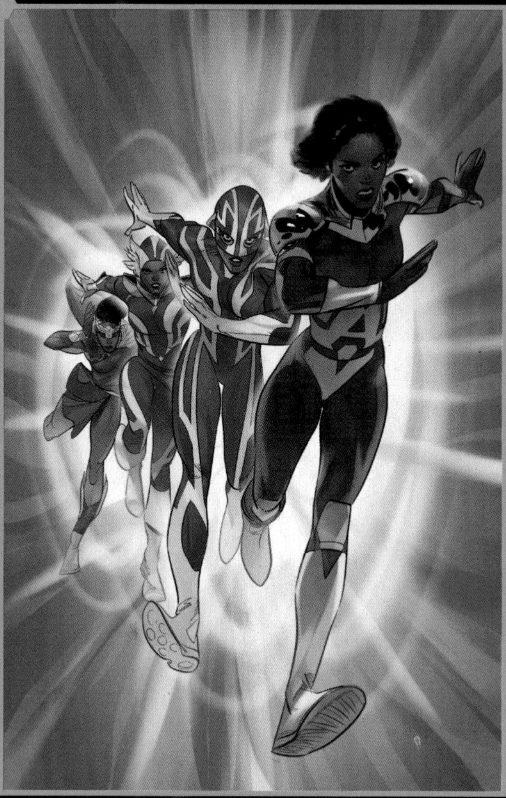

#1 VARIANT BY **OTTO SCHMIDT**

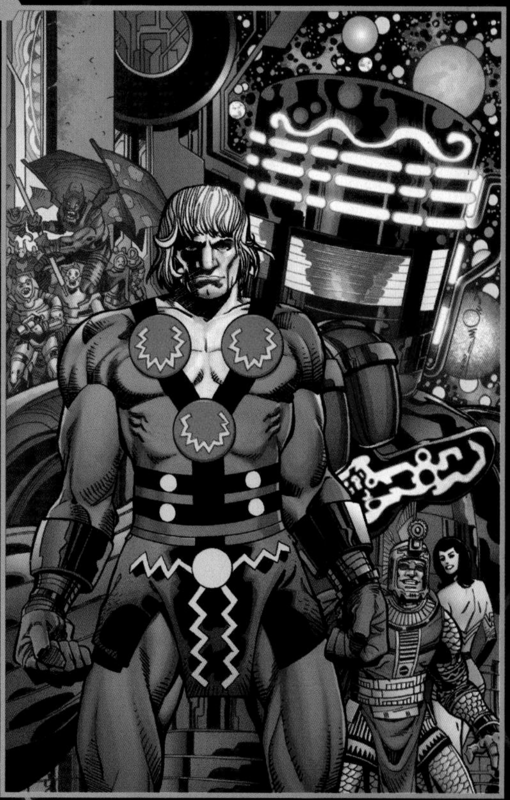

#1 VARIANT BY **WALTER SIMONSON & LEN O'GRADY**

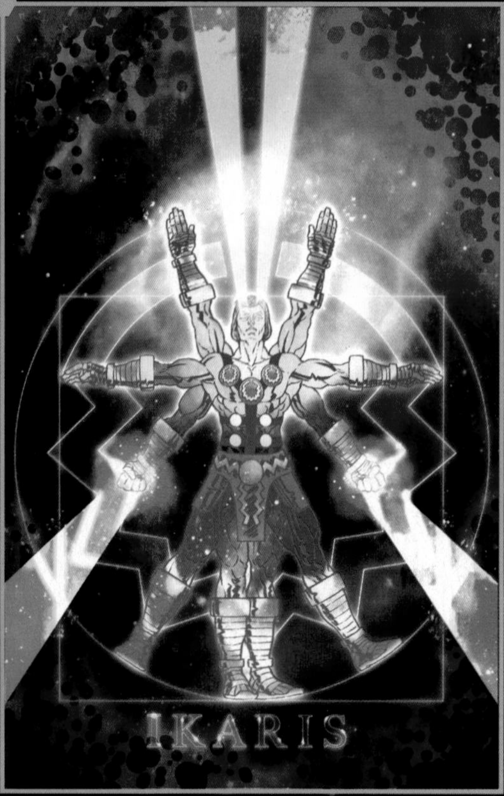
IKARIS

#1 VARIANT BY **SUPERLOG**

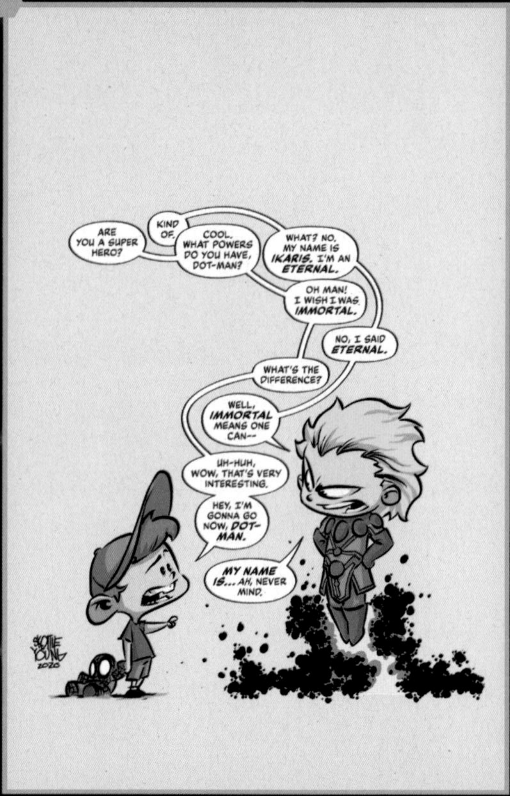
ARE YOU A SUPER HERO?
KIND OF.
COOL. WHAT POWERS DO YOU HAVE, DOT-MAN?
WHAT? NO. MY NAME IS IKARIS. I'M AN ETERNAL.
OH MAN! I WISH I WAS IMMORTAL.
NO, I SAID ETERNAL.
WHAT'S THE DIFFERENCE?
WELL, IMMORTAL MEANS ONE CAN--
UH-HUH, WOW, THAT'S VERY INTERESTING.
HEY, I'M GONNA GO NOW, DOT-MAN.
MY NAME IS... AH, NEVER MIND.
SKOTTIE YOUNG 2020

#1 VARIANT BY **SKOTTIE YOUNG**

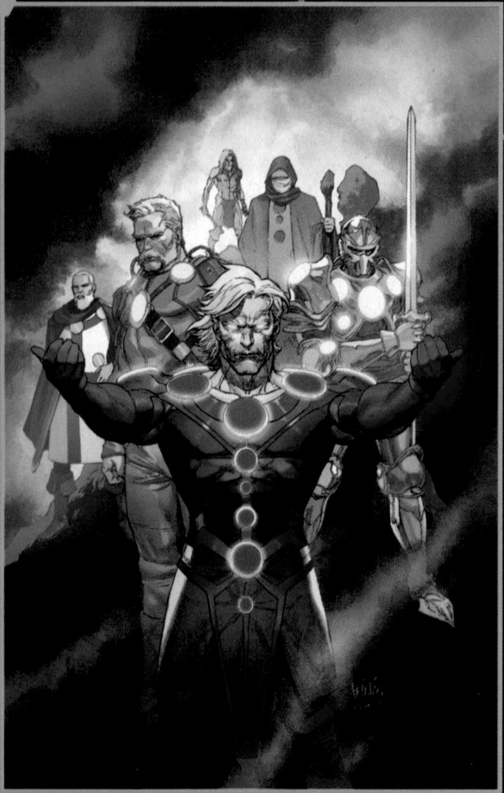

#1 VARIANT BY **LEINIL FRANCIS YU**
& SUNNY GHO

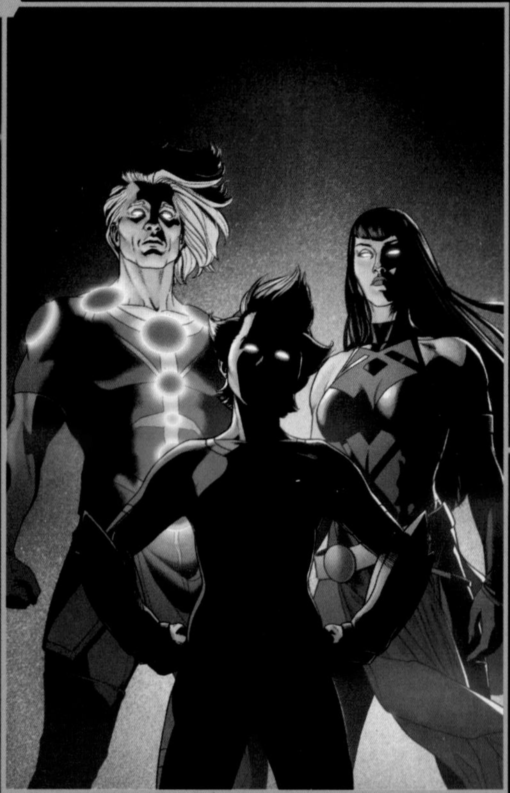

#2 VARIANT BY **JAMIE McKELVIE**
& MATTHEW WILSON

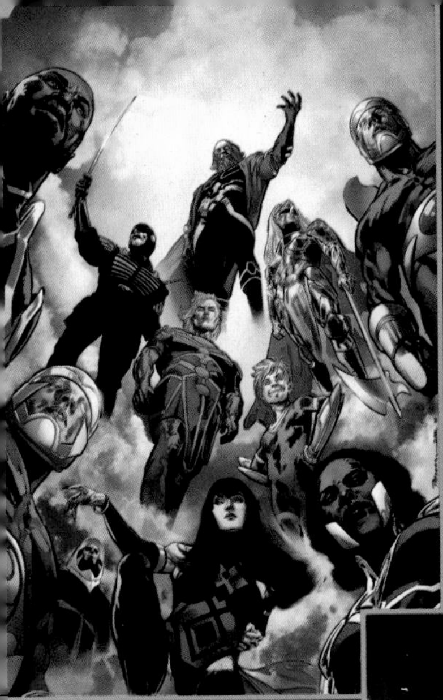

#2 VARIANT BY
PHIL JIMENEZ
& FRANK D'ARMATA

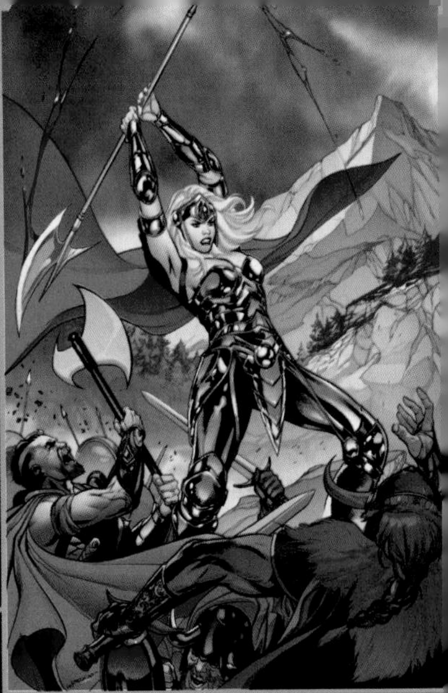

#3 VARIANT BY
EMA LUPACCHINO
& DAVID CURIEL

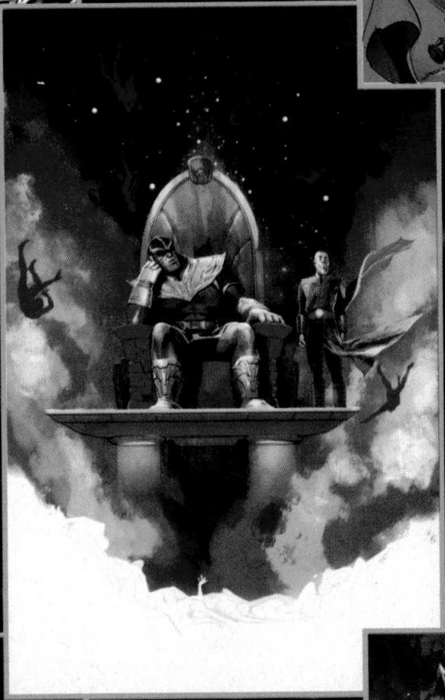

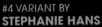

#4 VARIANT BY
STEPHANIE HANS

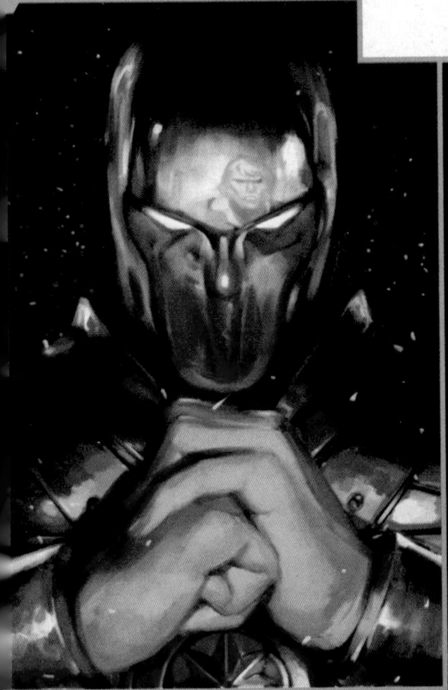

#5 VARIANT BY **GERALD PAREL**

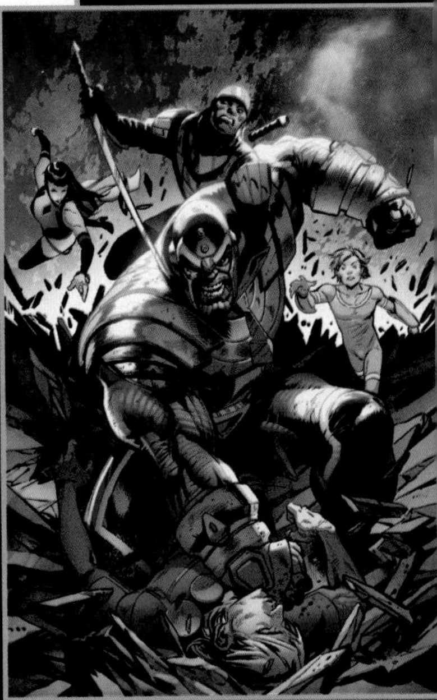

#6 VARIANT BY **GEOFF SHAW**
& MARTE GRACIA

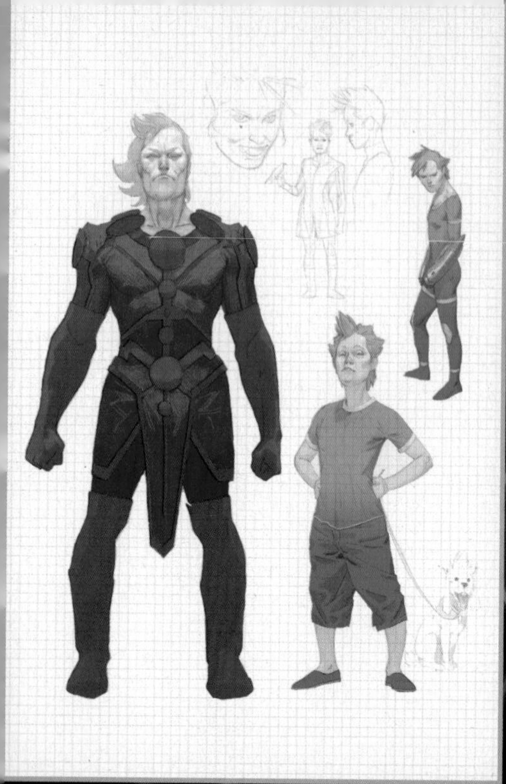

#1 DESIGN VARIANT BY **ESAD RIBIĆ**

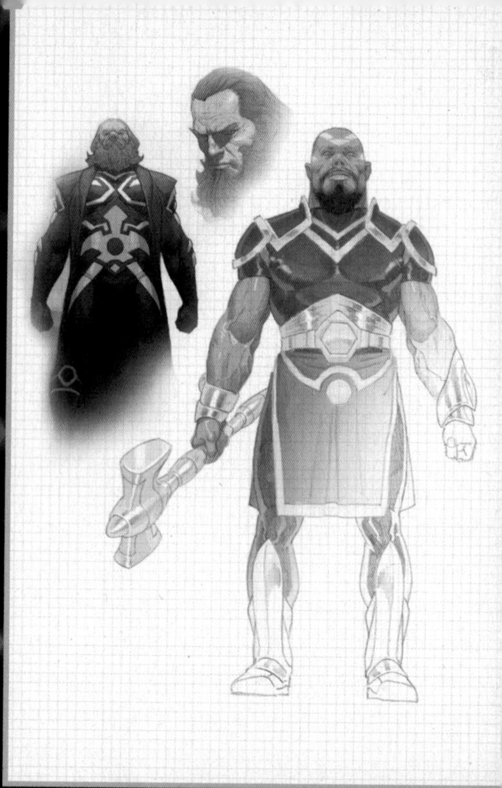

#2 DESIGN VARIANT BY **ESAD RIBIĆ**

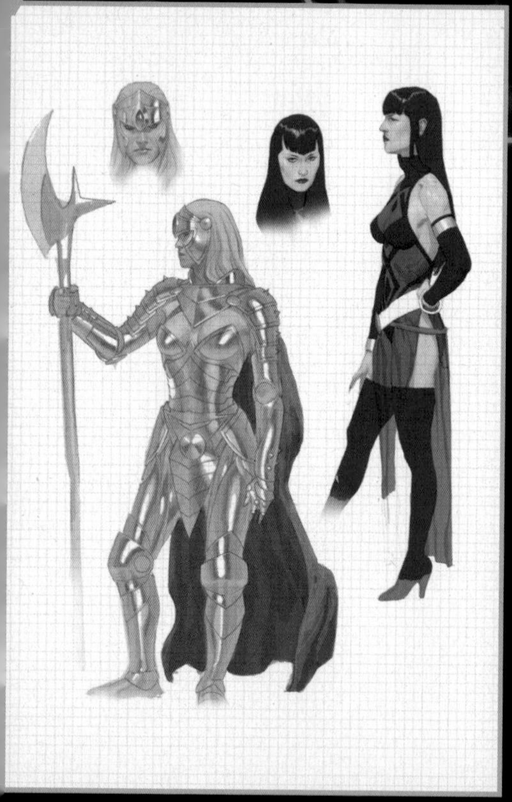

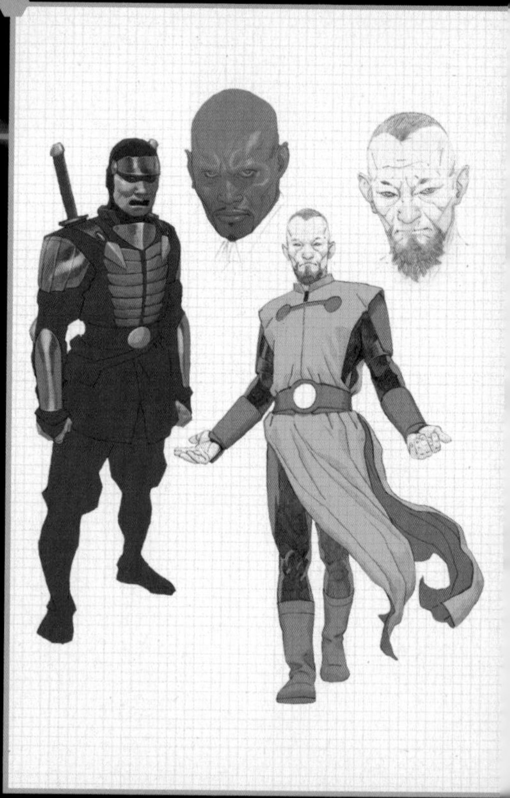

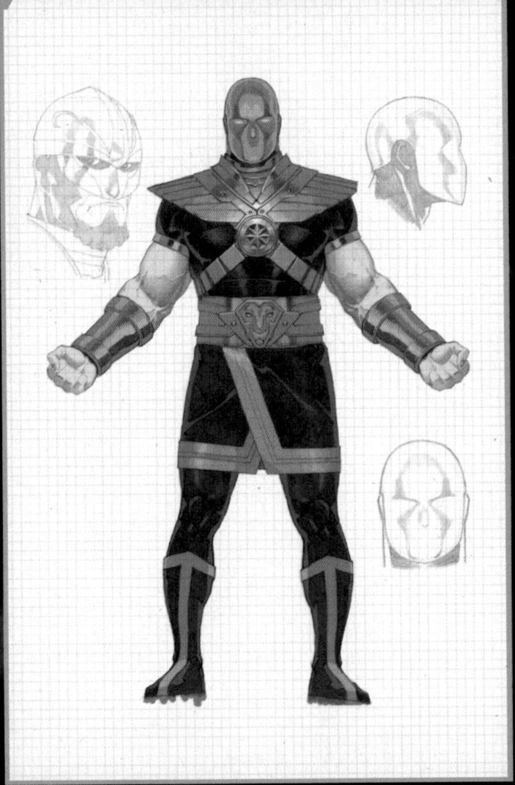

#5 DESIGN VARIANT BY **ESAD RIBIĆ**

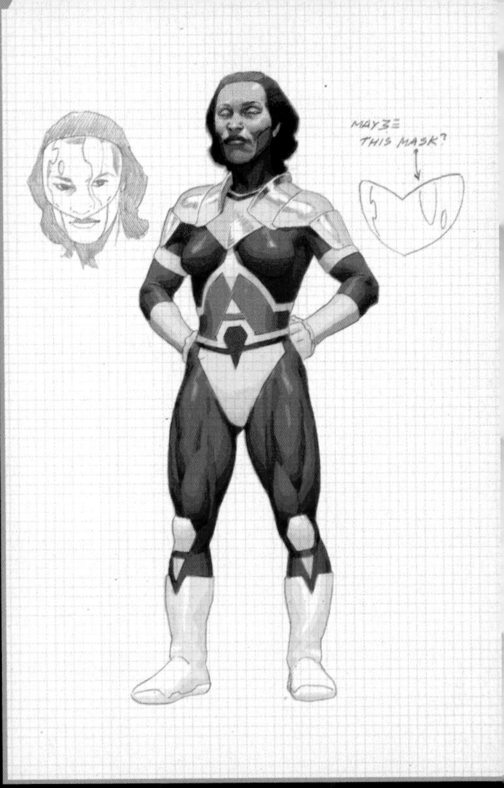
MAYBE
THIS MASK?

#6 DESIGN VARIANT BY **ESAD RIBIĆ**

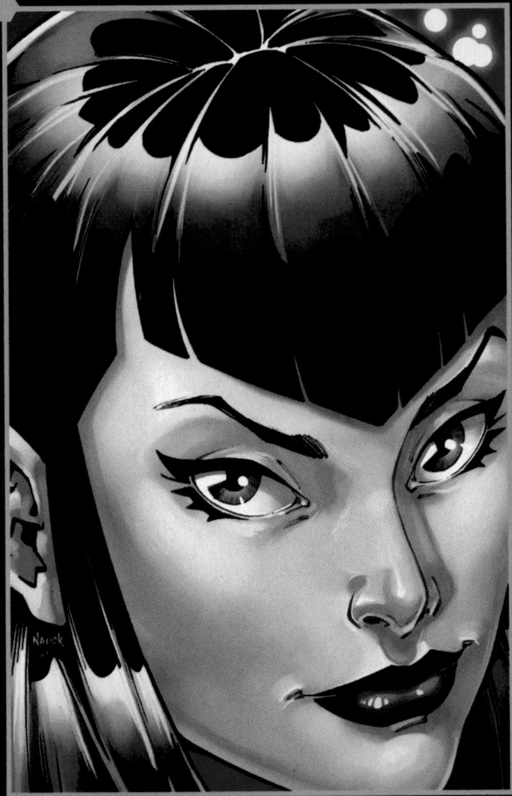
NAUCK

#1 HEADSHOT VARIANT BY **TODD NAUCK**
& **RACHELLE ROSENBERG**

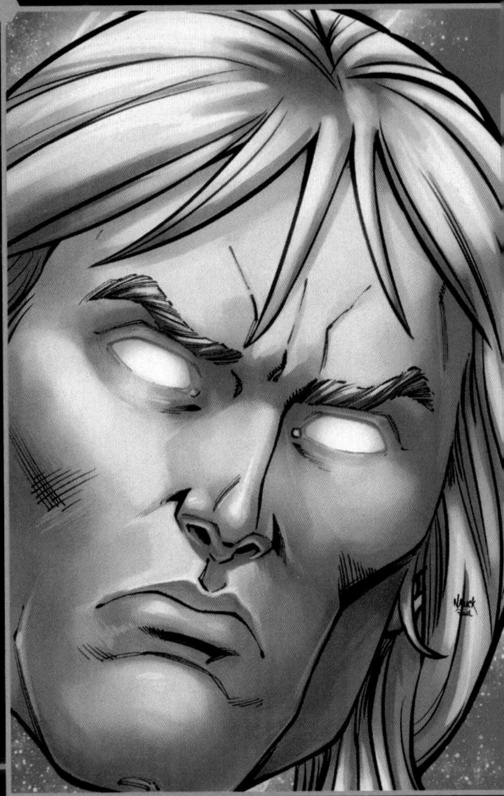

#2 HEADSHOT VARIANT BY **TODD NAUCK**
& **RACHELLE ROSENBERG**

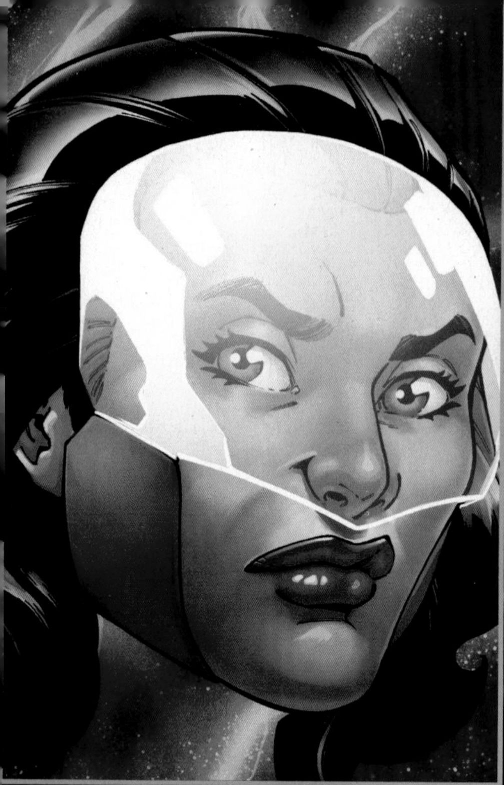

#3 HEADSHOT VARIANT BY **TODD NAUCK & RACHELLE ROSENBERG**

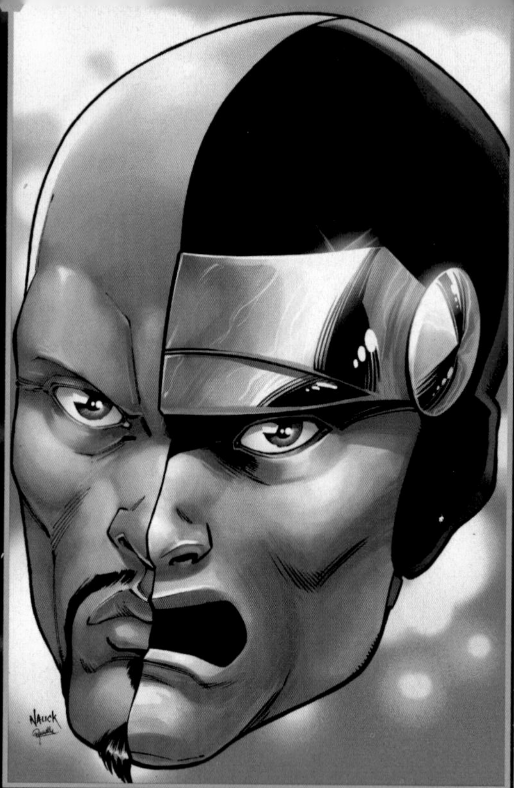
NAUCK

#4 HEADSHOT VARIANT BY **TODD NAUCK & RACHELLE ROSENBERG**

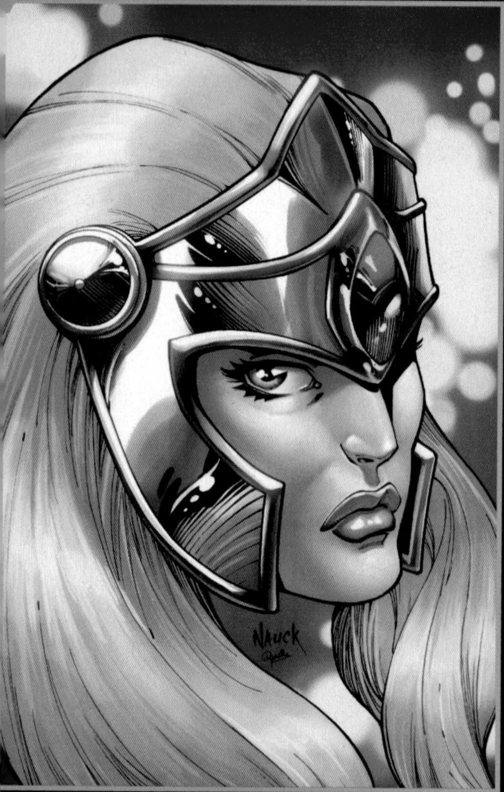
NAUCK

#5 HEADSHOT VARIANT BY **TODD NAUCK & RACHELLE ROSENBERG**

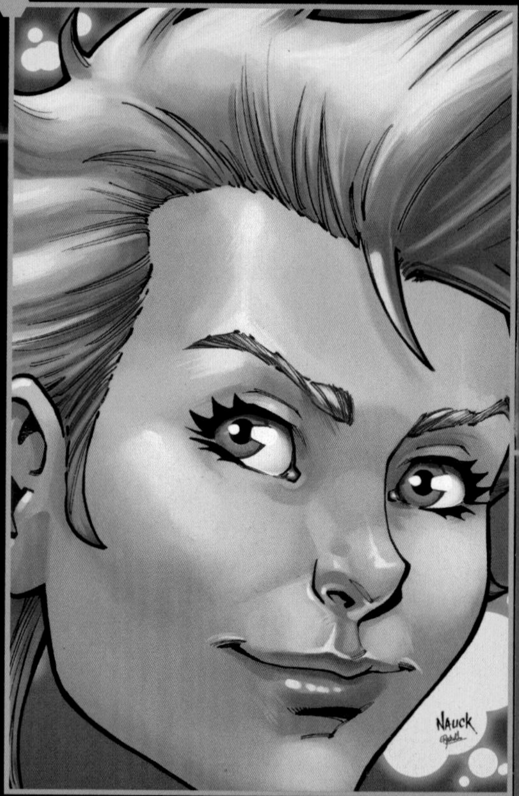
NAUCK

#6 HEADSHOT VARIANT BY **TODD NAUCK & RACHELLE ROSENBERG**